In a groundbreaking exploration of the impostor phenomenon, Cokley's curated volume is nothing short of a scholarly triumph. Drawing on over 4 decades of research, Cokley's piercing analysis and collaboration with scholars redefine the landscape of research in this area, charting a compelling course that not only reviews but significantly expands our understanding. By delving into underexplored areas such as the context in which the impostor phenomenon develops, the conditions under which it manifests, and the practical implications of these findings, this collection becomes a must-read resource for psychologists, educators, and anyone intrigued by the science behind feeling like a fraud or adopting a "fake it until you make it" mentality. This work signals the future of impostor phenomenon research, providing a comprehensive road map for navigating the complexities of self-doubt and authenticity.

—**Helen A. Neville, PhD,** Professor, Educational Psychology and African American Studies, and President, Society of Counseling Psychology, University of Illinois Urbana-Champaign

The
IMPOSTOR
PHENOMENON

The
IMPOSTOR
PHENOMENON

Psychological Research, Theory, and Interventions

Edited by
KEVIN COKLEY

AMERICAN PSYCHOLOGICAL ASSOCIATION

Copyright © 2024 by the American Psychological Association. All rights reserved. Except as permitted under the United States Copyright Act of 1976, no part of this publication may be reproduced or distributed in any form or by any means, including, but not limited to, the process of scanning and digitization, or stored in a database or retrieval system, without the prior written permission of the publisher.

The opinions and statements published are the responsibility of the authors, and such opinions and statements do not necessarily represent the policies of the American Psychological Association.

Published by
American Psychological Association
750 First Street, NE
Washington, DC 20002
https://www.apa.org

Order Department
https://www.apa.org/pubs/books
order@apa.org

Typeset in Charter and Interstate by Robert Kern, TIPS Publishing Services, Carrboro, NC

Printer: Gasch Printing, Odenton, MD
Cover Designer: Anthony Paular Design, Newbury Park, CA

Library of Congress Cataloging-in-Publication Data

Names: Cokley, Kevin O. (Kevin O'Neal), 1969- editor.
Title: The impostor phenomenon : psychological research, theory, and
   interventions / edited by Kevin Cokley.
Description: Washington, DC : American Psychological Association, [2024] |
   Includes bibliographical references and index.
Identifiers: LCCN 2023044301 (print) | LCCN 2023044302 (ebook) | ISBN
   9781433841439 (paperback) | ISBN 9781433841446 (ebook)
Subjects: LCSH: Imposter phenomenon. | BISAC: PSYCHOLOGY / Social
   Psychology | SOCIAL SCIENCE / Women's Studies
Classification: LCC BF637.I46 I47 2024 (print) | LCC BF637.I46 (ebook) |
   DDC 158.1--dc23/eng/20231211
LC record available at https://lccn.loc.gov/2023044301
LC ebook record available at https://lccn.loc.gov/2023044302

https://doi.org/10.1037/0000397-000

Printed in the United States of America

10 9 8 7 6 5 4 3 2 1

To Pauline Clance and Suzanne Imes,
whose work has inspired me and countless numbers
of students, researchers, and thought leaders.

Contents

Contributors	*ix*
Acknowledgments	*xi*

Introduction: The Importance of Empirical Research on the Impostor Phenomenon   **3**
Kevin Cokley

I. CONCEPTUAL, THEORETICAL, AND METHODOLOGICAL FOUNDATIONS   15

1. Impostor Phenomenon: Origins and Treatment   **17**
Pauline Clance and Suzann Lawry

2. An Overview of the Impostor Phenomenon: Definitional and Theoretical Considerations   **45**
Kevin Cokley, Keoshia Harris, Shaina Hall, and Myya Singletary

3. The Impostor Phenomenon and Mental Health   **61**
Ramya Garba, Carly Coleman, and Tia Kelley

4. Impostor Phenomenon and Burnout   **81**
Lizette Ojeda

5. The Impostor Phenomenon's Relation to Achievement at School and Work   **111**
Lauren A. Blondeau

6. Measurement Issues Related to the Impostor Phenomenon   **131**
Hwa Young Lee, Cheryl B. Anderson, Kevin Cokley, and Shine Chang

viii • *Contents*

II. POPULATIONS AND CONTEXTS   159

7. Gender and the Impostor Phenomenon   161
Kadie R. Rackley, Taylor Payne, Ashley Bennett, and Germine H. Awad

**8. Racism and the Impostor Phenomenon Among African
American Students: A Socioecological Analysis**   181
Donte Bernard

**9. A Mixed-Methods Study of Impostor Phenomenon
in a Hispanic-Serving Institution**   203
Olympia Caudillo and Rodolfo Rincones

**10. Impostor Phenomenon in Science, Technology, Engineering,
and Mathematics**   221
Devasmita Chakraverty

11. Impostor Phenomenon in Medicine   245
Devasmita Chakraverty

III. INTERVENTIONS AND TRENDS   267

**12. Critical Issues of the Impostor Phenomenon and
Interventions for Historically Marginalized People**   269
Lisa Orbé-Austin and Richard Orbé-Austin

**13. An Evolving Analysis of Impostor Syndrome From 1983 to
the Present: Implications for Clinicians and Researchers**   285
Valerie Young

**14. Research-Based Strategies for Combating the Impostor
Phenomenon in Higher Education**   309
Danielle Rosenscruggs and Laura Schram

15. Trends Within the Impostor Phenomenon Literature   341
Steven Stone-Sabali

Index   *363*

About the Editor   *385*

Contributors

Cheryl B. Anderson, PhD, Division of Cancer Prevention & Population Sciences, The University of Texas MD Anderson Cancer Center, Houston, TX, United States

Germine H. Awad, PhD, University of Michigan, Ann Arbor, MI, United States

Ashley Bennett, PhD, The University of Texas at Austin, Austin, TX, United States

Donte Bernard, PhD, Department of Psychological Sciences, University of Missouri, Columbia, MO, United States

Lauren A. Blondeau, PhD, Department of Statistics and Data Science, The University of Texas at Austin, Austin, TX, United States

Olympia Caudillo, EdD, The Graduate School, The University of Texas at El Paso, El Paso, TX, United States

Devasmita Chakraverty, PhD, Indian Institute of Management Ahmedabad, Ahmedabad, India

Shine Chang, PhD, Division of Cancer Prevention & Population Sciences and the Department of Epidemiology, The University of Texas MD Anderson Cancer Center, Houston, TX, United States

Pauline Clance, PhD, Professor Emerita, Department of Psychology, Georgia State University, Atlanta, GA, United States

Kevin Cokley, PhD, Department of Psychology, University of Michigan, Ann Arbor, MI, United States

x • *Contributors*

Carly Coleman, BA, Department of Educational Psychology, The University of Texas at Austin, Austin, TX, United States

Ramya Garba, PhD, Department of Psychiatry, Norton College of Medicine, State University of New York, New York, NY, United States

Shaina Hall, BS, Department of Educational Psychology, The University of Texas at Austin, Austin, TX, United States

Keoshia Harris, MA, Department of Educational Psychology, The University of Texas at Austin, Austin, TX, United States

Tia Kelley, BA, Department of Educational Psychology, The University of Texas at Austin, Austin, TX, United States

Suzann Lawry, PhD, Georgia State University, Atlanta, GA, United States

Hwa Young Lee, PhD, Division of Cancer Prevention & Population Sciences, The University of Texas MD Anderson Cancer Center, Houston, TX, United States

Lizette Ojeda, PhD, Department of Educational Psychology, Texas A&M University, College Station, TX, United States

Lisa Orbé-Austin, PhD, Dynamic Transitions Psychological Consulting, New York, NY, United States

Richard Orbé-Austin, PhD, Dynamic Transitions Psychological Consulting, New York, NY, United States

Taylor Payne, PhD, The University of Texas at Austin, Austin, TX, United States

Kadie R. Rackley, PhD, St. Edwards University, Austin, TX, United States

Rodolfo Rincones, PhD, Department of Educational Leadership and Foundations, The University of Texas at El Paso, El Paso, TX, United States

Danielle Rosenscruggs, MS, Department of Psychology, University of Michigan, Ann Arbor, MI, United States

Laura Schram, PhD, Rackham Graduate School, University of Michigan, Ann Arbor, MI, United States

Myya Singletary, MA, Department of Educational Psychology, The University of Texas at Austin, Austin, TX, United States

Steven Stone-Sabali, MEd, PhD, Department of Educational Studies, The Ohio State University, Columbus, OH, United States

Valerie Young, EdD, Impostor Syndrome Institute, South Hadley, MA, United States

Acknowledgments

It is exciting to be able to offer the first research-focused book on the impostor phenomenon. Editing this book has been an incredibly rewarding experience. When APA Publishing initially approached me about writing a book, I immediately thought that an edited book would offer the most comprehensive coverage of the impostor phenomenon. I was aware of the many researchers, scholars, and thought leaders who were doing outstanding work on the impostor phenomenon, and I believed their contributions and insights needed to be highlighted in the book. I want to thank the chapter authors for giving so graciously of their time and efforts. Without them this book would not be possible. I want to thank all of my students, past and present, who have helped shape my thinking about the impostor phenomenon.

The
IMPOSTOR
PHENOMENON

INTRODUCTION

The Importance of Empirical Research on the Impostor Phenomenon

KEVIN COKLEY

In 1978, Pauline Clance and Suzanne Imes introduced the term "impostor phenomenon" in the academic literature. They defined the term as an internal experience of intellectual phoniness. In 1985, Pauline Clance followed this groundbreaking article by writing a book titled *The Impostor Phenomenon: Overcoming the Fear That Haunts Your Success*. Based on her clinical experiences, this book traces the origins of the impostor phenomenon, addresses its psychological impact, and provides suggestions about how to overcome impostor feelings. At the time that Clance wrote the book, according to PsycINFO only six published articles and five unpublished dissertations had examined the impostor phenomenon. By 2000, there were 41 published articles and 32 dissertations, for an average of approximately 1.9 published articles and 1.5 dissertations per year since 1978. Although this was evidence of increasing interest, overall, the scholarly interest in the impostor phenomenon was still modest.

Fast-forward to 2022, and scholarly interest in the impostor phenomenon has grown tremendously. At the time of this writing there were 195 published articles, 147 dissertations, and 13 book chapters, for an average of approximately 4.4 articles and 3.3 dissertations per year. The increasing scholarly interest in the impostor phenomenon coincides with the rise of its popularity

https://doi.org/10.1037/0000397-001
The Impostor Phenomenon: Psychological Research, Theory, and Interventions,
K. Cokley (Editor)
Copyright © 2024 by the American Psychological Association. All rights reserved.

in popular culture. There has been a resurgence in attention paid to the impostor phenomenon, as evidenced by the market being flooded with self-help, pop psychology books on the impostor phenomenon (aka imposter syndrome in popular culture discourse). A number of famous people and celebrities (e.g., Michelle Obama, Tina Fey, Tom Hanks, Viola Davis, Maya Angelou, Lady Gaga, Jennifer Lopez) have publicly acknowledged their insecurities or that they feel like a fraud. A recent Google search for the terms "impostor phenomenon," "imposter phenomenon," "impostor syndrome," and "imposter syndrome" yielded results of 1.26 million, 2.25 million, 4.29 million, and 9.46 million, respectively.

The popularity of the impostor phenomenon is due to it being an immensely relatable topic, with an estimated 70% of people feeling like an impostor as commonly referenced from an article published in the *International Journal of Behavioral Science* (Sakulku & Alexander, 2011). In this article, the 70% figure is attributed to an article written in the *Chronicle of Higher Education*, not an actual empirical study (Gravois, 2007). In the Gravois article, the 70% reference is attributed to an unpublished survey by Pauline Clance and Gail Matthews. However, a recent synthesis of studies estimated that up to 82% of people experience impostor feelings (Bravata et al., 2020). The origins of the 70% figure in an unpublished source underscore the need for the empirical, evidence-based rationale of this book. Much of the conventional wisdom and popular culture discourse about the impostor phenomenon is driven by intuitive, common sense–based recommendations about how to cope with, and conquer, impostor feelings. There is no doubt a market for this type of pop psychology. However, similar to the 70% figure, much of the discourse about the impostor phenomenon is not rooted in, or informed by, empirical research.

MISINFORMATION IN POPULAR CULTURE

One of the challenges and frustrations of being a researcher and scholar on the impostor phenomenon is having to deal with misinformation and uninformed criticisms of the term. I do not characterize critiques of the term as necessarily challenging and frustrating because there are certainly legitimate critiques one can make. However, much of what is being said about the impostor phenomenon on social media and in popular culture is misleading and in some instances just wrong. Recently I was contacted by a fellow expert on the impostor phenomenon and contributor to this book, Dr. Lisa Orbé-Austin, regarding a TikTok video she had seen. The video, posted by @theconsciouslee, referenced a tweet posted on April 13, 2022, by @jewelsfromjuana, stating that she was no longer using the term "imposter syndrome." She made this decision because of a lecture she heard by @atachine, which informed her that the concept was created by two White women to explain why minoritized folks feel like outsiders or face self-doubt. @jewelsfromjuana continued by saying that this fraud feeling was a result of systemic bias and exclusion and that the academy created a term to cover up systemic bias and placed the blame on the person in minoritized communities rather than blaming the system. At the time this introduction was written, the TikTok video had been liked over 75,000 times and the tweet had been liked over 22,000 times, retweeted over 5,600 times, and quote tweeted 860 times. The claim that the term was created to explain why minoritized folks feel like outsiders or face self-doubt is simply not true as it pertains to people of color. If one carefully reads the Clance and Imes (1978) article, it clearly indicates that the focus was on mostly White women, not minoritized women or minoritized men. It is also not accurate to say that the academy (i.e., a reference to Pauline Clance's faculty status) created the term to cover up systemic bias. In fact, as elaborated later in their article, Clance and Imes recognized that societal stereotypes about women's intelligence exacerbated women's feelings of self-doubt. A critique can be made that they could have spent more time explicitly addressing systemic bias, especially as it relates to minoritized people, which is a nod to the role of the environment. However, it cannot reasonably be concluded from carefully reading their body of work that their motivation was to blame minoritized individuals rather than the system. They were always clear about the role of the sociocultural context of the impostor phenomenon. This mischaracterization of their motivation contributes to criticisms of the impostor phenomenon.

One of the more thoughtful popular culture critiques was made in an article published in the *Harvard Business Review* (Tulshyan & Burey, 2021). This article created quite the buzz on social media (e.g., it was shared over 67,000 times on Facebook). In the article, the authors argued that the original concept excluded the effects of systemic racism, classism, and xenophobia and that the answer to overcoming "imposter syndrome" is to fix the environment rather than to fix individuals. The authors criticized use of the word "imposter" for essentially being too heavy-handed (they describe the word as having undertones of "criminal fraudulence") when individuals were simply unsure or anxious. It should be remembered that Clance and Imes (1978) used this term to describe their clinical observations. The term "impostor" literally refers to a person who pretends to be someone else in order to deceive others, and the women Clance and Imes were working with often reported that they believed they had fooled people into thinking they were intelligent. Considered in this context, use of the word "impostor" is not unreasonable. In fact, the women

6 • *Kevin Cokley*

they worked with used the term "impostor" to describe their feelings. Tulshyan and Burey (2021) were also critical of the term "syndrome" after acknowledging that Clance and Imes originally used the term "impostor phenomenon." It would be helpful if critiques of the concept of impostorism would not use the term "impostor syndrome," as the word "syndrome" can serve to reify the criticism of pathologizing normal, warranted feelings.

INDIVIDUAL VERSUS ENVIRONMENT

The critique of the impostor phenomenon focusing on the individual rather than the environment has been extended by McGee et al. (2022), who argued that it is really racism and oppression, camouflaged as impostor syndrome, that negatively harms minoritized individuals. McGee is particularly critical of the impostor phenomenon/syndrome construct, as she derisively believes it has been used to peddle interventions that focus on individuals thinking or breathing their way out of impostor feelings (McGee et al., 2022). McGee's critique has some merit, and the impact of racism and oppression on impostor feelings is addressed throughout this book. In fact, every talk that I give on the impostor phenomenon among BIPOC (Black, Indigenous, People of Color) individuals addresses the challenges of overcoming lack of representation, racially hostile environments, discrimination, and marginalization. That said, I also believe there are problems with reducing the impostor phenomenon to only bias, racism, and oppression. I disagree that impostor feelings would no longer exist among Black students if structural, institutional, and everyday racism were eradicated, as suggested by McGee et al. (2022). For example, some empirical research indicates that Black students attending historically Black colleges and universities also experience impostor feelings (Bernard et al., 2020). Reducing the impostor phenomenon to only racism is a *cultural misattribution bias*, which limits our scientific understanding of human nature among BIPOC individuals by only focusing on how the cultural context shapes human behavior and psychological functioning while ignoring or dismissing how individual-level processes also shape human behavior and psychological functioning (Causadias et al., 2018). In other words, as powerful as the cultural context of racism is in influencing or causing the impostor phenomenon, BIPOC individuals are not immune from being shaped by psychological processes. The problem with this cultural misattribution is that it (unwittingly) stereotypes the behavior of BIPOC individuals as homogenous and *only* being influenced by race and culture, while (unwittingly) privileging the behavior of White people as normative. Stated another way, reducing the impostor phenomenon to racism suggests that BIPOC individuals can only have thoughts and feelings in reaction to racism, whereas the thoughts and feelings of White people are viewed within the context of being unique individuals. This critique of the impostor phenomenon has created a false dichotomy in a focus on the individual versus the environment. Human behavior is complex, and interventions should never be reduced to either the individual level or the environmental level. The focus should always be both–and, which is consistent with a diunital logic and worldview promoted by Afrocentric psychologists (Myers, 1988).

A UBIQUITOUS EXPERIENCE?

As this book was close to completion, I was contacted by another fellow expert on the impostor phenomenon and contributor to this book, Dr. Valerie Young, regarding a recently published article on the impostor syndrome in *The New Yorker*. The title of the article is "Why Everyone Feels Like They're Faking It." The teaser description summarizes the article as follows: "The concept of Impostor Syndrome has become ubiquitous. Critics, and even the idea's originators, question its value." The article immediately caught my attention because the subtitle suggested that Pauline Clance and Suzanne Imes were now questioning its value (Jamison, 2023). This was confusing to me because nowhere have I seen Clance or Imes make any statements suggesting that they were starting to question its value (they do have feelings about using the term "impostor syndrome," but to my knowledge they have never questioned the utility of the impostor phenomenon). The article is an interesting exploration of the ubiquity of the impostor syndrome concept and how Clance and Imes never imagined how popular the concept would become. Some interesting and not well-known historical facts are shared (e.g., the original impostor phenomenon paper kept getting rejected before being accepted into the journal *Psychotherapy: Theory, Research, and Practice*). The article identifies clinical interventions utilized by Clance and Imes (e.g., gestalt therapy's empty-chair technique).

However, the most provocative part of the article was the discussion about the Whiteness of the impostor syndrome and how many women of color did not identify with the construct and questioned why White women were experiencing impostorism when essentially there were many examples of successful White women for them to see. Jamison (2023) cited a Black physician who talked about how she had been "misdiagnosed" with impostor syndrome when the reality was that she was just recognizing the impact of having connections and privilege (which she did not have). The Black physician read Clance and Imes's (1978) paper and said that, as a Black woman, she could not find herself in the paper. Jamison went on to say that Clance and Imes agree with many of the critiques of Tulshyan and Burey (2021) but believe that using the term "syndrome" pathologizes and distorts their original idea. Jamison offered an additional critique of the impostor syndrome from her mother, for whom the concept did not resonate and who suspected that women of her generation actually felt underestimated rather than struggled with proving themselves.

Jamison (2023) stated that although most of the critics of impostor syndrome are women of color, many people of color still identify with the experience. At the end of the article, she reverted back to using the term "impostor phenomenon" and concluded that it is "an inescapable part of being alive" (Jamison, 2023, para. 49). Although generally a thoughtfully written article, curiously Jamison did not present any specific details about Clance and Imes supposedly questioning the value of the impostor phenomenon. Although Jamison understands the problems and challenges of the word "syndrome," her continued use of the word "syndrome" throughout the article underscores the concerns that Clance and Imes have about distorting their original idea. The question of whether the impostor phenomenon is relevant to people of color is a question best addressed through careful empirical research rather than personal anecdotes.

UNRESOLVED ISSUES

Although much of the popular culture debate about the impostor phenomenon focuses on its applicability to people of color and whether it is racialized, there are many other important theoretical, empirical, and methodological questions about the impostor phenomenon that have not been satisfactorily answered or have equivocal answers. For example, is the impostor phenomenon part of one's identity, as suggested by Matthews and Clance (1985)? Is the impostor phenomenon a stable personality trait or predisposition, or is it an affective experience created by circumstances (state) of being evaluated too highly (McElwee & Yurak, 2010)? The contributors in this book either explicitly or implicitly endorse belief in the ubiquity of the impostor phenomenon, yet there are theoretical questions about the impostor phenomenon's utility as a distinct psychological entity. In other words, if the impostor phenomenon is everywhere and experienced by nearly everyone, is it really a useful and distinct psychological construct? In this book we take the position that the impostor phenomenon is commonly experienced by many people but the sociocultural context is important to consider. The impostor phenomenon is experienced differently and has different implications depending on the individual, group, and social context.

Some scholars have raised questions about the theoretical assumptions of the impostor phenomenon and suggested that behaviors attributed to impostors have a self-presentational element (i.e., impostors believe there are interpersonal benefits from presenting as an impostor; e.g., Leary et al., 2000). It is often stated that women are more susceptible to impostor feelings, yet research is equivocal on this. More recently it has been suggested that members of ethnic minorities are more susceptible to impostor feelings, but it is not clear if all empirical studies support this. There are also concerns about the quality of the measurement of the impostor phenomenon, with questions raised about its dimensionality and whether existing measures are inadequate to capture a racialized form of impostor feelings among racial and ethnic minorities. Increasingly questions are being asked about how the impostor phenomenon impacts participation in science, technology, engineering, mathematics, and medicine. One of the most commonly asked questions about the impostor phenomenon is what can be done about it. However, relatively little empirical work has been done on interventions specific to impostor phenomenon. Finally, given the resurgence of interest in the impostor phenomenon, what is the state of the field and where is it going? This brings us to the importance of this book.

The debates, misunderstandings, mischaracterizations, and unanswered questions surrounding the impostor phenomenon underscore the need for a book that addresses the aforementioned theoretical, empirical, and methodological issues and critiques. Currently there is no such book in existence for researchers and practitioners to reference. This book is envisioned as filling that gap. The goals of this book include the following:

- to provide a critical review of empirical studies on the impostor phenomenon,
- to provide a review of the major issues involved with researching the impostor phenomenon,
- to highlight areas of agreement along with tensions and disagreement among scholars and practitioners, and
- to be a research-based resource for individuals who are engaged in impostor phenomenon research and interventions.

Many of the contributors to this book are among the leading scholars and thought leaders on the impostor phenomenon. Many of the contributors conduct empirical research on the impostor phenomenon, and others engage in interventions that are informed by empirical research and years of clinical work and educational outreach. Some of the contributors have included personal narratives that describe how they became involved in work on the impostor phenomenon. The contributors agree on many issues. Perhaps most importantly, there is consensus that the impostor phenomenon is *not* a psychiatric disorder (and therefore should not be considered for inclusion in the *Diagnostic and Statistical Manual of Mental Disorders*), unlike some researchers who advance the position that the impostor phenomenon is a psychiatric disorder (e.g., Bravata et al., 2020).[1] However, there are some tensions and places of disagreement that are worthy of continued discussion (e.g., use of the term "impostor syndrome"). Ultimately, I believe that healthy debate is good for the field.

OVERVIEW OF THE BOOK

This book is divided into three sections. Part I: Conceptual, Theoretical, and Methodological Foundations includes six chapters. In Chapter 1, Clance and Lawry discuss the origins of the impostor phenomenon. They address issues of terminology, express concerns around the mislabeling of the originating work, and provide an overview of the state of impostor phenomenon intervention. They also directly address the sociocultural context of the impostor phenomenon and provide an example of a sociocultural-level intervention. In Chapter 2, Cokley et al. provide an overview of definitional and theoretical considerations of the impostor phenomenon, address misconceptions and limitations of the impostor phenomenon construct, and introduce the idea of a racialized impostor phenomenon. In Chapter 3, Garba et al. provide a broad overview of the extant literature on the mental health correlates of the impostor phenomenon and specifically discuss anxiety, depression, perfectionism, and self-esteem. In Chapter 4, Ojeda reviews the few empirical studies linking the impostor syndrome to burnout syndrome, provides an overview of the common factors that may affect both, and offers recommendations for further research and implications for practice. In Chapter 5, Blondeau reviews findings linking the impostor phenomenon with school and work achievement and proposes mediating roles of mental health, personality, self-efficacy, and self-regulation. In Chapter 6, Lee et al. provide a general description of the psychometric properties of impostor phenomenon measurement scales, discuss the methodological limitations and controversies of the most well-known impostor phenomenon instruments, and propose new directions for improving assessment of the impostor phenomenon.

Part II: Populations and Contexts includes five chapters. In Chapter 7, Rackley et al. review the literature on impostorism and gender. They focus on studies examining gender differences, discuss moderators that may help

---

[1] I was an author on this paper, but I do not agree with the position that the impostor phenomenon is a psychiatric disorder.

explain gender differences, and conclude by suggesting future directions in impostorism and gender research. In Chapter 8, Bernard examines the impostor phenomenon among African American students and interrogates how racism may inform the development and maintenance of impostor feelings. In Chapter 9, Caudillo and Rincones present a mixed-methods study of the impostor phenomenon in a Hispanic-serving institution and note that impostor phenomenon research at these institutions is lacking. In Chapter 10, Chakraverty reviews the impostor phenomenon in science, technology, engineering, and mathematics fields, with an emphasis on BIPOC individuals and underrepresented groups such as first-generation students. She also discusses the personality trait nature versus the environmental influence of the impostor phenomenon, strategies to overcome impostor feelings, and suggestions for future research. In Chapter 11, Chakraverty reviews research on the impostor phenomenon in medicine, focusing on graduate students, MD-PhD students, residents, physicians, physician assistants, and veterinarians. She proposes strategies to overcome impostor feelings along with suggestions for future research.

Part III: Interventions and Trends has four chapters. In Chapter 12, Orbé-Austin and Orbé-Austin discuss critical issues and concerns related to the impostor phenomenon when it is experienced by marginalized groups. They explore how the impostor phenomenon may be experienced differently by distinct marginalized groups and discuss interventions they have found to be particularly useful for historically marginalized people. In Chapter 13, Young discusses the origins and evolution of an established educational intervention for the impostor "syndrome," which she proposes can offer areas of future research and future considerations for clinicians, coaches, and others who work with clients. In Chapter 14, Rosenscruggs and Schram discuss the impostor phenomenon within higher education contexts. Informed by the literature and their work designing and facilitating impostor phenomenon workshops, they share strategies regarding how higher education institutions can effectively and efficiently deliver student-facing impostor phenomenon interventions. In Chapter 15, Stone-Sabali provides an overview of the publication and topical trends within the impostor phenomenon literature. He summarizes a bibliometric investigation of the impostor phenomenon literature (e.g., identifying most cited authors and most cited articles) and concludes with implications for future directions.

It would be nearly impossible to comprehensively cover every important issue pertaining to the state of empirical research on the impostor phenomenon. As this book is being written, new issues (e.g., Is the impostor phenomenon actually beneficial?; Tewfik, 2022), scales (e.g., Impostor Phenomenon

Assessment; Walker & Saklofske, 2023), and researchers (e.g., Tewfik, 2022) have emerged. That said, this book will serve as a primer on the state of impostor phenomenon research. It is hoped that this book will be a foundational resource for scholars, researchers, clinicians, and practitioners and will inspire new research questions and future research agendas.

REFERENCES

Bernard, D. L., Jones, S. C. T., & Volpe, V. V. (2020). Impostor phenomenon and psychological well-being: The moderating roles of John Henryism and school racial composition among Black college students. *Journal of Black Psychology, 46*(2–3), 195–227. https://doi.org/10.1177/0095798420924529

Bravata, D., Watts, S., Keefer, A., Madhusudhan, D., Taylor, K., Clark, D., Nelson, R., Cokley, K., & Hagg, H. (2020). Prevalence, predictors, and treatment of impostor syndrome: A systematic review. *Journal of General Medicine, 35*(4), 1252–1275. https://doi.org/10.1007/s11606-019-05364-1

Causadias, J. M., Vitriol, J. A., & Atkin, A. L. (2018). Do we overemphasize the role of culture in the behavior of racial/ethnic minorities? Evidence of a cultural (mis)attribution bias in American psychology. *American Psychologist, 73*(3), 243–255. https://doi.org/10.1037/amp0000099

Clance, P. R., & Imes, S. A. (1978). The imposter phenomenon in high achieving women: Dynamics and therapeutic intervention. *Psychotherapy: Theory, Research & Practice, 15*(3), 241–247. https://doi.org/10.1037/h0086006

Gravois, J. (2007, November 9). You're not fooling anyone. *The Chronicle of Higher Education.* https://www.chronicle.com/article/youre-not-fooling-anyone/

Jamison, L. (2023, February 6). Why everyone feels like they're faking it. *The New Yorker.* https://www.newyorker.com/magazine/2023/02/13/the-dubious-rise-of-impostor-syndrome

Leary, M. R., Patton, K. M., Orlando, A. E., & Wagoner Funk, W. (2000). The impostor phenomenon: Self-perceptions, reflected appraisals, and interpersonal strategies. *Journal of Personality, 68*(4), 725–756. https://doi.org/10.1111/1467-6494.00114

Matthews, G., & Clance, P. R. (1985). Treatment of the impostor phenomenon in psychotherapy clients. *Psychotherapy in Private Practice, 3*(1), 71–81. https://doi.org/10.1300/J294v03n01_09

McElwee, R. O., & Yurak, T. J. (2010). The phenomenology of the impostor phenomenon. *Individual Differences Research, 8*(3), 184–197.

McGee, E. O., Botchway, P. K., Naphan-Kingery, D. E., Brockman, A. J., Houston, I. I., & White, D. T. (2022). Racism camouflaged as impostorim and the impact on Black STEM doctoral students. *Race, Ethnicity and Education, 25*(4), 487–507. https://doi.org/10.1080/13613324.2021.1924137

Myers, L. J. (1988). *Understanding an Afrocentric world view: Introduction to an optimal psychology.* Kendall/Hunt.

Sakulku, J., & Alexander, J. (2011). The impostor phenomenon. *International Journal of Behavioral Science, 6*(1), 75–97.

Tewfik, B. (2022). The impostor phenomenon revisited: Examining the relationship between workplace impostor thoughts and interpersonal effectiveness at work. *Academy of Management Journal, 65*(3), 988–1018. https://doi.org/10.5465/amj.2020.1627

Tulshyan, R., & Burey, J.-A. (2021, February 11). Stop telling women they have imposter syndrome. *Harvard Business Review.* https://hbr.org/2021/02/stop-telling-women-they-have-imposter-syndrome

Walker, D. L., & Saklofske, D. H. (2023). Development, factor structure, and psychometric validation of the impostor phenomenon assessment: A novel assessment of impostor phenomenon. *Assessment, 30*(7), 2162–2183. https://doi.org/10.1177/10731911221141870

PART I CONCEPTUAL, THEORETICAL, AND METHODOLOGICAL FOUNDATIONS

1

IMPOSTOR PHENOMENON
Origins and Treatment

PAULINE CLANCE AND SUZANN LAWRY

I grew up in the hills of Appalachia, where my elementary school had one teacher for several grades, all taught in the same room, and high school stopped at 11th grade. Many did not get out of high school, and there were few options other than coal mining. I remember always loving school, being an avid reader, being the first female senior class president through beating the captain of the football team, and graduating third in my class. Despite this, a high school counselor warned me to expect to get "no better than Cs" in college.

When I entered college, I had many doubts and fears. I feared failure and kept expecting to get one of those Cs. Yet I succeeded and graduated cum laude. I had some excellent professors and mentors who believed in me and encouraged me to go to graduate school. Getting into a graduate school for a PhD in clinical psychology was highly competitive at that time, 1960, especially for a woman. Very few women were selected, but I was admitted to the University of Kentucky. It was a time when the philosophy was to set up a competitive culture by accepting more students than would complete the program, with a clear and stated expectation that many would fail. In an orientation, we were told, "Look around you. Only a small number of you will survive the first year." There were 15 or so in my class, and six of us decided to form a study group; we had a motto that we would "Collaborate and Graduate." We had a proseminar class

---

https://doi.org/10.1037/0000397-002
The Impostor Phenomenon: Psychological Research, Theory, and Interventions,
K. Cokley (Editor)
Copyright © 2024 by the American Psychological Association. All rights reserved.

in which each professor taught their specialty area. The reading lists were long, and the material was hard. After 2-hour examinations every 2 weeks, our study group would go out and have a beer or coffee. After the first exam, I felt relief and hoped I had done okay, but as we talked about it, I got more frightened. I remembered questions where I was uncertain of my answers. When someone in the group shared something they wrote, I asked myself, "Why didn't I think of that?" My doubt and anxiety grew.

I would say, "Oh, I think I failed. I'm really worried." Then, when the test grades came back, I actually did as well as my study mates and sometimes even better. After about three times of doing this with them, they began saying, "Don't pull that 'woe is me, I'm going to fail' stuff again with us!" So I began to hide my doubts. I still worried and had anxiety and sleeplessness about my performance, but I rarely, if ever, voiced it.

With my history, it was easy for me to understand my own self-doubts about being smart enough. I did not have the educational background of my peers; my faculty and peers did not share my identities; and more concretely, successful people were telling me not to expect to make it. Yet I graduated; I got my PhD. Only three or four others in my class of 15 graduated with me. With these statistics, it was also easy to worry about when others would figure out I did not really belong in the academy.

Carrying that worry with me, I began my career as a psychologist and landed a position at a small, mostly White, liberal arts college with competitive admission standards. I taught at the college part-time, and I provided therapy to students the rest of the week. In one therapy session, a student said, "I feel like an impostor [beside all these other outstanding students]." I began to notice a pattern that many female students expressed considerable doubt about their intellectual abilities, especially when facing exams and experiences where they had to demonstrate their competence. These doubts persisted in spite of high test scores, repeated success, praise, and positive feedback from their professors; this was an experience I understood deeply.

As a result of my experiences with these students, a colleague, Dr. Suzanne Imes, and I began to discuss and study this experience in other women. We found that highly successful women, who had earned PhDs in their various specialties, who were respected in their professions, and who were recognized for their academic excellence did not experience an internal sense of their own success. We labeled this experience impostor phenomenon (IP) and published our findings in the *Journal of Psychotherapy: Theory, Research, and Practice* (Clance & Imes, 1978). Later at Georgia State University, I developed the Clance Impostor Phenomenon Scale (CIPS; Clance, 1985). The CIPS has now been translated into 36 languages and serves as a gold standard to

IP. Research using the CIPS comes from over 59 countries from the large to the small: Armenia, Australia, Bangladesh, Bosnia and Herzegovina, Bulgaria, Canada, Dominica, Greece, Holland, India, Iran, Israel, Java, Lebanon, Malaysia, Mexico, Nepal, Nigeria, Pakistan, the Philippines, Poland, Saudi Arabia, Slovenia, South Africa, Thailand, the United Arab Emirates, the United Kingdom, the West Indies (Lesser Antilles), and more. I have authored two books in this area, *The Impostor Phenomenon: Overcoming the Fear That Haunts Your Success* (1985a) and *The Impostor Phenomenon: When Success Makes You Feel Like a Fake* (1985b). The seminal book was published well before the internet even existed, and now it can be found online as an audiobook. IP has resonated with successful people from all walks of life, including academia, business, entertainment, health care, pop culture, and even politics, to name a few. I state these facts to emphasize that IP is a very real experience of many high-achieving people; it is an experience that has continued to be relevant across place, discipline, identity, and culture for over 40 years, and there is no indication of it slowing down.

—Pauline Rose Clance, PhD

THE ORIGIN STORY

It is important to open this chapter on treating IP with the life story of Dr. Pauline Rose Clance to underscore several key points upon which our discussion about intervention is predicated. Growing up in Appalachian mining country, identifying as female, experiencing poverty and an underresourced educational system, being a first-generation college student, and yet still succeeding in the overwhelmingly male, economically privileged academy of the 1960s and 1970s set the stage for Dr. Clance's own experience of IP and a deep recognition of the powerful influence of social location. Her individual success defies not only overtly stated expectations by her school counselor and graduate faculty but also persistent systemic expectations based on her intersecting identities. Similarly, the original research was predominately based on White women's experiences in academia, which was a place they were not expected to be in at the time, much less to succeed in (Clance & Imes, 1978). Reviews of 4 decades of subsequent research have underscored the powerful relationship between IP and sociocultural context (Bravata et al., 2020; Gottlieb et al., 2020; Yaffe, 2023). Thus, it is deeply troubling that recent discourse, often fueled by mainstream media, mischaracterizes IP as an individual-level construct that is somehow separate from social location. Sociocultural context was, and always should be, foundational in understanding IP to prevent its occurrence and develop effective intervention.

Secondly, her life history can be utilized to clarify a persistent confusion of terms that also has implications for intervention. Dr. Pauline Rose Clance and Dr. Suzanne Imes are the original founders who identified this construct and coined it the "impostor phenomenon" (Clance & Imes, 1978). After their founding work, the term "impostor *syndrome*," at times spelled "impos*ter* syndrome," surfaced. This second term has often been used by the lay public and is easily found on the internet, social media, podcasts, and lay publications. These sources often add some of their own conceptualizations but retain a close tie to the originating work. As academic discourse struggles to effectively move information from the Ivory Tower to the lay public, IP stands as a clear testament that doing so is achievable; IP has truly become a household word. Certainly, this popularity has had clear clinical benefits in breaking the silence and isolation that historically shroud this experience. Despite this success story, the multiple terms have also created confusion that yields problematic implications for treatment.

The Story of Terminology and Treatment Implications

Drs. Clance and Imes chose both terms, "impostor" and "phenomenon," quite intentionally. As noted earlier, the term "impostor" honors a woman's voice in her poignant description of her experience, which was also powerfully felt by other accomplished women, at the very inception of this line of research. To clarify, feeling like an impostor is differentiated from being one (Ferrari, 2005) and is not used to imply being incompetent or having success that is not commensurate with ability. Instead, the word "impostor" brings to sharp relief the perplexing yet defining feature of the IP construct; the individual feels like a fraud despite the truth that they are, in fact, highly successful.

While Clance and Imes were both broadly trained as clinical psychologists, they were also deeply embedded in the humanistic, existential, and gestalt traditions of the 1960s and 1970s. To align with those traditions, they considered using the term "impostor *experience*"; however, they chose the term "phenomenon" to underscore that IP is not a completely transitory experience but rather one that can persist and, importantly, echo the experience of others in ways that are similar yet phenomenologically unique. Given that this phenomenon emerged from very private disclosures of academically successful women breaking gender barriers at the time, it was especially important to both Clance and Imes to not use a term that could pathologize these women's contextualized experiences (Clance & O'Toole, 1987). Moreover, the definition of the word "phenomenon" evokes an experience that is deeply sensed, about which not all is known, and yet exists; this is a persistent truth about IP to this day even with the 40 years of subsequent research.

In a clarifying discussion about the choice of terminology, it is also important to highlight a term that was intentionally not used: "disorder." Although a critique of the role of the *Diagnostic and Statistical Manual of Mental Disorders* in pathologizing responses to oppression is beyond the scope of this writing, the use of the term "syndrome" or "disorder" reflects a sharp deviation from the founding work. These terms suggest a level of individual dysfunction that we do not see in clinical practice. Moreover, providers' adoption of such a mischaracterization can mistakenly narrow intervention to target the individual as the only unit of change. Finally, such framing absolves oppressive systems in creating the fertile conditions that keep IP alive and well. Exclusive use of individual-level framing denies IP's origin story, neglects a growing literature that demonstrates the powerful influence of context, and thwarts effective conceptualization and intervention; for all these reasons, such framing should be avoided.

Individual-level framing has, rightfully, drawn critique (Tulshyan & Burey, 2021); however, such critique is often leveled at a misrepresentation of the IP construct. In contrast, IP was always meant to be framed as a *contextualized experience*. This misperception needs definitive correction to support forward momentum to integrate the literature, identify IP's complex etiology and maintenance factors, and ultimately generate effective intervention. In truth, the totality of one's lived experiences are inextricably linked with one's experience of IP. Academic research has demonstrated the connection between IP and oppression in an expanding range of diverse samples (Bernard et al., 2017; Chao et al., 2012; Clance et al., 1995; Peteet, Brown, et al., 2015; Stone et al., 2018) and is developing a more nuanced understanding of its role in the distress experienced by these communities (Austin et al., 2009; Cokley et al., 2017; Ewing et al., 1996; Peteet, Montgomery, & Weekes, 2015).

Clarification of Terms for Academic and Clinical Discourse

Due to the increasing mislabeling of the original work, the task of locating and connecting the literature base has become unnecessarily complicated. This is even more problematic when one considers that IP research crosses multiple academic disciplines, databases, and languages. Due to this state of the literature, when developing key word algorithms, researchers are encouraged to include the terms "impostor phenomenon," "impostor syndrome," and "impostorism" (all with and without "er" spelling) to access the full range of relevant literature. Additionally, although the initial and gold standard for measuring IP remains the CIPS, there has been some confusion about its usage. To clarify and to ensure the legacy of the founding work, those wanting to use the scale should request permission at www.paulineroseclance.com, give appropriate acknowledgment, use the correct term and spelling (impostor phenomenon), utilize a score of 62 or higher as the cut-off for clinical severity, and always report the CIPS scores that are used to create categorical variables for analyses.

In sum, use of the term "impostor phenomenon" was a deeply personal and intentional choice that poignantly describes the perplexing and persistent experience of feeling like a fraud despite clear evidence to the contrary. The broad resonance of IP has spurred considerable dialogue in academic, public, and social media forums, and notably, the role of systemic oppression has often been obfuscated over time. To be clear, the etiology of IP is understood as a common reaction to a cumulation of experiences and negative messages that occur in personal, professional, and sociocultural domains across a life. The terms "syndrome" or "disorder" are not only misnomers but also create negative, pathologizing implications for the public, clinicians, and researchers alike, which can, in turn, serve to maintain and perpetuate oppression.

AN OVERVIEW OF THE STATE OF IMPOSTOR PHENOMENON INTERVENTION

In initial writing, conceptualization and treatment for IP was seen as a collaborative endeavor to discern how a client's interpersonal and social contexts formed IP so that therapy could "begin to unravel this mystery" (Clance et al., 1995, p. 87). This early call to examine how IP is uniquely made, and to adapt the treatment accordingly, is still applicable today. Unfortunately, investigations into intervention are notably lacking despite the plethora of research into the occurrence of IP and its correlates. The lack of intervention research is even more perplexing when one considers the sustained academic and public interest from a variety of disciplines across the globe for over 40 years. Indeed, two literature reviews document a marked increase in publications about IP across the last decade (Bravata et al., 2020; Gottlieb et al., 2020). The lack of intervention literature could plausibly be due to a publication bias against null findings; however, this hypothesis would certainly be contrary to our clinical experience of IP being quite responsive to treatment. Fortunately, there has been a recent move to begin to build IP intervention literature to fill this gap, although currently intervention has largely been conducted in nonclinical populations (Chang et al., 2022; Fainstad et al., 2022; Haskins et al., 2019; Hutchins & Flores, 2021; Magro, 2022; Zanchetta et al., 2020).

THE CLANCE IMES IMPOSTOR PHENOMENON CYCLE: A PHENOMENOLOGICAL PICTURE

Clance (1985a) described a predictable cycle that appears to play a critical role in how IP is maintained despite evidence to the contrary. Anecdotally in clinical work, we have found that interrupting the cycle at multiple junctures can help reduce the severity of IP, so we present it here to frame our discussion on intervention. The IP cycle described in previous work (Clance, 1985a) was visually adapted for this publication (Figure 1.1).

Achievement Task in Context

Many achievement tasks set in motion a predictable, self-perpetuating IP cycle. These tasks can range from postgraduate training, to applying for a promotion, to even being asked to serve as an expert. There have been illuminating investigations into the types of achievement tasks that trigger IP and for whom. Hutchins and Rainbolt (2017) found women report high IP responses to challenges of their work from positions of power, like a supervisor or a tenure review board, whereas men report heightened IP responses to challenges of their work from students or colleagues. Additionally, IP has been linked with stereotype threat (Cokley et al., 2015). These data support the influence of social location on the types of achievement tasks that can trigger IP feelings, cognitions, and behaviors.

FIGURE 1.1. Clance Imes Impostor Phenomenon Cycle

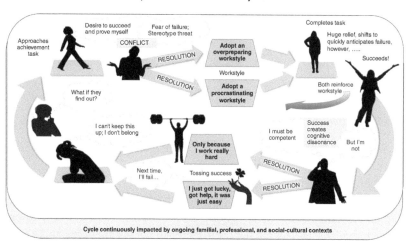

Note. Copyright 2023 by Pauline Clance and Suzann Lawry. Used with permission.

Drive for Success and Fear of Failure Conflict

These individuals value achievement and typically describe feeling excited and drawn to challenging tasks. Some are also motivated to prove themselves or excel against a negative stereotype about a salient part of their identity (Cokley et al., 2015; Stone et al., 2020). Almost immediately, IP fears, doubts, and shame can replace that draw. They begin to predict failure from not being intelligent, talented, or competent enough. Certainly, their personal and professional contexts can shape the costs of such imagined failures, for example, "If this doesn't get funded, I can just hear them saying I didn't deserve it. I'm the only Black faculty," "Most women don't even get an interview," or "I'll have to tell my family I failed." Sometimes, at this juncture, clients solve this internal conflict by avoiding the achievement task altogether. Indeed, some research suggests that experiencing high levels of IP correlates with staying in positions where tasks can be performed perfectly, which can limit career mobility and satisfaction (Neureiter & Traut-Mattausch, 2017; Neureiter et al., 2017; Vergauwe et al., 2015). Ultimately, these individuals do commit to many achievement tasks successfully while carrying this internal conflict.

Workstyle Choice

Some address the internal conflict between their achievement drive and fear of failure by engaging in an overpreparing workstyle. They start tasks early, rewrite obsessively, and drop all self-care routines to drive toward the perfect product. For others, they develop a workstyle of initial procrastination, that is then followed by a period of frenzied intense work; this also produces an exceptional product. Interestingly, there is some suggestion that men, as a group, may use more procrastination than women do in response to IP (Hutchins et al., 2018; Hutchins & Rainbolt, 2017). Clinically, we also see some clients vacillate between the two styles.

Task Completion and Success

Regardless of workstyle, the work itself is intense and filled with anxiety and fear, so when it is finally over, these individuals are exhausted and flooded with relief. The enormity of this relief serves as a negative reinforcer of their workstyle. The relief is also quickly replaced as they begin anticipating negative feedback due to their self-doubt about their abilities. These anxieties can be, and often are, exacerbated by their environment, for example, microaggressions about intelligence, lack of representation of salient identities, and pressure to succeed from families. In sharp contrast to these negative expectations, they experience success. The experience of success also reinforces the emotionally, intellectually, and physically exhausting workstyle. Unfortunately, these workstyles, repeatedly reinforced in these ways across time, often then function as deeply held, rigid rituals or superstitions. Similarly, they are commonly never tested.

Cognitive Dissonance: Success and Negative Self-Evaluations

The success experience creates uncomfortable cognitive dissonance. The objective success does not match their negative self-evaluation of their intelligence, talent, or competence. These negative self-evaluations have typically been formed over a lifetime influenced by biological, individual, familial, and sociocultural contexts. Negative self-evaluations are also created and/or magnified by current professional contexts, for example, competitive work norms; hostile environments filled with microaggressions; and lack of diversity, equity, and inclusion (DEI).

Resolving Dissonance Using Externalizing Narratives

For individuals experiencing IP, they often resolve this cognitive dissonance by externalizing their success and attributing it to a myriad of causes that are unrelated to their abilities, for example, luck, their likeability, the task being too easy, or excessive hard work rather than talent (Clance, 1985a). Stone et al. (2018) found notable differences when examining this important feature of this cycle, attributions of success, in Black college students. Some of these students also reported crediting their success to their faith, receiving support, and interpreting positive feedback as a reflection of the evaluator's underlying lowered racist expectations of their performance. Notably, others in their sample also articulated attributing success to an empowered rechanneling of their experiences of oppression. This work provides important nuance in how IP and the Clance Imes IP cycle is experienced by Black students in the academy, attributions of success, and the unique sociocultural pressures they carry. The provider is encouraged to listen carefully to the unique ways each client tosses away their success to effectively intervene at this juncture.

Persistent Anticipation of Impostor Status Becoming Known

In these ways, an individual's beliefs about their impostor status are maintained through a repetitive cycle initiated by a drive for success and fear of failure, exhausting workstyle choices, multiple reinforcement schedules, and ultimately external attributions of their eventual success. Each step of the cycle is continuously influenced by one's historical and current personal, professional, and sociocultural contexts. In these ways, the cycle becomes self-perpetuating and leaves individuals with a persistent lack of belonging among their comparably successful peers and fears of being discovered as an impostor.

AN INTEGRATED AND MULTILEVEL APPROACH TO IMPOSTOR PHENOMENON INTERVENTION

Due to this complexity, conceptualization and treatment require a collaborative and multilevel approach that is adapted to each client's unique experience of IP, values, treatment beliefs, stage of change, and preferences. Until an evidence-based treatment literature emerges, providers should integrate what is known about IP, relevant evidence-based treatments, and their client's unique lived experience to guide their work. The remainder of this chapter makes an effort to describe such an integration. The clinical examples in this chapter have been created from common clinical themes; no clinical material used herein reflects a single client. However, the composite examples do hold authority of countless encounters with IP across a collective 70 years of clinical practice, teaching, and supervision, so they elucidate very real and typical IP experiences and responses to intervention.

Clinical Presentation

It is important to remember that clients often hesitate to disclose IP and can present with other concerns (Clance & Imes, 1978; Magro, 2022; Matthews & Clance, 1985). Knowing a community's incidence rate can better prepare providers to recognize IP even when it is not initially disclosed. For example, high IP is reported in medical students and pharmacists (Gottlieb et al., 2020; Henning et al., 1998; Rosenthal et al., 2021); psychology graduate students (Tigranyan et al., 2021); Black, Latinx, and Asian college students (Cokley et al., 2013); and women (Meyer et al., 2015; Muradoglu et al., 2022). Similarly, knowing common markers, like exhibiting an overworking or procrastinating workstyle, can help providers avoid missing the presence of IP. Importantly, IP can also play key roles in other presenting concerns. For example, IP is often a better predictor of distress than minority stress (Cokley et al., 2013) or even mental health history (Henning et al., 1998). Finally, the comorbidity of IP with other learning and mental health concerns suggests screening is warranted for clients who do present with IP initially (Bravata et al., 2020; McGregor et al., 2008; Tigranyan et al., 2021).

Biological Level of Influence

IP is an embodied experience that impacts, and is impacted by, the body. Therefore, intervention should assess this dynamic influence to adequately address this level of influence.

Biological Conditions and Intervention

Physical conditions are important to assess because clients can misattribute biologically based challenges in ways that both shape and maintain IP. For example, college students who have undiagnosed attention-deficit/hyperactivity disorder often internalize their academic challenges as "stupidity" and their procrastination as "laziness," which can foster their experience of IP. Receiving an accurate diagnosis can help challenge these cognitions about their intellectual capacity. Additionally, by including medication or other biological intervention, subsequent behavioral interventions to address their procrastinating or obsessive workstyles can often be more effective.

Biological Impact of Impostor Phenomenon and Intervention

In addition to biological conditions shaping IP, it is also true that the experience of IP impacts the body. Physical descriptions of IP in therapy are often indiscernible from a fight-or-flight stress response, and for some, their trauma history (including race, gender, and other identity-based trauma), can exacerbate these physiological reactions. Consequently, for clients who present in these ways, providers are encouraged to utilize the variety of evidence-based practices available to help clients manage acute physiological arousal in response to IP triggers, for example, dialectical behavior therapy (DBT; Linehan, 2014), acceptance and commitment therapy (ACT; Hayes et al., 2011), cognitive behavioral therapy (Barlow et al., 2011), and the trauma literature (Horowitz, 2020; Resick et al., 2017).

Relatedly, this population's workstyles can chronically disrupt self-care routines. For example, pharmacists with high IP report regularly working over 80 hours per week (Sullivan & Ryba, 2020). Not surprisingly, there is a growing literature demonstrating a positive correlation between IP and burnout (Clark et al., 2022; Crawford et al., 2016; Hutchins & Rainbolt, 2017; Vergauwe et al., 2015). Thus, interrupting a client's exhausting workstyle and supporting their self-care routines are often integral to effective IP treatment. For some, a negative self-schema and conditions of worth fuel these patterns, and humanistic, dynamic, and emotion-focused therapy (EFT) strategies can be helpful (Greenberg, 2011; Levenson, 2010; Rogers, 1957). For others, interventions such as existentialism (Yalom, 1980) and more recently ACT (Hayes et al.,

2011) can help clients who struggle with the perpetual task of crafting a life of meaning and renewal. Other clients may find relief by being able to recognize and externalize burdensome stereotypes of strength or by framing self-care as resistance to oppression (Comas-Díaz, 2020; Crocket, 2013). Still other clients may benefit from approaches that target self-care behaviors, for example, cognitive behavioral therapy's behavioral activation (Santos et al., 2021) or motivational interviewing (Miller & Rollnick, 2013). Finally, with clients for whom traditional White Western psychotherapeutic interventions do not resonate, accessing the power of image making, metaphor, and spiritual rituals to expand awareness of their needs, recognize the impact of context, and motivate empowered change can be useful (Comas-Díaz, 2020; Hayes et al., 2011; Jung, 1961).

A Composite Case Example: Biological-Level Intervention
"Breah" was a respected author who entered therapy emotionally and physically depleted wanting to find a way to live her "best life." Over time, she painfully disclosed an incessant workstyle that, to her, proved an inherent lack of talent. Despite her exhaustion, she resisted changing these work patterns. Eventually, utilizing her metaphor, she was invited to make a list of what her best life would include. Starting with an empty circle, she was then asked to fill it with pie-shaped wedges for each item on her list and make each proportionately sized to reflect the space each occupied in her life. As she worked, she suddenly looked up, experientially realizing, "There is no way I can fit all of me in!" This exercise created more openness to reduce her work hours, which, she found, did not reduce the quality of her work. This fact challenged her former IP beliefs about her abilities and workstyle choices, and she began to embrace a life of doing a little less, feeling a lot better, and enjoying her talent.

Psychological Level of Influence

Given the dynamic connection between cognitions, emotions, and behaviors, many approaches target these factors. Certainly, working on specific IP cognitions, emotions, and behaviors can help clients embrace their power to change their experience of distress. At the same time, providers should take care to avoid exclusive individual-level framing that can inadvertently blame clients for their reactions to situational contexts.

Cognitive Factors and Intervention
To borrow a well-used phrase from Dr. Clance, clients must "use their intelligence about their intelligence." Once metacognition is developed, clients are

positioned to engage in cognitive restructuring, positive reframing/cognitive reappraisals, and mindful awareness/radical acceptance to reduce distress (Barlow et al., 2011; Beck & Beck, 1995; Hayes et al., 2011; Linehan, 2014). Originally, Matthews and Clance (1985) suggested the utility of cognitive restructuring to support internalized, global, and permanent attributions of success experiences and, inversely, more externalized, specific, and temporary attributions of failure experiences; this continues to be a pragmatic guide to IP intervention (Abramson et al., 1978; Beck & Beck, 1995). Doing so also counters unrealistic social comparisons, beliefs in a fixed mindset (Dweck, 1999), dichotomous definitions of success and failure, and equating performance with self-worth, which can help maintain IP.

To challenge IP cognitions, providers are encouraged to utilize familiar cognitive restructuring strategies (Barlow et al., 2011; Beck & Beck, 1995; Ellis & Dryden, 1987). One effective application of these approaches is gathering evidence against IP cognitions by asking trusted others for honest and specific feedback. Relatedly, exploring how clients measure themselves, and against whom, can facilitate clients crafting new measures that are more commensurate with their realities. Another strategy is to experientially challenge impostor narratives by having meaningful discussions with others who also struggle with IP and whose competencies they can more clearly see (Hutchins & Flores, 2021; Matthews & Clance, 1985). Similarly, the authentic and judicious use of therapist disclosure about IP can be used effectively. Lastly, experiential enactments using the empty-chair technique can also be used to challenge IP cognitions of having fooled supervisors or of positive evaluations being wrong. In this application, clients first imagine their respected faculty, mentors, and supervisors who gave them positive feedback sitting at one big table. Then they elaborate on the image, for example, their names, what they are wearing, how they sit. Next, the client tells these evaluators how their judgments were all wrong. Finally, the client describes how each person would likely respond. Experiential enactments, like this one, can bring the client's full embodiment of IP to the therapy room so cognitive challenges, albeit from imagined voices of their past, are more impactful. Some helpful cognitive themes that often emerge include: the intellect is multifaceted and unevenly developed for everyone; social comparisons erase inevitable differences in experience and context, mistakes are a gift and inherent in learning; if others are worthy of respect, then their positive evaluations are too; and importantly, one's value is not dependent upon performance.

In addition to restructuring cognitions, facilitating positive reframes (cognitive reappraisals) can also bring some relief, for example, working hard *is part of* competence (rather than evidence of incompetence); persistent luck, by definition, *is not luck*; and support from faith or others *allows optimal performance to emerge*. Others respond to psychoeducation, for example, as people achieve, the resulting change in peer group can feel like a drop in competency, despite there being no actual change in ability. Similarly, learning the Dunning–Kruger effect can help clients reframe that knowing what you do not know is a sign of intelligence rather than a sign of incompetence. Finally, knowing that those who struggle with IP are a smart, hardworking, respected, and accomplished group can help individuals adjust beliefs about what their IP signals about themselves.

Despite efforts at cognitive restructuring and reappraisals, IP cognitions can be persistent. Moreover, some clients do not respond well to these cognitive interventions. At such times, approaches that encourage mindful awareness and acceptance of IP cognitions can be helpful (Hayes et al., 2011; Linehan, 2014). For example, an ACT diffusion technique encourages clients to give their IP thoughts a name, for example, "There's 'Impostor Brain.' Remember, it lies." By doing so, the thought can pass without further cognitive elaboration or experiencing the typical emotional and behavioral reactions.

For targeting IP cognitions, Zanchetta et al. (2020) added an important contribution to IP intervention literature in a study designed to enhance a growth mindset (Dweck, 1999). The intervention, delivered through a one-to-one coaching group and a training group, significantly reduced CIPS scores when compared with a no intervention group. Further, the one-to-one coaching group showed more reduction in CIPS at a 5-month follow-up. Chang et al. (2022) also targeted a growth mindset to help reduce IP; they used a 90-minute workshop format at a summer STEM (science, technology, engineering, and mathematics) research program. In qualitative interviews after the program, participants reported relief at learning about IP and being better able to challenge their IP cognitions; however, quantitative measures of IP were unchanged. The responses to two questions used to measure a growth mindset did significantly improve. Interestingly, there was an interaction between time and gender for IP, wherein women reported increased levels of IP and men reported decreased levels. These data contrast with findings from Zanchetta et al. The measures they used may clarify these findings. Specifically, the two questions measuring growth mindset emphasized meritocracy beliefs: (a) "Becoming a top, productive scientist is possible for everyone through effort and practice" and (b) "Success in science is pretty much related to how much effort a person makes" (Chang et al., 2022, p. 4). One way to interpret these findings is that the intervention may have increased meritocracy beliefs in female participants (which would deny the impact of sexism in STEM), and this in turn may have increased their CIPS score. In contrast, male participants, who do not experience the impact of sexism in STEM, would benefit from enhanced meritocracy beliefs, and thus their CIPS scores were reduced. These findings suggest the relationship between growth mindset, meritocracy, IP, and social location may be more nuanced than assumed, and this complexity should be integrated into intervention. Additionally, the differences in outcome between Zanchetta et al. and Chang et al. suggest meaningful change in IP may require sustained intervention and social connections over time, which also has implications for intervention.

Hutchins and Flores (2021) utilized cognitive processing therapy (Resick et al., 2017) to design an intervention to reduce IP that was delivered across two 2-hour workshops. The intervention group was compared with an IP psychoeducation group and an unrelated professional training group. Only the intervention group showed significant reductions on the CIPS, and these gains were maintained at a 3-month follow-up. In qualitative interviews with participants, factors named as efficacious included examining the impact of IP, understanding it to be a common experience, being able to recognize the Impostor Mind, challenging and interrupting these narratives, and receiving social support. Participants also spontaneously described having discussed the topic at their work after the workshops, suggesting there may have been a systemic impact as well. Importantly, participants identified talking about IP in dyads, which occurred in the intervention group only, as the most effective component. The efficacy of this cognitive processing therapy-informed intervention suggests aligning IP intervention with the robust trauma intervention literature may be a productive approach.

Emotional Factors and Intervention

For some, especially men, IP correlates with avoidant styles of coping (Hutchins et al., 2018; Hutchins & Rainbolt, 2017); avoidance can certainly interfere with accessing and processing one's emotional life. For other clients, the emotional impact of IP is quite accessible and may even need regulation strategies. Consequently, providers are encouraged to draw from familiar emotion-focused approaches to help access, soothe, tolerate, and regulate the emotional distress of IP. Certainly, the use of accurate empathy, unconditional positive regard, and therapist congruence and authenticity is foundational (Norcross & Lambert, 2018; Rogers, 1957) because many clients are suffering with IP in silence, isolation, and invalidating environments. Thus, providing authentic, empathic validation is both corrective and paves the way for clients to self-soothe. Another avenue for self-soothing and reducing associated feelings of shame and isolation is psychoeducation. In therapy, when clients begin to destigmatize their experience by understanding it has a name and all the situational factors that have contributed to it, they overwhelmingly experience some relief; this is congruent with recent findings (Chang et al., 2022; Hutchins & Flores, 2021). When utilizing psychoeducation, providers should be careful about prematurely framing IP as a completely normal experience; doing so can function to invalidate extreme levels of suffering that some clients endure. An alternative is giving clients the CIPS, which can serve to both legitimize their experience as well as clarify and acknowledge that individuals experience a range of severity. When doing so, a cut-off score of 62 indicates clinically significant distress (Chrisman et al., 1995). Framing IP as a common experience, embedded in a context, that is experienced on a continuum of severity should be integrated into treatment.

In addition to psychoeducation, using approaches that target detachment from suffering, emotional tolerance, and regulation skills can also assist clients in addressing the emotional storms IP can bring. For example, the use of self-compassion (Patzak et al., 2017) or the Buddhist practice of Metta Bhavana, also known as loving kindness meditation, can help clients detach from IP and soothe their emotional reactivity. Based on older Eastern traditions, DBT's emotion tolerance and regulation modules (Linehan, 2014), as well as the radical acceptance strategies from ACT (Hayes et al., 2011), can also be useful. Relatedly, when clients can identify the types of tasks, people, experiences, and contexts that predictably trigger their IP feelings, they can choose to proactively cope (e.g., enhance self-care routines, get trusted feedback, garner spiritual and/or social supports, prime competent narratives, problem solve).

Although strategies for detaching, tolerating, and regulating emotions are often needed, framing emotions as valid reactions to needs and experiences can be critical for effective intervention. Dynamic, EFT, and other emotion-focused traditions offer interventions that align with this framing. For example, using dynamic Socratic exploration to prompt insight about how current IP triggers connect to early childhood experiences and then helping clients differentiate their current context and current resources from their past can help reduce emotional reactivity, generate self-compassion, and prompt behavioral change. Using an EFT approach, clients are supported to uncover, validate, and soothe their unmet needs that are signaled by emotions; in the case of IP, this underlying need is often to feel good enough to be loved. An effective EFT enactment is to have clients give an imagined, younger version of themselves soothing messages about success, failure, and self-worth. Clinically, it is our experience that because IP is a deeply felt narrative, more emotion-focused interventions such as these are needed for lasting, transformative change.

Before leaving a discussion on the distressing emotional components of IP, it is also important for providers to address the frequent absence of positive emotions about achievement. For example, many clients with high IP do not attend graduation ceremonies, celebrate with loved ones, or even share their accomplishments. In therapy, when they do disclose a valued success, they often quickly change the subject or submerge their joy and pride. Having a provider notice, deepen, and help amplify these positive feelings can be a powerful corrective experience for many clients whose families or systems may discourage such expression.

Behavioral Factors and Intervention

It is deeply human to resist the very change we seek. One common example of this is seen in client resistance to changing their exhausting work routines. Even small changes can feel like risking failure and being exposed as an impostor. Providers must honor this felt risk and utilize effective strategies to navigate resistance. These include Socratic exploration to stimulate insight (Levenson, 2010), decisional balance sheets of the pros/cons of change (Barlow et al., 2011), and motivational interviewing strategies that help uncover a client's unique motivations to support their goals for change (Miller & Rollnick, 2013). As with any good therapy, honoring and exploring the function of resistance can pave the road to client-centered empowered change.

After working through resistance, clients are better positioned to engage in needed behavioral changes. Utilizing exposure principles (Barlow et al., 2011), providers can support clients in making small behavioral changes to approach tasks they typically avoid and begin to adjust their workstyle. When these changes do not make them fail and, at the same time, improve their lives, their anticipatory fears decrease and they gain more behavioral flexibility. Approaching feared tasks can also be supported with mindfulness and diffusion strategies (Hayes et al., 2011). Finally, for some, behavioral skill deficits may need to be addressed before approaching tasks. By supporting clients to take behavioral risks, to fail, to learn, and to risk again, essentially learning to fail, providers can help clients break their fear of failure and open pathways for empowered, valued living.

A Composite Case Example: Psychological-Level Intervention

"Jasmine" had long been underemployed and overworked, and she entered therapy feeling completely exhausted. She described a vicious cycle of completing work, only to discount her findings and start over with more complex questions. She anticipated her boss would evaluate her work as "too elementary" and avoided submitting fully completed projects for review. Using Socratic collaborative exploration, she recognized that by overworking she was devaluing herself—just as her system did. In developing metacognition about her work pattern, she also recognized *all* science dynamically unfolds, and thus her own scientific inquiry would as well. This reframe allowed her to begin to submit her work. Each submission served as a behavioral exposure, and she noticed her anticipatory anxiety decreased. Moreover, being familiar with her IP cycle and her patterns of tossing her success, she was able to make more internal, stable, and realistic attributions when receiving positive feedback from her boss that helped maintain the changes.

Sociocultural Levels of Influence

Historical and current contexts contribute to the etiology and maintenance of IP (Bravata et al., 2020; Muradoglu et al., 2022). The exact clinical picture of how families, professional environments, and systems of oppression impact any single client is, understandably, quite diverse. This reality necessitates a careful and collaborative effort between providers and clients to tailor intervention accordingly.

Familial Context and Intervention

Internalized messages of self-worth, success, and failure inform how clients experience IP. Sometimes families can play a protective role against IP, for example, valuing a child regardless of achievement, celebrating success and supporting failures, and preparing children to navigate systemic oppression. For others, when success is required and failure is a source of shame, or when clients are compelled to excel against critical family narratives, families can set the stage for IP. Additionally, a client's success can also create family conflicts, for example, survival guilt, competitive dynamics, and geographical losses. These family dynamics can certainly shape a client's experience of IP. Fortunately, externalizing unhelpful narratives from families should be familiar terrain for providers, and these same methods are applicable to IP, for example, addressing conditions of worth (Rogers, 1957), core pain and self-schemas (Greenberg, 2011), and core beliefs (Barlow et al., 2011); breaking interpersonal patterns (Carr, 2000); and externalizing negative narratives that are passed down through families (Comas-Díaz, 2020; Crocket, 2013).

This clinical picture of the importance of upbringing is reflected in the literature that underscores the protective role that racial identity and parenting can play (Bernard et al., 2017; Cokley et al., 2017; Ewing et al., 1996; Lige et al., 2017; Peteet, Montgomery, & Weekes, 2015; Wang et al., 2020). Other research reveals how low support, low expressiveness, and high demand from parents can be associated with higher IP (Langford & Clance, 1993; Yaffe, 2023). Additionally, families who communicate model minority and meritocracy myths may, inadvertently, encourage internal attributions of discrimination and systemic barriers, which can in turn heighten IP. Such messages, along with survivor guilt, have been associated with high IP (Austin et al., 2009; Canning et al., 2020; Cokley et al., 2013; Henderson et al., 2020; Peteet, Montgomery, & Weekes, 2015).

Lastly, clients' current relational or parental status can also influence IP. Although high IP and role overload positively correlate for both women and men, women report their family role contributes more to their overall role overload and distress (Duxbury et al., 2018; West, 2014). This aligns with associations between high work–family conflict and higher IP scores (Crawford et al., 2016). These findings suggest gendered, unrealistic division of labor is fertile ground for IP, which is also seen in clinical work. Intervention in this context can target the family system (e.g., gender equity, accessing extended family supports, task delegation). When systemic change is not a desired or realistic option, it can be helpful to support clients in reframing their definitions of success in ways that are commensurate with their situational realities.

Professional Context and Intervention

There has been a considerable amount of research investigating the types of academic and professional settings that are associated with high IP. It is becoming clear that environments that value brilliance; no mistake culture; and individualistic, competitive norms likely foster high levels of IP (Canning et al., 2020; Gottlieb et al., 2020; Hutchins & Rainbolt, 2017; Muradoglu et al., 2022). Indeed, many Ivy League institutions have initiatives encouraging faculty to post their own rejection letters; one college even distributes a humorous, but poignant, Certificate of Failure that articulates the right to completely fail and still be a worthy human being (Bennett, 2017). Intervention in this context clearly requires providers to empathically acknowledge and validate the impact of such norms, policies, practices, and conditions. By doing so, providers utilize their therapeutic power to stand with clients against what is causing harm. Importantly, intervention at this level of influence should balance coping strategies with environmental change strategies to address client needs and preferences. Providers can support client coping and resilience with interventions that target valued living, social supports, self-care routines and/or spiritual practices, and crafting a life of meaning beyond their professional identity (Comas-Díaz, 2020; Hayes et al., 2011; Linehan, 2014; Yalom, 1980). Additionally, as low support from supervisors and mentors has been implicated in high levels of IP (Chakraverty et al., 2022; Deshmukh et al., 2022; Hutchins & Rainbolt, 2017; Peteet, Montgomery, & Weekes, 2015), helping clients build these connections can promote a needed sense of belonging and give them access to critical professional advice (Chakraverty et al., 2022; Keefer, 2015). In making systemic change, providers can utilize a client-driven problem-solving approach, for example, finding like-minded peers to set collaborative and supportive norms, collectively advocating for systemic change through a student or professional group, reporting harassment and abuse, or developing an exit plan.

Sociocultural Context and Intervention

Finally, the role of oppression and social location must be considered in comprehensive IP intervention. One common factor that we hear clinically, which has been clearly demonstrated in the literature, is the lack of representation of one's salient identities (Bernard et al., 2017; Deshmukh et al., 2022; Stone et al., 2018; West, 2014). It is easy to see how such lack of diversity can mistakenly appear to add external validation to false IP narratives about capacity and belonging and how this, in turn, can affect professional engagement. For example, a colleague, who has an illustrious STEM career, disclosed she finished her entire graduate training without asking a single question in class for fear that not only she, but also her gender, would be confirmed as inferior. Tragically, this is not an isolated occurrence, as research on stereotype threat and IP support this picture (Cokley et al., 2015). Lack of representation and negative stereotypes certainly set these dynamics in motion. For example, Henning et al. (1998) found men reported higher level of IP in nursing, the only female-dominated medical field investigated, whereas women reported higher IP in all the other, male-dominated, medical fields. These data underscore the central role oppression can play in IP.

To effectively intervene at this sociocultural level of influence, providers must wholeheartedly commit to embody the three tenets of *cultural humility* (Tervalon & Murray-García, 1998). To pragmatically apply this concept to IP intervention, the first tenet calls providers to continually develop knowledge and skills to work effectively with IP in marginalized communities and to regularly engage in critical self-reflective practice to address internalized bias (e.g., negative cultural stereotypes, meritocracy myths). The second tenet encourages providers to address issues of power and privilege within the therapeutic dyad (e.g., maintaining clients are experts of their IP experience, treatment collaboration, judicious self-disclosure to minimize power differentials). The final tenet underscores the need for providers to hold institutions accountable to address oppression that is embedded in norms, policies, and procedures that serve to foster IP. Peteet, Montgomery, and Weekes (2015) called for increased mentorship and DEI initiatives to reduce IP; this call aligns with this last tenet and underscores the provider's role as an agent of social change inside their academic or clinical settings.

In addition to embodying cultural humility, when targeting clients' internalization of negative stereotypes that heighten IP, providers are encouraged to use strategies from narrative therapy (Crocket, 2013) and liberatory psychology (Comas-Díaz, 2020). Haskins et al. (2019) provided an in-depth application of womanism to IP intervention that should be referenced by all providers—especially those working with clients who identify as BIPOC (Black, Indigenous, People of Color). Pragmatically, these approaches first support developing critical consciousness of oppressive messages that promote IP and facilitate rejecting them. These approaches also intentionally build positive counternarratives that affirm client identities, strengths, resilience, and power. For example, by acknowledging the sexism surrounding motherhood in a clinical setting, one author was able to strongly reject the validity of IP narratives about her commitment and began to embrace how being a mother enhanced her clinical efficacy. Finally, these approaches encourage clients to build supportive communities and collectively act toward social justice. For instance, we have been humbled by the countless clients who have powerfully engaged in developing DEI initiatives when this level of influence is included in treatment.

Investigations into intervention at this level of influence through workshops, trainings, and support groups have begun to be investigated. In response to high levels of IP in STEM, O'Connell et al. (2020) designed a workshop to develop critical consciousness of sexism and build communication skills. Surprisingly about half of the participants reported being unaware, or marginally aware, of how sexism in their institution and in their field created barriers for their success; this awareness improved over the workshop. In qualitative postinterviews, participants underscored the importance of holding institutions accountable for DEI initiatives over building women's communication skills. Another investigation at this level of influence offered a variety of intervention choices to participants including asynchronous trainings, one-to-one coaching, and unlimited written coaching, as well as a regular in-person support group (Fainstad et al., 2022). Following the 6-month intervention period, participants reported they were better able to challenge their IP narratives, valued meeting with each other to build more supportive norms, and appreciated the flexibility in being able to choose the format of engagement. This provides an important model of how to approach systemic-level intervention to target the conditions within which IP thrives.

A Composite Case Example: Sociocultural-Level Intervention
"Mateo" believed he was not smart enough to be a health provider and attributed his academic achievement to "just working hard." Given his huge case-load, based on expected patient quotas, he ruminated about missing something,

being fired, and having to tell his family. Initial intervention to normalize making some errors was met with strong resistance. When exploring the resistance, he disclosed that being perfect and exceeding expectations was a trusted strategy against anti-Latino sentiment. The White therapist apologized and acknowledged that mistakes carry very different costs for him, which she had not fully appreciated. Because remaining in the setting was necessary, he then explored feeling trapped and was invited to imagine what beloved deceased ancestors might advise. Quickly, he imagined them saying, "Faster isn't better." He then talked with his family, and eventually his employer, about seeing fewer clients. Although this entailed contributing less money to his family for a time, the slower pace allowed him to work in ways that matched his values and time to make an exit plan. Although feelings of IP were still intermittently present, he began to recognize the source, challenge its validity, and integrate his clients' positive feedback about his efficacy over statistics.

CONCLUSION

In summary, the term "impostor phenomenon" is the preferred term to honor its origin story, to connect the growing literature, and to maintain IP's framing as a contextualized experience. IP is both created and maintained by a host of biopsychosociocultural influences; consequently, conceptualization and intervention must be comparably complex. Unfortunately, the intervention literature has been remarkably slow to emerge. In this vacuum, providers should use the extant IP research but center on their clients' unique experiences to build accurate conceptualizations. By doing so, providers are positioned to draw from relevant evidence-based interventions to address each salient level of influence. Finally, providers are encouraged to engage in cultural humility and examine their own beliefs and practices that may foster IP in their clients, in their settings, and in themselves. Through shared liberation, we can cocreate spaces where self-worth and performance are never linked and all are free to grow and embrace lives that reflect one's values and motivations.

REFERENCES

Abramson, L. Y., Seligman, M. E., & Teasdale, J. D. (1978). Learned helplessness in humans: Critique and reformulation. *Journal of Abnormal Psychology, 87*(1), 49–74. https://doi.org/10.1037/0021-843X.87.1.49

Austin, C. C., Clark, E. M., Ross, M. J., & Taylor, M. J (2009). Impostorism as a mediator between survivor guilt and depression in a sample of African American college students. *College Student Journal, 43*(4, Pt. A), 1094–1109.

Barlow, D. H., Farchione, T. J., Fairholme, C. P., Ellard, K. K., Boisseau, C. L., Allen, L. B., & Ehrenreich, J. T. (2011). *Unified protocol for transdiagnostic treatment of emotional disorders: Therapist guide*. Oxford University Press.

Beck, J. S., & Beck, A. T. (1995). *Cognitive therapy: Basics and beyond*. Guilford Press.

Bennett, J. (2017, June 24). On campus, failure is on the syllabus. *New York Times*. https://www.nytimes.com/2017/06/24/fashion/fear-of-failure.html

Bernard, D. L., Hoggard, L. S., & Neblett, E. W., Jr. (2018). Racial discrimination, racial identity, and impostor phenomenon: A profile approach. *Cultural Diversity and Ethnic Minority Psychology, 24*(1), 51–61. https://doi.org/10.1037/cdp0000161

Bravata, D.M., Watts, S.A., Keefer, A.L., Madhusudhan, D.K., Taylor, K.T., Clark, D.M., Nelson, R.S., Cokley, K.O., & Hagg, H.K. (2020). Prevalence, predictors, and treatment of impostor syndrome: A systematic review. *Journal of General Internal Medicine, 35*(4), 1252–1275. https://doi.org/10.1007/s11606-019-05364-1

Canning, E. A., LaCosse, J., Kroeper, K. M., & Murphy, M. C. (2020). Feeling like an imposter: The effect of perceived classroom competition on the daily psychological experiences of first-generation college students. *Social Psychological and Personality Science, 11*(5), 647–657. https://doi.org/10.1177/1948550619882032

Carr, A. (2000). *Family therapy: Concepts, process and practice*. Wiley.

Chakraverty, D., Cavazos, J. E., & Jeffe, D. B. (2022). Exploring reasons for MD-PhD trainees' experiences of impostor phenomenon. *BMC Medical Education, 22*, Article 333. https://doi.org/10.1186/s12909-022-03396-6

Chang, S., Lee, H. Y., Anderson, C., Lewis, K., Chakraverty, D., & Yates, M. (2022). Intervening on impostor phenomenon: Prospective evaluation of a workshop for health science students using a mixed-method design. *BMC Medical Education, 22*(1), Article 802. https://doi.org/10.1186/s12909-022-03824-7

Chao, R. C.-L., Mallinckrodt, B., & Wei, M. (2012). Co-occurring presenting problems in African American college clients reporting racial discrimination distress. *Professional Psychology: Research and Practice, 43*(3), 199–207. https://doi.org/10.1037/a0027861

Chrisman, S. M., Pieper, W. A., Clance, P. R., Holland, C. L., & Glickauf-Hughes, C. (1995). Validation of the Clance Imposter Phenomenon Scale. *Journal of Personality Assessment, 65*(3), 456–467. https://doi.org/10.1207/s15327752jpa6503_6

Clance, P. R. (1985a). *The impostor phenomenon: Overcoming the fear that haunts your success*. Peachtree.

Clance, P. R. (1985b). *The impostor phenomenon: When success makes you feel like a fake*. Bantam Books.

Clance, P. R., Dingman, D., Reviere, S., & Stober, D. (1995). Impostor phenomenon in an interpersonal/social context: Origins and treatment. *Women & Therapy, 16*(4), 79–96. https://doi.org/10.1300/J015v16n04_07

Clance, P. R., & Imes, S. (1978). The impostor phenomenon in high achieving women: Dynamics and therapeutic intervention. *Psychotherapy: Theory, Research, & Practice, 15*(3), 241–247. https://doi.org/10.1037/h0086006

Clance, P. R., & O'Toole, M. (1987). The impostor phenomenon: An internal barrier to empowerment and achievement. *Women & Therapy, 6*(3), 51–64. https://doi.org/10.1300/J015V06N03_05

Clark, P., Holden, C., Russell, M., & Downs, H. (2022). The impostor phenomenon in mental health professionals: Relationships among compassion fatigue, burnout, and compassion satisfaction. *Contemporary Family Therapy: An International Journal, 44*(2), 185–197. https://doi.org/10.1007/s10591-021-09580-y

Cokley, K., Awad, G., Smith, L., Jackson, S., Awosogba, O., Hurst, A., Stone, S., Blondeau, L., & Roberts, D. (2015). The roles of gender stigma consciousness, impostor phenomenon and academic self-concept in the academic outcomes of women and men. *Sex Roles, 73*(9–10), 414–426. https://doi.org/10.1007/s11199-015-0516-7

Cokley, K., McClain, S., Enciso, A., & Martinez, M. (2013). An examination of the impact of minority status stress and impostor feelings on the mental health of diverse ethnic minority college students. *Journal of Multicultural Counseling and Development, 41*(2), 82–95. https://doi.org/10.1002/j.2161-1912.2013.00029.x

Cokley, K., Smith, L., Bernard, D., Hurst, A., Jackson, S., Stone, S., Awosogba, O., Saucer, C., Bailey, M., & Roberts, D. (2017). Impostor feelings as a moderator and mediator of the relationship between perceived discrimination and mental health among racial/ethnic minority college students. *Journal of Counseling Psychology, 64*(2), 141–154. https://doi.org/10.1037/cou0000198

Comas-Díaz, L. (2020). Liberation psychotherapy. In L. Comas-Díaz & E. Torres Rivera (Eds.), *Liberation psychology: Theory, method, practice, and social justice* (pp. 169–185). American Psychological Association. https://doi.org/10.1037/0000198-010

Crawford, W., Shanine, K., Whitman, M., & Michele Kacmar, K. (2016). Examining the impostor phenomenon and work–family conflict. *Journal of Managerial Psychology, 31*(2), 375–390. https://doi.org/10.1108/JMP-12-2013-0409

Crocket, K. (2013). Narrative therapy. In M. D. Spiegler and J. Frew (Eds.), *Contemporary psychotherapies for a diverse world* (1st rev. ed., pp. 459–500). Routledge.

Deshmukh, S., Shmelev, K., Vassiliades, L., Kurumety, S., Agarwal, G., & Horowitz, J. (2022). Imposter phenomenon in radiology: Incidence, intervention, and impact on wellness. *Clinical Imaging, 82*, 94–99. https://doi.org/10.1016/j.clinimag.2021.11.009

Duxbury, L., Stevenson, M., & Higgins, C. (2018). Too much to do, too little time: Role overload and stress in a multi-role environment. *International Journal of Stress Management, 25*(3), 250–266. https://doi.org/10.1037/str0000062

Dweck, C. S. (1999). *Self-theories: Their role in motivation, personality, and development.* Taylor and Francis/Psychology Press.

Ellis, A., & Dryden, W. (1987). *The practice of rational-emotive therapy (RET).* Springer Pub Co.

Ewing, K. M., Richardson, T. Q., James-Myers, L., & Russell, R. K. (1996). The relationship between racial identity attitudes, worldview, and African American graduate students' experience of the imposter phenomenon. *The Journal of Black Psychology, 22*(1), 53–66. https://doi.org/10.1177/00957984960221005

Fainstad, T., Mann, A., Suresh, K., Shah, P., Dieujuste, N., & Jones, C. D. (2022). Better together: A novel online physician group coaching program to reduce burnout in trainees: A randomized controlled trial. *Journal of General Internal Medicine, 37*(Suppl. 2), S204–S205. https://doi.org/10.1007/s11606-022-07653-8

Ferrari, J. R. (2005). Impostor tendencies and academic dishonesty: Do they cheat their way to success? *Social Behavior and Personality, 33*(1), 11–18. https://doi.org/10.2224/sbp.2005.33.1.11

Gottlieb, M., Chung, A., Battaglioli, N., Sebok-Syer, S. S., & Kalantari, A. (2020). Impostor syndrome among physicians and physicians in training: A scoping review. *Medical Education, 54*(2), 116–124. https://doi.org/10.1111/medu.13956

Greenberg, L. S. (2011). *Emotion-focused therapy.* American Psychological Association.

Haskins, N. H., Hughes, K. L., Crumb, L., Smith, A. R., Brown, S. S., & Pignato, L. (2019). Postmodern womanism: Dismantling the imposter phenomenon for Black American college students. *Negro Educational Review, 70*(1–4), 5–25.

Hayes, S. C., Strosahl, K. D., & Wilson, K. G. (2011). *Acceptance and commitment therapy: The process and practice of mindful change* (2nd ed.). Guilford Press.

Henderson, M., Shure, N., & Adamecz-Völgyi, A. (2020). Moving on up: "First in family" university graduates in England. *Oxford Review of Education, 46*(6), 734–751. https://doi.org/10.1080/03054985.2020.1784714

Henning, K., Ey, S., and Shaw, D. (1998). Perfectionism, the impostor phenomenon, and psychological adjustment in medical, dental, nursing and pharmacy students. *Medical Education, 32*(5), 456–464. https://doi.org/10.1046/j.1365-2923.1998.00234.x

Horowitz, M. (2020). *Treatment of stress response syndromes* (2nd ed.). American Psychiatric Association Publishing.

Hutchins, H., & Flores, J. (2021). Don't believe everything you think: Applying a cognitive processing therapy intervention to disrupting imposter phenomenon. *New Horizons in Adult Education and Human Resource Development, 33*(4), 33–47. https://doi.org/10.1002/nha3.20325

Hutchins, H. M., Penney, L. M., & Sublett, L. W. (2018). What imposters risk at work: Exploring imposter phenomenon, stress coping, and job outcomes. *Human Resource Development Quarterly, 29*(1), 31–48. https://doi.org/10.1002/hrdq.21304

Hutchins, H. M., & Rainbolt, H. (2017). What triggers imposter phenomenon among academic faculty? A critical incident study exploring antecedents, coping, and development opportunities. *Human Resource Development International, 20*(3), 194–214. https://doi.org/10.1080/13678868.2016.1248205

Jung, C. G. (1961). *Memories, dreams, and reflections*. Random House.

Keefer, J. (2015). Experiencing doctoral liminality as a conceptual threshold and how supervisors can use it. *Innovations in Education and Teaching International, 52*(1), 17–28. https://doi.org/10.1080/14703297.2014.981839

Langford, J., & Clance, P. R. (1993). The impostor phenomenon: Recent research findings regarding dynamics, personality and family patterns and their implications for treatment. *Psychotherapy: Theory, Research, Practice, Training, 30*(3), 495–501. https://doi.org/10.1037/0033-3204.30.3.495

Levenson, H. (2010). *Brief dynamic therapy*. American Psychological Association.

Lige, Q., Peteet, B., & Brown, C. (2017). Racial identity, self-esteem, and the impostor phenomenon among African American college students. *The Journal of Black Psychology, 43*(4), 345–357. https://doi.org/10.1177/0095798416648787

Linehan, M. (2014). *DBT training manual*. Guilford Press.

Magro, C. (2022). From hiding to sharing. A descriptive phenomenological study on the experience of being coached for impostor syndrome. *International Journal of Evidence Based Coaching and Mentoring, S16*, 68–80. https://doi.org/10.24384/0409-b325

Matthews, G., & Clance, P. R. (1985). Treatment of the impostor phenomenon in psychotherapy clients. *Psychotherapy in Private Practice, 3*(1), 71–81. https://doi.org/10.1300/J294v03n01_09

McGregor, L. N., Gee, G. D., & Posey, K. F. (2008). I feel like a fraud and it depresses me: The relation between the imposter phenomenon and depression. *Social Behavior and Personality, 36*(1), 43–48. https://doi.org/10.2224/sbp.2008.36.1.43

Meyer, M., Cimpian, A., & Leslie, S. (2015). Women are underrepresented in fields where success is believed to require brilliance. *Frontiers in Psychology, 6*, Article 235. https://doi.org/10.3389/fpsyg.2015.00235

Miller, W., & Rollnick, S. (2013). *Motivational interviewing: Helping people change* (3rd ed.). Guilford Press.

Muradoglu, M., Horne, Z., Hammond, M. D., Leslie, S.-J., & Cimpian, A. (2022). Women—particularly underrepresented minority women—and early-career academics feel like impostors in fields that value brilliance. *Journal of Educational Psychology, 114*(5), 1086–1100. https://doi.org/10.1037/edu0000669

Neureiter, M., & Traut-Mattausch, E. (2017). Two sides of the career resources coin: Career adaptability resources and the impostor phenomenon. *Journal of Vocational Behavior, 98*, 56–69. https://doi.org/10.1016/j.jvb.2016.10.002

Neureiter, M., Traut-Mattausch, E., Buse, K., & Di Fabio, A. (2016). An inner barrier to career development: Preconditions of the impostor phenomenon and consequences for career development. *Frontiers in Psychology, 7*, Article 48. https://doi.org/10.3389/fpsyg.2016.00048

Norcross, J. C., & Lambert, M. J. (2018). Psychotherapy relationships that work III. *Psychotherapy: Theory, Research, & Practice, 55*(4), 303–315. https://doi.org/10.1037/pst0000193

O'Connell, C., Eranki, P., & Landis, A. (2020). Empowering women's voices in STEM and banishing the inner impostor. *The International Journal of Diversity in Education, 21*(1), 75–87. https://doi.org/10.18848/2327-0020/CGP/v21i01/75-87

Patzak, A., Kollmayer, M., & Schober, B. (2017). Buffering impostor feelings with kindness: The mediating role of self-compassion between gender-role orientation and the impostor phenomenon. *Frontiers in Psychology, 8*, Article 1289. https://doi.org/10.3389/fpsyg.2017.01289

Peteet, B., Brown, C., Lige, Q., & Lanaway, D. (2015). Impostorism is associated with greater psychological distress and lower self-esteem for African American students. *Current Psychology, 34*(1), 154–163. https://doi.org/10.1007/s12144-014-9248-z

Peteet, B. J., Montgomery, L., & Weekes, J. C. (2015). Predictors of imposter phenomenon among talented ethnic minority undergraduate students. *The Journal of Negro Education, 84*(2), 175–186. https://doi.org/10.7709/jnegroeducation.84.2.0175

Resick, P. A., Monson, C. M., & Chard, K. M. (2017). *Cognitive processing therapy for PTSD: A comprehensive manual*. Guilford Press.

Rogers, C. R. (1957). The necessary and sufficient conditions of therapeutic personality change. *Journal of Consulting Psychology, 21*(2), 95–103. https://doi.org/10.1037/h0045357

Rosenthal, S., Schlussel, Y., Yaden, M., DeSantis, J., Trayes, K., Pohl, C., & Hojat, M. (2021). Persistent impostor phenomenon is associated with distress in medical students. *Family Medicine, 53*(2), 118–122. https://doi.org/10.22454/FamMed.2021.799997

Santos, M. M., Puspitasari, A. J., Nagy, G. A., & Kanter, J. W. (2021). Behavioral activation. In A. Wenzel (Ed.), *Handbook of cognitive behavioral therapy: Overview and approaches* (pp. 235–273). American Psychological Association. https://doi.org/10.1037/0000218-009

Stone, S., Saucer, C., Bailey, M., Garba, R., Hurst, A., Jackson, S. M., Krueger, N., & Cokley, K. (2018). Learning while Black: A culturally informed model of the impostor phenomenon for Black graduate students. *The Journal of Black Psychology, 44*(6), 491–531. https://doi.org/10.1177/0095798418786648

Sullivan, J. B., & Ryba, N. L. (2020). Prevalence of impostor phenomenon and assessment of well-being in pharmacy residents. *American Journal of Health-System Pharmacy, 77*(9), 690–696. https://doi.org/10.1093/ajhp/zxaa041

Tervalon, M., & Murray-García, J. (1998). Cultural humility versus cultural competence: A critical distinction in defining physician training outcomes in multicultural education. *Journal of Health Care for the Poor and Underserved, 9*(2), 117–125. https://doi.org/10.1353/hpu.2010.0233

Tigranyan, S., Byington, D. R., Liupakorn, D., Hicks, A., Lombardi, S., Mathis, M., & Rodolfa, E. (2021). Factors related to the impostor phenomenon in psychology doctoral students. *Training and Education in Professional Psychology, 15*(4), 298–305. https://doi.org/10.1037/tep0000321

Tulshyan, R., & Burey, J.-A. (2021, February 11). Stop telling women they have imposter syndrome. *Harvard Business Review.* https://hbr.org/2021/02/stop-telling-women-they-have-imposter-syndrome

Vergauwe, J., Wille, B., Feys, M., De Fruyt, F., & Anseel, F. (2015). Fear of being exposed: The trait-relatedness of the impostor phenomenon and its relevance in the work context. *Journal of Business and Psychology, 30*(3), 565–581. https://doi.org/10.1007/s10869-014-9382-5

Walker, A. (1983). *In search of our mothers' gardens: Womanist prose.* Harcourt Brace Jovanovich.

Wang, M. T., Henry, D. A., Smith, L. V., Huguley, J. P., & Guo, J. (2020). Parental ethnic–racial socialization practices and children of color's psychosocial and behavioral adjustment: A systematic review and meta-analysis. *American Psychologist, 75*(1), 1–22. https://doi.org/10.1037/amp0000464

West, L. M. (2014). "Something's gotta give": Advanced-degree seeking women's experiences of sexism, role overload, and psychological distress. *NASPA Journal About Women in Higher Education, 7*(2), 226–243.

Yaffe, Y. (2023). The association between familial and parental factors and the impostor phenomenon—A systematic review. *The American Journal of Family Therapy, 51*(5), 527–545. https://doi.org/10.1080/01926187.2021.2019140

Yalom, I. D. (1980). *Existential psychotherapy.* Basic Books.

Zanchetta, M., Junker, S., Wolf, A. M., & Traut-Mattausch, E. (2020). Overcoming the fear that haunts your success: The effectiveness of interventions for reducing the impostor phenomenon. *Frontiers in Psychology, 11*, Article 405. https://doi.org/10.3389/fpsyg.2020.00405

2

AN OVERVIEW OF THE IMPOSTOR PHENOMENON

Definitional and Theoretical Considerations

KEVIN COKLEY, KEOSHIA HARRIS, SHAINA HALL, AND MYYA SINGLETARY

In 1978, two psychologists, Pauline Clance and Suzanne Imes, published a short conceptual paper based on their clinical experiences working with approximately 150 highly successful women. These women came from various backgrounds, including law, medicine, social work, nursing, and university teaching. Yet, despite evidence of their competence, intelligence, and success, these women believed themselves to not be intelligent or competent. Clance and Imes (1978) thus coined the term "impostor phenomenon" (IP) to describe an internal experience of intellectual phoniness they believed was especially prominent among women. They stated that the women in their sample reported feeling overvalued by their colleagues and administrators, and they feared that some significant person would eventually find out that they were intellectual impostors. Since the introduction of IP, research and popular culture discourse on this topic has increased considerably. As interest has grown, we note the tensions, misrepresentations, and disagreements that characterize some of the research and much of the discourse on IP. Accordingly, we address these issues in this chapter and provide an overview of the IP construct. We review contextual and theoretical considerations, discuss misconceptions and limitations of the IP construct, and propose a reconceptualization of IP for minoritized individuals that we call a racialized impostor phenomenon.

https://doi.org/10.1037/0000397-003
The Impostor Phenomenon: Psychological Research, Theory, and Interventions,
K. Cokley (Editor)
Copyright © 2024 by the American Psychological Association. All rights reserved.

FAMILY DYNAMICS

The inability of these women to accept compliments or positive feedback and internalize their successes did not suddenly occur as adults. Clance and Imes observed that the roots of the impostor feelings could be traced back to early family dynamics. Their clinical observations indicated that impostors typically fell in one of two groups. In one group, a girl often had a sibling or relative who was viewed as being intelligent while the girl was viewed as being socially skilled or sensitive. This was frustrating to the girl, who hoped that her academic performance and accomplishments would prove to her family that she was intelligent. However, after still not being validated for her intelligence by her family, the girl began questioning her intelligence and internalizing self-doubts about her prior accomplishments. In the other group, a girl received the opposite treatment from her family. She was praised for her intelligence and accomplishments and received messages suggesting that she was a genius and that all work for her came easily. Despite receiving ostensibly positive messages, the girl nevertheless felt pressure because she could not live up to the incredibly high standards being placed upon her. She knew that work did not always come easily for her, which led to her feeling like a fraud and impostor.

GENDER CONSIDERATIONS

The focus on family dynamics for young girls would seem to indicate that Clance and Imes were cognizant of the different socialization processes that women and men experience. It is important to note that even within the context of different socialization processes, women in the sample reported that they were still expected to do well in school. Clance and Imes believed that the societal stereotype of women being less intelligent than men exacerbated the already-formed feelings of self-doubt cultivated by early family dynamics. This is noteworthy because they essentially identified family dynamics as the precipitating cause of impostor feelings and that societal stereotypes about women (and presumably other experiences of sexism and oppression, though they did not explicitly state this) exacerbated the impostor feelings being experienced by the girls. Clance and Imes called the family dynamics versus societal stereotypes of women's intelligence a "chicken or egg" problem that needed further research. This problem also has implications for the debate mentioned in the Introduction about whether the problem experienced by Black students in science, technology, engineering, and mathematics is IP or racism. Readers are referred to Chapter 7 for a more comprehensive discussion of gender and IP.

RACIAL AND ETHNIC CONSIDERATIONS

Much of the literature that examines IP among racially and ethnically minoritized groups largely focuses on Black/African American individuals. Further, scholarship that examines IP generally within populations of color often does not report racial and ethnic differences. Although there is a dearth of research that examines racial and ethnic differences in the experience and outcomes associated with IP, burgeoning literature suggests that racial and ethnic differences exist. Readers are referred to Chapters 8, 9, 10, 11, and 12 for a more comprehensive review and discussions of racial and ethnic considerations.

Overall, little research specifically focuses on racial and ethnic differences related to impostorism. It can be concluded that IP is experienced by people of color generally; however, sociocultural factors may make the experience of IP different between racial and ethnic groups. More research is needed to understand the racialized experience of impostorism within the context of diverse racial and ethnic minorities.

THEORETICAL CONSIDERATIONS

In a brief description of features that accompany IP beliefs among typical female clients, Clance and O'Toole (1987) identified the following 10 features:

- the impostor cycle
- introversion
- dread of evaluation
- terror of failure
- guilt about success
- great difficulty in internalizing positive feedback
- generalized anxiety
- overestimating others while underestimating oneself
- defining intelligence in a skewed manner
- false and nonaffirming family messages[1]

It is tempting to view the description of the features of IP, and scholarly writings on IP in general, as a scientific theory. By definition, a scientific theory is an explanation of a phenomenon that has been repeatedly tested and corroborated using the tenets of the scientific method. Theories that are well-established

---

[1]Individuals are encouraged to read Clance and O'Toole's (1987) article for a deeper description of these features.

48 • *Cokley et al.*

and have contributed to scientific knowledge have been subjected to rigorous scrutiny. When Clance and Imes (1978) coined the term "impostor phenomenon," they were trying to explain attitudes and behaviors they had repeatedly observed among high-achieving women. However, it is not clear that their goal was to propose a coherent scientific theory of IP.

The famous philosopher of science Karl Popper (1963) stated that for a theory to be considered scientific it must be testable and falsifiable. Pauline Clance and her collaborators set the tone for IP research through their early clinical observations and later correlational and nonexperimental research. This body of research established an important foundation of knowledge that has informed the vast majority of contemporary empirical IP research. However, clinical observations and correlational and nonexperimental research alone do not lend themselves to Popper's tenets of testability and falsifiability. In short, if there really were a theory of IP, it could not be adequately tested only using clinical observations and correlational and nonexperimental methods.

Let us assume there is enough existing descriptive information about IP to warrant calling it a testable scientific theory. In perhaps the most rigorously conducted study of IP, Leary et al. (2000) tested the presumed theoretical assumptions of IP. They identified three central characteristics or assumptions of IP. The primary assumption of IP is the sense of being an impostor or fraud and believing that others perceive oneself more positively than is warranted. The second defining assumption is that impostors fear that others will find out they are a fraud and thus view them as the impostor they believe they are. The third defining assumption is that impostors have difficulty internalizing their successes and continue to behave in ways that perpetuate their impostor feelings.

TESTING THE THEORETICAL ASSUMPTIONS

Leary et al. (2000) argued that these three assumptions are somewhat paradoxical. If impostors engage in self-deprecating behaviors (e.g., externalizing their successes, dismissing praise, openly admitting they are frauds), would not these behaviors be contradictory? In other words, if impostors fear that people will see them as frauds, the natural response should be to engage in behaviors that would make people see the impostor as highly competent. This would be a self-enhancement mechanism that serves to protect one's self-esteem. However, the theoretical assumption of IP is the opposite of this. The impostor engages in self-deprecating behaviors that are not consistent with someone who has concerns about protecting their self-esteem. Simply put, dismissing praise or externalizing your success could have the impact of confirming to people that you really are not that competent and perhaps you really are a fraud.

These concerns led Leary et al. (2000) to conduct a series of studies testing the theoretical assumptions underlying IP.[2] Social psychological constructs of self-appraisal (how a person evaluates themselves) and reflected appraisal (a person's perception of how others see and evaluate them) guided the conceptualization of the theoretical assumptions. The first study examined the assumption that others view impostors more positively than they really are and more positively than impostors evaluate themselves. Using a correlational approach, the authors found that impostorism scores were negatively correlated with self-appraisals, reflected appraisals, and the difference between self- and reflected appraisals as expected. However, the authors found that after removing the spurious relationship between impostor scale and difference scores, correlations were reduced to zero. Simply stated, impostorism was more a function of self-appraisal than of the discrepancy between self-appraisal and reflected appraisal. The authors also found that impostorism scores were highest among individuals who evaluated themselves negatively (self-appraisal) and who believed that others evaluated them negatively (reflected appraisal). This finding is the opposite of what was expected based on theoretical assumptions, which would be that the highest impostorism scores would be among individuals who evaluated themselves negatively while believing that others evaluated them positively.

The second study examined whether impostorism behaviors were really just interpersonal strategies to convey a particular social identity rather than what impostors truly believed about themselves. Leary et al. (2000) speculated that impostors may engage in self-deprecatory behaviors because there was some social value in them, rather than the impostors actually believing the negative self-appraisal (e.g., saying that one feels like an impostor could be beneficial in people lowering their expectations for you). The authors argued that this is important because "the viability of the impostor phenomenon as a theoretical construct depends on whether the behavioral concomitants of impostorism are best viewed as veridical expressions of one's self-perceptions or misrepresentations enacted for their social or personal beliefs" (Leary et al., 2000, p. 734). Put another way, are the self-deprecating behaviors of impostors due to the impostors really believing they are frauds and incompetent, or do the self-deprecating behaviors not really represent how the impostors evaluate themselves but instead serve some other purpose? An experimental design was

---

[2]Individuals are encouraged to read Leary et al.'s (2000) study for more details on the methods and analysis.

used that included impostorism as a continuous variable and three dichotomous variables: expected performance on a bogus test (lower vs. higher than participants' pretest predictions), publicity of response (public vs. private), and participant gender. Results indicated that the importance of doing well on the bogus test was a function of impostorism, expected performance, and response publicity. Doing well on the test was less important for high impostors than for low impostors when their responses were made public. However, when the responses were kept private, doing well was more important for high impostors than for low impostors. Leary et al. concluded that "impostors acted more like impostors are presumed to act when they thought others held low expectations for them and their behaviors were public" (Leary et al., 2000, p. 743). These findings were additional support for the hypothesis that there was a substantial self-presentational component for individuals identified as impostors. This is important because if the assumptions of IP are correct, impostors should act like impostors (e.g., expecting performance on a test to be low) both in public and in private. This was not supported by the findings.

In the third study, Leary et al. (2000) examined the possibility that there are two types of impostorism. They speculated that the first, *true impostorism*, is consistent with the original conceptualization of IP. Individuals view themselves less positively than they believe others do, which fuels their fear of being detected as a fraud. They speculated that the second, *strategic impostorism*, involves the use of self-representational tactics whereby the individual may self-denigrate to obtain some form of benefit (e.g., convey an impression of modesty, lower others' expectations). Contrary to a true impostor, Leary et al. proposed that strategic impostors say self-denigrating comments about themselves but do not believe the negative views. Both true and strategic impostors would score high on an impostorism scale, but true impostors perceive themselves less positively than others perceive them whereas strategic impostors perceive themselves as positively as they think other people perceive them but will typically claim to have more negative views of themselves compared with other people. Leary et al. speculated that both demonstrate self-denigration. The difference is that true impostors exhibit signs of impostorism regardless of whether the evaluative performance is known by other people (public) or not (private), whereas strategic impostors are more prone to exhibiting signs of impostorism when the evaluative performance is public.

Participants completed pretest measures of impostorism, self-appraisal, and reflected self-appraisals, and based on their responses they were classified as having either a negative discrepancy or positive discrepancy between their self- and reflected appraisals. In this classification, true impostors should have a negative discrepancy (i.e., self-appraisal minus reflected self-appraisal is negative, indicating that impostors rated themselves more negatively than they thought others did), whereas strategic impostors should have a positive discrepancy (i.e., self-appraisal minus reflected self-appraisal is positive, indicating that impostors rated themselves at least as positively as they thought others did). Participants also completed a bogus test of adaptive functioning, a questionnaire regarding their feelings about taking the bogus test, a state self-esteem inventory, and a measure of reported self-confidence. An experimental design was used where individuals randomly assigned to the private evaluation condition were told that no one could see how they scored on the bogus test, whereas individuals assigned to the public evaluation condition were told that the researcher would know how they had performed on the bogus test. Consistent with theory, results indicated that impostorism was negatively correlated with expressed self-confidence. However, there was an interaction effect showing that low impostors expressed greater self-confidence in the public evaluation condition than the private evaluation condition, whereas high impostors expressed less self-confidence in the public evaluation condition than the private evaluation condition. For individuals with a negative discrepancy, impostorism scores were negatively associated with expressed confidence. This was consistent with theoretical expectations. However, for individuals with a positive discrepancy, there was no association between their impostorism scores and expressed confidence. This was not consistent with theoretical expectations.

Overall, Leary et al. (2000) indicated that the results of the third study did not support one of the key theoretical tenets of IP: that people who score high on impostorism believe that others hold unrealistically favorable perceptions of them. The study also did not support their speculation of a distinction between a true versus strategic impostor. Rather than finding a distinction, support was only found for a strategic impostor. Taking all three studies together, Leary et al. concluded that the findings "suggest that the behaviors attributed to impostors have a notable self-presentational element; people may respond in the nonenhancing manner characteristic of impostors because they believe such tactics will have interpersonal benefits" (Leary et al., 2000, p. 751). Stated another way, people who report being or feeling like an impostor often do so because it benefits them in some way (e.g., it is a protective self-presentational strategy; it lowers others' expectations, making it less likely that you will fail and making a successful performance more noteworthy; it conveys a sense of modesty; it protects one's image in the face of a potential failure; it elicits encouragement and support from others). Leary et al. do not doubt the existence of IP; however, results of the three studies indicated some problems underlying the presumed theoretical assumptions.

MISCONCEPTIONS OF THE IMPOSTOR PHENOMENON

Since the original definition, many understandings have been proposed to describe the experience of impostorism. Along with advancements in our understanding, misconceptions about impostorism have been widely adopted and perpetuated through scientific literature, popular culture, public figures, and a plethora of blogs that populate a quick Google search (Stone-Sabali et al., 2023). The resurgence of research on IP has provided validation and space to have many overdue conversations about structural inequities, the historical oppression of people of color, and the psychological impact of chronic impostorism. Along with the positive outcomes, misconceptions about IP are also popular. It is imperative to address misconceptions to avoid perpetuating harm through misinformation. We have identified three key misconceptions about IP in the academic literature and in our popular culture that detract from the original conceptualization of the construct: (a) Self-doubt and impostorism are interchangeable, (b) IP is the same as impostor syndrome, and (c) impostorism is a mental health diagnosis. It is understandable how such misconceptions are adopted; impostorism is relatable, buzzworthy, impactful, and accessible to many groups of people. Research on IP has grown in prominence and popularity due, in part, to the aspect of self-doubt that resonates resoundingly with most of us, especially as members of racial minorities.

Misconception #1: Impostor Feelings Are the Same as Self-Doubt

It is important to differentiate impostorism from similar constructs that are also related to competence. Prior research has distinguished impostorism from constructs such as self-efficacy, social anxiety, and stereotype threat (Bernard & Stone-Sabali, 2022). We assert that an examination of the difference between self-doubt and impostor feelings is also necessary to add to previous conceptualizations. *Self-doubt* is unique because it involves ruminating about one's overall competence when receiving negative feedback about performance, which may lead to a person performing poorly in multiple domains (Braslow et al., 2012). Those experiencing impostorism may feel incompetent, but their high achievement provides contradictory evidence, such as doing well on an essay. Self-doubt has also been described as a stable and global construct, whereas impostorism is inconsistent and may not affect multiple life domains (Bernard & Stone-Sabali, 2022). Put another way, developing self-doubt can influence one's belief in competence overall and show up in multiple areas of life. Previous research on IP supports that impostor feelings are domain specific and inconsistent (Bernard & Stone-Sabali, 2022).

Distinguishing between self-doubt and impostorism is also important because feelings of self-doubt and impostorism may function differently for members of racial minorities. Self-doubt is a natural part of life, especially when attempting novel activities or receiving negative feedback (Braslow et al., 2012). For minoritized individuals, impostorism involves internalizing messages of inferiority from the environment and experiencing heightened anxiety and fear of being ostracized. Although feelings of impostorism are common, the misconception that feelings of impostorism are innocuous self-doubt minimizes the relationship between feelings of impostorism and racial discrimination (Andrews, 2020). We must ask: Is impostorism simply manageable self-doubt, legitimate feelings of not belonging, or an accurate reading of the environment that is not accepting? Dismissing self-doubt as solely an internal experience in this environment would be myopic and harmful. Accordingly, when considering experiences in people of color of feeling fraudulent and inferior, we must consider additional factors beyond internal self-doubt and investigate the environments people of color live and work in.

Misconception #2: Impostor Phenomenon Is Interchangeable With Impostor Syndrome

The language and terminology we use to describe the behaviors of others can have significant implications. In the literature, the words "impostor phenomenon" and "impostor syndrome" are used interchangeably; however, for psychologists these terms communicate different experiences. It appears that term preferences are often associated with where the term is published. Lay literature tends to use "impostor syndrome," whereas academic journals tend to use "impostor phenomenon" when referencing behaviors related to doubting one's intellectual abilities (Bravata et al., 2020).

IP implies a flexible approach to understanding the behaviors associated with feeling like a fraud. Rather than placing the blame within the individual, IP examines the individual's experience from a contextual lens with regard to sociopolitical aspects that may influence this perspective (Feenstra et al., 2020). IP normalizes these feelings and conveys that these feelings may change depending upon the setting you are placed within. Environments that have been deemed supportive have been less likely to incite feelings of being a fraud or fear of being found incompetent (Feenstra et al., 2020; Kark et al., 2022; Stone et al., 2018). This further shows how the feelings tend to be situational rather than omnipresent, arising in all the individual's roles. This does not discount the experience of those who may feel like a fraud in multiple roles. It is plausible that these individuals are in multiple environments that make it difficult to internalize their success.

Although some individuals using the term "impostor syndrome" do so responsibly and in a nonpathologizing manner consistent with our description of the term "impostor phenomenon" (e.g., Valerie Young, see Chapter 13), our concern is that the label of "impostor syndrome" implies an abnormal medical condition, which may be counterintuitive for high-achieving individuals. Some individuals may have difficulty processing what it means to have a syndrome and may be afraid to further engage in achievement-oriented tasks that they are very capable of doing well. The probability of them internalizing the "impostor syndrome" label becomes even greater if stigma begins to emerge around feeling like an impostor.

Misconception #3: Impostor Phenomenon Is a Diagnosable Mental Health Disorder

The misconception that IP is a mental health disorder can be traced directly from the widely used misnomer of "impostor syndrome." This misconception can be harmful because it implies pathology suggesting that professional treatment is needed to overcome impostor feelings. The implication that impostorism is a pathology can best be defined as the *medicalization* of impostorism, or "defining [constructs] in medical terms, described using medical language, understood through the adoption of a medical framework, or 'treated' with medical intervention" (Conrad, 2007, p. 5). Medicalizing impostor feelings may stigmatize normal behaviors, promote shame, and imply that treatment is necessary to become normal (Kaczmarek, 2019). When impostor syndrome is discussed, there is an underlying message that you have a dysfunctional behavior versus experiencing some difficulties (Ogunyemi et al., 2022). As of the publishing of this chapter, there has not been an identified empirical treatment to mitigate the features associated with impostorism, yet scholars have suggested various interventions that could be helpful to overcome the impostor syndrome (Magro, 2022). Furthermore, impostor syndrome is currently not in the American Psychiatric Association's *Diagnostic and Statistical Manual of Mental Disorders* (*DSM*); however, some researchers have recommended adding impostor syndrome to the *DSM* (Bravata et al., 2020). The omission of IP from the *DSM* could suggest that these features of feeling fraudulent and fearing failure are a common human experience that may not rise to the level of being considered a syndrome. It may also suggest that mitigating impostor feelings among people of color goes beyond individual treatment modalities and rather involves addressing institutional racism and individual distress simultaneously.

Medicalization of IP as a syndrome can also influence conflating impostorism with other syndromes. Articles that mention the term "impostor phenomenon" are referring to the original definition conceptualized by Clance and Imes (1978). Literature on Capgras syndrome has been equated with the experience of IP (Stone-Sabali et al., 2023). Capgras syndrome describes individuals who incorrectly assume that someone has been replaced with an impostor. Typically, this term appears when literature is discussing delusions associated with certain psychological disorders (e.g., paranoid schizophrenia) or with neurodegenerative diseases (e.g., Alzheimer's; Josephs, 2007). Ironically, the word "impostor" is used, yet the definition is starkly different from the IP description. Conflating these two terms could have negative ramifications for those who do experience IP and may be influenced by the medicalized nature of sources discussing the impostor syndrome. Individuals who identify with IP may be assumed to have delusions about their intellectual abilities. Not only does this have a negative connotation, but this invalidates the individual's experience and further medicalizes a term that was intended to describe a common occurrence among a group of women.

LIMITATIONS OF THE ORIGINAL IMPOSTOR PHENOMENON CONSTRUCT: RACIALIZED IMPOSTOR PHENOMENON

Research has demonstrated that the experience of feeling like a fraud can be influenced by the individual's environment and their perceived social position in society (Feenstra et al., 2020). The lack of representation within environments is also a factor that could heighten feelings of fraudulence. As a result of a nondiverse environment, individuals who do not share identities with the majority may begin to question their worth and may negatively evaluate interpersonal interactions. The analysis of IP provided in Feenstra et al. (2020) from multiple perspectives (social, individual, societal, institutional) showcases that the individual's lived experience as a result of their various identities is important to consider. Furthermore, individuals who hold multiple minoritized identities have been found to be more susceptible to impostor feelings than their colleagues (Jackson et al., 2022; Muradoglu et al., 2022). Thus, we propose an additional conceptualization of IP, the *racialized impostor phenomenon*. We define racialized IP as an internal experience of intellectual and professional self-doubt that occurs among racially minoritized people because of racist environmental experiences.

Individuals of color are often faced with the double conundrum of being hypervisible and invisible within their respective environments (Wilkins-Yel et al., 2019). Because individuals of color are typically underrepresented within their environments, any differences that exist between them and their peers are magnified. For some, this may make it difficult for them to feel as though they belong (Jackson et al., 2022). Alternatively, these same individuals may experience instances of invisibility where their opinions and concerns are not taken seriously (Jackson et al., 2022). Underrepresented groups learn to maintain an outward presentation of "having it all together" despite the uncertainties they may possess (Muradoglu et al., 2022). This desire to appear put together could stem from past experiences of seeking assistance and being met with unwanted resistance or dismissive comments (Jackson et al., 2022). Research has demonstrated that this is a common occurrence for people of color, which makes it even more difficult to overcome feelings associated with IP. Not only is there a lack of support for grievances that affect people of color, but their struggles may be used to suggest that they are not equipped to succeed in such a rigorous environment (Jackson et al., 2022). Thus, the experience of IP is likely to vary from that of their White counterparts.

When we reflect upon the treatment of minoritized and nonminoritized individuals' experiences within society, we find stark differences. The experience of minoritized individuals is often laden with more obstacles and need to debunk stereotypes that are circulated within the media (Williams, 2018). Given that *society* encompasses many settings, including our schools, neighborhoods, and access to resources (among others), it seems necessary to examine how race could affect certain phenomena as well.

Scholars have cautioned researchers from using a theoretical framework or model developed with a majority White sample to explain the experience of non-White individuals (French et al., 2020; White, 1970). Furthermore, scholars have encouraged researchers to examine these frameworks with a critical eye and adapt a more culturally informed approach when explaining behaviors. This is done in part to acknowledge that the experiences of minority groups within various settings include unique challenges, such as racial discrimination, which create an added level of stress for these groups (Bernard et al., 2018; Bravata et al., 2020). Thus, when using frameworks that have been developed on majority White or all White samples, researchers are implicitly equating their experiences with the experiences of minoritized samples.

As previously noted, research on IP was originally conducted on a predominantly White sample centered on gender. Studies have demonstrated that the original conceptualization of IP does not neatly explain the experience of minoritized populations (e.g., Stone et al., 2018). Furthermore, research has begun to explore differences among members of racial minorities with IP (Bernard et al., 2018; Cokley et al., 2017). The inclusion of cultural differences creates space for researchers to explore rather than pathologize the actions of people of color. Not only does studying the racial influence of certain experiences increase our understanding, but it helps to further advocate for these groups. Most importantly, conceptualizing impostorism as being racialized for minoritized individuals helps to validate their concerns and acknowledge that discrimination can have some adverse consequences (Bernard et al., 2018).

Research supports the association of psychosocial factors and impostor feelings. Bernard et al. (2018) proposed that racial discrimination is associated with IP through feelings of "otherness" and inferiority beliefs about racial minorities held by peers. Because otherness and discrimination are commonplace for people of color, internalizing a sense of being outcasted and undeserving is logical. It is also plausible that one may misconceive that racism and discrimination overshadow the phenomenon of feeling like an impostor. McGee et al. (2022) argued that because racism is ingrained in our systems and institutions, feelings of fraudulence are not impostorism but rather natural by-products of racism. McGee et al. are concerned that the traditional conceptualization of IP focuses too much on the individual, which could lead to blaming the victim for their impostor feelings. Other scholars have expressed similar concerns (Mullangi & Jagsi, 2019). However, arguing that feelings of fraudulence are simply racism does not account for the psychological experiences of people of color and the relationship between the environment and one's internal experience. In an effort to signify that both aspects are equally important to consider, racialized IP was conceptualized to extend beyond feelings of impostorism and highlight the constant, crippling fear of exposure and rejection that is mirrored and perpetuated in the environment. Conceptually, we argue that the internal experience of fraudulence in racial minorities does not have to be mutually exclusive with racism or impostorism; rather, it is a culmination of the external and internal experiences.

Given that we argue for the existence of a racialized IP, some may wonder if an argument can be made for a gendered IP. We do not believe that a separate term for gendered IP is necessary because of the fact that the very idea of IP is based on the experiences of women and rooted in sex differences research by attribution theorists (Deaux, 1976) and theoretical ideas about sex-role stereotypes. In other words, gendered IP is redundant with IP, whereas racialized IP is based on the experiences of racially minoritized individuals who were not part of the original conceptualization of IP.

CONCLUSION

Forty-five years after its introduction into the psychological literature, interest in IP continues to grow, making it one of the most popular psychological constructs to cross over into popular culture. The growing interest has resulted in IP being subjected to more scrutiny by researchers (and increasingly by lay people). Although we can feel confident about certain assumptions about IP (e.g., sense of being an impostor or fraud), Leary et al.'s (2000) study raises doubts about other IP assumptions (e.g., that impostors believe others hold unrealistically favorable perceptions of them). Additionally, preliminary evidence suggests there is a self-presentational component of IP wherein impostors strategically engage in behaviors because of some benefit (e.g., lowered expectations). In fact, Leary et al.'s study suggests that instead of the existence of true impostors (i.e., individuals who exhibit signs of impostorism in public and in private), there are only strategic impostors (i.e., individuals who exhibit signs of impostorism in public but not in private). Although Leary et al.'s study raises more questions than provides definitive answers, it underscores the need to conduct more studies that rigorously test the underlying assumptions of IP.

Psychologists and other individuals conducting IP research must be careful with the way they characterize IP. IP is more than self-doubt. Reducing or equating impostor feelings to self-doubt does not take into consideration how these two constructs may function differently among minoritized individuals, for whom impostor feelings are particularly susceptible to environmental cues. Terminology is also very important, and as psychologists we believe that using the term "impostor syndrome" has the unintended effect of medicalizing a normative experience in a way that Clance and Imes never intended in their conceptualization of IP.

Much more IP research needs to be conducted with minoritized groups. We need to better understand if there are truly differences in IP across racial and ethnic minorities, and we need to better understand how IP functions within minoritized groups. Finally, we propose that IP needs to be reconceptualized for racial and ethnic minorities as a racialized IP. Doing this takes the focus off the individual and rightfully focuses on how environmental stressors, such as racism and sexism, contribute to the impostor feelings experienced by minoritized individuals and women.

REFERENCES

Andrews, N. (2020). It's not imposter syndrome: Resisting self-doubt as normal for library workers. *In the Library With the Lead Pipe*. https://www.inthelibrarywiththeleadpipe.org/2020/its-not-imposter-syndrome/

Bernard, D. L., Hoggard, L. S., & Neblett, E. W., Jr. (2018). Racial discrimination, racial identity, and impostor phenomenon: A profile approach. *Cultural Diversity and Ethnic Minority Psychology, 24*(1), 51–61. https://doi.org/10.1037/cdp0000161

Bernard, D. L., & Stone-Sabali, S. (2022). Imposter syndrome in graduate school. In M. J. Prinstein (Ed.), *The portable mentor: Expert guide to a successful career in psychology* (3rd ed., pp. 102–118). Cambridge University Press. https://doi.org/10.1017/9781108903264.006

Braslow, M. D., Guerrettaz, J., Arkin, R. M., & Oleson, K. C. (2012). Self-doubt. *Social and Personality Psychology Compass*, *6*(6), 470–482. https://doi.org/10.1111/j.1751-9004.2012.00441.x

Bravata, D. M., Madhusudhan, D. K., Boroff, M., & Cokley, K. O. (2020). Commentary: Prevalence, predictors, and treatment of imposter syndrome: A systematic review. *Journal of Mental Health and Clinical Psychology*, *4*(3), 12–16. https://doi.org/10.29245/2578-2959/2020/3.1207

Clance, P. R., & Imes, S. A. (1978). The imposter phenomenon in high achieving women: Dynamics and therapeutic intervention. *Psychotherapy: Theory, Research, & Practice*, *15*(3), 241–247. https://doi.org/10.1037/h0086006

Clance, P. R., & O'Toole, M. A. (1987). The imposter phenomenon: An internal barrier to empowerment and achievement. *Women & Therapy*, *6*(3), 51–64. https://doi.org/10.1300/J015V06N03_05

Cokley, K., Smith, L., Bernard, D., Hurst, A., Jackson, S., Stone, S., Awosogba, O., Saucer, C., Bailey, M., & Roberts, D. (2017). Impostor feelings as a moderator and mediator of the relationship between perceived discrimination and mental health among racial/ethnic minority college students. *Journal of Counseling Psychology*, *64*(2), 141–154. https://doi.org/10.1037/cou0000198

Conrad, P. (2007). *The medicalization of society: On the transformation of human conditions into treatable disorders*. Johns Hopkins University Press. https://doi.org/10.56021/9780801885846

Deaux, D. (1976). Sex and the attribution process. In J. H. Harvey, W. J. Ickes, & R. F. Kidd (Eds.), *New directions in attribution research* (Vol. 1, pp. 335–352). Halstead Press Division, Wiley.

Feenstra, S., Begeny, C. T., Ryan, M. K., Rink, F. A., Stoker, J. I., & Jordan, J. (2020). Contextualizing the impostor "syndrome." *Frontiers in Psychology*, *11*, Article 575024. https://doi.org/10.3389/fpsyg.2020.575024

French, B. H., Lewis, J. A., Mosley, D. V., Adames, H. Y., Chavez-Duenas, N. Y., Chen, G. A., & Neville, H. A. (2020). Toward a psychological framework of radical healing in communities of color. *The Counseling Psychologist*, *48*(1), 14–46. https://doi.org/10.1177/0011000019843506

Jackson, A., Colson-Fearson, B., & Versey, H. S. (2022). Managing intersectional invisibility and hypervisibility during the transition to college among first generation women of color. *Psychology of Women Quarterly*, *46*(3), 354–371. https://doi.org/10.1177/03616843221106087

Josephs, K. A. (2007). Capgras syndrome and its relationship to neurodegenerative disease. *Archives of Neurology*, *64*(12), 1762–1766. https://doi.org/10.1001/archneur.64.12.1762

Kaczmarek, E. (2019). How to distinguish medicalization from over-medicalization? *Medicine, Health Care, and Philosophy*, *22*(1), 119–128. https://doi.org/10.1007/s11019-018-9850-1

Kark, R., Meister, A., & Peters, K. (2022). Now you see me, now you don't: A conceptual model of the antecedents and consequences of leader imposterism. *Journal of Management*, *48*(7), 1948–1979. https://doi.org/10.1177/01492063211020358

Leary, M. R., Patton, K. M., Orlando, A. E., & Wagoner Funk, W. (2000). The impostor phenomenon: Self-perceptions, reflected appraisals, and interpersonal strategies. *Journal of Personality, 68*(4), 725–756. https://doi.org/10.1111/1467-6494.00114

Magro, C. (2022). From hiding to sharing: A descriptive phenomenological study on the experience of being coached for impostor syndrome. *International Journal of Evidence Based Coaching and Mentoring, S16*, 66–80. https://doi.org/10.24384/0409-b325

McGee, E. O., Botchway, P. K., Naphan-Kingery, D. E., Brockman, A. J., Houston, S., & White, D. T. (2022). Racism camouflaged as impostorism and the impact on Black STEM doctoral students. *Race, Ethnicity and Education, 25*(4), 487–507. https://doi.org/10.1080/13613324.2021.1924137

Mullangi, S., & Jagsi, R. (2019). Imposter syndrome: Treat the cause, not the symptom. *JAMA, 322*(5), 403–404. https://doi.org/10.1001/jama.2019.9788

Muradoglu, M., Horne, Z., Hammon, M. D., Leslie, S. J., & Cimpian, A. (2022). Women—particularly underrepresented minority women—and early career academics feel like impostors in fields that value brilliance. *Journal of Educational Psychology, 114*(5), 1086–1100. https://doi.org/10.1037/edu0000669

Ogunyemi, D., Lee, T., Ma, M., Osuma, A., Eghbali, M., & Bouri, N. (2022). Improving wellness: Defeating impostor syndrome in medical education using an interactive reflective workshop. *PLOS ONE, 17*(8), Article e0272496. https://doi.org/10.1371/journal.pone.0272496

Popper, K. (1963). *Conjectures and refutations: The growth of scientific knowledge.* Routledge & Kegan Paul.

Stone, S., Saucer, C., Bailey, M., Garba, R., Hurst, A., Jackson, S. M., Krueger, N., & Cokley, K. (2018). Learning while Black: A culturally informed model of the impostor phenomenon for Black graduate students. *The Journal of Black Psychology, 44*(6), 491–531. https://doi.org/10.1177/0095798418786648

Stone-Sabali, S., Bernard, D. L., Mills, K. J., & Osborn, P. R. (2023). Mapping the evolution of the impostor phenomenon research: A bibliometric analysis. *Current Psychology.* Advance online publication. https://doi.org/10.1007/s12144-022-04201-9

White, J. L. (1970). Toward a Black psychology. *Ebony Magazine, 25*(11), 44–52.

Wilkins-Yel, K. G., Hyman, J., & Zounlome, N. O. (2019). Linking intersectional invisibility and hypervisibility to experiences of microaggressions among graduate women of color in STEM. *Journal of Vocational Behavior, 113*, 51–61. https://doi.org/10.1016/j.jvb.2018.10.018

Williams, D. R. (2018). Stress and the mental health of populations of color: Advancing our understanding of race-related stressors. *Journal of Health and Social Behavior, 59*(4), 466–485. https://doi.org/10.1177/0022146518814251

3 THE IMPOSTOR PHENOMENON AND MENTAL HEALTH

RAMYA GARBA, CARLY COLEMAN, AND TIA KELLEY

According to the American Psychological Association (APA), mental health is a "state of mind characterized by emotional well-being, good behavioral adjustment, relative freedom from anxiety and disabling symptoms, and a capacity to establish constructive relationships and cope with the ordinary demands and stresses of life" (APA, n.d.-c). Similarly, one of the most widely used definitions of mental health describes it as "a state of well-being in which the individual realizes his or her own abilities, can cope with the normal stresses of life, can work productively and fruitfully, and is able to make a contribution to his or her community" (World Health Organization, 2004, para. 1). Based on both definitions, it is clear that mental health is a ubiquitous and essential part of daily life. In turn, a myriad of factors may affect its condition or state. One such factor is that of self-perception, or the way in which individuals view themselves relative to others (e.g., "I am not smart"). Some of these views may reflect genuine self-knowledge, whereas others may be colored with varying degrees of distortion, potentially resulting in compromised health outcomes (Bem, 1972; Yurica & DiTomasso, 2005). Such is the case with the impostor phenomenon (IP; Clance & Imes, 1978).

Colloquially known as impostor syndrome, IP refers to the internal experience of intellectual phoniness (Clance & Imes, 1978). In other words, it is the tendency

https://doi.org/10.1037/0000397-004
The Impostor Phenomenon: Psychological Research, Theory, and Interventions,
K. Cokley (Editor)
Copyright © 2024 by the American Psychological Association. All rights reserved.

of high-achieving individuals to misattribute their tangible and/or visible success to external factors (i.e., luck or happenstance) rather than innate traits. This tendency, according to the literature, is due to feelings of perceived fraudulence or inadequacy (Clance & Imes, 1978). Although the term "syndrome" used in popular culture may imply a psychological disorder or clinical diagnosis, IP has never been classified as such by the American Psychiatric Association's *Diagnostic and Statistical Manual of Mental Disorders* or the World Health Organization's *International Statistical Classification of Diseases and Related Health Problems*. Rather, it has been described as a self-reinforcing psychological phenomenon in which individuals (a) doubt and/or dismiss their accomplishments and (b) fear being perceived and/or exposed as frauds. Thus, despite external evidence to the contrary, those experiencing impostor feelings or fears misattribute their success to luck, happenstance, and/or chance. Additionally, because they believe they have somehow deceived others into thinking they are indeed competent, they constantly fear that their perceived ineptness will be unearthed. They therefore tend to place an excessive amount of pressure on themselves to overperform and prove that they are worthy of success. As one might imagine, this phenomenon has been linked to unfavorable mental health outcomes, such as anxiety, depression, and low self-esteem (Cokley et al., 2013; Cusack et al., 2013; McGregor et al., 2008; Sakulku & Alexander, 2011).

Dating back to the 1970s, IP was initially believed to only affect professional, high-achieving women (Clance & Imes, 1978). However, its deleterious psychological effects have since been observed in culturally diverse adolescents, emerging adults, collegians, male professionals, and postgraduate trainees (e.g., Caselman et al., 2006; Chakraverty, 2020; Cokley et al., 2013; McClain et al., 2016; Oriel et al., 2004). The following chapter therefore provides the reader with a broad, foundational overview of extant literature on the mental health correlates of IP. Due to the achievement-related nature of IP, we first discuss the mechanics of this relationship among achievement-oriented populations (i.e., students and professionals). We then discuss specific mental health constructs that have most commonly been linked to IP in the literature: depression, self-esteem, anxiety, and perfectionism.

IMPOSTOR PHENOMENON AND MENTAL HEALTH IN STUDENTS

In recent decades, diagnosable mental illness among student populations has significantly increased (Keyes et al., 2012). This increase has been linked to comorbid or co-occurring academic and psychological challenges (Clemens et al., 2020; Storrie et al., 2010). Although IP has never been classified as a diagnosable disease, it has been linked to such challenges among collegians and other student populations (e.g., Austin et al., 2009; Cokley et al., 2013; Kumar & Jagacinski, 2006; McGregor et al., 2008; Peteet, Montgomery, & Weekes, 2015).

The college experience is rife with competition, achievement orientation, and self-evaluation (Pedrelli et al., 2015). In turn, it presents a plethora of opportunities for students to engage in self-doubt and self-examination. It is therefore unsurprising that IP is prevalent among the college student population. More specifically, feelings of impostorism have been associated with academic disengagement, persistent feelings of inadequacy, and an unhealthy pressure to succeed among collegians (Canning et al., 2020). It has also been linked to diagnosable mental health concerns, such as depression and anxiety. In a 2008 study, the self-doubt and negative thought patterns associated with IP were found to be consistent with the self-doubt and negative thought patterns that many individuals with mild depression experience, as measured by the Beck Depression Inventory (Beck et al., 1996; McGregor et al., 2008). Similarly, when examining broad mental health concerns among diverse collegians, Kananifar and colleagues (2015) found that those who reported high levels of impostorism also reported higher levels of anxiety, depression, psychosomatic symptoms, and social dysfunction. Finally, Fraenza (2016) also found that reported experiences of impostor feelings were associated with greater anxiety in a graduate student sample. Given the aforementioned prevalence of comorbid mental illness among this population, it is unsurprising that the presence and/or addition of impostor feelings has been linked to adverse psychological outcomes.

To a lesser extent, the psychological effects of IP have also been examined in younger student populations. Although extant research is currently sparse, results are generally consistent with those involving college students. For example, Caselman et al. (2006) concluded that their high school student sample experienced impostorism at a similar rate as adult populations. Furthermore, they found that global self-worth (i.e., self-esteem) was negatively correlated with impostor feelings. Relatedly, in a sample of 233 high school students, feelings of impostorism and a general tendency to cover up one's true self were associated with indices of psychological disturbance. That is, feelings of intellectual fraudulence, or the fear of being exposed as truly incompetent, were associated with a history of suicidal ideation and attempts among a group of male and female adolescents (Lester & Moderski, 1995). Finally, Caselman (2003) examined IP among adolescents attending suburban high schools in both Japan and the United States. When examining self-perception (i.e., scholastic self-perception, athletic self-perception, physical self-perception, behavioral self-perception, close friend self-perception, and global self-worth), the author found that low global self-worth significantly predicted greater impostor feelings for both Japanese and American adolescents.

As reflected in these studies, the relationship between IP and mental health is well established among the general student population. However, few studies have examined it among students of color. The few that have seem to identify a heightened predisposition to impostorism among this group. Relative to their peers, students of color report ubiquitous experiences with racism, discrimination, and the psychological effects of both. They are therefore more likely to report a heightened awareness of their perceived marginal status (Greer & Chwalisz, 2007; Peteet, Brown, et al., 2015). According to the literature, such perceptions may result in the tendency to internalize discriminatory experiences as evidence of perceived incompetence (D. L. Bernard et al., 2017). In other words, students of color are more susceptible to feeling like frauds when they perceive themselves to be routinely treated as such. As one can imagine, this propensity is likely magnified in primarily White spaces (e.g., historically White colleges/universities), where students of color represent visible minorities (Ewing et al., 1996; Peteet, Brown, et al., 2015).

It therefore makes logical sense that in the literature, Black, Indigenous, and students of color in primarily White spaces tend to report experiences of minority status stress and IP in tandem (D. L. Bernard et al., 2017; Cokley et al., 2013; McClain et al., 2016). For example, McClain et al. (2016) found that minority status stress, in conjunction with IP, created a more taxing psychological burden for Black collegians, as both minority status stress and IP were found to have an equally deleterious effect on their mental health. Relatedly, in their seminal 2013 study, Cokley and colleagues examined differences in minority status stress, impostor feelings, and mental health among a group of African American, Asian American, and Latin American collegians. They found that both IP and minority status stress strongly predicted psychological distress, with IP serving as the strongest predictor. In line with these results, another study found that psychological well-being predicted IP in high-achieving racial/ethnic minorities. More specifically, Peteet, Montgomery, and Weekes (2015) revealed that among a sample of high-achieving racial/ethnic minority students, the endorsement of a low racial/ethnic identity and low psychological well-being predicted higher levels of IP. Finally, a 2017 study found that African American women who reported a greater frequency of racially discriminatory experiences were most vulnerable to the negative effects of IP (D. L. Bernard et al., 2017). Taken together, these studies suggest that the combination of racialized stressors and impostor feelings make students of color particularly vulnerable to the negative psychological effects of IP. In other words, the combination of feeling like a fraud and being treated like one can result in heightened feelings of distress among historically marginalized and minoritized student populations. The link between IP and mental health is not exclusive to students, however. This association has also been found among employed populations.

IMPOSTOR PHENOMENON AND MENTAL HEALTH IN EMPLOYED POPULATIONS

Pressures associated with the work environment generally differ from those in educational settings (Colligan & Higgins, 2006). For example, employed individuals typically contend with time-limited performance evaluations in exchange for perceived financial security. Thus, relative to student populations, paid workers may uniquely contend with the fear of losing financial support in the event they are "found out" as incompetent frauds. Unsurprisingly, performance expectations have been conceptually and empirically linked to feelings of anxiety, self-doubt, and worry among this group (Clance & Imes, 1978). For example, heightened thoughts of self-doubt and perceived future incompetence have been linked to sadness and psychological distress among early career professionals (Hutchins, 2015; Oriel et al., 2004). Such psychological experiences have been captured and illuminated by the impostor cycle (Clance, 1985a).

Based on rich clinical observations, Clance (1985a) introduced a model to describe what she coined the impostor cycle (see Chapter 1). According to this model, when faced with achievement-oriented tasks, impostors typically experience anxiety, self-doubt, and worry, prompting overpreparation and/or procrastination. If said tasks are accomplished, they often attribute their success to high effort (i.e., from overpreparation) or luck (i.e., despite procrastination; Sakulku & Alexander, 2011). Said accomplishments are typically accompanied by positive feedback, prompting temporary relief. Such feedback, and in turn, relief, is often discounted, however, cycling impostors back to initial feelings of perceived fraudulence, self-doubt, and/or anxiety (Sakulku & Alexander, 2011). Extant research on employed populations seems to reflect elements of this cycle.

In a qualitative study exploring the experiences of female faculty members, Laux (2018) revealed that all participants endorsed feelings of impostorism throughout their tenure process. During said process, respondents recounted feelings of anxiety, self-doubt, and worry, prompting overpreparation. Additionally, despite having achieved relative success, respondents admitted to experiencing feelings of professional fraudulence and unworthiness. One participant stated, "I said I didn't feel like an impostor as much anymore . . . and then I realized, it's probably because mostly I feel pretty much like a failure in my career. Maybe, I feel that I was 'found out' or something, so while that is gone, the sense that I am not much of a success remains." Others reported concerns that they were only selected for professional opportunities (e.g., tenure) due to certain characteristics and identities over their qualifications (Laux, 2018).

After qualitatively investigating impostorism among college faculty, Hutchins and Rainbolt (2017) made similar observations. From the themes that emerged, they found that despite achieving high levels of tangible, intellectual success (i.e., advanced degrees), faculty members reported feeling like intellectual frauds. Furthermore, said feelings reportedly produced elevated levels of stress, chronic worries, and anxiety. Hutchins and colleagues (2018) extended these observations by examining the impact of IP on work outcomes. They discovered that employed impostors tend to use avoidant coping strategies in an attempt to evade, rather than eliminate, fraudulent feelings. They also found that such strategies were associated with greater emotional exhaustion and lower job satisfaction (Hutchins et al., 2018). Similarly, in a study examining impostorism in white-collar workers, Vergauwe and colleagues (2015) found that the consistent fear of being exposed as a fraud, coupled with persistent feelings of self-doubt and anxiety, were both reflected in lowered levels of overall job satisfaction.

In addition to low job satisfaction, IP has also been linked to work–family conflict (Crawford et al., 2016; Hutchins et al., 2018). This conflict is described as the negative influence work has on one's family life (Crawford et al., 2016). Crawford and colleagues (2016) found that among community college employees, greater IP led to greater emotional exhaustion, which in turn predicted greater challenges balancing work and family demands.

Finally, a study examining the relationship between IP and mental health identified organizational support as a moderating variable. In line with aforementioned studies, Haar and de Jong (2022) found that participants who reported higher IP also reported higher job depression and anxiety. However, perceived organizational support (POS) seemed to moderate the strength of both relationships. That is, workers who identified as high impostors and indicated high POS also reported lower mental health issues, whereas those who indicated low POS reported greater mental health issues (Haar & de Jong, 2022). In other words, employees who believed they possessed a sufficient amount of job-related support were less likely to experience the adverse psychological effects of IP.

IMPOSTOR PHENOMENON AND DEPRESSION

Depression is characterized as a negative affective state, ranging from unhappiness and discontent to extreme feelings of pessimism, despondency, and sadness. Individuals who struggle with depression may also experience difficulty concentrating or making decisions, withdrawal from social activities, and a lack of motivation (APA, n.d.-b; LeMoult & Gotlib, 2019). Depression, as measured by validated instruments, has been consistently linked to IP. That is, feelings of professional and/or personal fraudulence have been associated with feelings of extreme sadness and despondency.

In a mixed-method study involving postdoctoral trainees in science, technology, engineering, and mathematics, Chakraverty (2020) found that IP manifested as symptoms related to depression, such as hopelessness, unhappiness, academic social isolation, and feelings of unworthiness. One participant in the study stated, "If they really knew what was going on in my head, they would reject me from the lab, and I'd lose my job. That type of thing has made it difficult to get up in the morning." Similarly, in a sample of Black collegians, Austin and colleagues (2009) found that higher reports of impostorism predicted greater depression. Further, students who reported stronger survivor's guilt endorsed greater IP, which in turn predicted more self-reported depressive symptoms (e.g., interpersonal problems, negative affect, somatic symptoms). Survivor's guilt, as described in the study, is the guilt-ridden comparison of one's own (e.g., high-achieving Black students') successes to the perceived misfortunes of racially similar others (Wayment, 2004). According to the authors, the students who felt the most guilt about their perceived success were more likely to endorse stronger impostor feelings and, in turn, more depressive symptoms. This finding therefore echoes the aforementioned link between awareness of one's own minority status and possible psychological distress, or in this case, depression.

In an effort to fully comprehend the nuanced relationship between depression and IP, specific components of depression have also been examined. With a sample of undergraduate students, Lester (2013) uncovered a relationship between IP and various symptoms of depression, such as hopelessness, helplessness, and irrational rumination. Such symptoms were also related to past suicidal ideation, thereby demonstrating an association between IP and suicidal cognitions. In line with this finding, younger (e.g., high school) students who endorsed greater feelings of IP were also found to endorse previous suicidal ideation and attempts (Lester & Moderski, 1995). Furthermore, this relationship was also found among practicing physicians, such that a higher endorsement of IP was associated with a higher prevalence of suicidal ideation

(Shanafelt et al., 2022). The combined results of these studies further highlight the potentially distressing consequences associated with IP at varying stages of development.

In addition to substantiating a link between IP and symptoms of depression, the literature has also revealed a positive association between IP and the mood-related construct Neuroticism. Per the five-factor model of personality, Neuroticism is one of five dimensions of personality and is described as "the tendency to experience negative affect, such as depression, anxiety, and hostility" (Chae et al., 1995, p. 471). Due in part to the latent presence of depression within this construct, it has also been linked to IP (e.g., N. S. Bernard et al., 2002). In a study examining the association between IP and the five-factor model, N. S. Bernard and colleagues (2002) found a positive association between IP and neuroticism. Further, relative to other facets of neuroticism, depression had the strongest relationship to IP. Rosenthal et al. (2021) found a similar relationship among first-year medical students, thereby providing additional support for this link.

In addition to prompting episodic bouts of depression, IP has also been shown to have longer term effects. In a recent study, Sverdlik and colleagues (2020) found that impostor feelings at time of assessment predicted increases in self-reported depression over a 5-month period among doctoral students. This finding suggests that feelings of fraudulence may have longer term emotional effects. Thus, efforts to mitigate impostor feelings may in turn diminish extended depressive symptoms.

IMPOSTOR PHENOMENON AND SELF-ESTEEM

Self-esteem has been described as "the degree to which the qualities and characteristics contained in one's self-concept are perceived to be positive" (APA, n.d.-d). In turn, it reflects one's views of their capabilities and accomplishments, as well as their perceived success in living up to them. It is therefore unsurprising that IP has long been linked to self-esteem in the literature (e.g., Caselman et al., 2006; Neureiter & Traut-Mattausch, 2016; Schubert & Bowker, 2019). IP and self-esteem have also consistently demonstrated strong congruence, prompting speculation about possible construct overlap (Cozzarelli & Major, 1990; Hutchins et al., 2018; Thompson et al., 1998). However, extant literature has identified them as two distinct constructs (Chrisman et al., 1995).

The Clance Impostor Phenomenon Scale (Clance, 1985a) is commonly used to measure levels of impostorism (Cozzarelli & Major, 1990; Hutchins et al., 2018; Thompson et al., 1998). When Chrisman and colleagues (1995) compared the Clance Impostor Phenomenon Scale with measures of self-esteem, they found it to be highly congruent with both scales. However, they also found that there was a greater and stronger association between the two self-esteem scales. Their study therefore demonstrated that although self-esteem and IP share similar traits (e.g., feelings of unworthiness), their distinct differences (e.g., feelings of fraudulence) warrant classification of two unique constructs.

According to extant literature, high impostor feelings have consistently predicted lower self-esteem (e.g., Cozzarelli & Major, 1990; Schubert & Bowker, 2019). For example, in a study with Black college students, Peteet, Brown, et al. (2015) found that individuals who reported high impostorism were more likely to endorse items consistent with low self-esteem. Relatedly, in a study examining low self-esteem in both students and professionals, findings revealed that reports of low self-esteem predicted greater feelings of impostorism (Neureiter & Traut-Mattausch, 2016). Furthermore, Gadsby and Hohwy (2021) conducted an experimental study exploring IP, performance evaluation, and self-esteem among an adult population in the United Kingdom. The participants completed an online task and were asked to evaluate their performance, both objectively and comparatively. The authors found that participants with greater IP were more negative in their self-evaluations of said task. Additionally, they found that greater IP was linked to lower self-esteem among these individuals.

Because IP and low self-esteem embody similar underlying traits, such as self-doubt and feelings of inadequacy, they tend to co-occur interpersonally (LaDonna et al., 2018; Schubert, 2013). For example, Schubert and Bowker (2019) found that relative to individuals with stable high self-esteem, those who reported low and/or unstable self-esteem were more predisposed to feelings of fraudulence, incompetence, and inadequacy. Related research has also revealed that such individuals tend to utilize self-protection and self-enhancement strategies more often than those with stable self-esteem (Finez et al., 2012; Schubert, 2013). Extreme overpreparation and excessive efforts to meet high standards of personal achievement are examples of such strategies. In line with this finding, Want and Kleitman (2006) identified IP as the strongest predictor of a self-protection mechanism in their study. With a general adult population, they investigated the connection between IP, self-handicapping, and parental style. Self-handicapping, as described in the study, involves positioning a barrier in the way of a perceived evaluation in order to blame said barrier in the event of failure (Kelley, 1971; Want & Kleitman, 2006). Through self-handicapping, one's perceived incompetence or failure can then be attributed to external rather than internal conditions. Relative to self-efficacy, Want and Kleitman found that impostorism was the strongest predictor of self-handicapping.

IMPOSTOR PHENOMENON AND ANXIETY

Anxiety is defined as an emotion characterized by fearful apprehension and somatic symptoms of tension, in which an individual anticipates impending danger, catastrophe, or misfortune (APA, n.d.-a). Early clinical observations of IP frequently identify anxiety as one of several underlying mechanisms through which IP is developed and maintained (Clance & Imes, 1978).

Anxiety has been conceptualized as existing in two forms, trait and state (Levitt, 2015). Trait anxiety is specific to the self and describes one's predisposition for experiencing anxiety. State anxiety, on the other hand, is situational and can fluctuate from occasion to occasion (Levitt, 2015). Based on this conceptualization, generalized anxiety is considered trait anxiety, whereas specific anxieties or phobias (e.g., performance anxiety) are considered state anxiety. Studies have revealed associations between IP and both forms (Cokley et al., 2017; Kumar & Jagacinski, 2006; Topping & Kimmel, 1985; Yaffe, 2023).

As stated in previous sections, IP is based on the fear that one's perceived intellectual phoniness or incompetence will be discovered. In turn, it is characterized by hypervigilance about the impending moment or situation in which one's phoniness will be revealed. This elevated physiological state, in which one assesses potential threats, is rooted in anxiety. It is therefore unsurprising that Clance and Imes (1978) identified generalized anxiety symptoms, such as hypervigilance, excessive worry, and fatigue, as some of the most frequently reported symptoms among those experiencing IP. Such symptoms are now widely understood to be associated with the onset and maintenance of IP. Clance and Imes also delineated behavioral features that contribute to both the development and perpetuation of IP: diligence and hard work. The relationship between IP and anxiety can be traced to both.

In order to prevent perceived exposure as intellectual frauds, impostors often engage in persistent hard work and overpreparation, triggering what Clance and O'Toole (1987) refer to as the impostor cycle. In this cycle, the fear of impending exposure prompts impostors to work harder, typically resulting in high achievement. Ironically, this achievement only seems to further perpetuate the fear of being exposed, resulting in more hard work and overpreparation (Clance & Imes, 1978). Cognitive dissonance between an impostor's perceived skill set and ideals of success may underlie the motivation to combat anxiety with hard work and diligence (Langford & Clance, 1993).

As previously mentioned, impostors often hold incredibly high standards for themselves (Clance, 1985b). Due to such standards, they often approach new tasks with debilitating levels of anxiety (Clance et al., 1995). What is perhaps most interesting is that studies have shown that this association exists regardless of the perceived outcome of said tasks (Thompson et al., 1998). In other words, impostors experience high levels of anxiety even in situations in which they can expect to receive positive or noncritical feedback, such as within their area(s) of expertise. It is therefore clear that anxiety and IP are deeply intertwined (Clance & O'Toole, 1987; Oriel et al., 2004; Rohrmann et al., 2016; Sonnak & Towell, 2001; Tigranyan et al., 2021; see also Stone-Sabali et al., 2023).

IMPOSTOR PHENOMENON AND PERFECTIONISM

In the literature, perfectionism has been characterized by unrealistically high personal standards, overgeneralization of failures, stringent self-evaluation, and an all-or-nothing mentality (Hewitt & Flett, 1991). Such features have been conceptually and empirically linked to IP (Clance & Imes, 1978; Clance & O'Toole, 1987; Henning et al., 1998; Pákozdy et al., 2023). Expectedly, the vast majority of research on this relationship has been with samples of high-achieving undergraduate and graduate students in science, technology, engineering, and mathematics. For example, a sample of health profession students (i.e., medicine, dentistry, nursing, and pharmacy students) demonstrated high levels of both perfectionism and IP (Henning et al., 1998). Additionally, these two constructs served as strong positive predictors of psychological distress across all four groups. Although this study did not assess the predictive relationship between perfectionism and IP, results suggest that these two constructs are likely to co-occur among high-achieving individuals.

Perfectionism has also been conceptualized as a dichotomous construct, reflected by both adaptive and maladaptive features. The adaptive form is understood to be driven by a healthy desire for success and has been associated with more positive outcomes, such as flexible thinking and better mental health (Thomas & Bigatti, 2020). On the other hand, the maladaptive form is understood to be driven by the fear of failure and has been associated with more negative outcomes, such as IP and suicidal ideation (Brennan-Wydra et al., 2021; Cokley et al., 2018; Pannhausen et al., 2022; Vergauwe et al., 2015). Studies have found both maladaptive perfectionism and IP to be positively associated with depression, anxiety, and psychological distress (Thomas & Bigatti, 2020). For example, in a study looking at the impact of trait perfectionism on academic malfunctioning among graduate students, trait perfectionism predicted impostor feelings, academic stress, and communication anxiety (Cowie et al., 2018). In other words, graduate students who endorsed high levels of maladaptive perfectionism were more likely to report impostor feelings, feel stressed about their academics, and feel anxious about interpersonal communication in various academic situations.

Perfectionism has also been conceptualized as a construct with both intrapersonal and interpersonal characteristics (Cowie et al., 2018). In the literature, perfectionistic self-presentation is an example of interpersonal perfectionism in which an individual aims to conceal perceived imperfections from others. This behavior is therefore adopted to promote an air of perfection (Hewitt et al., 2003). Given the fear impostors have about others identifying their perceived imperfections, this form of perfectionism is especially relevant to the IP discussion. It is therefore unsurprising that a 2018 study identified interpersonal perfectionism (i.e., perfectionistic self-presentation) as an incremental predictor of IP beyond trait perfectionism. Further, within this sample of graduate students, both perfectionism and IP were associated with communication anxiety (Cowie et al., 2018). Few studies have examined perfectionistic self-presentation as it relates to IP. However, these preliminary findings suggest that there may be specific interpersonal features that undergird the relationship between IP and perfectionism.

Perfectionistic beliefs are among the most commonly endorsed symptoms among perceived impostors (Cromwell et al., 1990). In a sample of high-achieving high school students, impostors differed from nonimpostors in their tendency to endorse irrational beliefs associated with high self-expectations, anxious overconcern, and helplessness (Cromwell et al., 1990). Although perfectionism was not explicitly explored in this study, endorsement of high self-expectations and anxious overconcern are consistent with the characteristics of perfectionism (Hewitt & Flett, 1991). Relatedly, Thompson et al. (2000) explored the relationship between perfectionism and IP in a sample of undergraduate college students. When compared with nonimpostors, the impostor group demonstrated higher perfectionistic beliefs.

The well-established relationship between IP and perfectionism has been found to pose a threat to mental health. In fact, one study found that maladaptive perfectionism increases one's risk for IP, which in turn increases one's risk for suicide (Brennan-Wydra et al., 2021). Another study found that IP may be the mechanism through which perfectionism predicts anxiety (Wang et al., 2019). In a sample of college students, Wang et al. (2019) found that IP fully mediated the relationship between perfectionism and anxiety. In other words, the effect of perfectionism on anxiety was fully dependent on impostor feelings. In that same study, IP also partially mediated or explained the relationship between perfectionism and depression. That is, the deleterious psychological effects of perfectionism (i.e., depression and anxiety) were found to be due, in part, to a co-occurring endorsement of impostor feelings (i.e., perceived incompetence and fraudulence). Relatedly, Thompson et al. (2000) concluded that the impostors in their study were more likely to hold perfectionistic beliefs and endorse high levels of anxiety, further demonstrating the potentially deleterious effects of both perfectionism and IP.

CONCLUSION

Spanning almost 50 years of research, the IP and mental health literature is vast and diverse. Initially believed to only affect professional, high-achieving women, the deleterious psychological effects of IP have been observed in culturally diverse adolescents, emerging adults, collegians, male professionals, and postgraduate trainees, to name a few. The effects of IP have also been observed at schools, in the workplace, and within a myriad of interpersonal exchanges. Through such observations, IP has been linked to depression, anxiety, perfectionism, minority status stress, and low self-esteem.

Countless studies, as reflected in this chapter, have demonstrated the psychological relevance, complexity, and ubiquity of IP. However, there are clearly a number of empirical opportunities, such as the need for more racially/ethnically diverse samples, longitudinal designs, and the validation of targeted clinical interventions. Given the established connection between minority status stress and IP, investigating possible underlying factors (i.e., mediators) could help to uncover novel points of intervention. By leveraging the findings of outcome studies, such interventions could be targeted to address not only symptoms of IP but also comorbid clinical conditions, such as anxiety, low self-esteem, and depression. Finally, due to the potentially long-term effects of IP, longitudinal studies could also help to further elucidate and treat distal factors over time.

REFERENCES

American Psychological Association. (n.d.-a). Anxiety. In *APA dictionary of psychology*. Retrieved December 15, 2022, from https://dictionary.apa.org/anxiety

American Psychological Association. (n.d.-b). Depression. In *APA dictionary of psychology*. Retrieved December 15, 2022, from https://dictionary.apa.org/depression

American Psychological Association. (n.d.-c). Mental health. In *APA dictionary of psychology*. Retrieved December 15, 2022, from https://www.apa.org/topics/mental-health

American Psychological Association. (n.d.-d). Self-esteem. In *APA dictionary of psychology*. Retrieved December 15, 2022, from https://dictionary.apa.org/self-esteem

Austin, C. C., Clark, E. M., Ross, M. J., & Taylor, M. J. (2009). Impostorism as a mediator between survivor guilt and depression in a sample of African American college students. *College Student Journal, 43*(4, Pt. A), 1094–1109.

Beck, A. T., Steer, R. A., & Brown, G. K. (1996). *Manual for the Beck Depression Inventory-II (BDI-II)*. Psychological Corporation.

Bem, D. J. (1972). Self-perception theory. In *Advances in experimental social psychology* (Vol. 6, pp. 1–62). Academic Press. https://doi.org/10.1016/S0065-2601(08)60024-6

Bernard, D. L., Lige, Q. M., Willis, H. A., Sosoo, E. E., & Neblett, E. W. (2017). Impostor phenomenon and mental health: The influence of racial discrimination and gender. *Journal of Counseling Psychology, 64*(2), 155–166. https://doi.org/10.1037/cou0000197

Bernard, N. S., Dollinger, S. J., & Ramaniah, N. V. (2002). Applying the Big Five personality factors to the impostor phenomenon. *Journal of Personality Assessment, 78*(2), 321–333. https://doi.org/10.1207/S15327752JPA7802_07

Brennan-Wydra, E., Chung, H. W., & Angoff, N. ChenFeng, J., Phillips, A., Schreiber, J., Young, C., & Wilkins, K. (2021). Maladaptive perfectionism, impostor phenomenon, and suicidal ideation among medical students. *Academic Psychiatry, 45*, 708–715. https://doi.org/10.1007/s40596-021-01503-1

Canning, E. A., LaCosse, J., Kroeper, K. M., & Murphy, M. C. (2020). Feeling like an imposter: The effect of perceived classroom competition on the daily psychological experiences of first-generation college students. *Social Psychological and Personality Science, 11*(5), 647–657. https://doi.org/10.1177/1948550619882032

Caselman, T. D. (2003). *The imposter phenomenon among American and Japanese adolescents: Gender, self-perception, self-concept and social support variables* [Doctoral dissertation, Oklahoma State University]. ProQuest Information & Learning.

Caselman, T. D., Self, P. A., & Self, A. L. (2006). Adolescent attributes contributing to the imposter phenomenon. *Journal of Adolescence, 29*(3), 395–405. https://doi.org/10.1016/j.adolescence.2005.07.003

Chae, J. H., Piedmont, R. L., Estadt, B. K., & Wicks, R. J. (1995). Personological evaluation of Clance's Imposter Phenomenon Scale in a Korean sample. *Journal of Personality Assessment, 65*(3), 468–485.

Chakraverty, D. (2020). The impostor phenomenon among postdoctoral trainees in STEM: A U.S.-based mixed-methods study. *International Journal of Doctoral Studies, 15*, 329–352. https://doi.org/10.28945/4589

Chrisman, S. M., Pieper, W. A., Clance, P. R., Holland, C. L., & Glickauf-Hughes, C. (1995). Validation of the Clance Imposter Phenomenon Scale. *Journal of Personality Assessment, 65*(3), 456–467. https://doi.org/10.1207/s15327752jpa6503_6

Clance, P. R. (1985a). *The impostor phenomenon: Overcoming the fear that haunts your success*. Peachtree.

Clance, P. R. (1985b). The superwoman aspect and the perfectionistic male. In *The impostor phenomenon: When success makes you feel like a fake* (pp. 77–87). Bantam Books.

Clance, P. R., Dingman, D., Reviere, S. L., & Stober, D. R. (1995). Impostor phenomenon in an interpersonal/social context: Origins and treatment. *Women & Therapy, 16*(4), 79–96. https://doi.org/10.1300/J015v16n04_07

Clance, P. R., & Imes, S. A. (1978). The imposter phenomenon in high achieving women: Dynamics and therapeutic intervention. *Psychotherapy: Theory, Research, & Practice, 15*(3), 241–247. https://doi.org/10.1037/h0086006

Clance, P. R., & O'Toole, M. A. (1987). The imposter phenomenon: An internal barrier to empowerment and achievement. *Women & Therapy, 6*(3), 51–64. https://doi.org/10.1300/J015V06N03_05

Clemens, V., Deschamps, P., Fegert, J. M., Anagnostopoulos, D., Bailey, S., Doyle, M, Eliez, S., Hansen, A. S., Hebebrand, J., Hillegers, M., Jacobs, B., Karwautz, A., Kiss, E., Kotsis, K., Kumperscak, H. G., Pejovic-Milovancevic, M., Råberg Christensen, A. M., Raynaud, J.-P., Westerinen, H., & Visnapuu-Bernadt, P. (2020). Potential effects of "social" distancing measures and school lockdown on child and adolescent mental health. *European Child & Adolescent Psychiatry, 29*(6), 739–742. https://doi.org/10.1007/s00787-020-01549-w

Cokley, K., McClain, S., Enciso, A., & Martinez, M. (2013). An examination of the impact of minority status stress and impostor feelings on the mental health of diverse ethnic minority college students. *Journal of Multicultural Counseling and Development, 41*(2), 82–95. https://doi.org/10.1002/j.2161-1912.2013.00029.x

Cokley, K., Smith, L., Bernard, D., Hurst, A., Jackson, S., Stone, S., Awosogba, O., Saucer, C., Bailey, M., & Roberts, D. (2017). Impostor feelings as a moderator and mediator of the relationship between perceived discrimination and mental health among racial/ethnic minority college students. *Journal of Counseling Psychology, 64*(2), 141–154. https://doi.org/10.1037/cou0000198

Cokley, K., Stone, S., Krueger, N., Bailey, M., Garba, R., & Hurst, A. (2018). Self-esteem as a mediator of the link between perfectionism and the impostor phenomenon. *Personality and Individual Differences, 135*, 292–297. https://doi.org/10.1016/j.paid.2018.07.032

Colligan, T. W., & Higgins, E. M. (2006). Workplace stress: Etiology and consequences. *Journal of Workplace Behavioral Health, 21*(2), 89–97. https://doi.org/10.1300/J490v21n02_07

Cowie, M. E., Nealis, L. J., Sherry, S. B., Hewitt, P. L., & Flett, G. L. (2018). Perfectionism and academic difficulties in graduate students: Testing incremental prediction and gender moderation. *Personality and Individual Differences, 123*, 223–228. https://doi.org/10.1016/j.paid.2017.11.027

Cozzarelli, C., & Major, B. (1990). Exploring the validity of the impostor phenomenon. *Journal of Social and Clinical Psychology, 9*(4), 401–417. https://doi.org/10.1521/jscp.1990.9.4.401

Crawford, W. S., Shanine, K. K., Whitman, M. V., & Kacmar, K. M. (2016). Examining the impostor phenomenon and work–family conflict. *Journal of Managerial Psychology, 31*(2), 375–390. https://doi.org/10.1108/JMP-12-2013-0409

Cromwell, B., Brown, N., Sanchez-Huceles, J., & Adair, F. L. (1990). The impostor phenomenon and personality characteristics of high school honor students. *Journal of Social Behavior and Personality, 5*(6), 563–573.

Cusack, C. E., Hughes, J. L., & Nuhu, N. (2013). Connecting gender and mental health to imposter phenomenon feelings. *Psi Chi Journal of Psychological Research, 18*(2), 74–81. https://doi.org/10.24839/2164-8204.JN18.2.74

Ewing, K. M., Richardson, T. Q., James-Myers, L., & Russell, R. K. (1996). The relationship between racial identity attitudes, worldview, and African American graduate students' experience of the imposter phenomenon. *Journal of Black Psychology, 22*(1), 53–66. https://doi.org/10.1177/00957984960221005

Finez, L., Berjot, S., Rosnet, E., Cleveland, C., & Tice, D. M. (2012). Trait self-esteem and claimed self-handicapping motives in sports situations. *Journal of Sports Sciences, 30*(16), 1757–1765. https://doi.org/10.1080/02640414.2012.718089

Fraenza, C. B. (2016). The role of social influence in anxiety and the imposter phenomenon. *Online Learning, 20*(2), 230–243. https://doi.org/10.24059/olj.v20i2.618

Gadsby, S., & Hohwy, J. (2021). Negative performance evaluation in the imposter phenomenon: Content, cause, and authenticity. *PsyArXiv.* https://doi.org/10.31234/osf.io/4neaj

Greer, T. M., & Chwalisz, K. (2007). Minority-related stressors and coping processes among African American college students. *Journal of College Student Development, 48*(4), 388–404. https://doi.org/10.1353/csd.2007.0037

Haar, J., & de Jong, K. (2022). Imposter phenomenon and employee mental health: What role do organizations play? *Personnel Review.* Advance online publication. https://doi.org/10.1108/PR-01-2022-0030

Henning, K., Ey, S., & Shaw, D. (1998). Perfectionism, the imposter phenomenon and psychological adjustment in medical, dental, nursing and pharmacy students. *Medical Education, 32*(5), 456–464. https://doi.org/10.1046/j.1365-2923.1998.00234.x

Hewitt, P. L., & Flett, G. L. (1991). Perfectionism in the self and social contexts: Conceptualization, assessment, and association with psychopathology. *Journal of Personality and Social Psychology, 60*(3), 456–470. https://doi.org/10.1037/0022-3514.60.3.456

Hewitt, P. L., Flett, G. L., Sherry, S. B., Habke, M., Parkin, M., Lam, R. W., McMurtry, B., Ediger, E., Fairlie, P., & Stein, M. B. (2003). The interpersonal expression of perfection: Perfectionistic self-presentation and psychological distress. *Journal of Personality and Social Psychology, 84*(6), 1303–1325. https://doi.org/10.1037/0022-3514.84.6.1303

Hutchins, H. M. (2015). Outing the imposter: A study exploring imposter phenomenon among higher education faculty. *New Horizons in Adult Education and Human Resource Development, 27*(2), 3–12. https://doi.org/10.1002/nha3.20098

Hutchins, H. M., Penney, L. M., & Sublett, L. W. (2018). What imposters risk at work: Exploring imposter phenomenon, stress coping, and job outcomes. *Human Resource Development Quarterly, 29*(1), 31–48. https://doi.org/10.1002/hrdq.21304

Hutchins, H. M., & Rainbolt, H. (2017). What triggers imposter phenomenon among academic faculty? A critical incident study exploring antecedents, coping, and development opportunities. *Human Resource Development International, 20*(3), 194–214. https://doi.org/10.1080/13678868.2016.1248205

Kananifar, N., Seghatoleslam, T., Atashpour, S. H., Hoseini, M., Habil, M. H. B., & Danaee, M. (2015). The relationships between imposter phenomenon and mental health in Isfahan universities students. *International Medical Journal, 22*(3), 144–146.

Kelley, H. H. (1971). *Attribution in social interaction.* General Learning Press.

Keyes, C. L., Eisenberg, D., Perry, G. S., Dube, S. R., Kroenke, K., & Dhingra, S. S. (2012). The relationship of level of positive mental health with current mental disorders in predicting suicidal behavior and academic impairment in college students. *Journal of American College Health, 60*(2), 126–133. https://doi.org/10.1080/07448481.2011.608393

Kumar, S., & Jagacinski, C. M. (2006). Imposters have goals too: The imposter phenomenon and its relationship to achievement goal theory. *Personality and Individual Differences, 40*(1), 147–157. https://doi.org/10.1016/j.paid.2005.05.014

LaDonna, K. A., Ginsburg, S., & Watling, C. (2018). "Rising to the level of your incompetence": What physicians' self-assessment of their performance reveals about the imposter syndrome in medicine. *Academic Medicine, 93*(5), 763–768. https://doi.org/10.1097/ACM.0000000000002046

Langford, J., & Clance, P. R. (1993). The imposter phenomenon: Recent research findings regarding dynamics, personality and family patterns and their implications for treatment. *Psychotherapy: Theory, Research, Practice, Training, 30*(3), 495–501. https://doi.org/10.1037/0033-3204.30.3.495

Laux, S. E. (2018). *Experiencing the imposter syndrome in academia: Women faculty members' perception of the tenure and promotion process* [Doctoral dissertation, Saint Louis University]. ProQuest.

LeMoult, J., & Gotlib, I. H. (2019). Depression: A cognitive perspective. *Clinical Psychology Review, 69*, 51–66. https://doi.org/10.1016/j.cpr.2018.06.008

Lester, D. (2013). Irrational thinking in suicidal individuals: A general or a specific deficit? *Suicidologi, 18*(2). https://doi.org/10.5617/suicidologi.2220

Lester, D., & Moderski, T. (1995). The impostor phenomenon in adolescents. *Psychological Reports, 76*(2), 466–466. https://doi.org/10.2466/pr0.1995.76.2.466

Levitt, E. E. (2015). *The psychology of anxiety* (2nd ed.). Routledge. https://doi.org/10.4324/9781315673127

McClain, S., Beasley, S. T., Jones, B., Awosogba, O., Jackson, S., & Cokley, K. (2016). An examination of the impact of racial and ethnic identity, impostor feelings, and minority status stress on the mental health of Black college students. *Journal of Multicultural Counseling and Development, 44*(2), 101–117. https://doi.org/10.1002/jmcd.12040

McGregor, L. N., Gee, D. E., & Posey, K. E. (2008). I feel like a fraud and it depresses me: The relation between the imposter phenomenon and depression. *Social Behavior and Personality, 36*(1), 43–48. https://doi.org/10.2224/sbp.2008.36.1.43

Neureiter, M., & Traut-Mattausch, E. (2016). An inner barrier to career development: Preconditions of the impostor phenomenon and consequences for career development. *Frontiers in Psychology, 7*, Article 48. https://doi.org/10.3389/fpsyg.2016.00048

Oriel, K., Plane, M. B., & Mundt, M. (2004). Family medicine residents and the impostor phenomenon. *Family Medicine, 36*(4), 248–252.

Pákozdy, C., Askew, J., Dyer, J., Gately, P., Martin, L., Mavor, K. I., & Brown, G. R. (2023). The imposter phenomenon and its relationship with self-efficacy, perfectionism and happiness in university students. *Current Psychology*. Advance online publication. https://doi.org/10.1007/s12144-023-04672-4

Pannhausen, S., Klug, K., & Rohrmann, S. (2022). Never good enough: The relation between the impostor phenomenon and multidimensional perfectionism. *Current Psychology, 41*(2), 888–901. https://doi.org/10.1007/s12144-020-00613-7

Pedrelli, P., Nyer, M., Yeung, A., Zulauf, C., & Wilens, T. (2015). College students: Mental health problems and treatment considerations. *Academic Psychiatry, 39*(5), 503–511. https://doi.org/10.1007/s40596-014-0205-9

Peteet, B. J., Brown, C. M., Lige, Q. M., & Lanaway, D. A. (2015). Impostorism is associated with greater psychological distress and lower self-esteem for African American students. *Current Psychology, 34*(1), 154–163. https://doi.org/10.1007/s12144-014-9248-z

Peteet, B. J., Montgomery, L., & Weekes, J. C. (2015). Predictors of imposter phenomenon among talented ethnic minority undergraduate students. *The Journal of Negro Education, 84*(2), 175–186. https://doi.org/10.7709/jnegroeducation.84.2.0175

Rohrmann, S., Bechtoldt, M. N., & Leonhardt, M. (2016). Validation of the impostor phenomenon among managers. *Frontiers in Psychology, 7*, Article 821. https://doi.org/10.3389/fpsyg.2016.00821

Rosenthal, S., Schlussel, Y., Yaden, M., DeSantis, J., Trayes, K., Pohl, C., & Hojat, M. (2021). Persistent impostor phenomenon is associated with distress in medical students. *Family Medicine, 53*(2), 118–122. https://doi.org/10.22454/FamMed.2021.799997

Sakulku, J., & Alexander, J. (2011). The imposter phenomenon. *International Journal of Behavioral Science, 6*(1), 73–92.

Schubert, N. (2013). *The imposter phenomenon: Insecurity cloaked in success* [Doctoral dissertation, Carleton University]. Carleton University Institutional Repository. https://doi.org/10.22215/etd/2013-06249

Schubert, N., & Bowker, A. (2019). Examining the impostor phenomenon in relation to self-esteem level and self-esteem instability. *Current Psychology, 38*(3), 749–755. https://doi.org/10.1007/s12144-017-9650-4

Shanafelt, T. D., Dyrbye, L. N., Sinsky, C., Trockel, M., Makowski, M. S., Tutty, M., Wang, H., Carlasare, L. E., & West, C. P. (2022). Imposter phenomenon in U.S. physicians relative to the U.S. working population. *Mayo Clinic Proceedings, 97*(11), 1981–1993. https://doi.org/10.1016/j.mayocp.2022.06.021

Sonnak, C., & Towell, T. (2001). The impostor phenomenon in British university students: Relationships between self-esteem, mental health, parental rearing style and socioeconomic status. *Personality and Individual Differences, 31*(6), 863–874. https://doi.org/10.1016/S0191-8869(00)00184-7

Stone-Sabali, S., Uanhoro, J. O., McClain, S., Bernard, D., Makari, S., & Chapman-Hilliard, C. (2023). Impostorism and psychological distress among college students of color: A moderation analysis of shame–proneness, race, gender, and race–gender interactions. *Current Psychology*. Advance online publication. https://doi.org/10.1007/s12144-023-04579-0

Storrie, K., Ahern, K., & Tuckett, A. (2010). A systematic review: Students with mental health problems—A growing problem. *International Journal of Nursing Practice, 16*(1), 1–6. https://doi.org/10.1111/j.1440-172X.2009.01813.x

Sverdlik, A., Hall, N. C., & McAlpine, L. (2020). PhD imposter syndrome: Exploring antecedents, consequences, and implications for doctoral well-being. *International Journal of Doctoral Studies, 15*, 737–758. https://doi.org/10.28945/4670

Thomas, M., & Bigatti, S. (2020). Perfectionism, impostor phenomenon, and mental health in medicine: A literature review. *International Journal of Medical Education, 11*, 201–213. https://doi.org/10.5116/ijme.5f54.c8f8

Thompson, T., Davis, H., & Davidson, J. (1998). Attributional and affective responses of impostors to academic success and failure outcomes. *Personality and Individual Differences, 25*(2), 381–396. https://doi.org/10.1016/S0191-8869(98)00065-8

Thompson, T., Foreman, P., & Martin, F. (2000). Impostor fears and perfectionistic concern over mistakes. *Personality and Individual Differences, 29*(4), 629–647. https://doi.org/10.1016/S0191-8869(99)00218-4

Tigranyan, S., Byington, D. R., Liupakorn, D., Hicks, A., Lombardi, S., Mathis, M., & Rodolfa, E. (2021). Factors related to the impostor phenomenon in psychology doctoral students. *Training and Education in Professional Psychology, 15*(4), 298–305. https://doi.org/10.1037/tep0000321

Topping, M. E., & Kimmel, E. B. (1985). The imposter phenomenon: Feeling phony. *Academic Psychology Bulletin, 7*(2), 213–226.

Vergauwe, J., Wille, B., Feys, M., De Fruyt, F., & Anseel, F. (2015). Fear of being exposed: The trait-relatedness of the impostor phenomenon and its relevance in the work context. *Journal of Business and Psychology, 30*(3), 565–581. https://doi.org/10.1007/s10869-014-9382-5

Wang, K. T., Sheveleva, M. S., & Permyakova, T. M. (2019). Imposter syndrome among Russian students: The link between perfectionism and psychological distress. *Personality and Individual Differences, 143*, 1–6. https://doi.org/10.1016/j.paid.2019.02.005

Want, J., & Kleitman, S. (2006). Imposter phenomenon and self-handicapping: Links with parenting styles and self-confidence. *Personality and Individual Differences, 40*(5), 961–971. https://doi.org/10.1016/j.paid.2005.10.005

Wayment, H. A. (2004). It could have been me: Vicarious victims and disaster-focused distress. *Personality and Social Psychology Bulletin, 30*(4), 515–528. https://doi.org/10.1177/0146167203261892

World Health Organization. (2004). *Promoting mental health: Concepts, emerging evidence, practice: Summary report.* https://apps.who.int/iris/handle/10665/42940

Yaffe, Y. (2023). How do impostor feelings and general self-efficacy co-explain students' test-anxiety and academic achievements: The preceding role of maternal psychological control. *Social Psychology of Education, 26*, 925–943. https://doi.org/10.1007/s11218-023-09767-1

Yurica, C. L., & DiTomasso, R. A. (2005). Cognitive distortions. In A. Freeman, S. H. Felgoise, C. M. Nezu, A. M. Nezu, & M. A. Reinecke (Eds.), *Encyclopedia of cognitive behavior therapy* (pp. 117–122). Springer. https://doi.org/10.1007/0-306-48581-8_36

4 IMPOSTOR PHENOMENON AND BURNOUT

LIZETTE OJEDA

High achievers who struggle to internalize their accomplishments despite clear evidence of their competence likely experience a debilitating phenomenon known as the impostor phenomenon (i.e., impostor syndrome, impostorism; Clance & Imes, 1978). Highly talented individuals may feel like intellectual frauds if they doubt that their achievements are a direct result of their intellect. Instead of taking credit for their accomplishments, they attribute their success to external factors, such as luck, or other reasons unrelated to their intellect, like being likable or knowing the right people and receiving favors. They may believe that their success is a natural result of how hard and long they worked for it and that, if they were skilled enough, it should not have taken them as long as it did compared with colleagues. In addition, a person who feels like a fraud may downplay the significance of their achievements and believe that people make too much of a big deal about what they have accomplished. The incongruence between how high achievers see themselves and how others see them intellectually often brings forth uncomfortable impostor feelings. They may fear that at any point, someone will figure out that they are not as capable as they thought they were. Unlike with achievements, failures are often attributed to their own doing and seen as proof that they are not as good as they look on paper (Thompson et al., 1998).

https://doi.org/10.1037/0000397-005
The Impostor Phenomenon: Psychological Research, Theory, and Interventions,
K. Cokley (Editor)
Copyright © 2024 by the American Psychological Association. All rights reserved.

People who experience impostor syndrome often base their sense of self-worth on how successful others perceive them to be (LaDonna et al., 2018). If an individual believes that they gave it their all yet did not succeed, then it must be because they did not have what it took after all. Thus, individuals with impostor feelings may be less likely to make moves that risk failure or being seen as an intellectual phony at the cost of putting themselves up for desired potential opportunities. For example, a person might not pursue a promotion in order to not risk rejection, even if colleagues believe that they are qualified for it. Such risk may be too much to bear if their confidence in their competence may take a hit. This in turn may perpetuate their belief that they are not smart enough or as skilled as people may think. Additionally, they may engage in self-sabotaging behaviors as a means to protect themselves from potential failure. In essence, individuals who overidentify with work tend to believe that their value is determined by accolades and recognition. Therefore, people with impostor syndrome may work excessively hard until they are certain that receiving skills-based scrutiny is unlikely. They may also resist seeking help so that their limiting self-beliefs about their abilities are not confirmed by their colleagues. Such immense self-imposed pressure to ensure success may lead to debilitating stress, which may put one's performance at risk and reinforce impostor feelings.

The chronic fear of making a mistake and therefore being exposed as an intellectual fraud can raise anxiety and stress levels (Cowman & Ferrari, 2002). According to the job demands–resources model (Demerouti et al., 2001), job demands and resources influence worker well-being and performance. They consist of physical, psychological, social, and organizational factors that may help or hinder one's achievements at work, personal sense of accomplishment, and stress levels. Such outcomes may depend on demand frequency (constant demands), quantity (multiple demands), intensity (high-stakes demands), and duration (continuous demands) of a worker's roles and responsibilities. A heavy workload that is paired with the fear of not meeting expectations and a lack of adequate resources to help meet demands can lead to feelings of inadequacy.

The conservation of resources theory (Hobfoll, 1989) sheds light on the importance of accessing and protecting personal resources (e.g., self-efficacy, resilience, coping strategies), social resources (e.g., support system), and organizational resources (e.g., learning and development programs), which are essential to successfully navigate work–life challenges. The model suggests that loss of such resources can result in a ripple effect and downward spiral, which may decrease goal success and increase stress. Workers who feel like a fraud may risk depleting their internal resources, such as self-confidence, and avoid seeking external resources, such as support at work, in an effort to prevent being perceived as incompetent to their own determinant, thus increasing the likelihood of burnout from managing demands with insufficient resources (Whitman & Shanine, 2012).

The impostor phenomenon can be considered a psychological job demand to maintain one's perceived mask of competence, and such impostor feelings may increase work exhaustion (McGarry et al., 2022). The pressure to perform exceptionally well combined with the fear of being found out as a fraud can be depleting, overwhelming, and stressful—all signs of burnout. *Burnout* is a prolonged debilitating psychological syndrome known as the unsuccessful management of chronic and excessive work-related stress (World Health Organization, 2019). It is often mistakenly used interchangeably with stress; however, burnout occurs over an undetermined amount of time as the *result* of unresolved chronic stress high in frequency, intensity, severity, and duration. Impostorism and burnout have some similarities in that they both involve negative self-evaluation and self-doubt. For instance, the impostor phenomenon includes frequent feelings of self-doubt and fear of being exposed as incompetent, whereas burnout can lead to self-critical thoughts, a sense of inadequacy, and a loss of confidence in one's abilities.

The combination of feeling intellectually inadequate and the fear of being unmasked as such can create a reciprocal cycle between impostor syndrome and burnout. That is, when a person feels like an impostor, they may put in more time, effort, and energy to prove their abilities, which may lead to burnout. When a person is burnt out, they are more likely to make mistakes, in turn leading to increased self-doubt. This interplay persists as they work hard to prove themselves and burn themselves out along the way. According to a Gallup report on the causes and cures of burnout, 80% of workers experience burnout at varying levels of severity (Gallup, 2020). Given the prevalence and detrimental effects of burnout, awareness of the main reasons, signs, and consequences, including impostor feelings, is key.

The common first sign of burnout is overwhelming physical and emotional exhaustion from unmanaged chronic stress (Maslach & Leiter, 2016). An attempt to minimize levels of exhaustion often involves detachment from work, decreased drive to do one's best work, and cynicism or negative attitudes at work. Disengagement may worsen if a worker feels ineffective, unproductive, or unaccomplished at work, leading to lost confidence and disappointment in oneself. As a result, they may experience a career crisis, which can include questioning one's career path, job dissatisfaction, and a lost sense of identity. An attempt to escape the main source of stress may result in the decision to lean back, step down, take a leave of absence, quit, or walk away from one's career altogether.

Burnout syndrome and impostor phenomenon often co-occur. A person who believes they are not as competent as they appear may be more likely to use their time, energy, and effort in excess to maintain their reputation as a skilled worker, therefore placing them at risk of burnout, particularly in the form of emotional exhaustion. Impostor feelings may contribute to disengagement at work if a worker does not want to be too visible and risk saying or doing something that reveals their phoniness. Furthermore, impostor syndrome may contribute to professional inefficacy if they are hyperfocused on their deficiencies despite a high level of job performance. Conversely, burnout syndrome can worsen impostor syndrome if a worker is too emotionally depleted to sustain concentration and minimize distractions and interruptions. Decreased mental capacities can diminish a sense of professional accomplishment through lack of confidence in one's ability to perform well at work, which in turn may contribute to impostor feelings. In essence, the burnout-based decreased sense of accomplishment can lead to questioning one's competence (Maslach & Leiter, 2016).

Surprisingly, few empirical studies have been conducted on the reciprocal relationship between impostor syndrome and burnout syndrome. As a result, scientist–practitioners may rely mainly on anecdotal rather than scientific data to inform the creation and application of evidence-based interventions to help prevent and intervene with debilitating impostor feelings and feelings of exhaustion at their intersection. Nonetheless, the limited scientific literature does suggest a statistically significant correlation between the impostor phenomenon and burnout among medical and mental health professionals (Clark et al., 2022; Legassie et al., 2008; Liu et al., 2022), but there remains little empirical knowledge on the interaction between impostorism and burnout among professionals in other industries, such as science, technology, engineering, and mathematics, and workers in general. The following is an overview of the various factors that may affect impostor syndrome and burnout, including individual factors, marginalization, workplace factors, work–life imbalance, work–family conflict, and stress management. In addition, recommendations for research and implications for practice are discussed.

INDIVIDUAL FACTORS

Impostorism can stem from various factors, including perfectionistic tendencies, cultural and societal expectations, family dynamics, early experiences of failure, or belonging to a marginalized group. Additionally, personality traits such as high sensitivity to criticism or a need for external validation can contribute to the development of impostor feelings.

Family Upbringing

High performance expectations during childhood can influence susceptibility to both impostor syndrome (Clance et al., 1995) and presumably burnout if praise was primarily given for academic success. A decreased sense of self-worth can develop if caregivers express disappointment in the child for not getting good enough grades. As a result, self-worth becomes dependent on external validation and overidentification with performance-based praise. If a person was raised by parents who modeled a stronger dedication to work than family and/or if they were rewarded by their parents for their hard work, this generational cycle may persist, influencing continued overwork and overidentification with work for generations to come.

Perfectionism

Research has found that people who have impostor feelings often have perfectionistic tendencies (Pannhausen et al., 2022). The intense fear of being discovered as a fraud may drive an individual to strive for excellence to compensate for their perceived lack of competence. They may exhibit excessive self-criticism, constantly setting unrealistically high standards for themselves, and experience anxiety related to their performance and achievements. Similar to impostor syndrome, perfectionism stems from external factors such as cultural expectations, early experiences, or high expectations from others (Gong et al., 2016). However, unlike impostor syndrome, perfectionism may also originate from a combination of genetic predispositions, personality traits, and a need to maintain control (Gong et al., 2016). Whereas people with impostor feelings are often motivated by the desire to avoid failure and negative evaluation from others, people with perfectionistic tendencies are often motivated by the desire to avoid making mistakes if they perceive their sense of worth is contingent upon meeting their own high standards. The expectation for perfection may increase self-criticism if one focuses on what is wrong or missing that could threaten their success rather than the competencies they have. Perfectionistic tendencies can lead to overworking if individuals find it difficult to disconnect from work and are compelled to work until "it's just right." In addition, if workers do not want to risk coworkers discovering that they are flawed, they may work more, work alone, and not ask for help, particularly in instances of performance evaluation. The irrational belief that being perfect gains approval, combined with impostor feelings as a result of difficulty meeting unrealistic high standards and followed by working excessively to fulfill self-imposed expectations, may in turn bring forth burnout. Striving for perfection hinders timely action, and therefore it is important to objectively determine when it is time to stop perfecting. Working toward developing higher self-esteem can help decrease the negative impact of perfectionism on impostorism (Cokley et al., 2018).

Indecision

Decision making relies on a cost–benefit analysis and whether a person perceives that they have enough information to make the best decision (Bruine de Bruin et al., 2007). Impostor syndrome has been found to decrease confidence in one's decisions (Aparna & Menon, 2022). Some people may be more confident in their decisions because they rely on their internal resources, such as previous experiences, knowledge, and skills. Those who are less confident in their ability to make the best decision may rely on external resources to guide them, such as accumulating more information, expending effort in data gathering, and seeking advice from multiple people to get multiple perspectives that can help them make a more informed decision. The cognitive load of thinking through all the options, pros, cons, and scenarios can increase exhaustion from overthinking decisions. As a result, decision making may be procrastinated in the presence of impostor feelings. Fear-based delays in decision making may worsen a given issue if putting it off exacerbates it or brings forth added challenges.

Workaholism

Workaholism is the compulsive need to work excessively and difficulty disconnecting from work (Griffiths, 2011), especially if it is the main source of one's sense of self-worth (McMillan et al., 2001). Workaholic tendencies consist of overworking, overcommitting, and overidentifying with work. When faced with urgent work matters, workaholism may compel workers to spend their limited time at work rather than with family (Snir & Zohar, 2008). As with impostor syndrome, being raised by highly demanding caregivers who focus more on the one B instead of several As contributes to self-doubt and may minimize the value of the As as proof of success. If caregivers are dissatisfied with their performance and focus on what does not demonstrate competency, they are more likely to work harder as a means to feel worthy. In essence, the need for external validation and recognition often results in a person taking on more work to get more praise.

Core Self-Evaluations

The fundamental bottom line of overall self-evaluation of personal value and worth (self-esteem) may be determined by one's perceived ability to remain calm and manage difficult emotions (e.g., anxiety, anger, depression) when under pressure (emotional stability), the ability to successfully handle hard tasks and stressful demands (self-efficacy), and the ability to exert control across various situations (personal control; Chaturvedi & Chander, 2010; Judge, 2009). Given that low self-esteem is related to impostor feelings (Cokley et al., 2018), even the highest achieving workers may doubt their value is enough despite looking good on paper. Workers with low self-esteem may be more likely to deprioritize themselves. For example, they may be less likely to take breaks and engage in sustainable self-care, which puts them at higher risk for burnout. If a person does not feel good about themselves, they are more likely to feel like an impostor and therefore more likely to work longer and harder than is necessary. People with low self-efficacy are not as confident in their ability to complete a given task. This can discredit their accomplishments and increase their propensity to work extra hard to make up for their perceived incompetence. Individuals experiencing impostor feelings are more likely to have a fear of being found out and a fear of failure. People with high self-esteem may be less likely to overwork themselves because they may recognize that this may come at a cost to their well-being. Naturally, if an individual values one-self, they are more likely to take care of themselves and therefore be less likely to experience burnout.

Character Strengths

The ability to identify, use, and leverage one's personal strengths may help decrease burnout (Allan et al., 2019) and impostor feelings. People with impostor syndrome may be less likely to see the significance of their strengths and therefore minimize them. In contrast, people who are clear on what they are good at may be less likely to feel like a fraud if they focus more on their strengths than weaknesses. Personal strengths may also mitigate burnout symptoms by leaning on what they do well if applied to producing quality work in potentially less time and with less stress. Knowing one's personal strengths may also help reduce "comparison-itis," which is related to impostor feelings when a worker compares themselves with others who they think are more skilled than them. As a result, they are more likely to overwork to reduce the competence gap they perceive between them and coworkers. Therefore, it is recommended that a strengths assessment be taken to identify top personal strengths. Additionally, reflecting on what comes easiest to a worker can help them identify patterns that may speak to the role of their strengths in their work. People with impostor feelings may not realize that their strengths are assets that have helped them have more success and less stress. The ability to do a task without much

MARGINALIZATION

High rates of impostor syndrome among high achievers with marginalized identities are due in part to stereotypes and assumptions about cultural group status, power, belonging, and competence. Such biases can come across as overt "isms," such as sexism, racism, ableism, and classism, as well as microaggressions, which are day-to-day slights, insults, putdowns, invalidations, and offensive behaviors (Sue et al., 2007). This can add the mental load of hypervigilance in which one is on alert about experiencing potential microaggressions and confusion as to whether they experienced an actual microaggression or they are overreacting and being too sensitive.

Marginalized employees may feel like the spokesperson or token representative for their cultural group, especially if they are one of the first, the few, or the only in their position, team, or organization as a whole. As a trailblazer paving the path for others within their cultural group, excessive work may be the result of concern that subpar performance might negatively affect opportunities for coworkers from their cultural group. In addition, they might feel like a spotlight is on them and that coworkers are waiting for them to conform to a negative stereotype that can affect their sense of belonging and professional potential. In essence, marginalized workers who experience ethnic- and race-related stress may have self-doubt in intellectual abilities and work harder to prove themselves, which may increase the risk for burnout.

Stereotype Confirmation Concern

Workers belonging to equity-deserving communities may experience stereotype confirmation concern (Contrada et al., 2001), which is the concern that they are confirming a stereotype about their cultural group, which makes them less likely to express a need for assistance or help with a given challenge so as not to confirm this assumption about their culture. For instance, a Black, Indigenous, or person of color (BIPOC) working mother may hesitate to miss work when her child is sick if she is concerned that she will not be seen as dedicated because of parenting responsibilities. The accumulation of such experiences may lead marginalized workers to internalize stereotypes and seek to prove that they are beyond negative assumptions about their abilities by working harder so as to not slip and confirm shortcomings to others or themselves.

First Generation Success Stress

Individuals who are the first in their family to graduate from college might question if they belong at their job and whether they have what it takes to do well. This may lead to overworking to prove themselves. Marginalized workers may feel responsible to represent their culture favorably so that generalizations are not made about people from their cultural background. Among immigrant families, the value of a strong work ethic is often prominent. Adult children of immigrant parents from collectivistic cultures may perpetuate the hard work mentality and add more pressure to perform because their work represents their family. A person who was raised in a working-class family may tend to have an internal drive to work hard and believe that if they work hard enough, it will result in upward mobility and career advancement. There may be a belief that members of the "upper class don't experience impostor syndrome because they grew up knowing that they belonged in any space they occupied. Anyone outside of that circle is going to experience some level of insecurity" (Crosara, 2022, p. 2).

WORKPLACE FACTORS

Although the number of hours worked can contribute to the risk of burnout, the bigger factor is the amount of mental energy exerted during those hours. Excessively dealing with high-stakes matters at work and difficulty managing crises can deplete mental resources because of the workload involved. Risk for burnout can increase from lack of job–person fit, which can particularly be caused by an incongruence with workload expectations, lack of control, coworker conflict, lack of recognition, and unfairness, as well as a mismatch of core values between the employee and their employer (Maslach & Leiter, 1997).

Job Role-Related Stress

A lack of clear understanding of the complexity of one's job duties can cause role confusion. Confused workers might not ask for clarification on ambiguity in their role so that they do not come across as incapable of doing their job duties without handholding during a learning curve. Role-related stress may increase if there is a skill gap preventing them from performing job duties well compared with colleagues. Given that impostor syndrome involves feeling inadequate at work despite evidence to the contrary, it is possible that the perceived competency deficiency is not because of a lack of sufficient skills but due to the belief that one is not knowledgeable enough. As a result, workers may take on additional trainings and certifications to lessen the perceived skills gap. This can add pressure to perform and increase time commitment to work. Difficulty acclimating to change and transitions may lead to emotional depletion and decrease perceived personal accomplishment as one learns how to perform new duties, particularly if they are not given resources to transition to change.

Micromanagement

A lack of autonomy with how, when, and where one works, despite producing on-time high quality work, can lead to burnout because an employee is not given the flexibility to arrange their schedule in a way that is conducive to work–life balance. Micromanaged workers whose work is scrutinized are more likely to feel incompetent and work under high levels of stress because of performance-based pressure. A lack of autonomy and role-appropriate decision-making power, coupled with feeling criticized or corrected, can mistakenly be interpreted as evidence that one is unable to perform at the expected skill level. One may think that if they were doing a great job, then their boss would not be focused on how expectations are met as long as results are achieved. Striving to do the job right according to one's supervisor adds a dimension of work-related stress that can become difficult to manage. One's role and presence at work may become a source of frustration, pressure, stress, and disillusionment, which may lead to disengagement. This may be reflected in absenteeism (i.e., absent from work) and presenteeism (i.e., present but inattentive), which then contribute to turnover and retention problems.

Psychological Safety

Feeling safe to speak up and not be shut down by others can buffer burnout. When workers are comfortable voicing an opinion despite the risk of being wrong, they are not as held back by potential repercussions. Without psychological safety (Edmondson & Lei, 2014), a person may start to question their competence and believe that if they were good enough, their perspective would be valued. Feeling unsafe psychologically at work and perceiving the work environment to be toxic can be emotionally taxing and contribute to isolation and disengagement. In addition, they might internalize critical or judgmental responses if they perceive that they are among the few who feel silenced or that their thoughts are not important to coworkers. A person with impostor feelings may compare themselves with others who they perceive as more respected, which can lead to working harder until they feel their voice is not only heard but requested and valued. Furthermore, psychological safety and feeling heard may help prevent burnout (Kerrissey et al., 2022).

Effort-Reward Imbalance

Impostor feelings and burnout may be more likely to occur if a person believes they are putting in more effort at work without receiving expected corresponding levels of recognition (Siegrist, 2002). Relatedly, excessive demands and low self-esteem have been found to lead to burnout (Basińska & Wilczek-Rużyczka, 2013). Employees who perceive an equitable balance between efforts and rewards may be more likely to stay committed to their work, even if they are overworking in a demanding, fast-paced environment that requires a high level of effort from them. Lack of sufficient and regular performance feedback beyond statements such as "Keep up the good work" can confuse a worker. On the one hand, they receive minimal constructive feedback and are told they are performing as expected, but on the other hand, their good performance has not resulted in merits. As a result, a worker may work even harder to prove that their impact is valuable and in turn be rewarded with the recognition and respect they seek. Once one realizes that this approach is not working, they are more likely to disengage from their work role and workplace altogether. This can be intensified by perceived unfairness, such as being passed over for promotion for a coworker who they perceive is not as competent or committed as them. When this type of situation happens frequently and/or intensely, a worker may put in less effort than they previously did due to the high cost to self that is not worth the low gain in rewards.

WORK-LIFE IMBALANCE

Employees with multiple roles (e.g., worker–caregiver) and responsibilities (e.g., job and family duties) may be more likely to experience work–life imbalance and burnout from multiple simultaneous demands from separate settings (e.g., workplace and home life). Work–life imbalance may be caused by being stretched too thin by both domains. Work–life balance is often mistakenly thought of as an equal distribution of time between work life and personal life, but it also includes satisfaction with work and life domains and effective navigation between work and life roles based on the importance placed on each, which can change over time (Brough et al., 2014; Greenhaus et al., 2003, 2006).

Stress can be elevated as a result of three types of conflict from being stretched too thin between one's work role and personal life, often resulting in the sacrifice of one over the other. Role conflict can be (a) time-based, resulting from difficulty in allocating sufficient time needed to successfully complete work or family responsibilities; (b) strain-based, caused by having insufficient energy to put into work and family obligations at the cost of one or the other; (c) behavior-based, in which the way one behaves in their work or family role is not conducive for one or the other (Greenhaus & Beutell, 1985). Theoretically but not empirically studied, work–life conflict may be applicable to impostor syndrome. For instance, time-based conflict may occur if the amount of time dedicated to perfecting a project to avoid being revealed as a phony takes time away from one's personal life. Strain-based conflict may increase stress levels if more energy is put into assuring that a project will not be criticized and therefore reveal incompetence, reducing mental presence with family members.

WORK-FAMILY CONFLICT

Work–family conflict is often a result between difficulty meeting demands that conflict with expectations at work and with family. More specifically, *family-to-work conflict* occurs when family matters interfere with work responsibilities, and *work-to-family conflict* occurs when work duties begin to interfere with family life. This may be heightened by anxiety about potentially harming one's position at work or even losing it all together, which may in turn make it difficult to provide financially for one's family. As a result, they may spend overtime at work and/or bring their work home, cutting into family involvement and emotional presence if they are physically occupied with or mentally distracted by work issues during time when they want to be fully present with loved ones.

Given potential anxiety about job security, the decision to dedicate more of oneself at work may be rationalized as ultimately being for the sake of their family's financial stability. Although time away from family in and of itself may cause turmoil, what may matter more is the level of strain and conflict, regardless of how much or little their family time is reduced to. If left unaddressed, this decision can damage relationships and even disintegrate families.

Work-to-Family Conflict

An overwhelming amount of stress due to job duties can cause conflict with home life responsibilities. Work-to-family conflict occurs when work duties spill over into family life. At work, one may be expected to not only fulfill their own role duties but also oversee that team members fulfill their responsibilities. Confidence in one's ability to meet work expectations may become harder to navigate depending on the level of stress they have from multiple responsibilities (e.g., their own, their team's, their family's) and the strain endured from insufficient time, energy, or resources to perform well. Emotional exhaustion often occurs as a result of trying to fulfill several obligations with several people, often simultaneously. It becomes more difficult to keep up the pace at work, and those prone to impostor feelings may begin to worry that others will discover that they are not cut out to handle their responsibilities as once thought. This brings forth anxiety about the perception coworkers and managers have of them, which may taint their reputation as a dedicated hard worker and result in fear of not being promoted, getting demoted, or even being fired. Given these perceived high stakes and overidentification with work, one may begin to invest more of their time, focus, energy, and effort in work than they do in their personal lives. This can cause tension between work–life role expectations.

Family-to-Work Conflict

Family-to-work conflict may arise if a worker worries that family obligations make it difficult to engage, be present, and perform at work beyond the bare minimum and compared with coworkers. It occurs when family matters spill over at work and interfere with one's job commitments and expected level of performance. This is particularly challenging for caregivers in general and even more so for primary- or single-income households, single parents with limited family support to help with child care, and "sandwich generations" in which an employee must simultaneously take care of their children and aging parents. A worker may have to take personal time off, use up sick hours, or lose income altogether if they are unable to attend work or if they have to leave work abruptly due to family issues that cannot wait until after work. As a result of decreased presence and visibility at work, people with impostor syndrome may become concerned about their reputation as a skilled and committed worker.

STRESS MANAGEMENT

Some manageable levels of stress that are not chronic, pervasive, or excessive can help people stay on top of their work and take healthy measures to perform well. However, when a person's stress levels increase beyond their capacity to tolerate and ameliorate, they may be more likely to believe that they are not cut out to do their job and/or work even harder with the hope that doing so will reduce stress and address the stressors faster than if they worked at a slower pace. This constant way of stress-based working behavior may eventually lead to burnout.

Performance Anxiety

Workers are more likely to have performance anxiety if they believe that, if they do not perform their job well, they will be seen as incompetent and work excessively to alleviate the anxiety and added stress that such concern can cause. Relatedly, fear of negative consequences based on performance-related perceptions are likely to occur. For instance, fear of failure is likely if one fears failing at their job and therefore revealing their inadequacy. The belief that one might fail at an important undertaking may contribute to procrastination (Parlade & Karayigit, 2022), not because they do not take work seriously but because they resist facing a task perceived as too difficult to perform successfully, which may increase impostor feelings. Understanding various types of failure feelings is key to help address performance-related fear more intentionally. Such fear includes (a) fear of shame, embarrassment, and judgment; (b) fear of incompetence; (c) fear of an uncertain future; (d) fear of lost positive impact and influence; and (e) fear of disappointing or upsetting important others (Parlade & Karayigit, 2022).

Fear of rejection can occur when individuals feel anxiety about being turned down by colleagues and passed up for promotion by supervisors. If they fear that their ideas will be dismissed or rejected, they are less likely to speak up so as to not risk their reputation as a competent worker and therefore reveal that they are a fraud. Of significance, a study on rejection sensitivity and burnout conducted a 21-month follow-up on symptoms and found that individuals who were more sensitive to rejection compared with those who were not were 119% more likely to burn out (Bianchi et al., 2015).

Fear of success, a less recognized form of fear, is known as the fear that one's continued success will come at a cost to their personal life and relationships. The perceived cost of success may include fear of causing jealousy, fear of being exploited, fear of being excluded or rejected, fear of overwhelming responsibilities, and fear of pressure to perform. Coined as *success syndrome*, fear of success originally attributed to high athletic performers can be applied to high professional achievers in the workplace (Ogilvie, 1968). More specifically, fear of success comprises (a) social and emotional isolation, (b) guilt of self-assertion under competition, (c) fear of discovering one's true potential, (d) fear of surpassing someone admired, and (e) pressure to sustain or surpass one's own previous performance and success (Ogilvie, 1968). High performers who fear further success may believe that they will have to work harder to maintain success, which may take up more of their personal time and create greater work-to-family conflict. Performance anxiety can affect a worker's level of visibility at work if they feel uncomfortable being in the spotlight because now others have their eyes on them and can judge their performance abilities. Unaddressed anxiety about one's work performance may lead to increased impostor feelings and emotional exhaustion. In essence, success phobia may make it difficult for high performers to perform even better if they fear potential negative outcomes as a result of further success (Ogilvie & Tutko, 1966).

Communication Styles

Interpersonal conflict is one of the top stressors that people experience, which is more difficult to control because it also involves other people who they may believe are unreasonable and unworkable. Conflict with colleagues can be influenced by one's communication skills and heightened if one perceives they are not being heard or respected. There are four types of communication styles, of which only one is most effective for performance: (a) aggressive communication expressed through combative, toxic, and punitive means; (b) passive communication based on a worker's silence that can be influenced by people-pleasing tendencies and conflict aversion; (c) passive-aggressive communication, which occurs when a worker communicates in an indirectly aggressive way; and (d) assertive communication, which is a direct, calm, and respectful expression of needs (Sigroha, 2021). A self-assertion style of communication is the most conducive at work.

People with impostor syndrome may be susceptible to a passive communication style if they believe that the other person knows best and they do not want to counterargue and risk being wrong and looking like a fool. As a result, they are more likely to tolerate interpersonal conflict, which may include doing additional work in an attempt to decrease tension.

Coping Strategies

The way a worker copes with work-related stress can help or harm their mental health based on an attempt to solve a problem and manage emotions (Carver et al., 1989; Folkman & Moskowitz, 2004). Coping strategies fall under two overarching types, namely, problem-focused and emotion-focused coping. *Problem-focused coping* is often used when a person sees that the problem is solvable. This may include getting advice and resources, eliminating nonpriorities

96 • Lizette Ojeda

and competing demands, strategic planning, implementing the plan, taking timely rather than premature action, and knowing when to ask for assistance. *Emotion-focused coping* tends to be used when a person believes they will have to endure the problem and thus just deal with it. This can include emotional social support, positive reframing, and making meaning out of the situation. However, maladaptive emotion-focused coping can include venting, withdrawal, denial, avoidance, suppression of one's feelings, and substance use.

Assertiveness and Boundaries

A person may avoid asserting their needs or setting boundaries as a form of self-preservation. In particular, they may be conflict-avoidant and passive because they think that addressing conflict requires confrontation and a hostile approach. However, healthy confrontation includes being able to express how one feels about a given situation that is not working for them and being able to respectfully bring this to others' attention and make requests that meet their particular needs. Individuals with impostorism do not want to risk upsetting someone despite transgressions made toward them. As a result, it becomes difficult to set and assert healthy boundaries. They may believe that saying no and setting expectations for how they should be treated will have negative ramifications, such as a ruined reputation, retaliation, rejection, or even job loss if they are perceived as a difficult person to work with who complains in excess and whose views and values are not a beneficial fit with the company culture. Difficulty saying no may also be a result of not wanting to come across as a worker who cannot "handle the heat" or does not have the competence to complete a given request. The accumulation of continuously taking on tasks and keeping their frustration in instead of voicing it can lead to increased exhaustion, irritability, and resentment. Those with impostor syndrome may be less likely to assert their needs if they doubt themselves, regardless of how much their accomplishments speak for themselves. For example, a person may think, "Who am I to say 'no' to my boss?" if they believe their boss knows best given their status and power differential. They may believe that, if they are being questioned or confronted, they must not be doing a good enough job because a matter was brought to their attention. As a result, they may put in more effort to address constructive feedback or complaints received so they can avoid continued conflict and preserve their confidence in their competence. Burnout may occur if they continue with the facade that they are not bothered by others' unwanted behaviors toward them, particularly if they perceive that they do not have sufficient stake in the ground or are not in a position of power to advocate for themselves and set boundaries, especially with those in authority, such as their supervisor.

It may be difficult to identify and enforce boundaries if individuals have a strong work ethic; are team oriented; and do not want to be seen as slacking, coasting, or uncommitted at work. A desire to belong may make it difficult to enforce boundaries if coworkers and managers do not set boundaries for themselves. For instance, it may be harder for a worker to set a boundary around not working evenings and weekends if they feel pressure to log on after hours because others at work do. This in turn can contribute to work–life imbalance and burnout. People with impostor feelings may make more microcommitments and take on more tasks in an attempt to prove themselves professionally and avoid being perceived as incompetent.

Negative Consequences of Burnout

The path to burnout occurs gradually rather than suddenly. Thus a person with impostor feelings might not realize that they have been on the path to burnout (Riethof & Bob, 2019) until negative consequences occur due to prolonged stress severe enough to damage one's physical and mental health, their personal life and relationships, and their career (Salvagioni et al., 2017). It is often difficult to recognize the damage that the unmanaged excessive accumulation of chronic stress has on a worker's life overall. As a result, it becomes harder and takes longer to recover from burnout. Individuals with impostor feelings who reach the state of high-stakes burnout may experience debilitating physical, psychological, relational, and professional consequences.

Physical Health

The first and most recognized negative impact of burnout is commonly physical consequences. However, it has been suggested that by this point, emotional resources have been depleted and exhaustion has begun to deteriorate physical health (Lheureux et al., 2016). A review of the negative effects of burnout on physical health found consensus on high-risk consequences such as increased risk for coronary heart disease (high cholesterol and blood pressure, obesity, Type II diabetes), migraines, gastrointestinal problems (gastroesophageal reflux disease, irritable bowel syndrome), respiratory infections (cold, flu, sinusitis, bronchitis, pneumonia), and musculoskeletal pain (chronic neck, shoulder, back, and joint pain); increased sensitivity to pain overall; increased frequency, intensity, severity, and duration of sickness; and increased risk of hospitalization (Salvagioni et al., 2017).

Mental Health

Compared with physical health, mental health consequences of burnout are less likely to be recognized sooner if a person interprets their psychological problems as a sign of not having thick skin and being emotionally weak. Furthermore, the stigma attached to mental health disorders may prevent people from acknowledging signs of deteriorating well-being. Common psychological consequences include insomnia, anxiety, and depression (Salvagioni et al., 2017). Workers with limited internal resources (e.g., resilience, resourcefulness) who experience self-doubt may be more likely to suffer from burnout. In contrast, resourceful people are more likely to believe that they have a high level of control over finding a solution to a stressful situation. Resilient people are able to bounce back from adversity and therefore may be more likely to withstand stressors than those who lack this important internal resource. Perseverance, or persistence to work through factors affecting one's success, can be helpful or harmful based on the approach used. For instance, perseverance may help people with impostor syndrome believe that, as long as they do not give up, they will acquire the knowledge they believe they need to succeed. It can also help decrease disengagement if they keep their eyes on the prize. However, persistence may contribute to continued excess work, which can cause or worsen burnout. Perseverance may show up as a need to push through an excessive state of stress, especially if a worker believes that not doing so may expose them as intellectually incompetent. A person may not realize the negative impact overwork has on other aspects of their life until issues become too debilitating to ignore.

Personal Relationships

When a person is unable to function at their best physically and/or mentally, their personal life and relationships are likely to suffer. Depending on the level of severity, physical ailments may make it difficult for individuals to be fully physically present in active social activities. Feeling like an impostor may contribute to lack of presence in one's personal life if much time and energy is spent on learning and perfecting work to assure that their impostor mask does not get revealed. This is important because stress levels can be lowered through the combination of stress-reducing hormones released during physical activities and the social support and connection that may protect against isolation. Individuals who have reached a state of exhaustion and disengagement may lack motivation to engage with others outside of work as a source of fulfillment that they might not find elsewhere if there are no other outlets available for them to turn to.

Career

Burnout may lead to job dissatisfaction; absence from work; and an inability to do one's job, do it well, and do more challenging work successfully (Salvagioni et al., 2017). Burnt out workers may be more likely to commit mistakes that might not have occurred had their energy not been depleted. High-achieving burnt out employees who make micromistakes or a critical mistake could diminish their sense of self because their current level of performance is not aligned with their past accomplishments. Impostor feelings may threaten one's professional efficacy and add pressure to perform, which can in turn result in working harder and longer. However, this may not be the case once a worker reaches the state of burnout. Due to burnout-based cynicism, they may ask themselves, "What's the point?" Even hard workers with a strong work ethic may start to care less about their performance because they do not see the payoff in their efforts and the reinforcement of hard work-based recognition has decreased and therefore no longer serves as a motivator to remain committed to their work.

If other important areas of one's life have been negatively impacted by the interaction between impostor syndrome and burnout, such as overall health (i.e., physical and mental) and personal relationships, one may start to question if their career is even worth the continued hard work at the expense of their nonwork life. As a result of persistent feelings of incompetence, those with impostor syndrome may feel less satisfaction with their job as a form of learned helplessness. Feeling like an impostor with constant self-imposed pressure to perform may lead to chronic stress, affecting not just the person but also those around them.

Job dissatisfaction may occur as a result of disillusionment at work, despite previous eagerness to make an impact at work and the fulfillment and meaning they found through their career. A worker whose identity had been largely based on their career is likely to question who they are besides their career and therefore set them on a path to reconnect with and reprioritize themselves. If a worker does not realize that the decreased work ethic and commitment to their career may be due to impostor syndrome and burnout rather than themselves directly, they are more likely to feel guilt for receiving income when they feel checked out at work. One may also feel grief about losing the passion they once had in their career. As a result, one is at greater risk of leaning back, stepping down, or even quitting their job.

INDIVIDUAL RECOMMENDATIONS FOR BURNOUT PREVENTION

Individuals who prioritize their needs may be less likely to burn out because they attempt to prevent stress levels from getting severe enough to negatively impact them. This may be difficult if a person has the belief that doing so would be self-centered and not reflective of a team player. Unfortunately, it is not until a person reaches near rock bottom that they realize they have to prioritize themselves because stress is negatively affecting important areas of their life. Self-advocacy and self-care are two overarching skills that may help prevent burnout.

Self-Advocacy

People who suffer in silence are more likely to struggle with impostor feelings and push through problems. Therefore, advocating for oneself is paramount. Self-advocacy can include identifying needs, communicating concerns, and asserting oneself in unfavorable situations so that their needs are made known and addressed.

Assertive Communication

Learning assertive communication skills can help increase one's confidence in their effective ability to voice their needs to others at work or in their personal life. For instance, one can communicate using "I" instead of "you" statements to help decrease defensiveness and avoid contributing to conflict with another person. For example, instead of saying, "You did not do your part of the project on time, and now it has piled up on me, and you made me fall behind," one can say, "I want to make sure we complete the project successfully, and I need your part of the work soon so I can make sure I do my part well and in a timely manner. Can you submit it today?"

Boundaries

One suggestion to minimize overcommitment tendencies is to recognize that when one says yes to something, this is an automatic no to something else (e.g., sleep, family time, hobbies) because there is no "25th hour" in the day. Making a list of values that a person does not want to be violated and behaviors that cross their boundaries can help create more clearly delineated instances in which they will turn down a request. For example, a nonnegotiable may be work-free weekends.

A situation-dependent boundary is based on a number of considered factors such as who is the requester and the level of importance, magnitude, and time commitment of the request that is determined on a case-by-case basis. A flexible boundary aims to maintain one's personal preference for how to handle various requests that cross a boundary but allows for making intentional exceptions when the costs outweigh the benefits of boundary enforcement. For instance, a person may prefer to regularly block off their lunch hour but be flexible on an as-needed basis. For example, a meeting might need to be scheduled that requires their presence, and the lunch hour is the only time everyone else is available. It is important to be aware if accommodating others at the expense of one's boundary violation is due to true flexibility or a result of people-pleasing and peer pressure. Enforcing boundary levels consistently may reduce excessive requests at work that are above and beyond their responsibility. However, occasional exceptions may result in intermittent reinforcement that inadvertently causes an unwanted behavior to continue. This is because one has conditioned others that, every once in a while, they will meet their request, and therefore others should approach them with requests because they know they will eventually say yes.

Self-Care

Self-care includes honoring one's values so that one's sense of worth is not primarily based on their career success. When personal values are violated or have been pushed to the back burner, it becomes harder to identify when the potential value of hard work ethic takes precedence over other values, such as personal growth, health, and family unity.

Personal Time Off

Taking time off work may be difficult if one perceives it will have negative ramifications, such as falling behind at work. A person who feels like a fraud may have difficulty taking time off for family, let alone themselves, if they believe that doing so would set them behind in their skills or that colleagues may think they are undedicated. Repeated and prolonged instances in which time off is not taken can lead to the disintegration of one's body, mind, or personal life. At this point, a person may believe that they have no choice but to take time off. The risk of reaching this point can be minimized if precautionary measures are taken to engage in rest and recuperation from stress. Time off should be taken as a method of prevention rather than intervention. By the time the damage of excessive chronic stress has been done, it will be harder and take longer to recover from burnout.

Workers might not recognize that colleagues see them as stressed out until their boss requests that they take time off because it is affecting work quality. This may result in anxiety if one believes they have been found out and are now viewed as someone who cannot keep up at work and therefore is less competent. It is important to note that taking time off and returning to the same situation that caused excessive stress in the first place will not prevent burnout. Thus, sustainable changes must be made after rest or burnout recovery. Realigning with one's values, enforcing boundaries, and scheduling in nonnegotiable self-care activities can help stop the stress cycle that inevitably leads to burnout, decreased performance, and prolonged impostor feelings.

Sleep

Sleep self-sabotage, also known as revenge bedtime procrastination, may occur when a worker postpones sleep despite needing and wanting more sleep. The 3Ss (i.e., scroll, snack, sip) are signs of purposely pushing back sleep time because daily pressures and responsibilities result in stress being too overwhelming and exhausting. As a result, one seeks downtime and engagement in low pressure, passive, and mindless activities. The "scroll" tendency occurs when a person chooses to spend time scrolling through social media or television at the expense of sleep time. "Snack" or "sip" tendencies occur when a person uses comfort food and alcohol, respectively, as a way to cope with stress. Engaging in these types of behaviors can cause guilt if a person criticizes themselves for wasting time doing unproductive activities instead of catching up on sleep or even work. Once any of the 3Ss becomes a habit, it can lead to a slippery slope of increased sleep deprivation and disengagement from loved ones because one would rather engage in passive activities and have time for themselves after a day of what seems like endless requests at work and home. Adequate restful sleep cannot be overstated. Lack of sufficient quality sleep may negatively affect one's mood and ability to tolerate a certain level of stress that would not be likely without adequate sleep. Furthermore, social support may decrease because of isolation that often comes with engaging in any of these stress-numbing behaviors during "me time." An unhealthy relationship with food and alcohol increases risk of developing addictions that can lead to obesity and alcoholism, which then worsen stressful problems, strip resources to better manage high demands, decrease job performance and relationship quality, and deteriorate physical (e.g., headaches, fatigue) and mental health (e.g., insomnia, mood disorders).

Given the potential risks that result from using escape methods to decompress from a stressful day, it is recommended that workers evaluate their sleep hygiene by tracking the quantity and quality of their sleep. A sleep tracker can determine not only hours spent in bed but also how many of those hours were restful. Bedtime routines that help decrease sleep deprivation include no screen time at least 1 hour before the identified best bedtime because the blue light that emits from screens (e.g., phone, tablet, television) can affect sleep quality. In addition, one should avoid food consumption 3 hours before sleep, especially heavy, greasy, and acidic foods, which can affect the digestive system and in turn disrupt sleep quality. Alcohol is mistakenly seen as a sedative, and although alcohol consumed 4 hours before bedtime might help one fall asleep more easily and quickly, sleep quality suffers, particularly rapid-eye-movement sleep (Yules et al., 1967). In essence, insufficient regular high-quality sleep can hinder performance, which may contribute to impostor feelings and spending more time at work because a worker is unable to perform at their best due to sleep deprivation, rather than their competence or time management.

ORGANIZATIONAL RECOMMENDATIONS FOR BURNOUT PREVENTION

Impostor syndrome has been found to increase work–family conflict when a person feels emotionally exhausted (Crawford et al., 2016). Furthermore, employees who do not perceive support from their organization are more likely to experience emotional exhaustion that contributes to work–family conflict. Therefore, it is essential that organizations support their employees so they can reduce conflict between work and family roles by helping them decrease feelings of impostorism and emotional depletion.

Person-Centered Resources

Organizations that provide multiple types of support and resources may be more likely to maintain their job performance and job satisfaction, as well as prevent burnout. Resources play a critical role in preventing burnout when workers can access, keep, and use a given resource. One of the most helpful types of resources to help decrease impostor feelings is social support (Barr-Walker et al., 2020). This can include creating an inclusive environment that promotes a sense of belonging, which is particularly important for talent with marginalized identities. Social support can also include team-building activities that may help decrease isolation and increase engagement. A powerful source of support includes mentorship programs within and outside the organization. Upon hiring, part of the onboarding process can include a buddy system in which the new hire is paired with a peer who can help them become acclimated during the transition into a new role within a new work environment. A mentor within the organization can help a worker navigate the ropes at work and help guide them at work. This requires a trusting relationship in which evaluation will not be part of the mentoring process. Otherwise, people with impostor feelings may not be as open about their challenges because they do not want to come across as incompetent to their mentor. Given the challenges that can come with an internal mentor, providing opportunities for external mentorship is key. A mentor who is detached from the organization and can provide objective feedback and expert guidance can help a worker be more open and honest because what they share does not carry high stakes for their employment.

Access to tangible and intangible resources can help set workers up for success and protect against burnout. For example, nap rooms at work can help employees recharge to boost productivity. In addition, offering flexibility and autonomy to workers is one of the most important workplace factors that can help prevent burnout. This is because the focus is on successful and timely job completion rather than micromanaging when, where, and how a job gets done. People will also be more committed to their organization if there are policies that help maintain work–life balance. For instance, a 4-day work week can reduce stress levels and increase workplace happiness. Furthermore, flexibility with when and where a worker works can help parents be able to take time off during the day for doctor appointments and school activities. This can help workers maintain good health and be more present for their child(ren). For employees, the time taken off to attend to their personal life can be traded for working a few extra hours to make up the time. The ability to work from home as needed can also help with work–life integration.

Learning and Development

Learning and development programs can be a resource for workers who need to develop skills to help prevent or recover from burnout, as well as impostor feelings that hold high-potential talent back from stepping into and thriving in leadership. For example, communication skills training can help reduce workplace conflict due to miscommunication that can be stressful or trigger impostor feelings if one fears that what they want to convey may not be made competently or taken seriously. Access to executive coaching can help leaders learn ways to navigate their role from an objective perspective, serve as a sounding board, and provide tools to prevent burnout. Excessive unmanageable stress not only affects the leader but also can trickle down to those they manage and/ or decrease their management abilities because their resources are depleted.

Workplace Culture

Unspoken rules and expectations should be identified and addressed because they may increase performance anxiety if left unclear, perpetuating impostor feelings and increasing risk for burnout. For instance, a manager who sends emails on evenings, weekends, and vacations indirectly sends the message that work comes before personal life. Even if a manager has vocalized that employees should not work after hours, if their behavior shows otherwise, this stated policy will be ineffective because a worker does not want to stand out and go against the grain. Doing so may put the spotlight on them, increasing performance anxiety and impostor feelings due to fear that their perceived incompetence will be revealed. Many organizations offer unlimited paid time off, but this can backfire if employees postpone taking time off until they finish a near-perfect project as a way to ease impostor feelings. As with working after hours, if the workplace has an unspoken culture of not taking paid time off, people may be less likely to take time off when needed and more likely to burn out.

Indeed, it can be difficult to avoid impostor feelings and burnout when there is a lack of perceived control over stressors as a result of too many demands and not enough resources. Access to relevant evidence-based tools may help weaken the discrepancy between a high achiever who doubts their intellect and colleagues who see them as competent. The combined stress of worrying that one's intellectual phoniness will be revealed and feeling chronically overwhelmed by never-ending responsibilities is a recipe for debilitating impostor syndrome and burnout. Signs of impostor syndrome may include intellectual self-doubt, indecision, procrastination, fear of failure, self-sabotage, and lack of self-advocacy (Holmes et al., 1993). For burnout, signs may include overall fatigue, energy depletion, emotional exhaustion, frustration, cynicism, resentment, lack of motivation, decreased job performance, and increased disengagement from work (Goodman et al., 2018; Maslach & Leiter, 2016). In essence, being on high alert about colleagues finding out that one is not yet ready to successfully take on a major project puts excessive strain on one's mental resources, which makes it harder to handle hard situations well in general. For workers, impostor syndrome and burnout syndrome can cost a highly successful professional their body, mind, relationships, and career. For organizations, impostor syndrome and burnout can cause retention, advancement, and engagement problems once an employee becomes worn out, mentally checked out, and full of performance self-doubt.

CONCLUSION

The relationship between impostor phenomenon and burnout reveals a complex interplay between psychological patterns and chronic work-related stress. Impostorism, characterized by self-doubt and fear of being exposed as a fraud despite evidence of competence, can contribute to the development and progression of burnout, which in turn can exacerbate impostor feelings. As individuals strive for success, their ambition and drive can lead to work overload, neglecting self-care, and a loss of control over their tasks. Emotional exhaustion, cynicism, and detachment follow, and impostor feelings and fear of failure intensify. This vicious cycle erodes self-confidence, promotes disengagement, and perpetuates chronic exhaustion. Recognizing and addressing the combined impact of the impostor phenomenon and burnout is crucial for promoting well-being and fostering healthier work environments, as well as helping workers do their best work as their most confident and mentally well selves. Through targeted interventions, support, and self-care practices, workers can break free from the burnout–impostor syndrome cycle and cultivate a healthier relationship with themselves and their work.

REFERENCES

Allan, B. A., Owens, R. L., & Douglass, R. P. (2019). Character strengths in counselors: Relations with meaningful work and burnout. *Journal of Career Assessment, 27*(1), 151–166. https://doi.org/10.1177/1069072717748666

Aparna, K. H., & Menon, P. (2022). Impostor syndrome: An integrative framework of its antecedents, consequences and moderating factors on sustainable leader behaviors. *European Journal of Training and Development, 46*(9), 847–860. https://doi.org/10.1108/EJTD-07-2019-0138

Barr-Walker, J., Werner, D. A., Kellermeyer, L., & Bass, M. B. (2020). Coping with impostor feelings: Evidence based recommendations from a mixed methods study. *Evidence Based Library and Information Practice, 15*(2), 24–41. https://doi.org/10.18438/eblip29706

Basińska, B. A., & Wilczek-Rużyczka, E. (2013). The role of rewards and demands in burnout among surgical nurses. *International Journal of Occupational Medicine and Environmental Health, 26*(4), 593–604. https://doi.org/10.2478/s13382-013-0129-8

Bianchi, R., Schonfeld, I. S., & Laurent, E. (2015). Interpersonal rejection sensitivity predicts burnout: A prospective study. *Personality and Individual Differences, 75*, 216–219. https://doi.org/10.1016/j.paid.2014.11.043

Brough, P., Timms, C., O'Driscoll, M. P., Kalliath, T., Siu, O.-L., Sit, C., & Lo, D. (2014). Work–life balance: A longitudinal evaluation of a new measure across Australia and New Zealand workers. *The International Journal of Human Resource Management, 25*(19), 2724–2744. https://doi.org/10.1080/09585192.2014.899262

Bruine de Bruin, W., Parker, A. M., & Fischhoff, B. (2007). Individual differences in adult decision-making competence. *Journal of Personality and Social Psychology, 92*(5), 938–956. https://doi.org/10.1037/0022-3514.92.5.938

Carver, C. S., Scheier, M. F., & Weintraub, J. K. (1989). Assessing coping strategies: A theoretically based approach. *Journal of Personality and Social Psychology, 56*(2), 267–283. https://doi.org/10.1037/0022-3514.56.2.267

Chaturvedi, M., & Chander, R. (2010). Development of emotional stability scale. *Industrial Psychiatry Journal, 19*(1), 37–40. https://doi.org/10.4103/0972-6748.77634

Clance, P. R., Dingman, D., Reviere, S. L., & Stober, D. R. (1995). Impostor phenomenon in an interpersonal/social context: Origins and treatment. *Women & Therapy, 16*(4), 79–96. https://doi.org/10.1300/J015v16n04_07

Clance, P. R., & Imes, S. A. (1978). The imposter phenomenon in high achieving women: Dynamics and therapeutic intervention. *Psychotherapy: Theory, Research, & Practice, 15*(3), 241–247. https://doi.org/10.1037/h0086006

Clark, P., Holden, C., Russell, M., & Down, H. (2022). The impostor phenomenon in mental health professionals: Relationships among compassion fatigue, burnout, and compassion satisfaction. *Contemporary Family Therapy, 44*, 185–197. https://doi.org/10.1007/s10591-021-09580-y

Cokley, K., Stone, S., Krueger, N., Bailey, M., Garba, R., & Hurst, A. (2018). Self-esteem as a mediator of the link between perfectionism and the impostor phenomenon. *Personality and Individual Differences, 135*, 292–297. https://doi.org/10.1016/j.paid.2018.07.032

Contrada, R. J., Ashmore, R. D., Gary, M. L., Coups, E., Egeth, J. D., Sewell, A., Goyal, T. M., & Chasse, V. (2001). Measures of ethnicity-related stress: Psychometric properties, ethnic group differences, and associations with well-being. *Journal of Applied Social Psychology, 31*(9), 1775–1820. https://doi.org/10.1111/j.1559-1816.2001.tb00205.x

Cowman, S., & Ferrari, J. (2002). Am I for real? Predicting impostor tendencies from self-handicapping and affective components. *Social Behavior and Personality, 30*(2), 119–125. https://doi.org/10.2224/sbp.2002.30.2.119

Crawford, W. S., Shanine, K. K., Whitman, M. V., & Kacmar, K. M. (2016). Examining the impostor phenomenon and work–family conflict. *Journal of Managerial Psychology, 31*(2), 375–390. https://doi.org/10.1108/JMP-12-2013-0409

Crosara, N. (2022, June). Working class pride. *Diva*, 56–57.

Demerouti, E., Bakker, A. B., Nachreiner, F., & Schaufeli, W. B. (2001). The job demands–resources model of burnout. *Journal of Applied Psychology, 86*, 499–512. https://doi.org/10.1037/0021-9010.86.3.499

Edmondson, A. C., & Lei, Z. (2014). Psychological safety: The history, renaissance, and future of an interpersonal construct. *Annual Review of Organizational Psychology and Organizational Behavior, 1*, 23–43. https://doi.org/10.1146/annurev-orgpsych-031413-091305

Folkman, S., & Moskowitz, J. T. (2004). Coping: Pitfalls and promise. *Annual Review of Psychology, 55*, 745–774. https://doi.org/10.1146/annurev.psych.55.090902.141456

Gallup. (2020). *Employee burnout: Causes and cures.* https://www.gallup.com/workplace/282659/employee-burnout-perspective-paper.aspx

Gong, X., Paulson, S. E., & Wang, C. (2016). Exploring family origins of perfectionism: The impact of interparental conflict and parenting behaviors. *Personality and Individual Differences, 100*, 43–48. https://doi.org/10.1016/j.paid.2016.02.010

Goodman, A., Suhail, F. K., Ganesan, D., Bernshteyn, M., Cortese, A., Coronado, C, & Knohl, S. J. (2022). Twelve steps for starting a support group for women resident physicians. *Physician Leadership Journal, 9*(1), 37–42. https://doi.org/10.55834/plj.8798561243

Greenhaus, J. H., Allen, T. D., & Spector, P. E. (2006). Health consequences of work–family conflict: The dark side of the work–family interface. In P. L. Perrewé & D. C. Ganster (Eds.), *Employee health, coping and methodologies* (pp. 61–98). Elsevier Science/JAI Press. https://doi.org/10.1016/S1479-3555(05)05002-X

Greenhaus, J. H., & Beutell, N. J. (1985). Sources of conflict between work and family roles. *Academy of Management Review, 10*(1), 76–88. https://doi.org/10.2307/258214

Greenhaus, J. H., Collins, K. M., & Shaw, J. D. (2003). The relation between work–family balance and quality of life. *Journal of Vocational Behavior, 63*(3), 510–531. https://doi.org/10.1016/S0001-8791(02)00042-8

Griffiths, M. D. (2011). Workaholism: A 21st-century addiction. *The Psychologist, 24*(10), 740–744.

Hobfoll, S. E. (1989). Conservation of resources: A new attempt at conceptualizing stress. *American Psychologist, 44*(3), 513–524. https://doi.org/10.1037/0003-066X.44.3.513

Holmes, S. W., Kertay, L., Adamson, L. B., Holland, C. L., & Clance, P. R. (1993). Measuring the impostor phenomenon: A comparison of Clance's IP Scale and Harvey's I-P Scale. *Journal of Personality Assessment, 60*(1), 48–59. https://doi.org/10.1207/s15327752jpa6001_3

Judge, T. A. (2009). Core self-evaluations and work success. *Current Directions in Psychological Science, 18*(1), 58–62. https://doi.org/10.1111/j.1467-8721.2009.01606.x

Kerrissey, M. J., Hayirli, T. C., Bhanja, A., Stark, N., Hardy, J., & Peabody, C. R. (2022). How psychological safety and feeling heard relate to burnout and adaptation amid uncertainty. *Health Care Management Review, 47*(4), 308–316. https://doi.org/10.1097/HMR.0000000000000338

LaDonna, K. A., Ginsburg, S., & Watling, C. (2018). "Rising to the level of your incompetence": What physicians' self-assessment of their performance reveals about the imposter syndrome in medicine. *Academic Medicine, 93*(5), 763–768. https://doi.org/10.1097/ACM.0000000000002046

Legassie, J., Zibrowski, E. M., & Goldszmidt, M. A. (2008). Measuring resident well-being: Impostorism and burnout syndrome in residency. *Journal of General Internal Medicine, 23*, 1090–1094. https://doi.org/10.1007/s11606-008-0536-x

Lheureux, F., Truchot, D., & Borteyrou, X. (2016). Suicidal tendency, physical health problems and addictive behaviours among general practitioners: Their relationship with burnout. *Work & Stress, 30*(2), 173–192. https://doi.org/10.1080/02678373.2016.1171806

Liu, R. Q., Davidson, J., Van Hooren, T. A., Van Koughnett, J. A. M., Jones, S., & Ott, M. C. (2022). Impostorism and anxiety contribute to burnout among resident physicians. *Medical Teacher, 44*(7), 758–764. https://doi.org/10.1080/0142159X.2022.2028751

Maslach, C., & Leiter, M. P. (2016). Understanding the burnout experience: Recent research and its implications for psychiatry. *World Psychiatry, 15*(2), 103–111. https://doi.org/10.1002/wps.20311

Maslach, C., & Leiter, M. P. (1997). *The truth about burnout.* Jossey Bass.

McGarry, T., Stevens, M., & Eme-Power, J. (2022). The clandestine cost of feeling like a fake: Imposter phenomenon and workplace presenteeism. *Academy of Management Annual Meeting Proceedings, 2022*(1), Article 2442.

McMillan, L. H., O'Driscoll, M. P., Marsh, N. V., & Brady, E. C. (2001). Understanding workaholism: Data synthesis, theoretical critique, and future design strategies.

International Journal of Stress Management, 8(2), 69–91. https://doi.org/10.1023/A:1009573129142

Ogilvie, B. C. (1968). The unconscious fear of success. *Quest, 10*(1), 35–39. https://doi.org/10.1080/00336297.1968.10519643

Ogilvie, B. C., & Tutko, T. A. (1966). *Problem athletes and how to handle them.* Pelham Books.

Pannhausen, S., Klug, K., & Rohrmann, S. (2022). Never good enough: The relation between the impostor phenomenon and multidimensional perfectionism. *Current Psychology, 41*(2), 888–901. https://doi.org/10.1007/s12144-020-00613-7

Parlade, J., & Karayigit, C. (2022). Examining procrastination and fear of failure among college students. *Cognition, Brain, Behavior, 26*(4), 199–213. https://doi.org/10.24193/cbb.2022.26.11

Riethof, N., & Bob, P. (2019). Burnout syndrome and logotherapy: Logotherapy as useful conceptual framework for explanation and prevention of burnout. *Frontiers in Psychiatry, 10*, Article 382. https://doi.org/10.3389/fpsyt.2019.00382

Salvagioni, D. A. J., Melanda, F. N., Mesas, A. E., González, A. D., Gabani, F. L., & Andrade, S. (2017). Physical, psychological and occupational consequences of job burnout: A systematic review of prospective studies. *PLOS ONE, 12*(10), Article e0185781. https://doi.org/10.1371/journal.pone.0185781

Siegrist, J. (2002). Effort-reward imbalance at work and health. In P. L. Perrewé & D. C. Ganster (Eds.), *Historical and current perspectives on stress and health* (pp. 261–291). JAI Elsevier. https://doi.org/10.1016/S1479-3555(02)02007-3

Sigroha, A. G. (2021). The impact of styles of communication on employees' performance in hospitals of national capital region of India. *Turkish Online Journal of Qualitative Inquiry, 12*(3), 5103–5109.

Snir, R., & Zohar, D. (2008). Workaholism as discretionary time investment at work: An experience-sampling study. *Applied Psychology, 57*(1), 109–127. https://doi.org/10.1111/j.1464-0597.2006.00270.x

Sue, D. W., Capodilupo, C. M., Torino, G. C., Bucceri, J. M., Holder, A. M. B., Nadal, K. L., & Esquilin, M. (2007). Racial microaggressions in everyday life: Implications for clinical practice. *American Psychologist, 62*(4), 271–286. https://doi.org/10.1037/0003-066X.62.4.271

Thompson, T., Davis, H., & Davidson, J. (1998). Attributional and affective responses of impostors to academic success and failure outcomes. *Personality and Individual Differences, 25*(2), 381–396. https://doi.org/10.1016/S0191-8869(98)00065-8

Whitman, M. V., & Shanine, K. K. (2012). Revisiting the impostor phenomenon: How individuals cope with feelings of being in over their heads. In P. L. Perrewé, J. R. B. Halbesleben, & C. C. Rosen (Eds.), *The role of the economic crisis on occupational stress and well being* (Vol. 10, pp. 177–212). https://doi.org/10.1108/S1479-3555(2012)0000010009

World Health Organization. (2019). *Burn-out an "occupational phenomenon": International Classification of Diseases* [Departmental news]. https://www.who.int/news/item/28-05-2019-burn-out-an-occupational-phenomenon-international-classification-of-diseases

Yules, R. B., Lippman, M. E., & Freedman, D. X. (1967). Alcohol administration prior to sleep: The effect on EEG sleep stages. *Archives of General Psychiatry, 16*(1), 94–97. https://doi.org/10.1001/archpsyc.1967.01730190096012

5

THE IMPOSTOR PHENOMENON'S RELATION TO ACHIEVEMENT AT SCHOOL AND WORK

LAUREN A. BLONDEAU

The impostor phenomenon (IP) is a self-belief of intellectual phoniness. Impostors believe that their successes are due to temporary means such as luck or charm rather than their own ability. Early researchers of the construct theorized that impostorism would inhibit success for its sufferers. Yet, in the intervening 4 decades, only a handful of studies have directly investigated the relation between IP and achievement. The present chapter reviews these findings in school, work, and laboratory settings. Results indicate that impostorism relates not only to an increase in grade-point average (GPA) for women and female students but also to a reluctance to join advanced courses. Findings at work reveal that IP associates primarily with negative outcomes, especially in certain environments. Interestingly, impostors and nonimpostors do not differ in their achievements in experimental settings. The second part of the chapter proposes the mediating role of mental health, personality, self-efficacy, and self-regulation on the impostorism–achievement association. Prior studies have shown that each of these theorized mediators has a strong relation with both IP and success separately. Overall, the existing literature has found some associations between impostorism and achievement; the present chapter proposes that that relation may be more nuanced.

https://doi.org/10.1037/0000397-006
The Impostor Phenomenon: Psychological Research, Theory, and Interventions,
K. Cokley (Editor)
Copyright © 2024 by the American Psychological Association. All rights reserved.

THE IMPOSTOR PHENOMENON'S RELATION TO ACHIEVEMENT AT SCHOOL AND WORK

In her groundbreaking work, Pauline Clance identified several accomplished women who felt undeserving of their current successes and positions (Clance & Imes, 1978). Despite their high abilities, the individuals felt their achievements were due to temporary means such as luck or charm. Clance termed this experience the "impostor phenomenon" and described it as "the internal experience of intellectual phoniness" (Clance & Imes, 1978, p. 1). Impostors feared any mistake would reveal them to be undeserving of their current achievements, a fear that resulted in mental health issues such as anxiety or depression (Clance, 1985; Clance & Imes, 1978). In order to avoid these negative emotions, the impostors engaged in behaviors such as procrastination or maladaptive perfectionism when faced with a new undertaking. If individuals had procrastinated, they could explain their poor performance as a result of insufficient time-on-task, rather than due to a lack of ability. Conversely, some impostors dealt with their discomfort and fear by working exceptionally hard to ensure that their product was perfect. Clance (Clance & O'Toole, 1987) posited that these self-protective behaviors, along with the associated negative affect, would result in reduced achievement in individuals suffering from IP. Indeed, she stated that impostors could be identified by their low accomplishments, despite their high capabilities (Clance & O'Toole, 1987).

In the intervening years, researchers have investigated correlates of IP, yet few have actually investigated its association with objective achievement. In the present chapter, we consider measurable rewards for reaching a goal at school or work, such as high grades or promotions. The handful of studies that have researched the association between impostorism and achievement have found mixed results. We review the scant literature relating these variables in school, work, and experimental settings. Next, we review important constructs related to both IP and achievement separately. We argue that these variables may act as mediators, as they strongly suggest an association between impostorism and achievement. Overall, more research into IP must be done to understand its effect on achievement.

CURRENT RESEARCH ON IMPOSTORISM AND ACHIEVEMENT

Although many researchers have posited a relation between IP and achievement, research linking the two constructs is scarce. A few studies have investigated measurable outcomes in an academic or work setting, whereas others have given participants experimental tasks to complete. In high school and college, some limited studies indicate that impostorism affects achievement for women or female students but not for men or male students. Interestingly, IP may have beneficial and/or deleterious effects for this population. The findings from a work setting differ, however. There, IP negatively relates to different achievements such as promotions, positive appraisals, and scholarly productivity. Finally, when participants were given achievement tasks to complete in a laboratory setting, impostors and nonimpostors did not differ in their accuracy or time-on-task. Based on these limited studies, impostorism seems to be most salient in an academic environment for women and girls or a work environment for everyone. More information about the findings is given next.

Academic Environments

A few studies have investigated the relation between IP and achievement in academic settings. In a recent study, Shreffler and colleagues (2021) analyzed scores on a comprehensive licensing exam given to students after completing their 2nd year of medical school. The researchers found no difference in exam scores across levels of impostorism. Participants experiencing few, moderate, frequent, or intense feelings of IP did not significantly differ in their achievement on the medical test. This nonsignificant finding may be due to the limited variety of scores on the exam. In an elite population such as medical school students, the majority are high-achieving and fared well on the exam. As most participants earned close to the same score, researchers could not find differences among the four impostor group levels. Importantly, the authors chose not to include sex or gender in their analysis, variables that may have moderated their results.

Other studies have looked at the relation between IP and GPA in high school or undergraduate courses. Impostorism did not relate to GPA for Canadian undergraduates (September et al., 2001) or U.S. undergraduates (Kumar & Jagacinski, 2006). Both studies used self-reported GPA as a background variable to control for ability; yet, if impostors are experiencing a reduction in achievement relative to nonimpostors, then their achievement scores may not truly reflect ability. The findings indicate that participants experiencing high amounts of IP had the same level of achievement (as measured by their cumulative GPA) as low impostors.

Interestingly, other studies indicate that the correlation between impostorism and GPA may be moderated by sex or gender. Cokley and colleagues (2015) found that IP positively predicted GPA for undergraduate women but not men in their study. Similarly, King and Cooley (1995) found a significant positive correlation between high school GPA and impostorism scores for female but not male undergraduates. In both of these studies, the women who felt like impostors had higher GPAs than nonimpostors. They may have been engaging in maladaptive perfectionistic behaviors to ensure their impostorism would not be discovered, thus ensuring a high GPA as well. Whereas these women were reporting their successes as due to luck or chance, their GPA indicates the opposite to be true. Cumulative GPA shows a pattern of achievement over several years; these impostors would have had to maintain their good luck over many semesters. Yet despite the evidence indicating their superior achievement, the women still reported higher feelings of impostorism.

But whereas IP positively related to GPA scores, it also had negative associations at school. Clance and O'Toole (1987) reported that undergraduate women were less likely to enroll in honors courses than men, despite being equally as talented. The authors argued that impostorism was limiting the women from achieving their full potential despite their high qualifications. Once the women in question learned about IP, more enrolled in the honors courses. Clance and O'Toole theorized that impostorism prevents women from excelling more than it does men. Therefore, the relation between IP and achievement in academic settings may be especially salient for women or girls. (See Chapter 7 for more information regarding gender and impostorism.)

Workplace Environments

As in academic settings, very few studies of IP's relation to achievement exist for a work environment. However, a handful of researchers have investigated IP as it relates to salary, promotion, or evaluation in the workplace. Although most research on these variables produced significant results, findings relating impostorism to salary are mixed. A 2016 study (Neureiter & Traut-Mattausch, 2016b) of working adults in Austria found that impostorism and salary were negatively correlated. Employees experiencing higher levels of IP had significantly lower salaries due to their low adaptability and knowledge of the job market. Notably, however, Hudson and González-Gómez (2021) did not find a relation between impostorism and salary in their study of employed adults in the United States.

The same two studies (Hudson & González-Gómez, 2021; Neureiter & Traut-Mattausch, 2016b) investigated impostorism's relation to promotions at work. Both found a negative association such that people reporting high levels of IP also had significantly fewer past promotions than nonimpostors. The two findings taken together indicate that people high on impostorism may have similar salaries to low impostors, despite having fewer promotions. The impostors may be succeeding in their current positions at work (as indicated by their salary), even though they may not have as high a position as a nonimpostor.

Other than salary and promotions, evaluations provide another measure of achievement for many employees. When being appraised by supervisors or students, impostors are more likely to receive negative feedback. Hudson and González-Gómez (2021) found that workers high on impostorism also had fewer positive work appraisals than low impostors. Similarly, students evaluated professors with high impostorism more negatively than low impostor professors (Brems et al., 1994). For whatever reason, the impostors were perceived as less competent than their low impostor colleagues, a finding which may explain their lower promotion rate.

One possible explanation for the low evaluations for professors may be that they are self-handicapping by procrastinating or avoiding work altogether. Indeed, Wester and colleagues (2020) found that high levels of impostorism hindered scholarly productivity for U.S. professors. Those participants who reported intense impostor feelings created fewer manuscripts and books than did individuals with lower impostorism.

Overall, employees with impostorism have smaller salaries, fewer promotions, lower evaluations, and reduced scholarly activity. That is, IP is negatively related to many achievements necessary to succeed at a job. In the school and work environments, Clance and O'Toole's (1987) hypothesis was correct: Impostorism is keeping people from reaching their highest potential, a relation that may be especially true for women or girls.

Experimental Findings

Whereas some researchers have measured achievements that naturally exist in the real world, others have given participants experimental tasks to complete. In these artificial environments, researchers are better able to control extraneous variables and find causal relations between IP and achievement. If IP relates to achievement in the real world, it is likely to do so in a controlled environment as well. Interestingly, in the laboratory settings, task outcomes did not relate to impostorism. For example, Thompson et al. (2000) gave undergraduates a modified Stroop Color–Word Interference Test (Stroop, 1938). In the high-mistakes condition, the participants were prompted to say either the text of a written color word or its ink color. For instance, if the word "BLUE" was written in red ink, participants should respond "blue" in the text condition and "red" in the ink condition. This test has been shown to be difficult for participants and results in many mistakes. The authors expected that impostors would fare worse than their peers due to increased anxiety and concern over mistakes. However, impostors and nonimpostors did not significantly differ in their reaction times or number of errors on the Stroop test. Although the two groups differed on several psychological constructs, their actual achievement scores were the same.

Other studies have found no relation between impostorism and experimental achievement on academic tasks. For instance, Want and Kleitman (2006) measured undergraduate participants' impostor scores, and then gave them an analogy test to complete. Just like in the Stroop test study, level of impostorism did not relate to accuracy on the analogies. Moreover, Badawy and colleagues (2018) tasked participants with answering questions from the Graduate Record Exam (GRE). The findings indicated that accuracy and time answering the items were unrelated to their impostorism scores. Interestingly, these results may be moderated by sex and accountability, as men in high-accountability conditions answered fewer questions correctly than women in the same condition.

In a recent study, Hudson and González-Gómez (2021) gave participants a paperclip and had them come up with as many uses as possible for it. This task is designed to measure both the quantity and creativity of responses. The researchers expected that impostors would fare poorly on this task, as creativity requires risk-taking and failure, two behaviors that impostors avoid. The results showed that impostorism levels were unrelated to how many different purposes the participants produced for the use of the paperclip. Notably, however, individuals with low levels of IP were able to think of more creative uses than high-level impostors. The authors argued that impostors were experiencing greater shame, an emotion that reduced the psychological resources needed to be creative. So, whereas those participants high on impostorism were still able to successfully complete the task, the quality of their responses was not as high as their peers. These findings, although statistically significant, are not strong evidence that IP results in achievement differences.

Overall, the research on experimental tasks indicates that impostorism does not relate to achievement in a lab environment. This discrepancy may be due to several factors. First, the artificial setting of a lab may not generalize to the real world. Some studies (Badawy et al., 2018) have found impostorism to be especially detrimental in high-stakes or high-accountability environments. It is possible that IP did not affect achievement for the undergraduates in the lab settings because the tasks were low-stakes and primarily anonymous. In the real world, performing poorly on an assignment at school or at work has negative consequences. A failure on the experimental task, however, probably would not affect the impostor's self-concept or expose them as a phony; therefore, their impostorism would become less detrimental in their assessments.

Role of Climate on Impostorism

Some research has shown that impostorism may be especially harmful to achievement in certain climates. For instance, Hudson and González-Gómez's (2021) study revealed that organizational structure moderated the association between shame and creativity. For impostors, working in a mechanistic organizational environment (one with centralized decision making) resulted in reduced creativity in their output. The restrictive climate resulted in greater deleterious effects of impostorism. Furthermore, in the same study, people with high levels of IP were more likely to experience shame when in certain experimental conditions. In a population of adult workers, impostors who were exposed to the judgment of others and failed at a task reported higher shame than other participants. Badawy and colleagues (2018) found similar results in undergraduate students. Impostors did worse on GRE questions when they were told that their professor would see their result and they were given negative feedback. In both studies, a perceived failure and social exposure resulted in reduced achievement for impostors. These situations seem to be especially detrimental to people who fear being exposed as phonies.

Summary of Current Research

Few studies have directly investigated the relation between IP and achievement. Of the handful that have, the findings are somewhat mixed. In an academic environment, impostorism and achievement have a stronger association for women and female students. IP relates to higher overall grades for this population but a reduced likelihood to enroll in honors courses. At work, impostors experience lower salaries, fewer promotions, and more negative evaluations than nonimpostors. This environment may have some of the highest consequences for being exposed as a phony; thus, IP may affect achievement more strongly here than at school or in the lab. Impostors who fail at work risk experiencing major life consequences such as being fired or earning a negative evaluation. Conversely, impostors who fail in an artificial setting such as a laboratory presumably receive few penalties for their poor performance. This difference may explain the negative relation of impostorism to achievement at work but not in the lab. Overall, much more research needs to be conducted to understand the causal effect of IP on achievement.

POSSIBLE MEDIATORS OF IMPOSTORISM AND ACHIEVEMENT

Aside from the aforementioned studies, research into impostorism's relation to achievement is scarce, yet several studies suggest that a strong link may exist. IP has strong connections to variables known to affect achievement, including constructs as varied as mental health, personality, self-efficacy, and self-regulation. In separate studies, these same variables relate to reduced achievement. Therefore, it is highly likely that the proposed variables mediate the relation between impostorism and achievement at work and school.

Whereas these constructs have been shown to relate to IP and achievement independently, only one study (Neureiter & Traut-Mattausch, 2016b) has directly researched their mediational role between the variables. In that research, career self-management variables mediated the relation between impostorism and salary and promotions at work. Impostors experienced reduced self-management in their career optimism, adaptability, and knowledge. Those variables, in turn, led to a lower salary and fewer promotions. The present chapter considers the mediating role of varied constructs on IP.

Mental Health

Probably the variables most studied in their relation to IP consider psychological well-being. People experiencing impostorism often report elevated levels of depression (e.g., Chrisman et al., 1995), anxiety (e.g., Badawy et al., 2018), and shame (e.g., Hudson & González-Gómez, 2021), all variables that can affect achievement as well.

Numerous studies have found that people high on IP also experience high levels of depression. For instance, Clance (1985; Clance & Imes, 1978) reported that the impostors in her research overgeneralized any situational failure as evidence of their own overall inadequacies. This belief in themselves as failures led to depression and extreme self-criticism. Clance's work implies that impostorism beliefs (and subsequent failures) cause depression, a finding that Hu and colleagues' (2019) study supports. However, some research indicates that the directionality may be reversed. For example, Tigranyan and colleagues (2021) found that depression positively and significantly predicted impostorism levels. Regardless of causality, impostors have repeatedly reported higher incidences of depression than nonimpostors (Bernard et al., 2002; Chrisman et al., 1995; McGregor et al., 2008).

Aside from relating positively to impostorism, depression also associates negatively with achievement. For instance, Riglin and colleagues' (2014) meta-analysis found that depression in adolescents (aged 10–17) related to lower grades or school failure. A subsequent meta-analysis (Wickersham et al., 2021) came to a similar conclusion: In children aged 4 to 18, depression was associated with lower achievement, primarily measured as test scores. Students with clinical depression do not fare well in school.

In work environments, people with depression report reduced achievement as well. Depressed employees experience greater absenteeism, productivity loss, and performance deficits when compared with their nondepressed colleagues (Lerner & Henke, 2008). These shortfalls may, in turn, lead to unemployment, lower salaries, or fewer promotions for the worker. In sum, impostors are more likely to report being depressed, a state that has been linked to lower achievement at school and work. These findings strongly suggest that depression may mediate a relation between IP and achievement.

Similarly, nearly every study measuring IP and anxiety has found a positive correlation between the two variables. Impostorism has been linked to anxiety from the beginning stages of the construct. In her early work on IP, Clance (1985; Clance & Imes, 1978) identified a common occurrence known as the impostor cycle. As part of this experience, impostors feel a short-lived elation after success, but that emotion is quickly followed by anxiety over their ability to replicate the achievement. Subsequent studies have confirmed these results: Impostors consistently report greater anxiety than nonimpostors.

The impostor's anxiety may be short-lived and due to situational factors (state anxiety) or more of a long-lasting personality characteristic (trait anxiety). Like in Clance's (1985) work, several studies have reported impostorism's relation to state anxiety, especially as it applies to assessment situations. For example, Cusack and colleagues (2013) found that impostors reported greater test anxiety. Kumar and Jagacinski's (2006) study replicated these results and found that the relation between impostorism and test anxiety was especially strong in women. Overall, numerous studies have confirmed that impostors experience high levels of state anxiety, especially when being evaluated.

But an impostor's anxiety is not limited to situational environments, and several researchers have found that people experiencing IP also have greater trait anxiety (e.g., Topping & Kimmel, 1985). Tigranyan and colleagues (2021) reported greater generalized anxiety in the impostors in their study of psychology doctoral students. Interestingly, however, levels of generalized anxiety did not predict IP when other variables were considered. In sum, impostors report greater state and trait anxiety than nonimpostors, and this emotion may affect their achievement. Indeed, Clance and O'Toole (1987) theorized that the increased anxiety that impostors experience may cause them to settle for certain successes, rather than attempt to achieve higher goals.

Several studies have shown a negative relation between anxiety and school and work successes. For example, a recent meta-analysis (Brumariu et al., 2022) found that students with anxiety had lower overall academic achievement and academic self-concept than individuals without anxiety. Not surprisingly, the anxious students were also less likely to complete high school. The relation between anxiety and achievement continues into the work environment as well. Waghorn and colleagues' (2005) research on Australian adults found that employees with anxiety had impaired work performance and reduced work trajectory. Additionally, people with anxiety disorders were less likely to participate in the labor force, a finding that parallels Lerner and Henke's (2008) research on depressed adults. Although these studies do not directly measure IP's effects on achievement, the relation between impostorism and anxiety and between anxiety and achievement suggests a strong association may exist.

Moreover, impostors are very likely to experience shame at work and school. People experiencing impostorism often feel shame after failure, though some impostors report the negative emotion even before any kind of assessment. Cowman and Ferrari's (2002) research found that shame-proneness strongly predicted impostorism in undergraduate students. In Hu and colleagues' (2019) sample of first-year medical students, high impostorism strongly related to greater feelings of shame and embarrassment. Employees from the United Kingdom and Germany reported shame after experiencing failures at work (Hudson & González-Gómez, 2021). Langford and Clance (1993) proposed that impostors experience high levels of negative emotion because they are overly concerned with how others perceive them. Impostors may be embarrassed by their purported inadequacies and experience shame when a failure confirms their shortfalls.

Impostors experience high levels of shame, and a handful of studies have found this emotion to result in reduced achievement. In a 2004 study (Pekrun et al., 2004), German undergraduates' midterm exam scores negatively related to shame. Students reporting higher shame did worse on the exam than their peers. These findings were replicated in a later study (Pekrun et al., 2009). One study (Hudson & González-Gómez, 2021) found shame to mediate the relation between impostorism and creativity in an experimental task given to employees. Workers experiencing high levels of IP produced less creative marketing slogans than their colleagues due to the impostors' increased shame.

Numerous studies have found an association between IP and negative emotions such as depression, anxiety, and shame. Impostorism as a whole seems to relate to overall poor mental health. Additionally, negative affect can lead to reduced achievement at school and work. These findings together suggest that poor mental health may mediate the relation between high levels of IP and low achievements.

Personality

Another possible mediator of impostorism and achievement is personality. Some studies have found that individuals with certain personalities are likely to report high levels of IP. For instance, impostors tend to have a strong fear of failure and engage in maladaptive perfectionism. Research suggests that these same variables may inhibit achievement in people with impostorism. Thus, personality traits such as fear of failure and perfectionistic concerns may mediate a negative relation between IP and achievement.

In their initial work, Clance and Imes (1978) theorized that IP had a fear of failure as its basis. People high on impostorism worked hard to avoid making mistakes, lest that failure expose them as the frauds they believed themselves to be (Clance, 1985; Clance & O'Toole, 1987). Indeed, studies have shown that fear of failure predicted impostorism in both undergraduate (Ross et al., 2001) and working adult populations (Neureiter & Traut-Mattausch, 2016a). Given an impostor's fear of failure, Cozzarelli and Major's (1990) finding that impostors reacted more negatively to failure than nonimpostors is not surprising. Individuals experiencing IP experience a "terror of failure" (Clance & O'Toole, 1987, p. 57) because they believe that any misstep will expose them for the frauds they believe themselves to be.

As impostors both fear failure and discount their own abilities (Cozzarelli & Major, 1990), they may be less likely to attempt to achieve at a level commensurate with their skills. Impostors may not try to reach high-level goals, instead settling for easier achievements with a greater certainty of success. They fear failure, as it may expose their self-perceived inabilities; thus, they only engage in activities where they know they will succeed. The impostor's fear of failure leads to reduced achievement at school and at work.

Indeed, studies have shown a negative relation between fear of failure and achievement. Schmalt (1999, 2005) found that individuals reporting higher fear of failure also had lower school grades. After finishing their university course work, students high in fear of failure were less likely to have a job lined up than students without that fear (Abele et al., 1999). In an experimental study, Lerche and colleagues (2018) found that fear of failure was negatively related to information accumulation and learning rates. Undergraduates high on fear of failure were slower and less accurate in reporting correct answers in a color-naming task.

Interestingly, some studies show the relation between fear of failure and achievement to be moderated by gender. Wach and colleagues (2015) reported that fear of failure predicted lower math grades for girls only. Additionally, Borgonovi and Han (2021) found that high-achieving girls reported greater fear of failure than high-achieving boys. These gendered findings relating fear of failure and achievement may account for the differential effects of IP on achievement. Girls and women may be more likely to experience fear of failure or may be more affected by its detrimental effects.

Several studies have found that impostorism positively relates to maladaptive perfectionism in students and employees (e.g., Caselman et al., 2006; Cusack et al., 2013; Henning et al., 1998; Hu et al., 2019; Rohrmann et al., 2016; Thompson, 1998, 2000). One way that impostors cope with the negative emotions associated with the construct is by overpreparing their work, as they fear that any mistakes may reveal their impostor status (Clance & Imes, 1978; Lane, 2015). Vergauwe and colleagues (2015) found maladaptive perfectionism to predict IP strongly in their sample of Belgian workers. A later study (Tigranyan et al., 2021) replicated these results in PhD students. In both a work and academic environment, impostors engage in perfectionistic behaviors and beliefs to deal with their internal turmoil. Unfortunately, these actions may, in turn, result in reduced achievement levels.

Findings indicate a negative relation between perfectionistic concerns and academic achievement. Individuals with perfectionistic concerns experience high fear of making a mistake and react negatively when they do fail (Madigan, 2019). Perfectionists often engage in procrastination (Sirois et al., 2017) and suffer with academic burnout (Hill & Curran, 2016). They report high levels of rumination and anxiety (Burcaş & Creţu, 2021; Hewitt & Flett, 1991). The behavior and psychological turmoil associated with perfectionistic concerns may explain the negative relation with academic achievement. Overall, several studies have shown a strong association between impostorism and perfectionism and between perfectionism and reduced achievement. These findings strongly suggest that perfectionism may mediate a link between impostorism and lowered achievement. Individuals with personalities related to fearing failure or experiencing perfectionism may be especially prone to impostorism. That relation, in turn, may lead to a reduction in achievement at school and work.

Self-Efficacy

Impostors tend to lack a positive self-concept, an issue that may result in lower achievement as well. People with impostorism tend to have reduced self-efficacy, a belief that one has the skills and ability to be successful in a given area (Bandura, 1986). This conviction may, in turn, mean that the impostors fail to achieve their full potential at school or work.

Numerous studies have shown a negative relation between IP and self-efficacy, such that impostors do not believe they can be successful in certain areas. This association has been found in Belgian employees (Vergauwe et al., 2015), U.S. academics (Muradoglu et al., 2022), U.S. doctoral students (Tao & Gloria, 2019), and Austrian undergraduates (Neureiter & Traut-Mattausch, 2017). People who feel like impostors do not think they have the ability to succeed in a given area, even if they have attained high achievements in the past.

Not surprisingly, self-efficacy positively relates to achievement in many areas. That is, if students believe they will be successful, they often are, regardless of their abilities. Richardson and colleagues (2012) found that, of the 50 measures they considered in their meta-analysis, performance self-efficacy had the strongest correlation with undergraduate GPA. Academic self-efficacy also positively related to GPA. Mao and colleagues (2021) replicated these findings for science success and found that self-efficacy had the largest effect size on learning achievement in science. Notably, as with fear of failure, self-efficacy often displays sex or gender differences. Huang's (2013) study found that male students reported significantly higher self-efficacy than female students in the stereotypically masculine domains of math and computers. However, female students had higher language arts self-efficacy. These sex disparities may account for the differential effects of impostorism on achievement. In sum, IP is highly related to self-efficacy, a construct that, in turn, predicts achievement. Impostors are less likely to believe they can be successful, thereby possibly inhibiting their accomplishments.

Self-Regulation

Finally, impostorism relates to a reduced ability of individuals to self-regulate. As self-regulation is integral in attaining success (Napiersky & Woods, 2018), impostors may experience fewer achievements. People with impostorism report poor self-discipline, career self-management, and career planning. They are likely to self-handicap through procrastination or disengagement. This inability to regulate their own path to achievement leads them to be less successful.

For the participants in Bernard and colleagues' (2002) study, impostorism related negatively to the self-discipline personality factor of Conscientiousness. That is, undergraduates who felt like frauds were also more likely to waste time and put off chores for later. As academic success often requires self-discipline (Duckworth & Seligman, 2005; Hagger & Hamilton, 2019), students who engage in these procrastinating behaviors may be less likely to do well in school.

Thus, impostors may have reduced academic achievement due to their lack of self-discipline. Furthermore, this relation carries over into the working world, where DuBrin (2001) found that self-discipline positively related to salary and career success. Self-discipline, often reduced in impostors, may be an integral part of achievement at work.

In a series of studies, Neureiter and Traut-Mattausch (2016a, 2016b, 2017) studied IP's relation to work-related outcomes in both students and employees in Austria. The researchers found that impostors had lower career self-management, career planning, and career striving than nonimpostors. This reduced self-regulation may inhibit achievement at work. In a cross-national study, Smale and colleagues (2019) found that proactive career behaviors, such as career self-management and career-enhancing strategies, positively predicted financial success. If impostors are limited in these proactive behaviors, they may be less likely to succeed at work.

People suffering from impostorism struggle to self-regulate. Although they excessively worry about failing, they ironically engage in behaviors that reduce their chances of succeeding. Many impostors employ procrastinating behaviors as a means of unconsciously self-handicapping, when, instead, self-discipline at completing the tasks would help them achieve their goals. Because of their reduced self-concept, impostors often eschew proactive career behaviors. They do not manage their careers well or plan for higher ones because they believe they do not deserve their current position. Unfortunately, this lack of self-discipline and planning may lead to fewer and lower achievements in their lives.

To date, only a handful of studies have investigated the relation between impostorism and achievement directly. However, research strongly suggests that different constructs may mediate the association. IP highly relates to mental well-being, personality factors, self-efficacy, and self-regulation. These variables, in turn, are associated with achievement. Future research should consider the mediating role of the constructs on the impostorism–achievement relation.

CONCLUSION

Research into IP and achievement has shown mixed results. In academic environments, impostorism as a whole does not relate to standardized test scores or GPA. However, studies that considered gender or sex as a moderator did find a link between IP and success for women. That is, in academic environments, impostorism related to greater achievement for women and female, but not men and male, students. IP may affect the different genders and sexes in different ways at school.

Work environments showed a slightly different pattern. Overall, impostorism negatively related to employees' achievement. Workers with high levels of IP reported fewer promotions, lower evaluations, and reduced productivity than employees with low levels of impostorism. Findings related to salary were mixed, however, with one study showing a negative association and another study showing no relation. At work, IP relates primarily to reduced achievement.

Interestingly, studies employing experimental designs failed to produce differing results for impostors and nonimpostors. Impostorism did not relate to accuracy or time answering questions on the Stroop test, analogies, or GRE. Impostors were, however, less creative in their responses finding uses for a paperclip. In these artificial lab environments, impostors may find that failure does not affect their overall self-worth. That is, they may feel that getting a question wrong will not expose them as a fraud as much as it would in an authentic environment such as work or school. The laboratory settings are low stakes, so the deleterious effects of impostorism might not be as salient.

Importantly, very little analysis on the effects of impostorism on achievement has been conducted, so these findings should be considered provisional until more studies can be conducted. Nevertheless, current research strongly suggests that a relation between the two variables exists.

Certain constructs, such as mental health, personality factors, self-efficacy, and self-regulation have shown strong associations with both IP and reduced achievement. Impostorism correlates with poor mental health in a variety of environments and cultures. People experiencing IP often report elevated depression, anxiety, and shame. These variables, in turn, relate to reduced achievement outcomes at school and work. Future studies should consider the mediating role of mental health on the impostorism–achievement relation.

Similar results can be found for personality traits, self-efficacy, and self-regulation. Fear of failure and perfectionistic tendencies strongly relate to IP. Moreover, these traits have shown negative associations with achievement at school and work. Impostors are very likely to fear failure and engage in maladaptive perfectionism, patterns that ironically reduce the likelihood of success. People experiencing impostorism also have low self-efficacy and poor self-regulation. These variables, too, relate to reduced achievement in varying environments. In the future, researchers should analyze the mediating role of these variables on the association between IP and achievement.

In sum, findings on impostorism and achievement are mixed. Research shows that IP has positive associations with GPA but negative relations to

126 • *Lauren A. Blondeau*

accelerated course-taking for women and girls. Impostorism has mostly delete-rious effects on work-related outcomes, such as promotions and evaluations. Yet, impostors and nonimpostors do not differ in their success on many experimental tasks. Further analysis of mediators of the impostorism–achievement association may help untangle these differential findings.

REFERENCES

Abele, A. E., Andrä, M. S., & Schute, M. (1999). Wer hat nach dem Hochschulexamen schnell eine Stelle? Erste Ergebnisse der Erlanger Längsschnittstudie (BELA-E) [Who is able to find employment after having finished a university exam? First results of the Erlangen longitudinal study (BELA-E)]. *Zeitschrift für Arbeits- und Organisationspsychologie, 43*(2), 95–101. https://doi.org/10.1026//0932-4089.43.2.95

Badawy, R. L., Gazdag, B. A., Bentley, J. R., & Brouer, R. L. (2018). Are all impostors created equal? Exploring gender differences in the impostor phenomenon–performance link. *Personality and Individual Differences, 131*, 156–163. https://doi.org/10.1016/j.paid.2018.04.044

Bandura, A. (1986). *Social foundations of thought and action: A social cognitive theory*. Prentice Hall.

Bernard, N. S., Dollinger, S. J., & Ramaniah, N. V. (2002). Applying the Big Five personality factors to the impostor phenomenon. *Journal of Personality Assessment, 78*(2), 321–333. https://doi.org/10.1207/S15327752JPA7802_07

Borgonovi, F., & Han, S. W. (2021). Gender disparities in fear of failure among 15-year-old students: The role of gender inequality, the organisation of schooling and economic conditions. *Journal of Adolescence, 86*(1), 28–39. https://doi.org/10.1016/j.adolescence.2020.11.009

Brems, C., Baldwin, M., Davis, L., & Namyniuk, L. (1994). The imposter syndrome as related to teaching evaluations and advising relationships of university faculty members. *The Journal of Higher Education, 65*(2), 183–193. https://doi.org/10.2307/2943923

Brumariu, L. W., Waslin, S. M., Gastelle, M., Kochendorfer, L. B., & Kerns, K. A. (2022). Anxiety, academic achievement, and academic self-concept: Meta-analytic syntheses of their relations across developmental periods. *Development and Psychopathology*, 1–17. https://doi.org/10.1017/S0954579422000323

Burcaş, S., & Creţu, R. Z. (2021). Multidimensional perfectionism and test anxiety: A meta-analytic review of two decades of research. *Educational Psychology Review, 33*(1), 249–273. https://doi.org/10.1007/s10648-020-09531-3

Caselman, T. D., Self, P. A., & Self, A. L. (2006). Adolescent attributes contributing to the impostor phenomenon. *Journal of Adolescence, 29*(3), 395–405. https://doi.org/10.1016/j.adolescence.2005.07.003

Chrisman, S. M., Pieper, W. A., Clance, P. R., Holland, C. L., & Glickauf-Hughes, C. (1995). Validation of the Clance Imposter Phenomenon Scale. *Journal of Personality Assessment, 65*(3), 456–467. https://doi.org/10.1207/s15327752jpa6503_6

Clance, P. R. (1985). *The impostor phenomenon: Overcoming the fear that haunts your success*. Peachtree.

Clance, P. R., & Imes, S. A. (1978). The imposter phenomenon in high achieving women: Dynamics and therapeutic intervention. *Psychotherapy: Theory, Research, & Practice, 15*(3), 241–247. https://doi.org/10.1037/h0086006

Clance, P. R., & O'Toole, M. A. (1987). The imposter phenomenon: An internal barrier to empowerment and achievement. *Women & Therapy, 6*(3), 51–64 https://doi.org/10.1300/J015V06N03_05

Cokley, K., Awad, G., Smith, L., Jackson, S., Awosogba, O., Hurst, A., Stone, S., Blondeau, L., & Roberts, D. (2015). The roles of gender stigma consciousness, impostor phenomenon and academic self-concept in the academic outcomes of women and men. *Sex Roles, 73*(9–10), 414–426. https://doi.org/10.1007/s11199-015-0516-7

Cowman, S. E., & Ferrari, J. R. (2002). "Am I for real?": Predicting imposter tendencies from self-handicapping and affective components. *Social Behavior and Personality, 30*(2), 119–125. https://doi.org/10.2224/sbp.2002.30.2.119

Cozzarelli, C., & Major, B. (1990). Exploring the validity of the impostor phenomenon. *Journal of Social and Clinical Psychology, 9*(4), 401–417. https://doi.org/10.1521/jscp.1990.9.4.401

Cusack, C. E., Hughes, J. L., & Nuhu, N. (2013). Connecting gender and mental health to imposter phenomenon feelings. *Psi Chi Journal of Psychological Research, 18*(2), 74–81. https://doi.org/10.24839/2164-8204.JN18.2.74

DuBrin, A. J. (2001). Career-related correlates of self-discipline. *Psychological Reports, 89*, 107–110. https://doi.org/10.2466/pr0.2001.89.1.107

Duckworth, A. L., & Seligman, M. E. P. (2005). Self-discipline outdoes IQ in predicting academic performance of adolescents. *Psychological Science, 16*(12), 939–944. https://doi.org/10.1111/j.1467-9280.2005.01641.x

Hagger, M. S., & Hamilton, K. (2019). Grit and self-discipline as predictors of effort and academic attainment. *British Journal of Educational Psychology, 89*(2), 324–342. https://doi.org/10.1111/bjep.12241

Henning, K., Ey, S., & Shaw, D. (1998). Perfectionism, the imposter phenomenon and psychological adjustment in medical, dental, nursing and pharmacy students. *Medical Education, 32*(5), 456–464. https://doi.org/10.1046/j.1365-2923.1998.00234.x

Hewitt, P. L., & Flett, G. L. (1991). Perfectionism in the self and social contexts: Conceptualization, assessment, and association with psychopathology. *Journal of Personality and Social Psychology, 60*(3), 456–470. https://doi.org/10.1037/0022-3514.60.3.456

Hill, A. P., & Curran, T. (2016). Multidimensional perfectionism and burnout: A meta-analysis. *Personality and Social Psychology Review, 20*(3), 269–288. https://doi.org/10.1177/1088868315596286

Hu, K. S., Chibnall, J. T., & Slavin, S. J. (2019). Maladaptive perfectionism, impostorism, and cognitive distortions: Threats to the mental health of pre-clinical medical students. *Academic Psychiatry, 43*(4), 381–385. https://doi.org/10.1007/s40596-019-01031-z

Huang, C. (2013). Gender differences in academic self-efficacy: A meta-analysis. *European Journal of Psychology of Education, 28*(1), 1–35. https://doi.org/10.1007/s10212-011-0097-y

Hudson, S., & González-Gómez, H. V. (2021). Can impostors thrive at work? The impostor phenomenon's role in work and career outcomes. *Journal of Vocational Behavior, 128*, Article 103601. https://doi.org/10.1016/j.jvb.2021.103601

King, J. E., & Cooley, E. L. (1995). Achievement orientation and the impostor phenomenon among college students. *Contemporary Educational Psychology, 20*(3), 304–312. https://doi.org/10.1006/ceps.1995.1019

Kumar, S., & Jagacinski, C. M. (2006). Imposters have goals too: The imposter phenomenon and its relationship to achievement goal theory. *Personality and Individual Differences, 40*(1), 147–157. https://doi.org/10.1016/j.paid.2005.05.014

Lane, J. A. (2015). The imposter phenomenon among emerging adults transitioning into professional life: Developing a grounded theory. *Adultspan Journal, 14*(2), 114–128. https://doi.org/10.1002/adsp.12009

Langford, J., & Clance, P. R. (1993). The imposter phenomenon: Recent research findings regarding dynamics, personality and family patterns and their implications for treatment. *Psychotherapy: Theory, Research, & Practice, 30*(3), 495–501. https://doi.org/10.1037/0033-3204.30.3.495

Lerche, V., Neubauer, A. B., & Voss, A. (2018). Effects of implicit fear of failure on cognitive processing: A diffusion model analysis. *Motivation and Emotion, 42*(3), 386–402. https://doi.org/10.1007/s11031-018-9691-5

Lerner, D., & Henke, R. (2008). What does research tell us about depression, job performance, and work productivity? *Journal of Occupational and Environmental Medicine, 50*, 401–410. https://doi.org/10.1097/JOM.0b013e31816bae50

Madigan, D. J. (2019). A meta-analysis of perfectionism and academic achievement. *Educational Psychology Review, 31*(4), 967–989. https://doi.org/10.1007/s10648-019-09484-2

Mao, P., Cai, Z., He, J., Chen, X., & Fan, X. (2021). The relationship between attitude toward science and academic achievement in science: A three-level meta-analysis. *Frontiers in Psychology, 12*, Article 784068. https://doi.org/10.3389/fpsyg.2021.784068

McGregor, L. N., Gee, D. E., & Posey, K. E. (2008). I feel like a fraud and it depresses me: The relation between the imposter phenomenon and depression. *Social Behavior and Personality, 36*(1), 43–48. https://doi.org/10.2224/sbp.2008.36.1.43

Muradoglu, M., Horne, Z., Hammond, M. D., Leslie, S.-J., & Cimpian, A. (2022). Women—particularly underrepresented minority women—and early-career academics feel like impostors in fields that value brilliance. *Journal of Educational Psychology, 114*(5), 1086–1100. https://doi.org/10.1037/edu0000669.supp

Napiersky, U., & Woods, S. A. (2018). From the workplace to the classroom: Examining the impact of self-leadership learning strategies on higher educational attainment and success. *Innovations in Education and Teaching International, 55*(4), 441–449. https://doi.org/10.1080/14703297.2016.1263232

Neureiter, M., & Traut-Mattausch, E. (2016a). An inner barrier to career development: Preconditions of the impostor phenomenon and consequences for career development. *Frontiers in Psychology, 7*, Article 48. https://doi.org/10.3389/fpsyg.2016.00048

Neureiter, M., & Traut-Mattausch, E. (2016b). Inspecting the dangers of feeling like a fake: An empirical investigation of the impostor phenomenon in the world of work. *Frontiers in Psychology, 7*, Article 1445. https://doi.org/10.3389/fpsyg.2016.01445

Neureiter, M., & Traut-Mattausch, E. (2017). Two sides of the career resources coin: Career adaptability resources and the impostor phenomenon. *Journal of Vocational Behavior, 98*, 56–69. https://doi.org/10.1016/j.jvb.2016.10.002

Pekrun, R., Elliot, A. J., & Maier, M. A. (2009). Achievement goals and achievement emotions: Testing a model of their joint relations with academic performance. *Journal of Educational Psychology, 101*(1), 115–135. https://doi.org/10.1037/a0013383

Pekrun, R., Goetz, T., Perry, R. P., Kramer, K., & Hochstadt, M. (2004). Beyond test anxiety: Development and validation of the Test Emotions Questionnaire (TEQ). *Anxiety, Stress, & Coping, 17*(3), 287–316. https://doi.org/10.1080/10615800412331303847

Richardson, M., Abraham, C., & Bond, R. (2012). Psychological correlates of university students' academic performance: A systematic review and meta-analysis. *Psychological Bulletin, 138*(2), 353–387. https://doi.org/10.1037/a0026838

Riglin, L., Petrides, K. V., Frederickson, N., & Rice, F. (2014). The relationship between emotional problems and subsequent school attainment: A meta-analysis. *Journal of Adolescence, 37*(4), 335–346. https://doi.org/10.1016/j.adolescence.2014.02.010

Rohrmann, S., Bechtoldg, M. N., & Leonhardt, M. (2016). Validation of the impostor phenomenon among managers. *Frontiers in Psychology, 7*, Article 821. https://doi.org/10.3389/fpsyg.2016.00821

Ross, S. R., Stewart, J., Mugge, M., & Fultz, B. (2001). The imposter phenomenon, achievement dispositions, and the five factor model. *Personality and Individual Differences, 31*(8), 1347–1355. https://doi.org/10.1016/S0191-8869(00)00228-2

Schmalt, H.-D. (1999). Assessing the achievement motive using the grid technique. *Journal of Research in Personality, 33*(2), 109–130. https://doi.org/10.1006/jrpe.1999.2245

Schmalt, H.-D. (2005). Validity of a short form of the Achievement-Motive Grid (AMG-S): Evidence for the three-factor structure emphasizing active and passive forms of fear of failure. *Journal of Personality Assessment, 84*(2), 172–184. https://doi.org/10.1207/s15327752jpa8402_07

September, A. N., McCarrey, M., Baranowsky, A., Parent, C., & Schindler, D. (2001). The relation between well-being, imposter feelings, and gender role orientation among Canadian university students. *The Journal of Social Psychology, 141*(2), 218–232. https://doi.org/10.1080/00224540109600548

Shreffler, J., Weingartner, L., Huecker, M., Shaw, M. A., Ziegler, C., Simms, T., Martin, L., & Sawning, S. (2021). Association between characteristics of impostor phenomenon in medical students and Step 1 performance. *Teaching and Learning in Medicine, 33*(1), 36–48. https://doi.org/10.1080/10401334.2020.1784741

Sirois, F. M., Molnar, D. S., & Hirsch, J. K. (2017). A meta-analytic and conceptual update on the associations between procrastination and multidimensional perfectionism. *European Journal of Personality, 31*(2), 137–159. https://doi.org/10.1002/per.2098

Smale, A., Bagdadli, S., Cotton, R., Dello Russo, S., Dickmann, M., Dysvik, A., Gianecchini, M., Kase, R., Lazarova, M., Reichel, A., Rozo, P., & Verbruggen, M. (2019). Proactive career behaviors and subjective career success: The moderating role of national culture. *Journal of Organizational Behavior, 40*(1), 105–122. https://doi.org/10.1002/job.2316

Stroop, J. (1938). Factors affecting speed in serial verbal reactions. *Psychological Monographs, 50*(5), 38–48. https://doi.org/10.1037/h0093516

Tao, K. W., & Gloria, A. M. (2019). Should I stay or should I go? The role of impostorism in STEM persistence. *Psychology of Women Quarterly, 43*(2), 151–164. https://doi.org/10.1177/0361684318802333

Thompson, T., Davis, H., & Davidson, J. (1998). Attributional and affective responses of impostors to academic success and failure outcomes. *Personality and Individual Differences, 25*(2), 381–396. https://doi.org/10.1016/S0191-8869(98)00065-8

Thompson, T., Foreman, P., & Martin, F. (2000). Impostor fears and perfectionistic concern over mistakes. *Personality and Individual Differences, 29*(4), 629–647. https://doi.org/10.1016/S0191-8869(99)00218-4

Tigranyan, S., Byington, D. R., Liupakorn, D., Hicks, A., Lombardi, S., Mathis, M., & Rodolfa, E. (2021). Factors related to the impostor phenomenon in psychology doctoral students. *Training and Education in Professional Psychology, 15*(4), 298–305. https://doi.org/10.1037/tep0000321

Topping, M. E., & Kimmel, E. B. (1985). The imposter phenomenon: Feeling phony. *Academic Psychology Bulletin, 7*(2), 213–226.

Vergauwe, J., Wille, B., Feys, M., De Fruyt, F., & Anseel, F. (2015). Fear of being exposed: The trait-relatedness of the impostor phenomenon and its relevance in the work context. *Journal of Business and Psychology, 30*, 565–581. https://doi.org/10.1007/s10869-014-9382-5

Wach, F.-S., Spengler, M., Gottschling, J., & Spinath, F. M. (2015). Sex differences in secondary school achievement—The contribution of self-perceived abilities and fear of failure. *Learning and Instruction, 36*, 104–112. https://doi.org/10.1016/j.learninstruc.2015.01.005

Waghorn, G., Chant, D., White, P., & Whiteford, H. (2005). Disability, employment, and work performance among people with *ICD-10* anxiety disorders. *The Australian and New Zealand Journal of Psychiatry, 39*(1–2), 55–66. https://doi.org/10.1080/j.1440-1614.2005.01510.x

Want, J., & Kleitman, S. (2006). Imposter phenomenon and self-handicapping: Links with parenting styles and self-confidence. *Personality and Individual Differences, 40*(5), 961–971. https://doi.org/10.1016/j.paid.2005.10.005

Wester, K. L., Vaishnav, S., Morris, C. W., Austin, J. L., Haugen, J. S., Delgado, H., & Umstead, L. K. (2020). Interaction of imposter phenomenon and research self-efficacy on scholarly productivity. *Counselor Education and Supervision, 59*(4), 316–325. https://doi.org/10.1002/ceas.12191

Wickersham, A., Sugg, H. V. R., Epstein, S., Stewart, R., Ford, T., & Downs, J. (2021). Systematic review and meta-analysis: The association between child and adolescent depression and later educational attainment. *Journal of the American Academy of Child & Adolescent Psychiatry, 60*(1), 105–118. https://doi.org/10.1016/j.jaac.2020.10.008

6 MEASUREMENT ISSUES RELATED TO THE IMPOSTOR PHENOMENON

HWA YOUNG LEE, CHERYL B. ANDERSON, KEVIN COKLEY, AND SHINE CHANG

Significant evidence from the literature suggests that the impostor phenomenon (IP) is inversely associated with academic (Cozzarelli & Major, 1990) and career success (Hutchins et al., 2018; Hutchins & Rainbolt, 2017), mental and physical health (Cokley et al., 2013, 2017), self-esteem and emotional intelligence (Ghorbanshirodi, 2012), and self-compassion (Patzak et al., 2017). Researchers often use scales comprising multiple items to characterize the IP experiences of individuals. Application of consistent scales to measure specific constructs across studies is useful for harmonizing measurement across different study populations in different settings and for making valid comparisons of results. Ideally, such scales consistently measure specified dimensions of constructs, such as IP, regardless of population and setting, to inform research and the development of interventions in meaningful ways. When supported by rigorous psychometric evaluation, the reliability and validity of scales provide critical confidence in the accurate measurement of such constructs and the resulting research.

This chapter was supported by a grant from the National Institutes of Health, National Institute of General Medical Sciences, R01 GM147064. The content is solely the responsibility of the authors and does not necessarily reflect the official views of the National Institutes of Health.

https://doi.org/10.1037/0000397-007
The Impostor Phenomenon: Psychological Research, Theory, and Interventions,
K. Cokley (Editor)
Copyright © 2024 by the American Psychological Association. All rights reserved.

132 • *Lee et al.*

To date, only a few IP scales have been developed and their psychometric properties evaluated. Description of the properties of a scale by psychometric evaluation reveals the capability of the scale to accurately measure a construct of interest. Psychometric evaluation assesses each item in a scale for strength to measure the construct or a subscale dimension of the construct, as well as the alignment of items that together capture the construct or subscale dimension. Some IP scales have not had adequate psychometric evaluation, and often researchers using these IP instruments have done so without evaluating them in their specific studies. Even if an instrument used in a study has been validated previously and deemed reliable, evaluation and report of the instrument's psychometric properties ensures appropriateness of the scale with each specific study sample. Without such psychometric scale evaluation, study results could be misleading. Thus, researchers' understanding of the psychometric properties of the instruments they use and reporting of these properties as part of their research results will improve overall knowledge of IP. Unfortunately, few published studies assessing IP instruments have fully addressed their psychometric properties.

This chapter first provides a general description of the psychometric properties of measurement scales to help researchers understand what to look for when selecting a reliable and valid instrument. Next, it discusses the psychometric properties of the most well-known IP instruments currently available, the methodological limitations of each scale, and controversies in IP measurement. Finally, new directions for improving assessment of IP are discussed.

MEASUREMENT TOOLS FOR PSYCHOMETRIC SCALE EVALUATION

In this section, we delve into the measurement of psychometric properties, specifically focusing on reliability and validity. The various types of reliability and validity that are widely used in IP studies are explored and described in detail.

Scale Reliability

Assessing reliability is one of the key measures for reporting the psychometric properties of a scale. *Reliability* is the quality of obtaining consistent results from a given scale or its stability of measurement. There are, in general, three types of reliability measures: *test–retest reliability*, which measures the consistency of items on a scale over time; *internal consistency*, which measures the homogeneity among items on a scale; and *interrater reliability*, which measures the homogeneity across observers who rate, code, or assess the same phenomenon. Most IP studies assess internal consistency (i.e., stability/consistency across items) rather than test–retest reliability and interrater reliability, both of which require administering the scale over two or more timepoints and ratings by two or more individuals, resources that may not be readily available in every study.

The most widely used tool to measure internal consistency is Cronbach's alpha (Cronbach, 1951). In observational studies, a Cronbach's alpha value above .70 for the early stages of research and .80 for basic research is commonly considered "adequate" (Nunnally & Bernstein, 1994). A Cronbach's alpha of around .90 is considered "excellent," but values over .90 indicate that the instrument, or subscale in a multidimensional measure, is unnecessarily redundant, that is, too many items are similarly worded (Streiner, 2003).

Clark and Watson (1995) indicated that a scale that consists of 20 or more items has a higher likelihood of achieving acceptable values of the coefficient alpha even when the instrument includes two distinct, unrelated constructs. Thus, interitem correlations and item-total correlations must also be considered to verify the internal consistency of the scale. Clark and Watson suggested that desirable interitem correlations range from .15 for a scale containing broader constructs (i.e., multidimensional constructs like Clance's IP scale) to .50 for a scale containing a narrower construct (i.e., unidimensional construct like Leary's IP scale).

Scale Validity

Along with reliability, validity is one of the most important psychometric properties to assess. There are four types of validity measures: *face* validity, *content* validity, *criterion* validity, and *construct* validity, but this chapter specifically focuses on construct validity, which is widely used to evaluate validity in IP studies.

Construct validity assesses the extent to which items measure what they are intended to measure. Construct validity can be obtained by measures of convergent validity, divergent validity (aka discriminant validity), dimensionality assessment from factor analysis, or nomological validity. *Convergent validity* is the measurement property that assesses whether the scale's measurement of the construct of interest is strongly associated with that of other scales that measure the same or related constructs. Several studies have shown positive or negative relationships of IP with mental health, personality, self-efficacy, depression, and other constructs (e.g., Cokley et al., 2013; Ghorbanshirodi, 2012). In addition, research has provided evidence of convergent validity by demonstrating a high correlation between a newly developed IP scale and existing validated IP scales (e.g., r values = .60 to .70, Leary et al., 2000b; McElwee & Yurak, 2007).

Divergent validity is the measurement property that assesses whether the scale's measurement of a construct of interest differs from other scales that measure different concepts. For example, one study provided evidence of divergent validity showing that the relationship between IP and a depression measure was weaker than the relationship between two depression measures (Kolligian & Sternberg, 1991).

Dimensionality (e.g., number of constructs), obtained through factor analysis to reduce multiple items into a smaller set of latent constructs (aka factors), is widely used to support the construct validity of a scale. Several studies have assessed the dimensionality of the Clance IP Scale (CIPS) as evidence of its construct validity through the two types of factor analysis, either exploratory factor analysis (EFA) or confirmatory factor analysis (CFA). EFA is a data-driven approach that does not require a prior assumption about the number of latent constructs in the scale. Researchers select an optimal number of latent constructs based on a criterion, such as an eigenvalue (the amount of variance in a set of items that is accounted for by a given factor). According to Worthington and Whittaker (2006), items with factor loadings less than .32 or items with factor loadings higher than $|.32|$ on two or more factors (i.e., cross-loading) should be removed. Items with cross-loadings with differences of less than .15 from the item's highest factor loading should also be removed from further analyses (Worthington & Whittaker, 2006).

CFA is used to assess the extent to which a hypothesized model, based on theory, fits the data. This hypothesized model is then tested to see whether the model fits the data using multiple fit indices, including the chi-square test (χ^2), comparative fit indices (CFI), Tucker–Lewis index (TLI), root-mean-square error of approximation (RMSEA), and standardized root-mean-square residual (SRMR). The most widely used general guideline is that CFI and TFI values greater than or equal to .95, RMSEA values less than or equal to .06, and SRMR values less than or equal to .08 indicate a good fit of the data (Hu & Bentler, 1999). A strength of CFA is that it can be used to assess how well an established model generalizes across groups (e.g., demographic groups, such as gender or race) or across time. Specifically, it can examine whether the same latent construct(s) is being measured across groups of interest (i.e., measurement invariance). To our knowledge, only one study (Ibrahim et al., 2021) has been conducted to assess the measurement invariance of an existing IP instrument, Ibrahim's Impostor Phenomenon Profile (IPP30; see detailed information later in the chapter). Researchers should understand the importance of measurement invariance and know that it is a critical issue when using the same questionnaire in different groups and comparing scores across groups.

Nomological validity refers to the extent to which predictions in a formal theoretical framework are confirmed. It is similar to predictive validity, but nomological validity is a combination of a scale's predictive validity to test a model containing several relationships among constructs. Nomological validity can be assessed by path analysis and structural equation modeling, which allow researchers to test direct and indirect paths specified in a model. Such analyses estimate whether a proposed model fits the data well using multiple fit indices, such as χ^2, CFI, RMSEA, TLI, and SRMR. For example, Ibrahim and colleagues (2022) reported evidence of nomological validity for their new IP scale, the IPP30, where being labeling as "talented" in childhood predicted learned helplessness beliefs indirectly through lower growth mindset beliefs. Learned helplessness positively predicted the IPP30, showing that all hypothesized relationships were significant at $p < .05$.

A BRIEF SUMMARY OF IMPOSTOR PHENOMENON SCALES: PSYCHOMETRIC PROPERTIES, USE OF SAMPLES, STRENGTHS, AND WEAKNESSES

This section provides a brief overview of the commonly used IP scales in chronological order, followed by a discussion of the strengths and weaknesses associated with each of these scales (see Table 6.1).

Harvey's Impostor Phenomenon Scale

In the published literature, the first IP scale was created by Harvey and Katz (1985). The Harvey IP Scale (HIPS) was empirically developed based on a systematic list of items appearing in reports by 178 high achieving women (Clance & Imes, 1978), theoretical observations of a "false self" concept by Harvey (1980), and survey data from a subsample of 41 Black high school women (Stahl et al., 1980). The initial pool was 21 items that were administered to 74 men and women graduate students and then to 72 men and women undergraduate students for cross-validation purposes (Harvey, 1981). The final 14 items were selected based on empirical clarity, item discrimination, and internal consistency. The scale uses a 7-point response format ranging from "not at all true" to "very true."

TABLE 6.1. Characteristics of Often-Used Impostor Phenomenon Scales

| | | | Reliability (Cronbach's alpha) | Construct validity | | |
Scale	Number of items	Publication year		Dimensionality	Convergent/divergent validity	Strengths and weaknesses
HIPS	14	1985	.34 to .91	Three-factor model is the best fitting model: 54.7% of variance explained	• Positively or negatively related but substantially different from the self-monitoring behaviors scale, trait anxiety, and the self-esteem scale (τ values = .41 to .42)	• Internal consistency varied across studies • Issue with several cross-loaded items • May not exhibit significant relationships with measures relevant to IP • Mixed with reversed-coded items, may be an issue of psychometric properties
CIPS	20	1985	.85 to .96	Results of factor structure varied, ranging from one- to four-factor models (with residual covariances or after removing a couple of items)	• Highly associated with another IP scale, PFS (r = .78) • Positively or negatively related but substantially different from depression, self-esteem, social anxiety, self-monitoring, self-evaluation, concerns over mistakes, doubts, anxiety, depression, and neuroticism (r values = .59 to .71)	• Widely used • High internal consistency • Issue with factor structure varies by different studies • Deleting items or adding residual errors varies by different studies • Issue with using a cutoff score • Luck construct may need to be reconsidered
PFS	51	1991	.85 to .95	Two-factor model is the best fitting model, indicating Inauthenticity and Self-Deprecation	• Highly associated with two other IP scales, HIPS and CIPS (r values = .76 to .86) • Positively or negatively related but substantially different from self-monitoring, depression, frequency of spontaneous fraudulent thoughts, and negative affect (r values = .29 to .61)	• High internal consistency • Rarely used • Too many items • Confirmatory factor analysis needed to clarify the factor structure • Items loaded on each factor can be exchangeable • No information about response options reported

Scale	Items	Year	Reliability	Factor structure	Validity	Notes
Leary's IP scale	7	2000	.87 to .94	One-factor model is the best fitting model; 73.4% of variance explained	Highly associated with two other IP scales, CIPS and PFS (r values = .87 to .94)	• Short seven-item scale • Rarely used • High internal consistency • Brings up an issue with the multidimensionality of IP as a construct • Fails to distinguish empirical finding of true versus strategic impostor
IPP	30	2022	.69 to .92 across the six subscales	Bifactor model is the best fitting model	• High correlations with another IP scale, CIPS (r = .78) • Positively or negatively related but substantially different from Learned Helplessness Scale, the Defensive Pessimism Questionnaire, growth mindset, and grit or perseverance/resilience (r values = .70 to .71)	• Unique approach to improving the measurement and conceptual clarity of IP • Most recent scale • Additional work needed
Short version of CIPS	10	2022	.93	One-factor model is acceptable	• Positively or negatively related but substantially different from job stress, turnover, job satisfaction, Extraversion, Agreeableness, Conscientiousness, Honesty-Humility (r values = .57 to .26)	• Removed ambiguities in both item wordings and response scale options • No comparison made with the original 20-item scale or with other existing IP scales

Note. HIPS = Harvey Impostor Phenomenon Scale; IP = impostor phenomenon; CIPS = Clance Impostor Phenomenon Scale; PFS = Perceived Fraudulence Scale; IPP = Impostor Phenomenon Profile.

Reliability

Harvey and Katz (1985) reported that the Cronbach's alpha coefficient was .81 for the first sample and .74 for the cross-validation sample. Other studies using this scale have reported Cronbach's alpha coefficients similar in magnitude, ranging from .70 to .75 (Hellman & Caselman, 2004; Leary et al., 2000b; Topping & Kimmel, 1985). One of these studies used 285 university faculty members and a version of the Harvey scale modified to reflect situations related to faculty (Topping & Kimmel, 1985). By contrast, Holmes and colleagues (1993) reported a Cronbach's alpha coefficient for the HIPS of .91 with 62 participants, of whom 48 were women and half of whom were clinically identified impostors referred by experienced clinicians. Edward and colleagues (1987) reported unacceptably low Cronbach's alpha coefficients, ranging from .34 using a sample of 50 undergraduate students. However, when evaluating IP as a multidimensional construct, Cronbach's alpha coefficients of HIPS subscales have ranged from .65 to .81 (Edwards et al., 1987).

Construct Validity

One study conducted an EFA to identify the factor structure of the HIPS and found that a three-factor solution fit best, accounting for 54.7% of variance explained by factors (Edwards et al., 1987). These factors were Impostor, Unworthy, and Inadequate. However, one item, "My personality or charm . . ." negatively loaded on the factor of Inadequate, and another item, "My public and private self . . ." cross-loaded on both Impostor and Inadequate, with factor loadings of .64 and .43, respectively. Topping and Kimmel (1985) reported that the HIPS had a significant moderate and positive relationship with the self-monitoring behaviors scale ($\tau = .18$) and trait anxiety ($\tau = .42$) but had a significantly negative relationship with the self-esteem scale ($\tau = -.41$; Topping & Kimmel, 1985).

Comments

The HIPS has not been widely used to measure IP due to its somewhat inconsistent results for internal consistency across studies and other issues with its validity. Low internal consistency may result from the many reverse-coded items in the scale. Concerning validity, several studies have identified issues with the construct validity of the HIPS, including that the HIPS scale may not significantly distinguish nonimpostors from impostors, compared with the CIPS (Holmes et al., 1993). The HIPS scale was also not found to have significant relationships between IP and other measures of interest (Chrisman et al., 1995; Flewelling, 1985; Kertay et al., 1991; Lawler, 1984).

Clance's Impostor Phenomenon Scale

The CIPS is well-known and has been widely used in clinical settings and research purposes for decades. After Clance and Imes (1978) used the term "impostor phenomenon" in a study of over 150 highly successful women, Clance developed a scale to measure IP. The CIPS measures the degree to which individuals experience a fear of failure, discount their ability, and attribute their success to luck (Clance, 1985a; Gibson-Beverly & Schwartz, 2008; Langford & Clance, 1993). The scale consists of 20 items, ranging from 1 (not at all true) to 5 (very true). The CIPS differs somewhat from the HIPS in that the CIPS was designed to evaluate more clinical symptoms or experiences than the HIPS. Clance and colleagues also added items that measure attributes and feelings (e.g., feeling less capable than peers and fear of evaluation), such that the scale assesses broader constructs than the HIPS does. Unlike the HIPS, all items are worded in the same direction, eliminating the need for reverse coding of items.

The CIPS can be used to describe IP using the sum of all 20 items to produce a total score ranging from 20 to 100 with higher scores indicating that an individual experiences more frequent and serious IP. The total score can be used to categorize individuals into one of three levels of IP based on a criterion suggested by Clance (1985a), whereas Holmes and colleagues (1993) proposed an alternative approach by recommending the use of a cutoff score of 62 to distinguish impostors from nonimpostors or to classify individuals into four different levels of IP experiences. As there is no established guideline or standard procedure for classifying individuals into levels of IP, researchers have used a variety of methods, such as the criterion suggested by Clance and the cutoff score recommended by Holmes and colleagues (e.g., Cozzarelli & Major, 1990; Levan et al., 2020; Thompson et al., 2000).

Reliability

The CIPS has been shown to have good reliability across most studies. Most reliability coefficients using the CIPS ranged from .85 to .96, which are considered acceptable (Freeman et al., 2022; Mak et al., 2019; McElwee & Yurak, 2007; Rohrmann et al., 2016). Despite this, it is important to note that caution is required in interpreting internal consistency if a unidimensional scale consists of more than 20 items.

Construct Validity

The construct validity of the CIPS has been established through factor analyses. Chrisman et al. (1995) conducted an EFA and identified three factors,

Luck, Fake, and Discount, after deleting two items (Items 1 and 2). They used a sample of 269 undergraduate students, 69% of whom were women. Similarly, a series of CFAs by H. Lee and colleagues (2022) revealed that the three-factor solution was the best fit after removing three items and allowing the inclusion of two residual covariances in the final model; the 959 participants in that study sample were students and professionals from STEM (science, technology, engineering, and mathematics) and medicine (x^2_{SB} [114] = 268.287, CFI = .948, TLI = .938, RMSEA = .055, SRMR = .038). After Kertay et al.'s (1991) study removed four items (1, 2, 19, and 20) with low interitem correlations, French and colleagues (2008) used this 16-item version of the CIPS and gathered CFA results that indicated that the two-factor model consisting of Fake/Discount and Luck was better than either the one- or three-factor models (CFI = .796, TLI = .963, SRMR = .057). The study participants in this research study were 1,271 engineering undergraduate students, mostly men (81%).

Several other studies found the CIPS to be unidimensional. Simon and Choi (2018) reported that CFA supported a one-factor structure with three residual covariances in a study involving 211 doctoral students in STEM fields. Freeman et al. (2022) conducted EFA with varimax rotation and concluded that a one-factor model fit best because 11 of the 20 items cross-loaded on both the first and the second factors and the loading values were above .3 (Worthington & Whittaker, 2006). In addition, Noskeau and colleagues (2021) conducted CFA yielding a one-factor solution after removing four items due to low factor loadings (Item 1 = .18, Item 2 = .28, Item 3 = .34, Item 20 = .41). This study included 211 working adults in the United Kingdom.

The CIPS has also been translated and adapted for use in multiple languages, including German, Korean, Japanese, and Hebrew. A couple of studies have evaluated the construct validity of these versions of the CIPS. For example, a three-factor model was found to be the best fitting model for the German version of the CIPS after removal of four items (Items 1, 2, 8, and 13), based on both EFA and CFA, in studies of 151 and 149 undergraduate students, respectively, most of whom were women (Brauer & Wolf, 2016). On the other hand, Jöstl and colleagues (2012) found that a one-factor solution with residual covariances among items was the best fitting model for the 16-item German version of the CIPS, based on a sample of 631 Austrian doctoral students (62% women). A recent report by Yaffe (2020) evaluated the construct validity of the Hebrew version of CIPS using both EFA and CFA. The sample was 248 female Hebrew-speaking students. After removing Item 2, the CFA results showed that a four-factor model was the best fitting model and that its factors accounted for 54.81% of the model's variance (RMSEA = .052 [.040, .063], SRMR = .054, TLI = .924, CFI = .935).

As described here, many studies have evaluated the construct validity of the CIPS; however, the results have been controversial across studies. Therefore, more research is needed to establish a clear guidance for the construct validity of the CIPS.

Despite the inconsistent results for dimensionality, a validation study of the CIPS demonstrated a high correlation between the CIPS and another IP scale, Perceived Fraudulence Scale ($r = .78$). In addition, the CIPS was found to be related to but substantially different from measures of depression (r values = $-.26$ to $.71$), self-esteem (r values = $-.59$ to $-.51$), social anxiety (r values = $.27$ to $.54$), and self-monitoring (r values = $-.33$ to $-.02$; Chrisman et al., 1995). Rohrmann and colleagues (2016) also indicated that CIPS is an independent construct, showing that the scale is separate from measures of core self-evaluation ($r = -.46$), concern over mistakes and doubts ($r = .57$), anxiety (r values = $.37$ to $.48$), depression (r values = $-.15$ to $.47$), and neuroticism ($r = .48$), even though these factors were highly related to the CIPS.

Comments

Using a cutoff score to distinguish impostors from nonimpostors raises several concerns. First, the choice of a cut-point to define IP is problematic because the arbitrary nature of a cut-point, which can vary depending on the sample composition, increases the likelihood of misclassifying participants by IP status. Second, using cut-point scores dividing observations into categories reduces a significant amount of information that is available when assessing the entire range of scores. Third, removing items that have lower interitem correlations before categorizing impostors versus nonimpostors raises issues with comparing results across studies and the generalizability of findings (Vergauwe et al., 2015). Therefore, it is important to consider these limitations when using cutoff scores to distinguish impostors from nonimpostors in research studies.

As reported in the construct validity, previous research to determine the factor structure of the CIPS has often involved dropping items to obtain better model fit or incorporating varied residual covariances. The specific practice of dropping items and adding residual covariances has varied across different studies.

Some have highlighted the number of items used to assess the Luck construct in the CIPS as a potential limitation. Luck is often assessed by only two or three items, far fewer items than for other constructs, such as "fear of failure" and "discount their ability." Developing more items to reflect Luck may be needed to provide a fuller understanding of the construct in IP (French et al., 2008). On the other hand, Levant and colleagues reported that the Luck construct was not prominent in a study of IP among 3rd-year medical students (Levant et al., 2020), and H. Lee and colleagues (2022) also raised a concern

142 • *Lee et al.*

that the construct of Luck may not be a major component of IP and instead only an empirical association with IP.

Kolligian and Sternberg's Perceived Fraudulence Scale

Having identified insufficient support for the psychometric properties of existing IP scales, Kolligian and Sternberg (1991) developed a new IP scale in which IP is conceptualized as *perceived fraudulence*, which "reflect[s] a relatively broad range of phenomenological tendencies associated with the experience" (Kolligian & Sternberg, 1991, p. 312). The authors defined impostorism as a self-perception of fraudulence, which consists of cognitive and affective components. Items included in the Perceived Fraudulence Scale (PFS) measure the extent to which individuals experience perceived intellectual phoniness with six subscales that include fraudulent ideation, depressive tendencies, self-criticism, social anxiety, achievement pressures, and self-monitoring skills.

A trial version of the PFS that contained 67 items was administered to 60 Yale undergraduates. It was reduced to 51 items based on item analysis processes through factor analyses to improve internal consistency and validity. The 51-item version was then administered to a sample of 50 undergraduates and a second sample of 100 college students (50 women and 50 men) for the purpose of cross-validation.

Reliability
The authors of the PFS reported Cronbach's alpha coefficients for the PFS subfactors, Inauthenticity and Self-Deprecation, were .95 and .85, respectively, for Study 1 and .86 and .92, respectively, for Study 2 (Kolligian & Sternberg, 1991). Leary and colleagues (2000b), in their use of the PFS, also reported an overall Cronbach's alpha coefficient of .88, but they used different response options from the original scale, ranging from "not at all characteristic of me" (1) to "extremely characteristic of me" (5). It should be noted that estimating Cronbach's alpha for the PFS scale, which contains 51 items, may not be informative, as a high reliability coefficient is almost certain to be achieved regardless of the quality of the items (Clark & Watson, 1995).

Construct Validity
Kolligian and Sternberg (1991) conducted EFA with varimax rotation and concluded that a two-factor model was the best solution for the PFS, which they labeled as Inauthenticity and Self-Deprecation.

Evidence of convergent validity was found by showing that the PFS constructs were related to self-monitoring, depression, frequency of spontaneous fraudulent thoughts, and negative affect (r values = .30 to .61). Chrisman et al. (1995) and Leary et al. (2000b) also found that the correlation coefficient between the PFS and HIPS was in the range of .76 to .83, and the correlation coefficient between the PFS and CIPS was in the range of .78 to .86. These correlations were statistically significant ($p < .001$). Evidence of divergent validity was determined by showing that two measures of depression were more highly related with each other (r = .80, $p < .001$) than with the PFS (r values = .52 to .53). Two measures of anxiety were also more highly related with each other (r = .61, $p < .001$) than with the PFS (r values = .29 to .58).

Comments

Two studies by Kolligian and Sternberg (1991) conducted EFA using the same 51 items of the PFS with different samples. The results of both studies showed that the two-factor model was the best solution, and the labels of each factor were the same for both studies. However, there were discrepancies in the number of items loading onto each factor and which specific items loaded onto each factor between the two studies. This raises concerns about the stability of the factor structure because items could be interchangeable across factors, reducing the ability of each factor to distinguish the defining concepts of the subfactors clearly. To address this, further study should conduct CFA to evaluate the factor structure. The PFS has not been as widely used as other IP scales, perhaps because it includes a larger number of items (51 items) than other scales. In addition, there is no information about response options of the scale in Kolligian and Sternberg's study.

Leary et al.'s Impostor Phenomenon Scale

Leary and colleagues (2000b) tested whether the central construct of IP could be empirically demonstrated through experimentation, believing that existing IP scales (e.g., CIPS, HIPS, PFS) measure not only the central concept of IP but also other relevant factors related to IP but not central to it. Thus, they developed a unidimensional scale reflecting the sense of being an impostor or a fraud (i.e., Inauthenticity). The scale consists of seven items using a 5-point response format ranging from "not at all characteristic of me" (1) to "extremely characteristic of me" (5). They mass-tested the seven-item IP scale at the beginning of the semester in all introductory psychology undergraduate students. As their work aimed to identify the central construct of IP, description provided about the process of developing the IP scale was not reported in their published paper. The Leary IP scale is available from Mark Leary's website at Duke University (Leary et al., 2000a).

Reliability
The scale showed high internal consistency, with Cronbach's alpha of .87 to .94, as reported in several studies (Freeman et al., 2022; Leary et al., 2000b; McElwee & Yurak, 2007).

Construct Validity
Leary and colleagues (2000b) used EFA, yielding a one-factor solution using seven items; this factor accounted for 73.4% of the model's variance. In addition, the authors stated that the scale showed evidence of construct validity that item response patterns did not differ by gender (no detailed information was reported in their paper). Two studies reported that the scale was highly correlated with existing IP scales, including HIPS, CIPS, and PFS (.70 to .80; Leary et al., 2000b), and had a correlation coefficient of .60 with the CIPS (McElwee & Yurak, 2007).

Comments
Leary and colleagues (2000b) highlighted that impostorism is highly related to self-view and use of interpersonal strategies to express one's self differently in private and public situations. This suggests that IP may consist of multidimensional constructs that describe different characteristics of IP (H. Lee et al., 2022). This work suggests that expressing doubt in one's own abilities to be successful again may be an interpersonal strategy used to lower other people's expectations, convey a sense of modesty, protect one's image in case of failure, and obtain social support from others. In other words, individuals with high impostorism are more likely to express themselves less positively in public situations, possibly because they are sensitive about how they express themselves—how they may be perceived—differently to people in different roles (e.g., boss, teacher, friends). Building on this concept, Leonhardt and colleagues (2017) evaluated the construct validity of IP for conceptual clarity. Their idea was to identify two types of impostors, true impostors and strategic impostors. *True impostors* were more likely to have a negative self-view, whereas strategic impostors were not. *Strategic impostors* had a strong tendency to use self-presentation strategies to get others to lower their expectations of them. H. Lee et al.'s (2022) study supported the findings that different groups of people with IP are characterized by different combinations of self-doubt and fear of evaluation and that, among individuals in STEM and medicine fields, fear rather than self-doubt may be more relevant as the defining feature of IP.

Leary et al.'s (2000b) work raises questions about the multidimensionality of IP as a construct and the self-presentation motives of respondents to IP measures, which invites further evaluation to clarify the defining features of

IP. Although their work attempted to distinguish between true and strategic impostors through experiments, it did not succeed in supporting their argument statistically at a significance level of .05. If IP is not unidimensional and existing IP scales cannot distinguish between true impostors and strategic impostors, then future efforts to improve existing IP scales or develop new ones are warranted.

Ibrahim et al.'s Impostor Phenomenon Profile

The IPP30 was developed by Ibrahim and colleagues (2021) to assess categories of cognitive patterns, emotions, and behavioral strategies identified in previous IP theory and research (Clance, 1985b; Clance & Imes, 1978; Harvey & Katz, 1985; Sakulku & Alexander, 2011). An initial item pool of 450 items, created by three experts, was administered to 303 German participants, 36% of whom were women. It was reduced to 31 items describing six factors identified through EFA and CFA. The six factors include (a) competence doubt (11 items), which measures self-doubt in one's competence and fear of failure; (b) working style (six items), which measures procrastination and "pre-crastination" (i.e., doing things early) tendencies on tasks; (c) alienation (three items), which measures feeling inauthentic and impression management; (d) other–self divergence (four items), which reflects feeling overrated by others; (e) ambition (four items), which reflects need to be successful and make a difference; and (f) need for sympathy (three items), which describes a need to be liked and considered helpful and sympathetic (Ibrahim et al., 2020). A 2021 study by the same authors involving 482 German participants (64% women) reported one item dropped from the ambition factor for a final 30-item IPP30 scale (Ibrahim et al., 2021). The response format uses a visual analog scale ranging from 1 ("does not apply in any aspect") to 100 ("applies completely"). An English version of the 30-item IPP30 (Ibrahim et al., 2022) was administered online via a crowdsourcing website for U.S. businesses (Amazon Mechanical Turk) to 407 employed, highly educated (91% bachelor's or master's degree) participants from the United States.

Reliability

Cronbach's alpha coefficients for the IPP31 ranged from .69 to .92 across the six subscales (Ibrahim et al., 2020). Due to the small number of items on most of the subscales, McDonald's omega ($\omega > .8$ is considered acceptable) was used as an alternative measure of reliability and ranged from .72 to .92 in the first sample and .72 to .94 in the cross-validation sample (Ibrahim et al., 2020, 2021). In the English-language IPP30 sample, omega ranged from .57 to .93

across subscales, with the lowest reliabilities on the Ambition (ω = .68) and Need for Sympathy (ω = .57) factors, as in the German IPP30, and an omega of .94 for the IPP30 total score (Ibrahim et al., 2022).

Construct Validity

A series of CFA that tested alternative models in three samples (approximately n = 400 each) by Ibrahim et al. (2020: 31 items, 2021: 30 items, 2022: 30 items) showed that a six-factor model was superior to a one-factor model. However, the CFI values across the three samples for the first-order, six-factor models were not relatively high (CFI = .91, .91, .85; RMSEA = .063, .061, .075, respectively). They concluded that a bifactor model was the best solution through a series of model comparisons in the 2021 German and the 2022 U.S. samples (CFI = .94, .90; RMSEA = .051, .063), supporting the multidimensionality of the IPP30, as well as the use of an IPP30 total score. The bifactor model hypothesizes a general factor that all items load on and six factors on which items of each factor load. Bifactor models can separate the general factor from the specific factors, including testing mean differences on factors beyond the general factor, and are more applicable when it is important to test whether specific factors predict other variables (e.g., outcomes) over and above the general factor (Chen et al., 2012). For the IPP30, measurement invariance (i.e., when factor loadings and items' intercepts are equivalent across groups) was supported across genders, with women scoring higher on the Competence Doubt and Need for Sympathy subscales and men higher on Ambition (Ibrahim et al., 2021).

The IPP30 total score has been found to have high correlations with the CIPS (r = .78) and internal-stable-global attributional style in negative situations (r values = .35, .28, .40, respectively by dimension; Ibrahim et al., 2021). It also correlates positively with the Learned Helplessness Scale (r = .71), the Defensive Pessimism Questionnaire (r = .62), and the Thought–Action Fusion Scale (r = .46) on superstitious beliefs (Ibrahim et al., 2022). The IPP30 total score has also been found to have negative correlations with measures of growth mindset (r = −.40) and grit or perseverance/resilience (r = −.70; Ibrahim et al., 2022).

Comments

The scale development work by Ibrahim and colleagues represents a unique approach to improving the measurement and conceptual clarity of IP. Their use of bifactor modeling, which is becoming more popular in psychological and psychiatric research, is particularly promising for determining the relation of common and separate facets of IP to external variables, such as possible antecedent and outcome variables of IP. However, additional work on this scale is needed. For example, consistently lower reliability scores for the Ambition and Need for Sympathy subscales (Ibrahim et al., 2021, 2022) and their weaker loadings on the general construct than on the two specific factors, including low correlations with the Competence Doubt and Alienation subscales (Ibrahim et al., 2021), which are perhaps the hallmarks of IP, warrant further study.

The 10-Item CIPS

Wang and colleagues (2022) reevaluated the CIPS to examine the multidimensionality of the scale. They first reanalyzed the 20-item CIPS data from Rohrmann et al. (2016; $n = 242$ German workers in leader positions, 37% women) to contrast the fit of four plausible models: a one-factor model, a three-factor model (Fake, Discount, Luck), a second-order factor with three first-order factors, and an exploratory bifactor model with a general factor and three subfactors. Overall results from the four models indicated that the 20-item CIPS data was best used as a one-factor, single score. The bifactor model was especially helpful in reaching this conclusion: McDonald's omega measuring reliability for the general factor was .91, whereas the omegas for the specific three factors ranged from .03 to .26; the explained common variance of the general factor was .78, indicating that 78% of the variance in the model was attributed to the general, one-factor. Thus, Wang et al. (2022) concluded that none of the three subscales were reliable enough to be reported or interpreted and that the total score was the optimal choice as most of its variance was attributed to the general factor in the bifactor model.

Next, to create a new, short, one-factor scale in Study 2, Wang et al. (2022) selected 10 items from the CIPS to cover its original three content domains. Considering explained common variance from the bifactor model using the Rohrmann et al. (2016) data and correlations among the variables, the three factors included Fake (four items), Discount (four items), and Luck (two items). The wording of some items was changed. For example, frequency wording, such as "often" and "sometimes," was deleted, and one of the "Luck" items was altered to reflect a more direct attribution of success to luck rather than competence ("I feel my success was due to some kind of luck rather than competence"). In addition, the original 5-point response scale was replaced with a 7-point frequency scale (1 = *never*, 2 = *rarely*, 3 = *occasionally*, 4 = *sometimes*, 5 = *frequently*, 6 = *usually*, 7 = *always*). The 10-item scale was administered online via Amazon Mechanical Turk, a global crowdsourcing website for businesses and their global workforce. The study sample included 294 working adults (55.8% female); however, the nationalities of participants and other demographic information were not reported.

148 • *Lee et al.*

Reliability
Cronbach's alpha for the CIPS-10 was .93 (Wang et al., 2022).

Construct Validity
Three models were fit to the data, a one-, two-, and three-factor model, all with three pairs of correlated residuals, as well as an exploratory bifactor model, which was attempted but did not converge. The three models had comparable fit, but the one-factor model was determined to be sufficient (RMSEA = .077, CFI = .962, SRMR = .037).

The CIPS-10 total score was found to correlate positively with the Emotionality factor of the HEXACO-104 (Honesty–Humility, Emotionality, Extraversion, Agreeableness, Conscientiousness, Openness to Experience; de Vries et al., 2016; K. Lee & Ashton, 2006) personality measure (r = .31), which reflects fear of physical dangers, anxiety in response to stress, need for emotional support from others, and empathy and sentimental attachments with others. It correlated negatively with four other HEXACO-104 subfactors— Extraversion (r = −.57), Agreeableness (r = −.29), Conscientiousness (r = −.26), Honesty–Humility (r = −.18)—and was not related to Openness to Experience (r = −.01). It was also positively related to job stress (r = .26), as well as turnover intention (r = .26), and negatively related to job satisfaction (r = −.25).

Comments
The CIPS-10 offers substantial improvements to the original 20-item CIPS, removing ambiguities in both item wordings and the response scale options. However, because both were derived from the original CIPS and literally are both a "chip off the old block," the debate on what is/are the central, defining feature(s) and dimensionality of IP will undoubtedly continue. In addition, they did not evaluate the relationship between the original CIPS scale and the new, short version of the CIPS.

An interesting finding from the Wang et al. (2022) Study 2 using the CIPS-10 concerned its unexpected negative correlation with the Honesty–Humility factor of the HEXACO-104. This factor has four subscales (Sincerity, Fairness, Greed Avoidance, Modesty), in which low scores (together with high scores on the CIPS-10) would suggest manipulative strategies for self-presentation and a strong sense of self-importance. More research to better understand the self-presentational aspects of IP is needed.

It is also important to note that concern over the correlated residuals in the CIPS-10 led the Wang group to further shorten the scale to six items (CIPS-6; RMSEA = .05, CFI = .99, SRMR = .02; see bolded items in Table 2 of Wang et al., 2022, and their Supplemental Material Section 5). Short IP scales like the CIPS-6 and the Leary IP scale (7 items) may better fit the needs of some researchers who wish to reduce participant burden, especially in certain situations, such as large-scale surveys with multiple constructs or repeated measures.

NEW DIRECTIONS FOR IMPOSTOR PHENOMENON METRICS

This section discusses the current IP scales used for measuring the IP, addressing the challenges involved in measuring IP and exploring potential future directions for IP studies.

Diversity Experience of Impostor Phenomenon

The growing research literature investigating IP, according to a systematic review by Bravata and colleagues (2020), has typically included small numbers of non-White participants in study samples. Only recently has research begun to examine IP experiences among racial and ethnic minorities in the United States, such as among Black college students (Cokley et al., 2013, 2017). As IP levels and correlates can differ by racial and ethnic groups, the influence of other domains of diversity, such as cultural (e.g., individualism vs. collectivism) and religious differences, remain to be explored. For example, Asians/ Asian Americans may use different self-presentation strategies (e.g., more modest) than other groups, and individuals may vary by religious affiliation in their strategies for internalizing success. Some argue that the existing conceptualization of the IP construct does not reflect relevant factors that contribute to the experience of IP in diverse groups. In Chapter 2, Cokley et al. argue that the original IP construct has limitations as it applies to the experiences of minoritized individuals. Qualitative studies among Black graduate students, for example, suggest that a reconceptualization of the IP construct may be needed to capture socioracial experiences (e.g., discrimination, marginalization) for a more culturally informed IP construct (Stone et al., 2018). Thus, Cokley et al. argue that a newly conceptualized racialized IP construct is needed. This would require the construction of a new racialized IP scale. Questions remain about whether a general racialized IP scale for all racially minoritized groups or group-specific racialized IP scales should be developed. For example, with the construct of racial microaggression, Nadal (2011) developed a racial and ethnic microaggressions scale for all people of color, and Lewis and Neville (2015) constructed a gendered racial microaggressions scale for Black women.

150 • *Lee et al.*

Multiple racialized IP scales will likely need to be developed both for people of color generally and also for specific groups.

Defining Impostor Phenomenon: Trait Versus State

An emerging controversy in IP research concerns the general tendency to regard IP as a trait, that is, as an individual difference that is generally stable over time and situations. To date, many of the items in widely used IP scales are worded to reflect IP as a trait and relatively independent of situations. However, many argue that the experience of IP is strongly influenced by situations, and some effort has been made to modify existing scales to address these aspects. For example, using the Japanese version of the CIPS, Fujie (2010) modified the scale to measure state IP by focusing on current IP feelings linked to three specific risk situations that include receiving evaluation, having a new experience, or having an unexpected success (Fujie, 2010). If existing scales do not capture IP at the state level and some situations or environments trigger people to feel more IP feelings (McElwee & Yurak, 2010; e.g., a new environment, a fixed mindset, racial discrimination, lack of belonging, being evaluated, the status of a particular perceiver), then future research needs to address the issues of trait versus state IP in scale development or modification.

It may be that conceptualizing IP as both trait and state forms is warranted, certainly at least until consensus is reached based on research evidence. Some would argue that some level of trait IP always exists, never goes away, and can be triggered to more substantial levels in certain environments or situations. It may be helpful to consider parallels to models of trait/state anxiety, such as Endler's multidimensional model of anxiety, which proposes that anxiety is a function of the interaction of person and situation variables (Endler et al., 1983). Endler suggested that situations congruent with specific dimensions of trait anxiety serve to induce corresponding state anxiety changes, that is, levels of state anxiety are dependent upon both the person (trait anxiety) and the stressful situation. Reflecting this perspective, the Endler Multidimensional Anxiety Scales include four dimensions of trait anxiety and two dimensions of state anxiety (Endler et al., 1989, 1991).

Another viable way of addressing trait versus state issues in IP research is to use statistical methods, such as latent state–trait theory. Introduced by Steyer and colleagues, this theory provides the theoretical framework and statistical techniques to quantify the amount of variance due to a trait, the situation or state, the interaction between trait and state, and measurement error (Steyer et al., 1992, 1999, 2015). By using structural equation modeling on data collected from the same individuals from at least two time points, estimates of consistency, occasion specificity, and reliability can be obtained for a given scale (e.g., Ziegler et al., 2009).

Exploring Dimensions of Impostor Phenomenon and Interpreting Scores

Current IP scales use a response scale that measures IP as a static trait, that is, the degree to which each individual item is characteristic of the respondent as a person (e.g., "not at all characteristic of me" to "extremely characteristic of me"). However, a strong case can also be made that measuring the frequency with which IP feelings are experienced (e.g., "never" to "always," as in the CIPS-10), how intense they are (e.g., "not at all intense" to "highly intense"), and how disruptive they are to respondents or how much they interfere with daily life (e.g., "not at all" to "extremely") can provide additional dimensions for understanding the experience and impact of IP feelings, particularly useful for developing interventions. Measuring coping self-efficacy can also provide important information to guide potential interventions, such as confidence in ability to deal with impostor feelings. Chang and colleagues (2022) found that summer research students were able to persist toward goals and challenging tasks because they reported being able to manage their feelings better following a brief intervention in spite of continuing to experience such feelings at the same levels as before the intervention.

In addition, recent studies have found that IP may not have only negative implications. For example, impostor thoughts can be a motivator that benefits job mastery and can improve interpersonal performance at work (Tewfik, 2022). However, Tewfik's (2022) studies focused only on the IP belief that others overestimate one's competence, which she considers the characteristic defining IP. Her work includes the development of a five-item IP measure of frequency (1 = *never* to 6 = *very frequently*) of beliefs that others overestimate one's competence. Leary and colleagues (2000b) suggested that among individuals reporting IP experiences, some may project impostor status, consciously or unconsciously, as an interpersonal strategy in public settings involving others, in order to reduce other peoples' expectations of them, to appear more modest, to obtain social support, or to protect their image or reputation from disappointment or embarrassment from failure.

CONCLUSION

This chapter has presented a comprehensive overview of the current state of IP measurement and has laid a foundation for future studies. Existing IP scales have generally demonstrated good reliability and validity where metrics were reported, and all have shown moderate to high correlations with one another and other relevant measures. Still, challenges to reliable and valid use of these scales remain to be addressed. Researchers should report the psychometric properties of the IP scale they use in their studies. This includes conducting a series of CFAs to identify the scale's factor structure, useful for greater understanding of scale structure in the absence of current consensus. Indeed, establishing the dimensionality of IP, whether uni- or multidimensional, as well as clarifying the defining features of IP, are key goals for improved insight into the mechanisms of IP and for development of informed interventions. In addition, a better understanding of measurement invariance is needed for the existing IP scales across groups that differ in demographic characteristics, cultural backgrounds, and other key characteristics. Importantly, the relatively unexplored issue of variability in the experience of impostor feelings—their frequency, intensity, and disruptive impact—may provide critical insight into understanding the state/trait aspects of the IP experience. Such understanding will inform design of interventions that can also capitalize on possible motivational benefits that some have reported related to IP feelings. In closing this chapter, we wish to remind our readers to strive for "theoretical clarity and empirical precision" in scale development and evaluation, sage advice from Clark and Watson (2019, p. 1424).

REFERENCES

Brauer, K., & Wolf, A. (2016). Validation of the German-language Clance Impostor Phenomenon Scale (GCIPS). *Personality and Individual Differences, 102,* 153–158. https://doi.org/10.1016/j.paid.2016.06.071

Bravata, D. M., Watts, S. A., Keefer, A. L., Madhusudhan, D. K., Taylor, K. T., Clark, D. M., Nelson, R. S., Cokley, K. O. & Hagg, H. K. (2020). Prevalence, predictors, and treatment of impostor syndrome: A systematic review. *Journal of General Internal Medicine, 35*(4), 1252–1275. https://doi.org/10.1007/s11606-019-05364-1

Chang, S., Lee, H. Y., Anderson, C., Lewis, K., Chakraverty, D., & Yates, M. (2022). Intervening on impostor phenomenon: Prospective evaluation of a workshop for health science students using a mixed-method design. *BMC Medical Education, 22*(1), Article 802. https://doi.org/10.1186/s12909-022-03824-7

Chen, F. F., Hayes, A., Carver, C. S., Laurenceau, J. P., & Zhang, Z. (2012). Modeling general and specific variance in multifaceted constructs: A comparison of the bifactor model to other approaches. *Journal of Personality, 80*(1), 219–251. https://doi.org/10.1111/j.1467-6494.2011.00739.x

Chrisman, S. M., Pieper, W. A., Clance, P. R., Holland, C. L., & Glickauf-Hughes, C. (1995). Validation of the Clance Imposter Phenomenon Scale. *Journal of Personality Assessment, 65*(3), 456–467. https://doi.org/10.1207/s15327752jpa6503_6

Clance, P. R. (1985a). *Clance Impostor Phenomenon Scale (CIPS)*. APA PsycTests. https://doi.org/10.1037/t11274-000

Clance, P. R. (1985b). *The impostor phenomenon: When success makes you feel like a fake.* Bantam Books.

Clance, P. R., & Imes, S. A. (1978). The imposter phenomenon in high achieving women: Dynamics and therapeutic intervention. *Psychotherapy: Theory, Research, & Practice, 15*(3), 241–247. https://doi.org/10.1037/h0086006

Clark, L. A., & Watson, D. (1995). Constructing validity: Basic issues in objective scale development. *Psychological Assessment, 7*(3), 309–319. https://doi.org/10.1037/1040-3590.7.3.309

Clark, L. A., & Watson, D. (2019). Constructing validity: New developments in creating objective measuring instruments. *Psychological Assessment, 31*(12), 1412–1427. https://doi.org/10.1037/pas0000626

Cokley, K., McClain, S., Enciso, A., & Martinez, M. (2013). An examination of the impact of minority status stress and impostor feelings on the mental health of diverse ethnic minority college students. *Journal of Multicultural Counseling and Development, 41*(2), 82–95. https://doi.org/10.1002/j.2161-1912.2013.00029.x

Cokley, K., Smith, L., Bernard, D., Hurst, A., Jackson, S., Stone, S., Awosogba, O., Saucer, C., Bailey, M., & Roberts, D. (2017). Impostor feelings as a moderator and mediator of the relationship between perceived discrimination and mental health among racial/ethnic minority college students. *Journal of Counseling Psychology, 64*(2), 141–154. https://doi.org/10.1037/cou0000198

Cozzarelli, C., & Major, B. (1990). Exploring the validity of the impostor phenomenon. *Journal of Social and Clinical Psychology, 9*(4), 401–417. https://doi.org/10.1521/jscp.1990.9.4.401

Cronbach, L. J. (1951). Coefficient alpha and the internal structure of tests. *Psychometrika, 16*, 297–334. https://doi.org/10.1007/BF02310555

de Vries, R., Tybur, J., Pollet, T., & Vugt, M. (2016). Evolution, situational affordances, and the HEXACO model of personality. *Evolution and Human Behavior, 37*(5), 407–421. https://doi.org/10.1016/j.evolhumbehav.2016.04.001

Edwards, P. W., Zeichner, A., Lawler, N., & Kowalski, R. (1987). A validation study of the Harvey Impostor Phenomenon Scale. *Psychotherapy: Theory, Research, & Practice, 24*(2), 256–259. https://doi.org/10.1037/h0085712

Endler, N. S., Edwards, J. M., & Kowalchuk, B. P. (1983). *The interaction model of anxiety assessed in a psychotherapy situation*. Southern Psychologist.

Endler, N. S., Edwards, J. M., Vitelli, R., & Parker, J. D. A. (1989). Assessment of state and trait anxiety: Endler Multidimensional Anxiety Scales. *Anxiety Research, 2*(1), 1–14. https://doi.org/10.1080/08917778908249322

Endler, N. S., Parker, J. D., Bagby, R. M., & Cox, B. J. (1991). Multidimensionality of state and trait anxiety: Factor structure of the Endler Multidimensional Anxiety Scales. *Journal of Personality and Social Psychology, 60*(6), 919–926. https://doi.org/10.1037/0022-3514.60.6.919

Flewelling, A. L. (1985). *The impostor phenomenon in individuals succeeding in self-perceived atypical professions: The effects of mentoring and longevity* [Unpublished master's thesis]. Georgia State University.

Freeman, K. J., Houghton, S., Carr, S. E., & Nestel, D. (2022). Measuring impostor phenomenon in healthcare simulation educators: A validation of the Clance Impostor Phenomenon Scale and Leary Impostorism Scale. *BMC Medical Education, 22*(1), Article 139. https://doi.org/10.1186/s12909-022-03190-4

154 • *Lee et al.*

French, B., Ullrich-French, S., & Follman, D. (2008). The psychometric properties of the Clance Impostor Scale. *Personality and Individual Differences, 44*(5), 1270–1278. https://doi.org/10.1016/j.paid.2007.11.023

Fujie, R. (2010). Development of the State Impostor Phenomenon Scale. *Japanese Psychological Research, 52*(1), 1–11. https://doi.org/10.1111/j.1468-5884.2009.00417.x

Ghorbanshirodi, S. (2012). The relationship between self-esteem and emotional intelligence with imposter syndrome among medical students of Guilan and Heratsi Universities. *Journal of Basic and Applied Scientific Research, 2*(2), 1793–1802.

Gibson-Beverly, G., & Schwartz, J. P. (2008). Attachment, entitlement, and the impostor phenomenon in female graduate students. *Journal of College Counseling, 11*(2), 119–132. https://doi.org/10.1002/j.2161-1882.2008.tb00029.x

Harvey, J. C. (1980). *Impostor phenomena among high achievers: The experience of true and false selves* [Unpublished special topics paper]. Temple University.

Harvey, J. C. (1981). *The impostor phenomenon and achievement: A failure to internalise success* [Unpublished doctoral dissertation]. Temple University.

Harvey, J. C., & Katz, C. (1985). *If I'm so successful, why do I feel like a fake: The impostor phenomenon*. St. Martin's Press.

Hellman, C. M., & Caselman, T. D. (2004). A psychometric evaluation of the Harvey Imposter Phenomenon Scale. *Journal of Personality Assessment, 83*(2), 161–166. https://doi.org/10.1207/s15327752jpa8302_10

Holmes, S. W., Kertay, L., Adamson, L. B., Holland, C. L., & Clance, P. R. (1993). Measuring the imposter phenomenon: A comparison of Clance's IP scale and Harvey's I-P scale. *Journal of Personality Assessment, 60*(1), 48–59. https://doi.org/10.1207/s15327752jpa6001_3

Hu, L., & Bentler, P. M. (1999). Cutoff criteria for fit indexes in covariance structure analysis: Conventional criteria versus new alternatives. *Structural Equation Modeling, 6*(1), 1–55. https://doi.org/10.1080/10705519909540118

Hutchins, H. M., Penney, L. M., & Sublett, L. W. (2018). What imposters risk at work: Exploring imposter phenomenon, stress coping, and job outcomes. *Human Resource Development Quarterly, 29*(1), 31–48. https://doi.org/10.1002/hrdq.21304

Hutchins, H. M., & Rainbolt, H. (2017). What triggers imposter phenomenon among academic faculty? A critical incident study exploring antecedents, coping, and development opportunities. *Human Resource Development International, 20*(3), 194–214. https://doi.org/10.1080/13678868.2016.1248205

Ibrahim, F., Münscher, J.-C., & Herzberg, P. Y. (2020). The facets of an impostor—Development and validation of the impostor-profile (IPP31) for measuring impostor phenomenon. *Current Psychology, 41*(6), 3916–3927. https://doi.org/10.1007/s12144-020-00895-x

Ibrahim, F., Münscher, J.-C., & Herzberg, P. Y. (2021). Examining the impostor-profile—Is there a general impostor characteristic? *Frontiers in Psychology, 12*, Article 720072. https://doi.org/10.3389/fpsyg.2021.720072

Ibrahim, F., Münscher, J.-C., & Herzberg, P. Y. (2022). The validation of the English Impostor-Profile 30 and the exploratory formulation of the learned helplessness model of the impostor phenomenon. *Acta Psychologica, 226*, Article 103589. https://doi.org/10.1016/j.actpsy.2022.103589

Jöstl, G., Steinberg, E., Lüftenegger, M., Schober, B., & Spiel, C. (2012). When will they blow my cover? The impostor phenomenon among Austrian doctoral students.

Zeitschrift für *Psychologie, 220*(2), 109–120. https://doi.org/10.1027/2151-2604/a000102

Kertay, L., Clance, P. R., & Holland, C. L. (1991). *A factor study of the Clance Impostor Phenomenon Scale* [Unpublished manuscript]. Georgia State University.

Kolligian, J., & Sternberg, R. J. (1991). Perceived fraudulence in young adults: Is there an "impostor syndrome"? *Journal of Personality Assessment, 56*(2), 308–326. https://doi.org/10.1207/s15327752jpa5602_10

Langford, J., & Clance, P. R. (1993). The imposter phenomenon: Recent research findings regarding dynamics, personality and family patterns and their implications for treatment. *Psychotherapy: Theory, Research, & Practice, 30*(3), 495–501. https://doi.org/10.1037/0033-3204.30.3.495

Lawler, N. K. (1984). *The impostor phenomenon in high achieving persons and Jungian personality variables* [Unpublished doctoral dissertation]. Georgia State University.

Leary, M. R., Patton, K. M., Orlando, A. E., & Wagoner Funk, W. (2000a). *Impostorism scale*. Duke University. https://sites.duke.edu/leary/files/2019/05/Impostorism.pdf

Leary, M. R., Patton, K. M., Orlando, A. E., & Wagoner Funk, W. (2000b). The impostor phenomenon: Self-perceptions, reflected appraisals, and interpersonal strategies. *Journal of Personality, 68*(4), 725–756. https://doi.org/10.1111/1467-6494.00114

Lee, H., Anderson, C. B., Yates, M. S., Chang, S., & Chakraverty, D. (2022). Insights into the complexity of the impostor phenomenon among trainees and professionals in STEM and medicine. *Current Psychology, 41*, 5913–5924. https://doi.org/10.1007/s12144-020-01089-1

Lee, K., & Ashton, M. C. (2006). Further assessment of the HEXACO Personality Inventory: Two new facet scales and an observer report form. *Psychological Assessment, 18*(2), 182–191. https://doi.org/10.1037/1040-3590.18.2.182

Leonhardt, M., Bechtoldt, M. N., & Rohrmann, S. (2017). All impostors aren't alike—Differentiating the impostor phenomenon. *Frontiers in Psychology, 8*, Article 1505. https://doi.org/10.3389/fpsyg.2017.01505

Levant, B., Villwock, J. A., & Manzardo, A. M. (2020). Impostorism in American medical students during early clinical training: Gender differences and intercorrelating factors. *International Journal of Medical Education, 11*, 90–96. https://doi.org/10.5116/ijme.5e99.7aa2

Lewis, J. A., & Neville, H. A. (2015). Construction and initial validation of the Gendered Racial Microaggressions Scale for Black women. *Journal of Counseling Psychology, 62*(2), 289–302. https://doi.org/10.1037/cou0000062

Mak, K. K. L., Kleitman, S., & Abbott, M. J. (2019). Impostor phenomenon measurement scales: A systematic review. *Frontiers in Psychology, 10*, Article 671. https://doi.org/10.3389/fpsyg.2019.00671

McElwee, R. O., & Yurak, T. (2007). Feeling versus acting like an impostor: Real feelings of fraudulence or self-presentation? *Individual Differences Research, 5*, 201–220.

McElwee, R. O., & Yurak, T. (2010). The phenomenology of the impostor phenomenon. *Individual Differences Research, 8*, 184–197.

Nadal, K. L. (2011). The Racial and Ethnic Microaggressions Scale (REMS): Construction, reliability, and validity. *Journal of Counseling Psychology, 58*(4), 470–480. https://doi.org/10.1037/a0025193

Noskeau, R., Santos, A., & Wang, W. (2021). Connecting the dots between mindset and impostor phenomenon, via fear of failure and goal orientation, in working adults.

Frontiers in Psychology, 12, Article 588438. https://doi.org/10.3389/fpsyg.2021.588438

Nunnally, J. C., & Bernstein, I. (1994). The assessment of reliability. *Psychometric Theory, 3*, 248–292.

Patzak, A., Kollmayer, M., & Schober, B. (2017). Buffering impostor feelings with kindness: The mediating role of self-compassion between gender-role orientation and the impostor phenomenon. *Frontiers in Psychology, 8*, Article 1289. https://doi.org/10.3389/fpsyg.2017.01289

Rohrmann, S., Bechtoldt, M. N., & Leonhardt, M. (2016). Validation of the impostor phenomenon among managers. *Frontiers in Psychology, 7*, Article 821. https://doi.org/10.3389/fpsyg.2016.00821

Sakulku, J., & Alexander, J. (2011). The impostor phenomenon. *International Journal of Behavioral Science, 6*(1), 73–92.

Simon, M., & Choi, Y.-J. (2018). Using factor analysis to validate the Clance Impostor Phenomenon Scale in sample of science, technology, engineering and mathematics doctoral students. *Personality and Individual Differences, 121*, 173–175. https://doi.org/10.1016/j.paid.2017.09.039

Stahl, J. M., Turner, H. M., Wheeler, A. E., & Elbert, P. (1980, September 1–5). *The "impostor phenomenon" in high school and college science majors* [Paper presentation]. American Psychological Association 88th Annual Convention, Montreal, Quebec, Canada.

Steyer, R., Ferring, D., & Schmitt, M. J. (1992). States and traits in psychological assessment. *European Journal of Psychological Assessment, 8*(2), 79–98.

Steyer, R., Mayer, A., Geiser, C., & Cole, D. A. (2015). A theory of states and traits—Revised. *Annual Review of Clinical Psychology, 11*, 71–98. https://doi.org/10.1146/annurev-clinpsy-032813-153719

Steyer, R., Schmitt, M., & Eid, M. (1999). Latent state–trait theory and research in personality and individual differences. *European Journal of Personality, 13*(5), 389–408. https://doi.org/10.1002/(SICI)1099-0984(199909/10)13:5<389::AID-PER361>3.0.CO;2-A

Stone, S., Saucer, C., Bailey, M., Garba, R., Hurst, A., Jackson, S. M., Krueger, N., & Cokley, K. (2018). Learning while Black: A culturally informed model of the impostor phenomenon for Black graduate students. *The Journal of Black Psychology, 44*(6), 491–531. https://doi.org/10.1177/0095798418786648

Streiner, D. L. (2003). Starting at the beginning: An introduction to coefficient alpha and internal consistency. *Journal of Personality Assessment, 80*(1), 99–103. https://doi.org/10.1207/S15327752JPA8001_18

Tewfik, B. (2022). The impostor phenomenon revisited: Examining the relationship between workplace impostor thoughts and interpersonal effectiveness at work. *Academy of Management Journal, 65*(3), 988–1018. https://doi.org/10.5465/amj.2020.1627

Thompson, T., Foreman, P., & Martin, F. (2000). Impostor fears and perfectionistic concern over mistakes. *Personality and Individual Differences, 29*(4), 629–647. https://doi.org/10.1016/S0191-8869(99)00218-4

Topping, M. E., & Kimmel, E. B. (1985). The imposter phenomenon: Feeling phony. *Academic Psychology Bulletin, 7*, 213–226.

Vergauwe, J., Wille, B., Feys, M., De Fruyt, F., & Anseel, F. (2015). Fear of being exposed: The trait-relatedness of the impostor phenomenon and its relevance in the work context. *Journal of Business and Psychology*, *30*, 565–581. https://doi.org/10.1007/s10869-014-9382-5

Wang, B., Andrews, W., Bechtoldt, M. N., Rohrmann, S., & de Vries, R. E. (2022). Validation of the Short Clance Impostor Phenomenon Scale (CIPS-10). *European Journal of Psychological Assessment*, 1–11. https://doi.org/10.1027/1015-5759/a000747

Worthington, R. L., & Whittaker, T. A. (2006). Scale development research: A content analysis and recommendations for best practices. *The Counseling Psychologist*, *34*(6), 806–838. https://doi.org/10.1177/0011000006288127

Yaffe, Y. (2020). Validation of the Clance Impostor Phenomenon Scale with female Hebrew-speaking students. *Journal of Experimental Psychopathology*, *11*(4), Article 2043808720974341. https://doi.org/10.1177/2043808720974341

Ziegler, M., Ehrlenspiel, F., & Brand, R. (2009). Latent state–trait theory: An application in sport psychology. *Psychology of Sport and Exercise*, *10*(3), 344–349. https://doi.org/10.1016/j.psychsport.2008.12.004

PART **II** POPULATIONS AND CONTEXTS

7 GENDER AND THE IMPOSTOR PHENOMENON

KADIE R. RACKLEY, TAYLOR PAYNE, ASHLEY BENNETT, AND GERMINE H. AWAD

The origins of the impostor phenomenon construct are rooted in Pauline Clance and Suzanne Imes's therapeutic work with over 150 high-achieving predominately White women who, despite their success, felt like impostors and devalued their achievements (Clance & Imes, 1978). As hypothesized by Clance and Imes (1978), early family dynamics and gender stereotypes may have partially influenced how successful women see themselves as impostors. Because the examination of this construct began with women, there is an assumption that there are widespread gender differences. It is clear that the impostor phenomenon has gendered components and influences. For example, factors such as gender socialization are important in how women judge their competence and make attributions about success (Park et al., 2008). Part of the difficulty with understanding and studying the impostor phenomenon in women is that the construct is partially influenced by many other important factors, such as perfectionism, gender socialization, attribution theory, self-schemas, personality, and family processes. Intersectional identities further nuance our understanding of the impostor phenomenon, as they may introduce factors that have previously not been examined in the literature.

This chapter reviews the literature on impostorism and gender. We discuss studies that have found a gender difference in experiences of the impostor

https://doi.org/10.1037/0000397-008
The Impostor Phenomenon: Psychological Research, Theory, and Interventions,
K. Cokley (Editor)
Copyright © 2024 by the American Psychological Association. All rights reserved.

phenomenon and present research that did not detect a gender difference for men and women. We discuss the moderators that may help explain gender differences and conclude the chapter by suggesting future directions that may address unanswered questions and provide further clarification of findings related to the role of gender in the experiences of the impostor phenomenon.

EMPIRICAL RESEARCH ON GENDER DIFFERENCES IN IMPOSTORISM

The empirical literature about gender differences in impostorism reveals more nuance than originally perceived. Clance and Imes (1978) conceptualized impostor phenomenon from their experiences with high-achieving female clients and originally considered it to be a phenomenon primarily experienced by women. However, subsequent research has produced mixed findings. Some impostor phenomenon research does show women experiencing higher levels of impostorism compared with their male peers (Cokley et al., 2018; Cowie et al., 2018; Cusack et al., 2013; Henning et al., 1998; King & Cooley, 1995; McGregor et al., 2008; Oriel et al., 2004). For example, undergraduate women reported higher impostorism and ability avoidance goals, or goals that avoid potentially demonstrating incompetence, and lower confidence in their intelligence compared with undergraduate men (Kumar & Jagacinski, 2006). A study of health profession students (e.g., medicine, dentistry, nursing, pharmacy) showed women's mean impostorism scores were higher than men's; however, both female and male health profession students reported high impostorism compared with other college students (Henning et al., 1998).

Other researchers found mean differences but also demonstrated that the relationship between gender and impostorism is more nuanced. For example, Muradoglu and colleagues (2022) found female academics reported higher impostor beliefs than their male peers; however, this relationship was moderated by racial background and perceptions of success in their field. Women in medical fields were more likely to report higher perfectionist competence related to impostorism, but there were no mean gender differences in overall impostorism scores (Ogunyemi et al., 2022). Patzak and colleagues (2017) found both men and women experienced impostorism, but women experienced it more severely. Domínguez-Soto and colleagues (2023) found an initial gender difference of women reporting higher impostorism, but further analysis indicated this gender difference was only significant for 1st-year engineering students compared with students further in their undergraduate or graduate programs. However, they found that the relationship between impostorism and transformational and passive leadership styles did not depend on gender.

Far more researchers have demonstrated no mean differences in impostorism by gender (Blondeau & Awad, 2018; Brauer & Wolf, 2016; Caselman et al., 2006; Castro et al., 2004; Cokley et al., 2013, 2015; Cowman & Ferrari, 2002; Fried-Buchalter, 1997; McClain et al., 2016; Rackley, 2018; September et al., 2001; Sonnak & Towell, 2001), including research using structured interviews among male therapeutic clients (Clance & O'Toole, 1987). One study even found the reverse trend, that male tenure-track faculty reported higher impostorism than their female counterparts (Topping & Kimmel, 1985). The researchers suggest this could possibly be explained by more societal barriers for women that may effectively weed out those experiencing impostorism or that impostorism for these faculty may be situational.

However, given that gender was part of the conceptualization of impostor phenomenon and that a considerable amount of the literature does demonstrate gender differences, we along with others in this area of study propose that the process of experiencing impostorism is gendered rather than simply explained by mean differences in the scale score. A lack of mean differences in impostorism does not necessarily mean this phenomenon operates the same way, regardless of gender. To that point, Cokley and colleagues (2015) emphasized that analyzing psychological processes when studying gender and impostorism is crucial because recent data show outcome differences by gender are smaller than conventionally assumed. Therefore, rather than differences between men and women, the impact of gendered experiences on mechanisms involved with the impostor phenomenon may be more significant.

GENDER DIFFERENCES IN IMPOSTORISM'S RELATIONSHIPS WITH OTHER VARIABLES

A substantial amount of the literature demonstrates that the relationship of impostorism with some other variables varies by gender even when mean differences are not found. For instance, Caselman and colleagues (2006) established that greater support from friends predicted lower impostorism for adolescents, but this connection seemed stronger for adolescent girls. They also found that, in addition to friend support, support from classmates more generally and strong self-perceptions of dependability predicted lower impostorism for adolescent girls but not for boys, suggesting more interdependent relationships and development for young girls.

Impostorism is often studied in the realm of academics, and impostor beliefs seem to have a gendered relationship with academic performance in terms of grades. Overall stronger impostor beliefs seem to predict higher grade-point average (GPA), but only for women (Cokley et al., 2015; King & Cooley, 1995). Further, Cokley and colleagues (2015) found impostorism directly predicts GPA for undergraduate women, but for men the influence was indirect. They demonstrated that, for men, stronger impostor beliefs predicted weaker academic self-concept, which in turn predicted more academic disengagement and subsequent lower GPA. One of the interpretations for this relationship is that individuals experiencing impostor beliefs often push themselves to work twice (or 3 times) as much to prove they belong or to ensure they will not fail and be "found out," and more time and attention spent on schoolwork often leads to better grades. King and Cooley's (1995) findings support this explanation. They found that whereas women and men did not differ in terms of GPA or number of hours spent on coursework outside of school, only women's stronger impostor beliefs predicted higher GPA and more hours spent on coursework. The gendered connection between impostor phenomenon and higher GPA for women makes sense given how girls are socialized. Young girls are taught to be agreeable and conscientious and to strive to make others happy, so they often complete their homework (to make their teachers happy) at higher rates than boys. This socialization paired with the cultural assumption that women do well academically when they work hard—because they lack the innate intellectual ability men inherit—facilitates earning higher grades. That same socialization might also amplify the connection between women's impostor beliefs and their efforts and subsequent academic performance, explaining the more direct connection between the two for women.

Some impostorism research has examined gendered relationships with performance attributions and outcomes beyond course grades. Chae and colleagues (1995) found stronger impostor beliefs correlated with stronger attributions of successful work performance to the nature of the situation (e.g., "It was an easy task") for men but not for women. Gender differences in these relationships are not always consistent. For example, Chae and colleagues also demonstrated that stronger impostor beliefs correlated to fewer attributions of successful work performance to individual effort only for men. However, Topping and Kimmel (1985) found the same relationship regardless of gender. For these studies, data were collected in Korea and the United States respectively, so cultural differences could at least partially explain this discrepancy.

Badawy and colleagues (2018) examined these concepts while manipulating the nature of performance feedback and the anticipated audience with whom that performance would be shared. They found women's and men's impostor beliefs interacted differently after receiving generated feedback that they had failed to answer Graduate Record Examinations questions correctly. After this feedback, impostor beliefs predicted higher anxiety for men, whereas impostorism predicted more effort and better performance for women. There were no significant relationships with these variables after feedback that participants had answered questions correctly. When the experiment involved sharing the individual's performance with their business course professor, impostorism predicted higher anxiety, reduced effort, and lower performance for men. Interestingly, impostorism did not relate to these outcomes for women. Badawy and colleagues suggested the impact of impostorism may be worse for men in the context of performance in the business domain because these outcomes are related to demonstrating competence in leadership and business, which gender stereotypes state men inherently possess. These men may have felt they could not live up to these societal expectations in this stereotypically male domain and thus engaged in self-handicapping.

Impostorism has also been studied beyond performance to determine relationships related to career aspirations and experiences. Blondeau and Awad (2018) found impostorism differentially influenced career perceptions for STEM (science, technology, engineering, and mathematics) undergraduates based on gender. They demonstrated that stronger impostor beliefs predicted weaker future intentions to work in a STEM field for men, independent of the positive effects of self-efficacy and interest in the domain. For women, only their interest in the field predicted whether they intended to work in their field after graduation, indicating impostorism did not affect women's STEM career aspirations as directly as it did for men's. Focusing on those already working in their careers, Hutchins and Rainbolt (2017) conducted a qualitative study of academic faculty who reported high impostorism scores. They found that men more often discussed that colleagues' implied or explicit statements questioning their training and expertise triggered impostorism beliefs. On the other hand, women more often endorsed that their own comparisons with colleagues regarding productivity and navigating the publication and grant process, including rejections and negative feedback, and handling other expectations during the pretenure period triggered their impostor beliefs. Additionally, women discussed coping with their impostorism by relying on social support and active methods, such as correcting cognitive distortions of success to address these thoughts, whereas men reported coping by avoidant methods, such as substance use and working harder.

Even though the focal points differ, these findings all indicate that we must move beyond simply looking for mean differences and examine the underlying psychological mechanisms by which impostorism differs by gender. In addition

INDIVIDUAL GENDERED TRAITS

As part of the conceptualization of impostor phenomenon, perceiving one's talents as unusual for someone of one's social group, such as gender or race, can contribute to the foundation of impostorism (Clance, 1985). For instance, Beard and Bakeman (2001) found that gender-nonconforming behaviors and expressions during childhood predicted impostorism for gay and bisexual men. They also found that parental interactions (both positive and negative) from childhood partially mediated this relationship, and in particular positive interactions with fathers predicted lower impostorism. The researchers suggested that early reactions to gender nonconformity may have made these men feel like they needed to hide aspects of themselves to not be rejected, fueling impostor beliefs. Further, they suggest parental reactions, particularly from these men's fathers, would especially inform these perceptions of gender role and expression authenticity and rejection.

Most of the impostorism research that examines specific gendered traits beyond identity focuses on gender role femininity and masculinity. For instance, Fassl and colleagues (2020) found that positive masculine traits (e.g., rationality, intelligence) predicted lower impostorism and negative feminine traits (e.g., anxiousness, self-doubt) predicted higher impostorism. Negative masculine traits (e.g., aggression, arrogance) and positive feminine traits (e.g., nurturing, empathy) were unrelated to impostorism. Additionally, negative femininity predicted engaging more in social comparisons, and social comparison orientation partially mediated the relationship between negative feminine traits and impostorism.

In particular, the societal bias favoring masculine traits might serve as a buffer when individuals perceive themselves as possessing some of those traits. September and colleagues (2001) compared Canadian undergraduates based on high or low identification with masculine and feminine traits. They found no mean gender differences in terms of masculine traits, which indicates that our orientations toward traits that are conventionally viewed as gendered do not always match with our gender expressions or biological sex. There were also no mean gender differences in impostorism scores. However, impostorism differed by participants' masculine traits. Specifically, students who rated themselves highly on masculine traits (e.g., leadership skills, assertiveness, rationality) reported lower impostorism and higher levels of well-being related to autonomy (September et al., 2001).

Further, it is important to consider interactions between gender identity and gender role orientation in terms of impostorism. Similarly, Patzak and colleagues (2017) found that 1st-year Austrian undergraduates who identified with feminine or undifferentiated gender role orientations (both low in masculine traits) reported stronger impostor beliefs than those who identified with masculine or androgynous gender roles (both high in masculine traits). When the authors conducted analyses on the entire sample, masculine gender role orientation predicted lower impostorism and feminine gender role orientation predicted higher impostorism. However, when these models were examined individually by participant gender, masculine traits did not predict impostorism for women and feminine traits did not predict impostorism for men. Patzak and colleagues suggested that including gender role orientation more comprehensively explains differences in impostorism than gender alone. They also demonstrated that self-compassion mediates the relationship between gender role orientation and impostorism, especially for feminine gender role orientation.

These findings suggest that there is something gendered about the process of experiencing impostorism. We should not limit our examinations of this gendered process to gender identity but also consider the role of gendered traits, roles, and conformity. In addition, we should also consider other aspects of our environment that might interact with gender norms and expectations.

CLIMATE GENDERED TRAITS

High-stakes environments that involve frequent evaluation, competition, and regular interactions with comparably capable and intelligent peers can magnify impostor beliefs (Clance, 1985). If those academic, work, or other professional climates also contain gendered elements, the gendered process of impostorism can interact with the pressures of a high-stakes environment. For example, Harvey and colleagues (1981) demonstrated that even without mean differences in impostorism by gender, people who reported their career as less typical for their gender were more likely to report higher impostorism. Similarly, Cokley and colleagues (2015) determined that greater awareness of gender stigma predicted stronger impostorism for both men and women. Further, Rackley (2018) demonstrated that different aspects of college climate predicted students' impostorism based on their gender. For women, gender stigma consciousness predicted higher impostorism and perceiving faculty as approachable predicted lower impostorism, but for men, only attributing their academic successes to reasons within their control related to lower impostorism.

Even gendered perceptions of workplace culture seem to relate to impostorism. Vial and colleagues (2022) found female academics were more likely to report higher impostorism when they perceived their field or workplace to emphasize innate aptitude or "brilliance" as a requirement for success. Additionally, these women were more likely to perceive this unspoken brilliance requirement as part of masculinity contest culture, a masculine-coded ruthless work culture that focuses on competition and dominance. In experiments using industry job postings, women more strongly anticipated they would experience impostorism in a job when postings referenced "natural intelligence" and other brilliance indicators, and they also expected that workplace to have a masculinity contest culture. Additionally, all participants regardless of gender anticipated stronger impostorism when hypothetical acquaintances indicated the workplace had a masculinity contest culture, but women experienced this anticipation more strongly. Vial and colleagues found these relationships did not change when the gender composition of employees favored women, so perceptions of workplace culture were the motivating factor.

Moreover, impostorism in academic and work climates can disproportionately affect women earlier in the school-to-career pipeline. Tao and Gloria (2019) found impostorism negatively related to women's reported persistence to complete their STEM doctoral program. However, self-efficacy in the program and perceptions of support and opportunities for collaboration in their training environment completely mediated this relationship. For these women, more impostor beliefs predicted lower self-efficacy and less supportive training environment perceptions, and those in turn predicted weaker persistence to complete their graduate program. In addition, Tao and Gloria found that the number of women represented in that program related to women's impostorism. Greater representation of women in the program predicted lower levels of impostorism. However, representation also moderated the relationship between impostorism and persistence. When women perceived their program to have at least a moderate representation of other women, the negative relationship between impostorism and persistence became stronger. The researchers interpret this finding to indicate that women experiencing impostorism in male-dominated programs might be able to explain those feelings as caused by lack of representation, whereas women who still experience impostorism in programs with greater female representation might think these feelings indicate something is wrong with them as an individual.

These findings indicate that gendered aspects of our environment can also influence the impact of impostorism, in addition to the role individual gendered traits and mechanisms that differ by gender may play. Other conditions and moderators can also affect the gendered experience of impostorism, such as intersections of gender and race, career field/field of study, and other marginalized identities such as first-generation college student (FGCS) status.

CONDITIONS FOR GENDER DIFFERENCES

Next we discuss moderators to consider when examining the experience of impostor phenomenon, specifically race and ethnicity, first-generation student status, and field of study or career field. Some of these topics are discussed more thoroughly in subsequent chapters (see Chapters 8 and 9 regarding race and ethnicity and Chapter 10 regarding career fields). However, we find it prudent to also briefly reference these topics here to highlight the importance of intersectional approaches to more fully understanding the relationship between gender and impostorism.

Women of Color

Recognizing that Clance and Imes's (1978) original study consisted of primarily White women and their experiences with impostor feelings, researchers have worked to expand the scholarship to understand how different demographic groups experience the phenomenon. Research has also shown that members of ethnic minority groups can be susceptible to these feelings, and researchers have expanded the literature by examining how cultural variables (e.g., minority status stress, ethnic identity, perceived discrimination, school racial composition) are related to the phenomenon (Bernard et al., 2017; Cokley et al., 2018; Peteet et al., 2015). Yet, despite these advances, there is a paucity of research examining the unique experiences of women of color and how women of color experience impostor feelings.

Too often, the public and academia have discussed impostorism as a phenomenon occurring at the individual level. This lens puts the burden on the individual and does not acknowledge the system or environment that the individual works within. Researchers such as Stone and colleagues (2018) have declared a need for development of more culturally informed models to understand how minoritized group members experience impostor feelings.

Research on how women of color experience the impostor phenomenon needs to be conducted using an intersectional lens. A limitation many quantitative studies have encountered while examining impostor feelings from a group differences perspective is that these studies examined either gender differences or racial/ethnic differences only (Bravata et al., 2020). Therefore, experiences of women of color are not properly represented in the quantitative literature on impostorism. Intersectionality views social categories, such as race, ethnicity, gender, and class, as intertwined and interrelated constructs that impact how an individual experiences the world and how the world interacts with the individual (Crenshaw, 1991). This intersectional lens can be applied to what researchers already know regarding how women and ethnically minoritized individuals experience the impostor phenomenon. One of the few intersectional studies related to gender and racial background found that women of color faculty experienced the highest level of impostorism compared with others. Muradoglu and colleagues (2022) found underrepresented minority women academics reported drastically higher impostorism when they perceived that their field emphasized innate brilliance as part of success. Although this did not fully explain the mean gender differences in impostorism, this model illustrated the increased severity of impostorism experienced by Latina and Black women academics.

By applying sophisticated quantitative analysis, Bernard and colleagues (2017) were able to longitudinally examine how frequency of and distress associated with experiences of racial discrimination and gender moderated the relations among impostor feelings and mental health. Only the interactions that combined all the moderators (gender, racial discrimination frequency/racial discrimination distress, and impostor feelings) yielded significant relations to depressive symptoms and interpersonal sensitivity (e.g., feeling misunderstood, inferior, or disliked by others). Black women who experienced high levels of impostor feelings and high frequencies of discrimination reported the highest level of depressive symptoms compared with their counterparts. The study highlighted ways in which gender–racial experiences can increase an individual's susceptibility to impostorism and how having impostor feelings influences the way they navigate their environments.

In regards to women of color and the impostor phenomenon, researchers should continue to look beyond simple group differences and examine the ways in which variables of interest can interact. By employing methodologies such as mediation and moderation analyses, researchers gain insights into how women of color experience impostorism. Researchers should push to have more intersectional studies, especially studies that occur outside of the academic environment and in other contexts, such as corporate or other workplace settings.

First-Generation College Students

Although there are many ways to define FGCSs, most researchers define someone as an FGCS if neither of their parents completed a four-year college degree (Cataldi et al., 2018; Holden et al., 2021). FGCSs make up one of the largest demographics in higher education, with studies estimating 25% to 30% of the enrolled undergraduate population are the first in their families to attend college (Cahalan & Perna, 2015; Cataldi et al., 2018). Studies have shown that FGCSs are more likely to identify as women, have a racially minoritized identity, and come from a low-income background (Center for First-Generation Student Success, 2019; Redford & Hoyer, 2017; Terenzini et al., 1996). As FGCSs are the first in their family to attend college, they might not start with the same level of navigational capital as continuing-generation students. FGCSs are able to successfully amass navigational capital throughout their college careers, but being the first person in a new environment trying to figure out how higher education works could contribute to the experience of impostorism among FGCSs.

There is much work to be done relating to FGCSs experiencing the impostor phenomenon. Current quantitative literature tends to take a group differences approach, though some studies are beginning to examine moderators and mediators that address those differences. Terenzini and colleagues (1996) suggested that FGCSs are more susceptible and experience higher levels of impostorism compared with their continuing-generation peers. In qualitative investigations of impostorism, Chapman (2017) demonstrated the majority of the interviewed nontraditional college students discussed experiencing impostorism and specifically related those feelings to difficulties in assimilating to their new identity as a college student. Further, they reported difficulty establishing a sense of belonging with their institution.

Career Field/Field of Study

The majority of the domain-specific research on women and impostorism has been conducted in fields related to STEM and medicine. Female students in STEM and medicine often report higher impostorism compared with their male counterparts (Alsaleem et al., 2021; Medline et al., 2022; Qureshi et al., 2017; Shill-Russell et al., 2022). This trend is echoed by the results of a narrative review finding that impostor feelings were more common among female doctors than male doctors (Freeman & Peisah, 2022). Additionally, interviews with STEM women indicate that impostor feelings are prevalent among this group (Dinin, 2017; McCullough, 2020) and demonstrate that imbalanced gender ratios in that field and workplace violence including microaggressions, harassment, and unwanted sexual attention based on gender seemed to perpetuate impostorism (Chakraverty & Rishi, 2022). Additional factors promoting feelings of impostorism for STEM college women include feeling as if they do not belong, being stereotyped and invalidated, and engaging in maladaptive coping strategies and demanding work habits (Trefts, 2019). Additionally, male-dominated environments may exacerbate the feeling of not belonging and lack of support. For example, research has found that male math students who have male professors received more career guidance in math compared with their female counterparts (Blondeau & Awad, 2017). Large-scale research is needed to further investigate how these factors contribute to impostorism among women in STEM and medicine and identify avenues of intervention. Many of these issues are reflective of systemic and historical gender bias within these fields.

Research investigating impostorism in relation to field of study also needs to examine the nature of these work environments and structural barriers. Academics' perceptions that success in their field partly relies on brilliance (conceptualized as an innate ability that cannot be learned) moderated gender differences in those academics' impostorism (Muradoglu et al., 2022). Mean differences by gender and career stage indicated women and early-career academics experience more impostorism, but these differences became more substantial when these academics also perceived innate talent to be required for success. This relationship impacted underrepresented minority women academics the hardest. Muradoglu and colleagues (2022) argued that their findings indicate impostorism should not be treated at an individual level but instead addressed at the environmental context level, in this case reframing field narratives of how to succeed. Specifically, they stated that "brilliance-oriented fields have failed to create an environment in which women, particularly those from groups underrepresented in academia, and early-career academics feel capable of succeeding" (Muradoglu et al., 2022, p. 1098).

Scholars in various fields (e.g., business, law) have argued that impostorism among women reflects broader, systemic issues resulting from gender bias ingrained in these fields. González (2020) explained, "If you feel that you don't belong in these hallowed marble halls—because you are not heterosexual, wealthy, cis-gender, white, thin, able-bodied, and/or citizen—it is because you do not, in fact, belong" (p. 236). Tulshyan and Burey (2021) argued that pathologizing impostorism assigns blame to the individual rather than the institution: "Impostor syndrome directs our view toward fixing women at work instead of fixing the places where women work" (p. 3). Salib (2022) further suggested that interventions aimed at reducing impostorism among women should be provided alongside an understanding that the factors contributing to their self-doubt are "external to them and . . . not an inherent flaw within them which impedes their growth" (p. 974).

FUTURE DIRECTIONS

Since Clance and Imes's (1978) initial conceptualization of the impostor phenomenon, we have expanded our understanding of how gender interacts with impostorism through the discussed empirical research. However, we still need more research to better understand the complexity of gender's influence on experiencing impostorism. We must move beyond assumptions of automatic gender differences and instead focus on understanding when and why gender differences occur. We also need to more broadly consider how gender influences impostorism to include gendered traits (beyond gender identity) within individuals and within our academic, work, and other professional climates. Further, we need to approach this future research with an intersectional lens. Next we give our recommendations for where we think this research needs to continue and expand, particularly into additional gendered academic and professional fields with intersectional approaches.

Domain-Specific Gaps

Researchers have begun to investigate impostorism among women within STEM fields—especially medicine—suggesting that specific aspects of STEM and medicine learning environments and social settings may contribute to women's self-doubt. Competitive environments, experiences of gender and sexual harassment, and underrepresentation of women within specific subfields are systemic barriers facing women in STEM and medicine today. These systemic factors warrant further investigation in understanding impostor feelings among women in STEM and medicine. Furthermore, more research is needed regarding impostorism among women in female-dominated and gender-balanced fields. It is unclear whether women experience differing levels of impostorism compared with men in fields such as nursing, education, and social services. Limited evidence suggests that impostorism may not differ between men and women in certain fields, such as dentistry (Khan & Khan, 2021). Similarly, Shill-Russell and colleagues (2022) found that number of female peers was not related to impostorism among women osteopathy students. Together, these findings suggest interactions of gender and domain climate with impostorism may be more complex than gender ratios alone.

Further Intersections

More research is needed to understand how gender interacts with other social identities—such as racial/ethnic identity, social class, sexual orientation, and generation status—to better understand the intersectional nature of impostorism for women. Socioeconomic status likely influences women's experience of impostor phenomenon. One study found that more privileged women reported feeling pressured to take on a *girl boss* mentality, described as "a narrative that overemphasizes individual responses to structural problems, leaning into neoliberal ideas of individual choice, personal responsibility and an emphasis on changing one's mindset in response to inequalities" (Murray et al., 2023, p. 11). Although girl-bossing may benefit some women, lower status women are predicted to experience greater feelings of self-doubt compared with more privileged women, especially in settings where social status is highly salient (e.g., college). Future research should investigate how cultural and social capital relates to impostorism among college women.

Sexual minority women may also experience impostorism because they may challenge traditional assumptions of femininity regarding personality (Lippa, 2005) and appearance (Krakauer & Rose, 2002). Affirming one's identity regarding sexual orientation may spill over and reduce feelings of self-doubt in other areas. More research is needed to also understand impostorism among sexual minority women.

Acculturation may influence feelings of impostorism among immigrant women. It is unclear how cultural stereotypes about academic ability interact with environments to affect impostorism. Attia (2019) suggested that immigrant college women experience *foreigner impostorism*, attributing feelings of impostorism to being from outside of the United States as they simultaneously acculturate and develop their professional identity. Research is needed to investigate the role acculturation plays in the development of impostor feelings among immigrant women.

Work experience gained over time may reduce feelings of self-doubt, and limited evidence suggests that age may influence feelings of impostorism. Medline and colleagues (2022) found that impostorism was lower among older medical students, and Clark and colleagues (2014) identified a similar pattern among research librarians. However, to date no studies have investigated whether these relationships differ for men and women. If job experience reduces women's experience of impostorism, interventions could aid women to advance specific job-related skills that they may have not otherwise developed due to systemic barriers, such as having reduced access to role models and mentors.

CONCLUSION

We need a more intersectional and nuanced understanding of how gender and impostor phenomenon interrelate. Research examining gender and impostorism must move beyond searching for differences in mean impostorism scores by gender. The extant literature shows those mean gender differences are equivocal at best but also that gender is still an integral part of how impostorism functions. Instead, we need to examine the underlying psychological and societal mechanisms through which impostorism operates. The influence of gender is not limited to our biological sex or our gender identity but instead interacts with conventionally gendered traits that individuals may possess, aspects of the environments and domains we work in, additional identities we hold, gendered stereotypes and socialization, and the societal mechanisms that perpetuate the impostor phenomenon. Thus, we should also not limit our examinations of gender and impostorism in the same way.

REFERENCES

Alsaleem, L., Alyousef, N., Alkaff, Z., Alzaid, L., Alotaibi, R., & Shaik, S. A. (2021). Prevalence of self-esteem and imposter syndrome and their associated factors among King Saud University medical students. *Journal of Nature and Science of Medicine*, *4*(3), 226–231.

Attia, M. (2019). *Sojourners in this place: An explanatory sequential mixed-methods study examining foreign-born and immigrant experiences of acculturation and professional identity development in counseling* (Publication No. 201019) [Doctoral dissertation, James Madison University]. JMU Scholarly Commons.

Badawy, R. L., Gazdag, B. A., Bentley, J. R., & Brouer, R. L. (2018). Are all impostors created equal? Exploring gender differences in the impostor phenomenon–performance link. *Personality and Individual Differences*, *131*, 156–163. https://doi.org/10.1016/j.paid.2018.04.044

Beard, A. J., & Bakeman, R. (2001). Boyhood gender nonconformity: Reported parental behavior and the development of narcissistic issues. *Journal of Gay & Lesbian Psychotherapy*, *4*(2), 81–97. https://doi.org/10.1300/J236v04n02_07

Bernard, D. L., Lige, Q. M., Willis, H. A., Sosoo, E. E., & Neblett, E. W. (2017). Impostor phenomenon and mental health: The influence of racial discrimination and gender. *Journal of Counseling Psychology*, *64*(2), 155–166. https://doi.org/10.1037/cou0000197

Blondeau, L. A., & Awad, G. H. (2017). Sex differences in career guidance of undergraduate math students and the relation to help-seeking behaviors. *Journal of Career Development*, *44*(2), 174–187. https://doi.org/10.1177/0894845316642866

Blondeau, L. A., & Awad, G. H. (2018). The relation of the impostor phenomenon to future intentions of mathematics-related school and work. *Journal of Career Development*, *45*(3), 253–267. https://doi.org/10.1177/0894845316680769

Brauer, K., & Wolf, A. (2016). Validation of the German-language Clance Impostor Phenomenon Scale (GCIPS). *Personality and Individual Differences, 102*(1), 153–158. https://doi.org/10.1016/j.paid.2016.06.071

Bravata, D., Madhusudhan, D., Boroff, M., & Cokley, K. (2020). Commentary: Prevalence, predictors, and treatment of imposter syndrome: A systematic review. *Journal of Mental Health & Clinical Psychology, 4*(3), 12–16. https://doi.org/10.29245/2578-2959/2020/3.1207

Cahalan, M., & Perna, L. (2015). *Indicators of higher education equity in the United States: 45 year trend report*. Pell Institute for the Study of Opportunity in Higher Education. https://files.eric.ed.gov/fulltext/ED555865.pdf

Caselman, T. D., Self, P. A., & Self, A. L. (2006). Adolescent attributes contributing to the imposter phenomenon. *Journal of Adolescence, 29*(3), 395–405. https://doi.org/10.1016/j.adolescence.2005.07.003

Castro, D. M., Jones, R. A., & Mirsalimi, H. (2004). Parentification and the impostor phenomenon: An empirical investigation. *The American Journal of Family Therapy, 32*(3), 205–216. https://doi.org/10.1080/01926180490425676

Cataldi, E. F., Bennett, C. T., & Chen, X. (2018). *First-generation students: College access, persistence, and postbachelor's outcomes*. National Center for Education Statistics. https://nces.ed.gov/pubs2018/2018421.pdf

Center for First-Generation Student Success. (2019). *First-generation college students: Demographic characteristics and postsecondary enrollment*. https://firstgen.naspa.org/files/dmfile/FactSheet-01.pdf

Chae, J.-H., Piedmont, R. L., Estadt, B. K., & Wicks, R. J. (1995). Personological evaluation of Clance's Imposter Phenomenon Scale in a Korean sample. *Journal of Personality Assessment, 65*(3), 468–485. https://doi.org/10.1207/s15327752jpa6503_7

Chakraverty, D., & Rishi, M. (2022). Impostor phenomenon and discipline-specific experiences of violence in science, technology, engineering, and mathematics. *Violence and Gender, 9*(1), 22–29. https://doi.org/10.1089/vio.2021.0025

Chapman, A. (2017). Using the assessment process to overcome imposter syndrome in mature students. *Journal of Further and Higher Education, 41*(2), 112–119. https://doi.org/10.1080/0309877X.2015.1062851

Clance, P. R. (1985). *The impostor phenomenon: Overcoming the fear that haunts your success*. Peachtree Publishers.

Clance, P. R., & Imes, S. A. (1978). The imposter phenomenon in high achieving women: Dynamics and therapeutic intervention. *Psychotherapy: Theory, Research, & Practice, 15*(3), 241–247. https://doi.org/10.1037/h0086006

Clance, P. R., & O'Toole, M. A. (1987). The imposter phenomenon: An internal barrier to empowerment and achievement. *Women & Therapy, 6*(3), 51–64. https://doi.org/10.1300/J015V06N03_05

Clark, M., Vardeman, K., & Barba, S. (2014). Perceived inadequacy: A study of the imposter phenomenon among college and research librarians. *College & Research Libraries, 75*(3), 255–271. https://doi.org/10.5860/crl12-423

Cokley, K., Awad, G., Smith, L., Jackson, S., Awosogba, O., Hurst, A., Stone, S., Blondeau, L., & Roberts, D. (2015). The roles of gender stigma consciousness, impostor phenomenon and academic self-concept in the academic outcomes of women and men. *Sex Roles, 73*(9–10), 414–426. https://doi.org/10.1007/s11199-015-0516-7

Cokley, K., McClain, S., Enciso, A., & Martinez, M. (2013). An examination of the impact of minority status stress and impostor feelings on the mental health of diverse ethnic minority college students. *Journal of Multicultural Counseling and Development*, *41*(2), 82–95. https://doi.org/10.1002/j.2161-1912.2013.00029.x

Cokley, K., Stone, S., Krueger, N., Bailey, M., Garba, R., & Hurst, A. (2018). Self-esteem as a mediator of the link between perfectionism and the impostor phenomenon. *Personality and Individual Differences*, *135*(1), 292–297. https://doi.org/10.1016/j.paid.2018.07.032

Cowie, M. E., Nealis, L. J., Sherry, S. B., Hewitt, P. L., & Flett, G. L. (2018). Perfectionism and academic difficulties in graduate students: Testing incremental prediction and gender moderation. *Personality and Individual Differences*, *123*(1), 223–228. https://doi.org/10.1016/j.paid.2017.11.027

Cowman, S. E., & Ferrari, J. R. (2002). "Am I for real?": Predicting impostor tendencies from self-handicapping and affective components. *Social Behavior and Personality*, *30*(2), 119–125. https://doi.org/10.2224/sbp.2002.30.2.119

Crenshaw, K. (1991). Mapping the margins: Intersectionality, identity politics, and violence against women of color. *Stanford Law Review*, *43*(6), 1241–1299. https://doi.org/10.2307/1229039

Cusack, C. E., Hughes, J. L., & Nuhu, N. (2013). Connecting gender and mental health to imposter phenomenon feelings. *Psi Chi Journal of Psychological Research*, *18*(2), 74–81. https://doi.org/10.24839/2164-8204.JN18.2.74

Dinin, A. J. (2017). *An exploration in theory of the storied experiences of women earning engineering Bachelor's degrees at a southern, research, predominantly White institution* (Publication No. 10758859) [Doctoral dissertation, North Carolina State University]. ProQuest Dissertations Publishing.

Domínguez-Soto, C., Labajo, V., & Labrador-Fernández, J. (2023). The relationship between impostor phenomenon and transformational leadership among students in STEM. *Current Psychology*, *42*(13), 11195–11206. https://doi.org/10.1007/s12144-021-02358-3

Fassl, F., Yanagida, T., & Kollmayer, M. (2020). Impostors dare to compare: Associations between the impostor phenomenon, gender typing, and social comparison orientation in university students. *Frontiers in Psychology*, *11*(1), Article 1225. https://doi.org/10.3389/fpsyg.2020.01225

Freeman, J., & Peisah, C. (2022). Imposter syndrome in doctors beyond training: A narrative review. *Australasian Psychiatry*, *30*(1), 49–54. https://doi.org/10.1177/10398562211036121

Fried-Buchalter, S. (1997). Fear of success, fear of failure, and the imposter phenomenon among male and female marketing managers. *Sex Roles*, *37*(11–12), 847–859. https://doi.org/10.1007/BF02936343

González, M. M. (2020). Queer battle fatigue, or how I learned to stop worrying and love the imposter inside me. *GLQ*, *26*(2), 236–238. https://doi.org/10.1215/10642684-8141802

Harvey, J. C., Kidder, L. H., & Sutherland, L. (1981, August). *The impostor phenomenon and achievement: Issues of sex, race, and self-perceived atypicality* [Paper presentation]. Association for the Study of Higher Education, Minneapolis, MN, United States.

Henning, K., Ey, S., & Shaw, D. (1998). Perfectionism, the impostor phenomenon and psychological adjustment in medical, dental, nursing and pharmacy students. *Medical Education, 32*(5), 456–464. https://doi.org/10.1046/j.1365-2923.1998.00234.x

Holden, C. L., Wright, L. E., Herring, A. M., & Sims, P. L. (2021). Imposter syndrome among first- and continuing-generation college students: The roles of perfectionism and stress. *Journal of College Student Retention.* Advance online publication. https://doi.org/10.1177/15210251211019379

Hutchins, H. M., & Rainbolt, H. (2017). What triggers imposter phenomenon among academic faculty? A critical incident study exploring antecedents, coping, and development opportunities. *Human Resource Development International, 20*(3), 194–214. https://doi.org/10.1080/13678868.2016.1248205

Khan, M. K., & Khan, K. R. (2021). Difference in the characteristics of imposter syndrome in dental students of preclinical and clinical phase. *Journal of Shalamar Medical & Dental College, 2*(1), 39–44. https://doi.org/10.53685/jshmdc.v2i1.19

King, J. E., & Cooley, E. L. (1995). Achievement orientation and the impostor phenomenon among college students. *Contemporary Educational Psychology, 20*(3), 304–312. https://doi.org/10.1006/ceps.1995.1019

Krakauer, I. D., & Rose, S. M. (2002). The impact of group membership on lesbians' physical appearance. *Journal of Lesbian Studies, 6*(1), 31–43. https://doi.org/10.1300/J155v06n01_04

Kumar, S., & Jagacinski, C. M. (2006). Imposters have goals too: The imposter phenomenon and its relationship to achievement goal theory. *Personality and Individual Differences, 40*(1), 147–157. https://doi.org/10.1016/j.paid.2005.05.014

Lippa, R. A. (2005). Sexual orientation and personality. *Annual Review of Sex Research, 16*(1), 119–153.

McClain, S., Beasley, S. T., Jones, B., Awosogba, O., Jackson, S., & Cokley, K. (2016). An examination of the impact of racial and ethnic identity, impostor feelings, and minority status stress on the mental health of Black college students. *Journal of Multicultural Counseling and Development, 44*(2), 101–117. https://doi.org/10.1002/jmcd.12040

McCullough, L. (2020). Barriers and assistance for female leaders in academic STEM in the U.S. *Education Sciences, 10*(10), 264–277. https://doi.org/10.3390/educsci10100264

McGregor, L. N., Gee, D. E., & Posey, K. E. (2008). I feel like a fraud and it depresses me: The relation between the imposter phenomenon and depression. *Social Behavior and Personality, 36*(1), 43–48. https://doi.org/10.2224/sbp.2008.36.1.43

Medline, A., Grissom, H., Guissé, N. F., Kravets, V., Hobson, S., Samora, J. B., & Schenker, M. (2022). From self-efficacy to imposter syndrome: The intrapersonal traits of surgeons. *JAAOS: Global Research and Reviews, 6*(4), 1–6. https://doi.org/10.5435/JAAOSGlobal-D-22-00051

Muradoglu, M., Horne, Z., Hammond, M. D., Leslie, S.-J., & Cimpian, A. (2022). Women—particularly underrepresented minority women—and early-career academics feel like impostors in fields that value brilliance. *Journal of Educational Psychology, 114*(5), 1086–1100. https://doi.org/10.1037/edu0000669

Murray, Ó. M., Chiu, Y.-L. T., Wong, B., & Horsburgh, J. (2023). Deindividualising imposter syndrome: Imposter work among marginalised STEMM undergraduates in the U.K. *Sociology, 57*(4), 749–766. https://doi.org/10.1177/00380385221117380

Ogunyemi, D., Lee, T., Ma, M., Osuma, A., Eghbali, M., & Bouri, N. (2022). Improving wellness: Defeating impostor syndrome in medical education using an interactive reflective workshop. *PLOS ONE, 17*(8), Article e0272496. https://doi.org/10.1371/journal.pone.0272496

Oriel, K., Plane, M. B., & Mundt, M. (2004). Family medicine residents and the impostor phenomenon. *Family Medicine, 36*(4), 248–252. https://fammedarchives.blob.core.windows.net/imagesandpdfs/fmhub/fm2004/April/Kathy248.pdf?q=impostor

Park, B., Smith, J. A., & Correll, J. (2008). "Having it all" or "doing it all"? Perceived trait attributes and behavioral obligations as a function of workload, parenthood, and gender. *European Journal of Social Psychology, 38*(7), 1156–1164. https://doi.org/10.1002/ejsp.535

Patzak, A., Kollmayer, M., & Schober, B. (2017). Buffering impostor feelings with kindness: The mediating role of self-compassion between gender-role orientation and the impostor phenomenon. *Frontiers in Psychology, 8*(1), Article 1289. https://doi.org/10.3389/fpsyg.2017.01289

Peteet, B. J., Montgomery, L., & Weekes, J. C. (2015). Predictors of imposter phenomenon among talented ethnic minority undergraduate students. *The Journal of Negro Education, 84*(2), 175–186. https://doi.org/10.7709/jnegroeducation.84.2.0175

Qureshi, M. A., Taj, J., Latif, M. Z., Zia, S., Rafique, M., & Chaudhry, M. A. (2017). Imposter syndrome among Pakistani medical students. *Annals of King Edward Medical University, 23*(2), 106–110. https://doi.org/10.21649/akemu.v23i2.1647

Rackley, K. R. (2018). *Examining the role of impostor phenomenon in the college experience* (Publication No. 28165898) [Doctoral dissertation, The University of Texas at Austin]. ProQuest Dissertations & Theses Global.

Redford, J., & Hoyer, K. M. (2017). *First-generation and continuing-generation college students: A comparison of high school and postsecondary experiences.* National Center for Education Statistics. https://nces.ed.gov/pubs2018/2018009.pdf

Salib, S. (2022). On gender bias and the imposter syndrome. *Journal of General Internal Medicine, 37*(4), 974. https://doi.org/10.1007/s11606-021-07318-y

September, A. N., McCarrey, M., Baranowsky, A., Parent, C., & Schindler, D. (2001). The relation between well-being, impostor feelings, and gender role orientation among Canadian university students. *The Journal of Social Psychology, 141*(2), 218–232. https://doi.org/10.1080/00224540109600548

Shill-Russell, C., Russell, R. C., Daines, B., Clement, G., Carlson, J., Zapata, I., & Henderson, M. (2022). Imposter syndrome relation to gender across osteopathic medical schools. *Medical Science Educator, 32*(1), 157–163. https://doi.org/10.1007/s40670-021-01489-3

Sonnak, C., & Towell, T. (2001). The impostor phenomenon in British university students: Relationships between self-esteem, mental health, parental rearing style and socioeconomic status. *Personality and Individual Differences, 31*(6), 863–874. https://doi.org/10.1016/S0191-8869(00)00184-7

Stone, S., Saucer, C., Bailey, M., Garba, R., Hurst, A., Jackson, S. M., Krueger, N., & Cokley, K. (2018). Learning while Black: A culturally informed model of the impostor phenomenon for Black graduate students. *The Journal of Black Psychology, 44*(6), 491–531. https://doi.org/10.1177/0095798418786648

Tao, K. W., & Gloria, A. M. (2019). Should I stay or should I go? The role of impostorism in STEM persistence. *Psychology of Women Quarterly, 43*(2), 151–164. https://doi.org/10.1177/0361684318802333

Terenzini, P. T., Springer, L., Yaeger, P. M., Pascarella, E. T., & Nora, A. (1996). First-generation college students: Characteristics, experiences, and cognitive development. *Research in Higher Education, 37*(1), 1–22. https://doi.org/10.1007/BF01680039

Topping, M. E., & Kimmel, E. B. (1985). The imposter phenomenon: Feeling phony. *Academic Psychology Bulletin, 7*(2), 213–226.

Trefts, S. (2019). *The imposter phenomenon in female, first-generation STEM majors* (Publication No. 13865876) [Doctoral dissertation, California Lutheran University]. ProQuest Dissertations Publishing.

Tulshyan, R., & Burey, J. A. (2021, February 11). Stop telling women they have imposter syndrome. *Harvard Business Review.* https://hbr.org/2021/02/stop-telling-women-they-have-imposter-syndrome

Vial, A. C., Muradoglu, M., Newman, G. E., & Cimpian, A. (2022). An emphasis on brilliance fosters masculinity-contest cultures. *Psychological Science, 33*(4), 595–612. https://doi.org/10.1177/09567976211044133

8

RACISM AND THE IMPOSTOR PHENOMENON AMONG AFRICAN AMERICAN STUDENTS

A Socioecological Analysis

DONTE BERNARD

Imposter syndrome isn't just an imaginary voice in our heads. We can hear it loud and clear when we receive almost daily messages from society that we truly don't belong.

–Jolie A. Doggett (2019, para. 8)

According to the National Center for Education Statistics (2022), college enrollment rates among African American college students between 2000 and 2018 rose from 31% to 37%, signaling that there has been tremendous growth in the number of African American students pursuing higher education degrees. Despite this encouraging trend, there are significant racial inequities in attainment outcomes, with African American students evidencing the lowest college completion rate (45.9%) relative to White (71.7%), Asian (67.2%), and Hispanic (55%) students (Shapiro et al., 2017). Although the driving factors behind these disparities are complex, scholars have highlighted that the pervasive and harmful effects of racism, defined as a system of beliefs, attitudes, institutional arrangements, and acts that tend to denigrate individuals or groups because of phenotypic characteristics (e.g., skin color) or ethnic group affiliation (Clark et al., 1999), reduce the likelihood of successful matriculation through graduation. Indeed, African American students navigate a litany of

https://doi.org/10.1037/0000397-009
The Impostor Phenomenon: Psychological Research, Theory, and Interventions,
K. Cokley (Editor)
Copyright © 2024 by the American Psychological Association. All rights reserved.

racism-related stressors that may lead students to internalize inaccurate beliefs that their intellectual ability is not on par with the students around them. These negative thinking patterns represent a widely studied construct known as the impostor phenomenon (IP), which represents a notable risk factor for poor psychosocial, academic, and vocational outcomes.

Over the past decade, there has been a surge of work that has highlighted the relevance of IP among African American college students and its association with racism-related experiences within the academy (see Bravata et al., 2020). Cultural frameworks building on this work highlight that IP among African American individuals does not exist in a vacuum but rather emanates as a product of racism and related stressors associated with one's marginalized status (Bernard & Neblett, 2018; Stone et al., 2018). Consistent with this literature, recent work posits that to understand the etiology of IP, one needs to look beyond the individual to consider the role of social structures and contextual influences that ultimately lead individuals to doubt their intellectual ability (Feenstra et al., 2020). Collectively, this literature challenges original conceptualizations of the person-centered origins of IP and underscores the need for more nuanced frameworks that consider how racism operates as a determinant of IP among African American college students. Thus, this chapter interrogates how the multifaceted nature of racism may inform the development and maintenance of IP among African American college students using a socioecological framework.

CONCEPTUALIZING IMPOSTOR PHENOMENON

IP refers to an individual's inability to internalize their own success and the concomitant belief that their self-perceived sense of incompetence and fraudulence will one day be exposed (Clance & Imes, 1978). As stated by Clance (1985), individuals struggling with IP have "extreme anxiety when they think they've made a mistake; they take drastic measures not to err or appear foolish in front of others" (p. 27). IP cognitions persist even in the face of objective success (e.g., high grades) and can lead individuals to discount their abilities by attributing them to external factors (e.g., luck, happenstance) over and above internal faculties. As a result, individuals who experience IP hold themselves to high self-imposed standards (e.g., unrealistic expectations) to counter the negative way they perceive themselves and the unfavorable way in which they believe they are perceived by others (Leary et al., 2000).

Although first coined to capture the sentiments of high-achieving White women, IP has been shown to be nearly ubiquitous, with prevalence estimates suggesting that over 80% of people in the United States will experience IP at some point in their lifetime (Bravata et al., 2020). Despite this prevalence, the period of emerging adulthood, and its overlap with the college transition, represents a particularly fertile time for IP to thrive (Lane, 2015). In the developmental period of early adulthood, individuals grapple with their identity and begin experiencing life in new environments outside of the familial context (Arnett, 2000). Thus, although the transition to and through emerging adulthood and the concomitant collegial experience is marked by exciting periods of identity exploration outside of the purview of family, it also represents perhaps the greatest period of psychological vulnerability and self-doubt as individuals attempt to navigate unfamiliar environments, adjust to new expectations, and engage in self-comparisons (Peer & McAuslan, 2016).

Although the college context may universally increase vulnerability for IP in all students, African American students and others from racially marginalized backgrounds may be particularly vulnerable. Specifically, research posits that African American students may be more susceptible to IP given that they are expected to grapple with their intellectual and personal identity, during an already vulnerable developmental period, within a society that commonly transmits racialized messages of inferiority, while simultaneously navigating the day-to-day challenges of college (e.g., academic stress, social stress; Arnett & Brody, 2008). Although the salience of such stressors may be particularly elevated among students attending predominantly White institutions (PWIs), students at historically Black colleges/universities (HBCUs) are not unaffected. In fact, students attending HBCUs have been found to report racism-related experiences as significant sources of stress (Greer, 2008), which can contribute to IP cognitions.

IMPOSTOR PHENOMENON AMONG AFRICAN AMERICAN STUDENTS

Increasingly, scholarship has documented that the heightened vulnerability for IP among African American young adults may be closely tied to unique, culturally relevant psychosocial factors. For instance, some studies have examined IP in the context of minority status stress defined as "the unique stressors experienced by minority students, which may include experiences with racism and discrimination, insensitive comments, and questions of belonging on a college campus" (McClain et al., 2016, p. 102). Scholarship examining the associations among IP and minority status stress have found that these two constructs are positively associated and that IP can have stronger or at least equivalent impact on the psychological adjustment of African American college students compared to minority status stress (Cokley et al., 2013; McClain et al., 2016). In a similar vein, studies have examined IP in the context of racial discrimination, considered by many to be among the most universal stressors that African American individuals must navigate throughout the lifespan (Pascoe & Smart Richman, 2009). Through multigroup path analyses, Cokley et al. (2017) found that the association between perceived discrimination and IP was stronger among African American and Latin American students in comparison to their Asian American peers. Similarly, Bernard and colleagues (2018) found a positive association between IP and decreased psychological adjustment over an 8-month period when African American young women reported high frequency of racial discrimination (or low levels of distress caused by discrimination).

Outside of race-related stress, scholars have also explored IP in relation to ethnic/racial identity, or the meaning and significance that one places on their race (Sellers et al., 1998). In one of the first empirical studies that sought to elucidate predictors of IP among African American students, Ewing and colleagues (1996) found that academic self-concept and immersion–emersion racial identity attitudes were negative predictors of IP. A more recent study found that higher levels of self-esteem mediated the association between racial identity and IP among African American college students (Lige et al., 2017). Furthermore, within a sample of African American and Hispanic college students, Peteet, Montgomery, and Weekes (2015) found that low ethnic identity and low psychological well-being positively predicted IP. Consistent with this cross-sectional research, longitudinal work has shown that certain profiles or patterns of racial identity significantly increased or decreased the extent to which individuals reported cognitions of IP over time (Bernard et al., 2018).

Other studies have focused on shedding light on IP in relation to psychological mechanisms separate from minority status stress and identity. For example, Austin et al. (2009) found that higher levels of academic survivors' guilt (i.e., feelings of guilt related to high academic achievement) exacerbated IP, such that IP mediated the association between survivors' guilt and depressive symptoms within a sample of African American college students attending an HBCU. Consistent with these findings, higher levels of IP have also been documented to predict lower levels of self-esteem and greater psychological distress among African American college students (Peteet, Brown, et al., 2015). Notably, recent work has also found IP to elevate use of maladaptive coping strategies and subsequent risk for social anxiety among African American students attending PWIs and HBCUs (Bernard et al., 2020). Collectively, this literature underscores that myriad factors unique to the African American experience play a significant role in influencing IP.

UNDERSTANDING THE ORIGINS OF IMPOSTOR PHENOMENON

Despite the increased relevance of IP among African American college students, its origins remain poorly understood. Prominent conceptualizations of the etiology of IP stem in large part from the initial clinical observations of Pauline Clance and Suzanne Imes, who suggested that IP is a consequence of familial messages received in childhood and gender-specific societal expectations (Clance et al., 1995; Clance & Imes, 1978). Although there is some support for this hypothesis (e.g., Cokley et al., 2015; King & Cooley, 1995), it is important to emphasize that work in this area has been conducted primarily within predominantly White samples. Thus, although these studies are certainly informative in unearthing factors that may contribute to IP, they incorrectly assume that such factors generalize to capture the experiences of African American individuals, and therefore overlook critical factors that may inform the development of IP among African American college students.

Emergent developmental models of IP among African American individuals suggest that cognitions of IP come to fruition for qualitatively different reasons compared with those of their White counterparts. Specifically, such models suggest that cognitions of intellectual incompetence are formulated, primarily, by socioracial factors. As an example, in elucidating potential pathways by which IP may develop among African American adolescents, Bernard and Neblett (2018) argued that IP development is closely tied to the pervasive nature of racism. Building on this assertion, Stone and colleagues (2018) noted that racism-related experiences at the individual (e.g., racial discrimination) and institutional (e.g., racial underrepresentation) level have significant psychosocial costs (e.g., feelings of isolation) that undergird self-doubt and perceptions of intellectual incompetence among African American graduate students. Together, this bourgeoning literature supports Clance et al.'s (1995) assertion that more attention is needed to understand how systems of oppression (i.e., racism) may contribute to IP among African American and other historically marginalized groups of undergraduate students.

PROMISE OF A SOCIOECOLOGICAL ANALYSIS

One specific framework that can be particularly useful in evaluating the multi-level impact of racism on the development of IP among African American college students is the socioecological model of health. Initially conceptualized as a violence prevention framework (Dahlberg & Krug, 2006), this model asserts that psychosocial outcomes (e.g., IP) are determined by complex interactions across the societal, community, relational, and individual level. In descending order, *societal*-level factors include educational and social policies, in addition to cultural norms. *Community*-level influences are characteristics associated with one's neighborhood, school, and workplace. *Relational*-level factors include close interpersonal interactions among peers and families. *Individual*-level factors include person-centered characteristics, such as sociodemographics and individualized beliefs and attitudes.

Interrogating the etiology of IP among African American college students through a socioecological perspective yields numerous benefits. First, such an approach moves beyond individual-level analyses of IP and instead frames its development as a product of complex interactions across ecological domains. Importantly, this framing is more in line with initial IP literature, which theorized that IP stems from the interplay between interpersonal and social contexts (Clance et al., 1995). Second, IP literature among African Americans tends to focus on its relationship with interpersonal socioracial experiences (e.g., racial discrimination), with little consideration as to how other forms of racism may shape the development of cognitions of intellectual incompetence. However, previous research has made clear that racism operates in distinct yet interrelated ways across individual, institutional, and cultural levels to exclude, isolate, and marginalize nondominant groups (Jones, 1972) and that macro manifestations of racism are equally if not more important to consider in the context of psychological outcomes (Harrell, 2000). Thus, the use of a socioecological framework facilitates opportunities to explicate how multiple manifestations of racism across micro and macro systems inform how African American students perceive themselves and others in college. Third, a socioecological analysis of IP provides space to acknowledge the inherent heterogeneity among African American college students. That is, African American students are not all affected by racism in the same way and may therefore exhibit differential vulnerability to IP as a function of their unique socioecological attributes.

RACISM AND IMPOSTOR PHENOMENON: A SOCIOECOLOGICAL ANALYSIS

The remainder of this chapter presents a socioecological analysis of racism as a multilevel determinant of IP among African American college students (Figure 8.1). Specifically, what follows is a review and synthesis of previous literature that delineates how racism functions across societal, community, relational, and individual domains to inform the development and maintenance of IP. In efforts to highlight that upstream macrolevel factors represent

FIGURE 8.1. A Socioecological Model of Factors Contributing to Impostor Phenomenon Among African American College Students

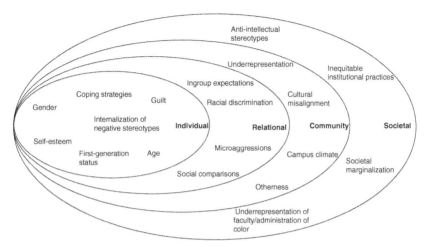

critical contributing factors to phenomena that are typically discussed at the person-centered level, the present analysis begins first at the societal level and progressively works downward to individual domains. Notably, although domains are discussed separately, racism can manifest in innumerable ways that permeate across socioecological domains. Further, it is important to acknowledge that the forthcoming discussion is by no means exhaustive but rather serves to highlight salient examples of how racism manifests across ecological systems to inform IP.

Societal-Level Risk Factors

At its most distal level, racism manifests in the form of structural policies, practices, and ideologies that serve to undermine how African American students see themselves and are perceived by others. Two key ways in which structural racism perpetuates these negative internal and reflected appraisals are gatekeeping of access to higher education and the reinforcement of negative stereotypes regarding the intellectual capacities of African American students.

Inequitable Access to College

Estimates suggest that over the past 20 years, the cost of attending a 4-year college full time has increased by nearly 180% (Hanson, 2023). Despite this substantial increase in cost, African American students are less likely to receive academic- or merit-based financial aid awards from the educational institution that they attend (Kelly & Adam, 2019). Further, African American college students are significantly more likely to receive registration sanctions (i.e., not being able to enroll in future courses or access academic transcripts) for not being able to cover tuition-related charges than any other student subgroup, regardless of financial merit or GPA (Curs et al., 2022). Thus, from the onset of their college journey, African American students must contend with academic institutional practices that transmit clear messages regarding who will be supported to attend college and who will not.

Although the financial burden of college may not obviously relate to IP development, a clear pattern of scholarship details clear links between these two issues. For example, African American college students have been found to report remarkably high levels of guilt for attending college due to the financial strain it may place on their families (Guiffrida, 2005). This guilt may also manifest as students grapple with the fact that their family may be struggling at home while they experience more privileges and opportunities in college (Moreno, 2021). Notably, IP has been theorized to stem, in part, from individuals experiencing successes that are unusual in their family (Clance, 1985), as they may experience guilt about their success while fearing they will let their family down (e.g., fears of failure). In support of this assertion, prior research has found that feelings of guilt among African American college students were predictive of IP and depressive symptoms (Austin et al., 2009).

Anti-Intellectual Stereotypes

Anchored within the historical legacy of antebellum slavery and Jim Crow, negative stereotypes that denigrate the intellectual aptitudes of African American individuals fundamentally shape how students come to perceive themselves both within and outside of the academy (Miller, 1995; Okeke et al., 2009). It is well documented that African American individuals face a wide range of negative stereotypes that deride their intellect, work ethic, morality, and humanity (Dixon & Rosenbaum, 2004). Unfortunately, because of these negative stereotypes, African American students are perceived as more problematic in school and subsequently disciplined (i.e., out-of-school suspensions) at significantly higher rates than their White peers (Skiba et al., 2022)—a trend that persists across all phases of education. In addition, non-Black teachers have been found to hold significantly lower expectations regarding the educational outlooks of African American students and to believe they are considerably less likely to complete a 4-year degree relative to White students (Gershenson et al., 2016).

The pervasive nature of stereotypes in contemporary society plays a significant role in shaping how students come to see their own ability. Concerningly, even when attending institutions with greater racial representation (i.e.,

HBCUs), African American students must contend with deficit-based narratives that question the rigor and quality of the education they receive (Commodore & Njoku, 2020). Research is replete with evidence documenting how the mere awareness of negative racialized stereotypes can compromise academic performance (i.e., stereotype threat) and perceptions of self-concept (Okeke et al., 2009). Accordingly, scholars have theorized that stereotype awareness may be a salient contributor to IP among African American students and others from historically marginalized backgrounds (Cokley et al., 2017).

Community-Level Risk Factors

As a community-level risk factor, racism serves to fundamentally alter the environmental characteristics of institutions of higher education in ways that can invalidate the experiences, strengths, and intellect of African American students. Discussed next are specific examples that outline how racism can confer risk for IP, particularly by creating campus community environments that make students feel unwelcomed, alienated, and marginalized.

Campus Underrepresentation

Scholars have extensively documented the challenges that African American students navigate within the college setting, particularly at PWIs. Among the most prominent challenges is the underrepresentation of same-race peers, faculty, and administration. The lack of representation on a college campus has been associated with more negative perceptions of campus climate, feeling less supported, and lower levels of belongingness among African American students (Rankin & Reason, 2005). The lack of representation within PWIs can also reinforce the salience of negative stereotypes regarding the intellectual capacity of African American students and reify the notion that "White students are seen as the norm and African American students [are seen] as the other in academia" (Peteet, Montgomery, & Weekes, 2015, pp. 157–158). Consequently, PWI attendance can engender feelings of otherness among African American students (Lige et al., 2017), which may help explain why they feel compelled to prove that they belong on campus by working harder than those around them (Solórzano et al., 2000). Thus, although African American students report comparable levels of academic competence relative to non-African American students (Leath & Chavous, 2018) and take steps to actively resist negative stereotypes (Fries-Britt & Griffin, 2007), they do so against a backdrop of more hostile racial climates, which may promote negative behavioral patterns (e.g., excessive hard work) and external attributions of success (e.g., I was only accepted into college because of my race) that characterize IP.

190 • *Donte Bernard*

Cultural Misalignment

According to Sue and Sue (2003), the cultural heritage of the dominant social group (i.e., White people) permeates mainstream social institutions, programs, and policies. Thus, it follows that the culture of college institutions in the United States reflects Eurocentric and Western worldviews that emphasize autonomy, individualistic motives (e.g., self-promotion), and competition (Tyler et al., 2008). However, these values are in direct opposition to Afrocentric cultural values such as communalism and harmony, in addition to culturally normative expressions of learning and communication (e.g., verve) that are salient within the African American community (Boykin, 1983; Parsons, 2008). As explained by Douglas et al. (2008), these cultural assets may be perceived as deficits within a "hegemonic, Western, epistemological framework" (p. 49) and can lead instructors to have lower academic expectations of African American college students. Even when African American students meet or surpass objective markers of success, their achievements are still often questioned by others and attributed to factors that negate their intellectual ability (McGee et al., 2022). Ultimately, the immersion into culturally invalidating academic institutions can be a culture shock for some African American students (Torres, 2009) and creates a prime context for students to internalize negative thoughts regarding their worth, intellect, and culture.

Relational-Level Risk Factors

Among African American students, the insidious nature of racism can also critically hinder positive interpersonal interactions with ingroup and outgroup members in ways that challenge appraisals of belonging, self-worth, and intellectual competence.

Racial Discrimination

According to a 2016 Pew Research study, over 80% of African Americans who have attended college report experiences of racial discrimination (Anderson, 2019), defined as personal and degrading actions perpetrated by members of a dominant racial group toward nondominant racial groups (Williams et al., 2003). Thus, it makes sense that experiences of racial discrimination are among the most frequently cited sources of stress among African American students in college, regardless of the racial composition of their institution (Greer, 2008; Pieterse et al., 2010). Although there is significant heterogeneity in individual perceptions of and responses to racial discrimination encounters, the adverse and cognitively taxing nature of these experiences is associated with a host of negative mental health (e.g., depression, anxiety, low self-esteem) and academic outcomes (e.g., low academic self-efficacy and academic motivation) that can persist as students matriculate through college (Benner et al., 2018). Chronic encounters of racial discrimination can profoundly affect self-perceptions of ability and have been directly related to the internalization of negative stereotypical beliefs about the intellect and ability of African Americans (D. James, 2022). In light of this work, prior research has postulated that experiences of racial discrimination can give rise to or reinforce feelings of self-doubt, feelings of otherness, beliefs of intellectual phoniness, and external attributions of success (Bernard et al., 2018), as well as the subsequent need to disprove negative societal stereotypes (McGee & Martin, 2011). In support of this notion, various manifestations of racial discrimination, including microaggressions (i.e., subtle expressions of race-based mistreatment), have been found to be among the most salient predictors of IP among students of color (Chakraverty, 2022; Cokley et al., 2017).

Ingroup Expectations

In addition to outgroup expectations and pressures, African American students are burdened with numerous ingroup challenges that can contribute to the development of IP. For example, work among graduate students of color has found that familial or community expectations of high achievement may create undue stress to not paint their community (which has been historically underrepresented in college) in a negative light (Craddock et al., 2011), thus fueling fears of negative evaluation and failure. Although positive ingroup expectations of high academic performance can certainly promote positive outcomes, the idealization or romanticization of students excelling within their academic studies may lead students to feel pressured to perform exceptionally well relative to those around them (Stone et al., 2018). Furthermore, exceeding in the academy can also be perceived by other ingroup members as conforming to Eurocentric norms, which may lead to cultural invalidations of "acting White" (Durkee et al., 2019). Concerningly, cultural invalidations from ingroup members can confer greater risk for negative psychosocial outcomes such as anxiety and depression compared with outgroup slights (Durkee & Gómez, 2022). One could imagine that such accusations of cultural inauthenticity could lead students to become particularly attuned to how they are perceived by both other ingroup and outgroup members. To this end, work has found that individuals high in IP are more likely to endorse interpersonal self-presentational behaviors, such as self-handicapping and self-deprecation, as a means to influence how they are perceived by others in evaluative contexts (Leary et al., 2000; McElwee & Yurak, 2010).

192 • *Donte Bernard*

Individual-Level Risk Factors

At the individual level, racism can inherently impede African American students' abilities to fend off the internalization of IP cognitions. Indeed, whether by limiting individual resources or by promoting the use of maladaptive coping strategies, racism represents a profound individual-level risk factor for IP.

First-Generation Status

Although risk for IP is universally elevated among students in college, risk is particularly high for those who are the first in their family to attend college (i.e., first-generation college students). First-generation students disproportionately stem from historically marginalized racial and ethnic backgrounds and from low-income communities (Redford & Mulvaney Hoyer, 2017). Relative to their continuing-generation peers, first-generation students generally report "limited anticipatory socialization related to college-going and within-college experiences" (Bettencourt et al., 2020, p. 755). As a result, first-generation students tend to report feeling less academically prepared and endorse more challenges adjusting to college culture and expectations in comparison to their continuing-generation peers (Engle et al., 2006). Further, first-generation college students have been found to report lower levels of belongingness and greater psychological adjustment concerns relative to non–first-generation students (Stebleton et al., 2014). Such concerns directly affect how first-generation students perceive themselves and their environment. For instance, recent work found that perceptions of classroom competition were more pronounced among first-generation students and were subsequently related to greater daily impostor endorsements relative to continuing-generation college students (Canning et al., 2020). Taken together, first-generation status and stressors associated with this status can uniquely inform IP development and also serve to amplify the community, relational, and structural racism-related stressors that contribute to IP.

Coping Strategies

It has been well-established that there are specific coping strategies that college students employ to combat daily hassles that may inadvertently contribute to IP. For instance, perfectionistic behaviors and thinking patterns are used to combat thoughts of intellectual incompetence (Pannhausen et al., 2022). Yet perfectionism is also highly correlated with extremely high standards of performance and hypercritical self-assessments (Flett et al., 2016), which can turn maladaptive. Indeed, maladaptive perfectionism can be characterized by unrealistic standards, self-criticism, and a heightened concern that mistakes will lead to negative perceptions from others (Frost et al., 1990). Thus, it makes sense that perfectionism is strongly associated with IP among college students (Cokley et al., 2018). Scholars have speculated that perfectionism among African American college students may stem from awareness of and motivations to disprove negative societal stereotypes (Elion et al., 2012). In this vein, high-effort coping strategies such as John Henryism (S. A. James et al., 1983), a culturally salient form of coping typified by excessive bouts of hard work to overcome general and racism-related stress, represent critical determinants of IP among African American college students (Bernard & Neblett, 2018). Although high-effort coping strategies such as John Henryism may bolster self-esteem (Stevens-Watkins et al., 2014) and perceptions of control (Hudson et al., 2016), many of the stressors that African American adolescents navigate are outside of their control (e.g., racial discrimination), which may render high-effort coping strategies such as John Henryism ineffective or even harmful (Neighbors et al., 2007). To this end, IP has been found to be positively associated with social anxiety, but only among students attending PWIs who reported higher levels of John Henryism (Bernard et al., 2020).

IMPLICATIONS

In the most basic sense, literature suggests that IP reflects a specific pattern of maladaptive thoughts that emerge in response to an internalized fear of negative evaluation. However, as discussed throughout this chapter, distilling IP down to a simple set of maladaptive cognitions represents an oversimplification of a construct that is closely tied to the prevalence of racism that permeates Western society and academic institutions. Accordingly, it is important to note that simply identifying as African American does not in itself increase risk for IP; rather, IP is linked with the socioecological risk factors that disproportionately burden African Americans. Thus, despite the popularity of person-centered conceptualizations of IP, this present work strongly aligns with the work of Feenstra and colleagues (2020), who underscored the need for future research to "examine contextual variables at the societal, institutional, and interpersonal levels, which may shape an individual's impostor feelings" (p. 4).

Relatedly, as researchers continue to unveil novel determinants and correlates of IP among African American and other communities of color, there is an increasingly compelling case for the need to reconceptualize how IP is measured and discussed in the literature. Indeed, despite the relevance of IP among historically marginalized communities, extant conceptualizations largely minimize or entirely overlook individual- and contextual-level culturally relevant factors that robustly predict IP, including issues of racism, underrepresentation, and alienation (Bernard et al., 2018; Cokley et al., 2013; Stone et al., 2018). Accordingly, our understanding of IP and its consequences among African Americans and other minoritized groups is insufficient. To this end, more work is needed to conceptually and empirically unpack how and why IP is pervasive and psychologically injurious among marginalized communities. To be sure, scholars have previously developed culturally informed frameworks to explicitly acknowledge the significance of race and racism as critical drivers of IP (Bernard & Neblett, 2018; Stone et al., 2018). Yet few studies have built from and upon these models to propose culturally relevant theoretical IP paradigms or measurement approaches that capture the unique ways in which IP may manifest.

Thus, to advance our understanding of IP among African American and other racially and ethnically marginalized communities, future scholarship has several priorities. First, drawing upon the work of DeCuir-Gunby and Schutz (2014), scholarship that formally reimagines or reconceptualizes how IP is operationalized in ways that more accurately align with historically marginalized communities is critically needed. Attempting to generalize a Eurocentrically derived construct to capture a phenomenon that has been shown to be qualitatively different among marginalized communities represents an antiquated practice that contributes to incomplete or substandard understandings of IP across different racial and ethnic groups. Second, issues related to racism, inequity, and marginalization are surprisingly largely absent from extant IP measures. In fact, in review of the five extant measures of IP developed to date (see Mak et al., 2019), only one scale by Walker and Saklofske (2023) included racism-related items. Even these are limited to only two questions related to affirmative action. Given this notable oversight, there is an immediate need for culturally derived measures that assess IP in ways that resonate with the unique experiences of African American and other students of color. Third, relatively little work has been done to map longitudinal pathways by which individual- and contextual-level factors shape IP, thus limiting the development of effective interventions to repudiate cognitions of intellectual incompetence. More work is needed to determine modifiable micro- and macrolevel mechanisms that can resist IP as students navigate through college.

CONCLUSION

In summary, IP represents a significant psychosocial concern among African American college students, regardless of the racial composition of the institution they attend. As presented within the present socioecological analysis, IP does not exist in a vacuum but rather represents a salient cognitive response to complex multilevel manifestations of racism that uniquely and collectively burden African American students (McGee et al., 2022). Thus, to reduce IP cognitions among African American students, it is equally if not of greater importance to focus on upstream macrolevel determinants of IP compared with downstream person-centered mechanisms that undergird IP.

REFERENCES

Anderson, M. (2019, May 2). *For Black Americans, experiences of racial discrimination vary by education level, gender*. Pew Research Center. https://www.pewresearch.org/fact-tank/2019/05/02/for-black-americans-experiences-of-racial-discrimination-vary-by-education-level-gender/

Arnett, J. J. (2000). Emerging adulthood: A theory of development from the late teens through the twenties. *American Psychologist, 55*(5), 469–480. https://doi.org/10.1037/0003-066X.55.5.469

Arnett, J. J., & Brody, G. H. (2008). A fraught passage: The identity challenges of African American emerging adults. *Human Development, 51*(5–6), 291–293. https://doi.org/10.1159/000170891

Austin, C. C., Clark, E. M., Ross, M. J., & Taylor, M. J. (2009). Impostorism as a mediator between survivor guilt and depression in a sample of African American college students. *College Student Journal, 43*(4, Pt. A), 1094–1109.

Benner, A. D., Wang, Y., Shen, Y., Boyle, A. E., Polk, R., & Cheng, Y.-P. (2018). Racial/ethnic discrimination and well-being during adolescence: A meta-analytic review. *American Psychologist, 73*(7), 855–883. https://doi.org/10.1037/amp0000204

Bernard, D. L., Hoggard, L. S., & Neblett, E. W. (2018). Racial discrimination, racial identity, and impostor phenomenon: A profile approach. *Cultural Diversity and Ethnic Minority Psychology, 24*(1), 51–61. https://doi.org/10.1037/cdp0000161

Bernard, D. L., Jones, S. C. T., & Volpe, V. V. (2020). Impostor phenomenon and psychological well-being: The moderating roles of John Henryism and school racial composition among Black college students. *The Journal of Black Psychology, 46*(2–3), 195–227. https://doi.org/10.1177/0095798420924529

Bernard, D., & Neblett, E. (2018). A culturally informed model of the development of the impostor phenomenon among African American youth. *Adolescent Research Review, 3*(3), 279–300. https://doi.org/10.1007/s40894-017-0073-0

Bettencourt, G. M., Manly, C. A., Kimball, E., & Wells, R. S. (2020). STEM degree completion and first-generation college students: A cumulative disadvantage approach to the outcomes gap. *The Review of Higher Education, 43*(3), 753–779. https://doi.org/10.1353/rhe.2020.0006

Boykin, A. W. (1983). The academic performance of Afro-American children. In J. Spence (Ed.), *Achievement and achievement motives* (pp. 321–371). Freeman.

Bravata, D. M., Watts, S. A., Keefer, A. L., Madhusudhan, D. K., Taylor, K. T., Clark, D. M., Nelson, R. S., Cokley, K. O., & Hagg, H. K. (2020). Prevalence, predictors, and treatment of impostor syndrome: A systematic review. *Journal of General Internal Medicine, 35*(4), 1252–1275. https://doi.org/10.1007/s11606-019-05364-1

Canning, E. A., LaCosse, J., Kroeper, K. M., & Murphy, M. C. (2020). Feeling like an imposter: The effect of perceived classroom competition on the daily psychological experiences of first-generation college students. *Social Psychological and Personality Science, 11*(5), 647–657. https://doi.org/10.1177/1948550619882032

Chakraverty, D. (2022). Impostor phenomenon and identity-based microaggression among Hispanic/Latinx individuals in science, technology, engineering, and mathematics: A qualitative exploration. *Violence and Gender, 9*(3), 135–141. https://doi.org/10.1089/vio.2021.0061

Clance, P. R. (1985). *The impostor phenomenon: When success makes you feel like a fake.* Bantam Books.

Clance, P. R., Dingman, D., Reviere, S. L., & Stober, D. R. (1995). Impostor phenomenon in an interpersonal/social context. *Women & Therapy, 16*(4), 79–96. https://doi.org/10.1300/J015v16n04_07

Clance, P. R., & Imes, S. A. (1978). The imposter phenomenon in high achieving women: Dynamics and therapeutic intervention. *Psychotherapy: Theory, Research, & Practice, 15*(3), 241–247. https://doi.org/10.1037/h0086006

Clark, R., Anderson, N. B., Clark, V. R., & Williams, D. R. (1999). Racism as a stressor for African Americans: A biopsychosocial model. *American Psychologist, 54*(10), 805–816. https://doi.org/10.1037/0003-066X.54.10.805

Cokley, K., Awad, G., Smith, L., Jackson, S., Awosogba, O., Hurst, A., Stone, S., Blondeau, L., & Roberts, D. (2015). The roles of gender stigma consciousness, impostor phenomenon and academic self-concept in the academic outcomes of women and men. *Sex Roles, 73*(9–10), 414–426. https://doi.org/10.1007/s11199-015-0516-7

Cokley, K., McClain, S., Enciso, A., & Martinez, M. (2013). An examination of the impact of minority status stress and impostor feelings on the mental health of diverse ethnic minority college students. *Journal of Multicultural Counseling and Development, 41*(2), 82–95. https://doi.org/10.1002/j.2161-1912.2013.00029.x

Cokley, K., Smith, L., Bernard, D., Hurst, A., Jackson, S., Stone, S., Awosogba, O., Saucer, C., Bailey, M., & Roberts, D. (2017). Impostor feelings as a moderator and mediator of the relationship between perceived discrimination and mental health among racial/ethnic minority college students. *Journal of Counseling Psychology, 64*(2), 141–154. https://doi.org/10.1037/cou0000198

Cokley, K., Stone, S., Krueger, N., Bailey, M., Garba, R., & Hurst, A. (2018). Self-esteem as a mediator of the link between perfectionism and the impostor phenomenon. *Personality and Individual Differences, 135*, 292–297. https://doi.org/10.1016/j.paid.2018.07.032

Commodore, F., & Njoku, N. R. (2020). Outpacing expectations: Battling the misconceptions of regional public historically Black colleges and universities. *New Directions for Higher Education, 2020*(190), 99–117. https://doi.org/10.1002/he.20370

Craddock, S., Birnbaum, M., Rodriguez, K., Cobb, C., & Zeeh, S. (2011). Doctoral students and the impostor phenomenon: Am I smart enough to be here? *Journal of Student Affairs Research and Practice, 48*(4), 429–442. https://doi.org/10.2202/1949-6605.6321

Curs, B. R., Harper, C. E., & Kumbal, J. (2022). Institutional inequities in the prevalence of registration sanctions at a flagship public university. *Journal of Diversity in Higher Education*. Advance online publication. https://doi.org/10.1037/dhe0000432

Dahlberg, L. L., & Krug, E. G. (2006). Violence: A global public health problem. *Ciência & Saúde Coletiva, 11*(Suppl.), 1163–1178. https://doi.org/10.1590/S1413-81232006000500007

DeCuir-Gunby, J. T., & Schutz, P. A. (2014). Researching race within educational psychology contexts. *Educational Psychologist, 49*(4), 244–260. https://doi.org/10.1080/00461520.2014.957828

Dixon, J. C., & Rosenbaum, M. S. (2004). Nice to know you? Testing contact, cultural, and group threat theories of anti-Black and anti-Hispanic stereotypes. *Social Science Quarterly, 85*(2), 257–280. https://doi.org/10.1111/j.0038-4941.2004.08502003.x

Doggett, J. A. (2019, October 10). *Imposter syndrome hits harder when you're Black.* Huffpost. https://www.huffpost.com/entry/imposter-syndrome-racism-discrimination_l_5d9f2c00e4b06ddfc514ec5c

Douglas, B., Lewis, C. W., Douglas, A., Scott, M. E., & Garrison-Wade, D. (2008). The impact of White teachers on the academic achievement of Black students: An exploratory qualitative analysis. *Educational Foundations, 22*, 47–62. https://files.eric.ed.gov/fulltext/EJ839497.pdf

Durkee, M. I., Gazley, E. R., Hope, E. C., & Keels, M. (2019). Cultural invalidations: Deconstructing the "acting White" phenomenon among Black and Latinx college students. *Cultural Diversity and Ethnic Minority Psychology, 25*(4), 451–460. https://doi.org/10.1037/cdp0000288

Durkee, M. I., & Gómez, J. M. (2022). Mental health implications of the acting White accusation: The role of cultural betrayal and ethnic-racial identity among Black and Latina/o emerging adults. *American Journal of Orthopsychiatry, 92*(1), 68–78. https://doi.org/10.1037/ort0000589

Elion, A. A., Wang, K. T., Slaney, R. B., & French, B. H. (2012). Perfectionism in African American students: Relationship to racial identity, GPA, self-esteem, and depression. *Cultural Diversity and Ethnic Minority Psychology, 18*(2), 118–127. https://doi.org/10.1037/a0026491

Engle, J., Bermeo, A., & O'Brien, C. (2006). *Straight from the source: What works for first-generation college students.* Pell Institute for the Study of Opportunity in Higher Education. https://eric.ed.gov/?id=ED501693

Ewing, K. M., Richardson, T. Q., James-Myers, L., & Russell, R. K. (1996). The relationship between racial identity attitudes, worldview, and African American graduate students' experience of the imposter phenomenon. *The Journal of Black Psychology, 22*(1), 53–66. https://doi.org/10.1177/00957984960221005

Feenstra, S., Begeny, C. T., Ryan, M. K., Rink, F. A., Stoker, J. I., & Jordan, J. (2020). Contextualizing the impostor "syndrome." *Frontiers in Psychology, 11*, Article 575024. https://doi.org/10.3389/fpsyg.2020.575024

Flett, G. L., Nepon, T., & Hewitt, P. L. (2016). Perfectionism, worry, and rumination in health and mental health: A review and a conceptual framework for a cognitive theory of perfectionism. In F. M. Sirois & D. S. Molnar (Eds.), *Perfectionism, health, and well-being* (pp. 121–155). Springer International Publishing. https://doi.org/10.1007/978-3-319-18582-8_6

Fries-Britt, S., & Griffin, K. (2007). The black box: How high-achieving Blacks resist stereotypes about Black Americans. *Journal of College Student Development, 48*(5), 509–524. https://doi.org/10.1353/csd.2007.0048

Frost, R. O., Marten, P., Lahart, C., & Rosenblate, R. (1990). The dimensions of perfectionism. *Cognitive Therapy and Research, 14*(5), 449–468. https://doi.org/10.1007/BF01172967

Gershenson, S., Holt, S. B., & Papageorge, N. W. (2016). Who believes in me? The effect of student–teacher demographic match on teacher expectations. *Economics of Education Review, 52*, 209–224. https://doi.org/10.1016/j.econedurev.2016.03.002

Greer, T. M. (2008). Racial and ethnic-related stressors as predictors of perceived stress and academic performance for African American students at a historically Black college and university. *The Journal of Negro Education, 77*(1), 60–71. https://www.jstor.org/stable/40034678

Guiffrida, D. (2005). To break away or strengthen ties to home: A complex issue for African American college students attending a predominantly White institution. *Equity & Excellence in Education, 38*(1), 49–60. https://doi.org/10.1080/10665680590907864

Hanson, M. (2023, June 25). *Average cost of college & tuition*. Education Data Initiative. https://educationdata.org/average-cost-of-college

Harrell, S. P. (2000). A multidimensional conceptualization of racism-related stress: Implications for the well-being of people of color. *American Journal of Orthopsychiatry, 70*(1), 42–57. https://doi.org/10.1037/h0087722

Hudson, D. L., Neighbors, H. W., Geronimus, A. T., & Jackson, J. S. (2016). Racial discrimination, John Henryism, and depression among African Americans. *The Journal of Black Psychology, 42*(3), 221–243. https://doi.org/10.1177/0095798414567757

James, D. (2022). An initial framework for the study of internalized racism and health: Internalized racism as a racism-induced identity threat response. *Social and Personality Psychology Compass, 16*(11), Article e12712. https://doi.org/10.1111/spc3.12712

James, S. A., Hartnett, S. A., & Kalsbeek, W. D. (1983). John Henryism and blood pressure differences among Black men. *Journal of Behavioral Medicine, 6*(3), 259–278. https://doi.org/10.1007/BF01315113

Jones, J. M. (1972). *Prejudice and racism*. Addison-Wesley.

Kelly, E., & Adam, T. (2019). *Trends in undergraduate nonfederal grant and scholarship aid by demographic and enrollment characteristics: Selected years, 2003–04 to 2015–16* [Web tables, NCES 2019-486]. National Center for Education Statistics. https://eric.ed.gov/?id=ED597396

King, J. E., & Cooley, E. L. (1995). Achievement orientation and the impostor phenomenon among college students. *Contemporary Educational Psychology, 20*(3), 304–312. https://doi.org/10.1006/ceps.1995.1019

Lane, J. A. (2015). The imposter phenomenon among emerging adults transitioning into professional life: Developing a grounded theory. *Adultspan Journal, 14*(2), 114–128. https://doi.org/10.1002/adsp.12009

Leary, M. R., Patton, K. M., Orlando, A. E., & Wagoner Funk, W. (2000). The impostor phenomenon: Self-perceptions, reflected appraisals, and interpersonal strategies. *Journal of Personality, 68*(4), 725–756. https://doi.org/10.1111/1467-6494.00114

Leath, S., & Chavous, T. (2018). Black women's experiences of campus racial climate and stigma at predominantly White institutions: Insights from a comparative and within-group approach for STEM and non-STEM majors. *The Journal of Negro Education, 87*(2), 125–139. https://doi.org/10.7709/jnegroeducation.87.2.0125

Lige, Q. M., Peteet, B. J., & Brown, C. M. (2017). Racial identity, self-esteem, and the impostor phenomenon among African American college students. *The Journal of Black Psychology, 43*(4), 345–357. https://doi.org/10.1177/0095798416648787

Mak, K. K., Kleitman, S., & Abbott, M. J. (2019). Impostor phenomenon measurement scales: A systematic review. *Frontiers in Psychology, 10*, Article 671. https://doi.org/10.3389/fpsyg.2019.00671

McClain, S., Beasley, S. T., Jones, B., Awosogba, O., Jackson, S., & Cokley, K. (2016). An examination of the impact of racial and ethnic identity, impostor feelings, and minority status stress on the mental health of Black college students. *Journal of Multicultural Counseling and Development, 44*(2), 101–117. https://doi.org/10.1002/jmcd.12040

McElwee, R. O., & Yurak, T. J. (2010). The phenomenology of the impostor phenomenon. *Individual Differences Research, 8*(3), 184–197.

McGee, E. O., Botchway, P. K., Naphan-Kingery, D. E., Brockman, A. J., Houston, S., & White, D. T. (2022). Racism camouflaged as impostorism and the impact on Black STEM doctoral students. *Race, Ethnicity and Education, 25*(4), 487–507. https://doi.org/10.1080/13613324.2021.1924137

McGee, E. O., & Martin, D. B. (2011). "You would not believe what I have to go through to prove my intellectual value!": Stereotype management among academically successful Black mathematics and engineering students. *American Educational Research Journal, 48*(6), 1347–1389. https://doi.org/10.3102/0002831211423972

Miller, L. S. (1995). The origins of the presumption of Black stupidity. *The Journal of Blacks in Higher Education, 9*, 78–82. https://doi.org/10.2307/2962640

Moreno, R. (2021). The guilt of success: Looking at Latino first-generation college students' experience of leaving home. *Journal of Hispanic Higher Education, 20*(2), 213–231. https://doi.org/10.1177/1538192719849756

National Center for Education Statistics. (2022). College enrollment rates. In *The condition of education 2020* (pp. 1–3). https://nces.ed.gov/programs/coe/pdf/coe_cpb.pdf

Neighbors, H. W., Njai, R., & Jackson, J. S. (2007). Race, ethnicity, John Henryism, and depressive symptoms: The national survey of American life adult reinterview. *Research in Human Development, 4*(1–2), 71–87. https://doi.org/10.1080/15427600701481004

Okeke, N. A., Howard, L. C., Kurtz-Costes, B., & Rowley, S. J. (2009). Academic race stereotypes, academic self-concept, and racial centrality in African American youth. *The Journal of Black Psychology, 35*(3), 366–387. https://doi.org/10.1177/0095798409333615

Pannhausen, S., Klug, K., & Rohrmann, S. (2022). Never good enough: The relation between the impostor phenomenon and multidimensional perfectionism. *Current Psychology, 41*, 888–901. https://doi.org/10.1007/s12144-020-00613-7

Parsons, E. R. C. (2008). Positionality of African Americans and a theoretical accommodation of it: Rethinking science education research. *Science Education, 92*(6), 1127–1144. https://doi.org/10.1002/sce.20273

Pascoe, E. A., & Smart Richman, L. (2009). Perceived discrimination and health: A meta-analytic review. *Psychological Bulletin, 135*(4), 531–554. https://doi.org/10.1037/a0016059

Peer, J. W., & McAuslan, P. (2016). Self-doubt during emerging adulthood: The conditional mediating influence of mindfulness. *Emerging Adulthood, 4*(3), 176–185. https://doi.org/10.1177/2167696815579828

Peteet, B. J., Brown, C. M., Lige, Q. M., & Lanaway, D. A. (2015). Impostorism is associated with greater psychological distress and lower self-esteem for African American students. *Current Psychology, 34*(1), 154–163. https://doi.org/10.1007/s12144-014-9248-z

Peteet, B. J., Montgomery, L., & Weekes, J. C. (2015). Predictors of imposter phenomenon among talented ethnic minority undergraduate students. *The Journal of Negro Education, 84*(2), 175–186. https://doi.org/10.7709/jnegroeducation.84.2.0175

Pieterse, A. L., Carter, R. T., Evans, S. A., & Walter, R. A. (2010). An exploratory examination of the associations among racial and ethnic discrimination, racial climate, and trauma-related symptoms in a college student population. *Journal of Counseling Psychology, 57*(3), 255–263. https://doi.org/10.1037/a0020040

Rankin, S. R., & Reason, R. D. (2005). Differing perceptions: How students of color and White students perceive campus climate for underrepresented groups. *Journal of College Student Development, 46*(1), 43–61. https://doi.org/10.1353/csd.2005.0008

Redford, J., & Mulvaney Hoyer, K. (2017). *First generation and continuing-generation college students: A comparison of high school and postsecondary experiences*. U.S. Department of Education. https://vtechworks.lib.vt.edu/handle/10919/83686

Sellers, R. M., Smith, M. A., Shelton, J. N., Rowley, S. A. J., & Chavous, T. M. (1998). Multidimensional model of racial identity: A reconceptualization of African American racial identity. *Personality and Social Psychology Review, 2*(1), 18–39. https://doi.org/10.1207/s15327957pspr0201_2

Shapiro, D., Dundar, A., Huie, F., Wakhungu, P. K., Yuan, X., Nathan, A., & Hwang, Y. (2017). *Completing college: A national view of student attainment rates by race and ethnicity—Fall 2010 cohort (Signature 12 supplement)*. National Student Clearinghouse Research Center. https://vtechworks.lib.vt.edu/handle/10919/89186

Skiba, R. J., Fergus, E., & Gregory, A. (2022). The new Jim Crow in school: Exclusionary discipline and structural racism. In E. J. Sabornie & D. L. Espelage (Eds.), *Handbook of classroom management* (3rd ed., pp. 211–230). Routledge.

Solórzano, D., Ceja, M., & Yosso, T. (2000). Critical race theory, racial microaggressions, and campus racial climate: The experiences of African American college students. *The Journal of Negro Education, 69*(1/2), 60–73. https://www.jstor.org/stable/2696265

Stebleton, M. J., Soria, K. M., & Huesman, R. L., Jr. (2014). First-generation students' sense of belonging, mental health, and use of counseling services at public research universities. *Journal of College Counseling, 17*(1), 6–20. https://doi.org/10.1002/j.2161-1882.2014.00044.x

Stevens-Watkins, D., Sharma, S., Knighton, J. S., Oser, C. B., & Leukefeld, C. G. (2014). Examining cultural correlates of active coping among African American female trauma survivors. *Psychological Trauma: Theory, Research, Practice, and Policy, 6*(4), 328–336. https://doi.org/10.1037/a0034116

Stone, S., Saucer, C., Bailey, M., Garba, R., Hurst, A., Jackson, S. M., Krueger, N., & Cokley, K. (2018). Learning while Black: A culturally informed model of the impostor phenomenon for Black graduate students. *The Journal of Black Psychology*, *44*(6), 491–531. https://doi.org/10.1177/0095798418786648

Sue, D. W., & Sue, D. (2003). *Counseling the culturally diverse: Theory and practice* (4th ed.). John Wiley & Sons.

Torres, K. (2009). "Culture shock": Black students account for their distinctiveness at an elite college. *Ethnic and Racial Studies*, *32*(5), 883–905. https://doi.org/10.1080/01419870701710914

Tyler, K. M., Uqdah, A. L., Dillihunt, M. L., Beatty-Hazelbaker, R., Conner, T., Gadson, N., Henchy, A., Hughes, T., Mulder, S., Owens, E., Roan-Belle, C., Smith, L., & Stevens, R. (2008). Cultural discontinuity: Toward a quantitative investigation of a major hypothesis in education. *Educational Researcher*, *37*(5), 280–297. https://doi.org/10.3102/0013189X08321459

Walker, D. L., & Saklofske, D. H. (2023). Development, factor structure, and psychometric validation of the Impostor Phenomenon Assessment: A novel assessment of impostor phenomenon. *Assessment*, *30*(7), 2162–2183. https://doi.org/10.1177/10731911221141870

Williams, D. R., Neighbors, H. W., & Jackson, J. S. (2003). Racial/ethnic discrimination and health: Findings from community studies. *American Journal of Public Health*, *93*(2), 200–208. https://doi.org/10.2105/AJPH.93.2.200

9
A MIXED-METHODS STUDY OF IMPOSTOR PHENOMENON IN A HISPANIC-SERVING INSTITUTION

OLYMPIA CAUDILLO AND RODOLFO RINCONES

The doctoral journey is challenging. Various factors influence degree completion, including a doctoral student's gender, ethnicity, generational status, socioeconomic background, and academic discipline (Flores & Park, 2015; Gardner, 2008, 2009; Golde, 1998; Lovitts, 2001; Sowell et al., 2008, 2015). Another factor that may also influence completion is the impostor phenomenon (IP). Studies indicate that IP may impede or hinder degree completion but not necessarily result in the termination of the academic career. Little is known about how doctoral students experience and coexist with IP.

The literature review revealed that most of the current research on IP is quantitative in nature. Research also revealed that certain student characteristics associated with nontraditional students, such as gender, ethnicity, and generational status, can predict the presence of IP. The existing literature lacks the voices of the students who experience IP, resulting in an omission that fails to reveal if reported impostor scores align with the descriptive impostor experiences.

https://doi.org/10.1037/0000397-010
The Impostor Phenomenon: Psychological Research, Theory, and Interventions,
K. Cokley (Editor)
Copyright © 2024 by the American Psychological Association. All rights reserved.

PURPOSE OF THE STUDY

The purpose of this mixed-methods study was to supplement current research with a study of IP among doctoral students enrolled in a Hispanic-serving institution (HSI), an institution with a predominantly non-White student population. Existing research on IP primarily focuses on the traditional undergraduate student enrolled in predominantly White institutions (PWIs). IP may not manifest in students enrolled in HSIs as it does among those in PWIs or in historically Black colleges and universities, but because this research is lacking, IP among students enrolled in HSIs remains undetermined.

The first objective of this study was to examine differences in IP by doctoral students' gender, generational status, and type of program. The second objective was to explore doctoral students' experiences of IP to develop a theoretical understanding of IP in an HSI. The third objective was to examine if qualitative interviews supported quantitative results and how those qualitative results served to contribute to a more comprehensive and nuanced understanding of IP.

SETTING

This study was conducted in an HSI located in the southwest region of the United States along the United States/Mexico border. The HSI primarily serves the educational needs of historically underrepresented students from varying social, cultural, and economic backgrounds. In fall 2020, Hispanic students accounted for 83% of the total enrollment. Approximately 49% of total enrolled students identified as first-generation. Female students accounted for 56% of the total enrollment. As of fall 2019, 1,043 students were enrolled in doctoral degree-granting programs.

LITERATURE REVIEW

IP is prevalent in academia, where intelligence is crucial to success. IP exists among students, faculty, librarians, administrators, and staff, all populations who inhabit higher education settings (Brems et al., 1994; Clark et al., 2014; Gibson-Beverly & Schwartz, 2008; Parkman, 2016; Zorn, 2005). Cope Watson and Smith Betts (2010) claimed that IP is "embedded in the institutional or systemic discourses that circulate in academic environments" (p. 1) and that due to its historical origins the climate in higher education is highly conducive to

IP. Historically women are relatively new to higher education, so they are often not highly visible in positions of leadership. This lack of female mentorship enables the emergence of impostor feelings among female students in higher education (Hoang, 2013).

Fear of success (FOS), studied by Horner in 1968, explored why women failed to achieve high-level goals in comparison to men. As a situational response, FOS emerged when a member of a gender achieved success in a field or discipline traditionally perceived as exclusive to the other gender (Bremer & Wittig, 1980; Caballero et al., 1975; Cherry & Deaux, 1978; Fried-Buchalter, 1997; Horner, 1973; Lentz, 1982; Levine & Crumrine, 1975; Pfost & Fiore, 1990; Piedmont, 1988). Women who participated in occupational fields traditionally perceived as male domains, such as higher education, experienced anxiety because they equated academic success with a loss of femininity or with possible social rejection (Bremer & Wittig, 1980; Caballero et al., 1975; Cherry & Deaux, 1978; Fried-Buchalter, 1997; Lentz, 1982; Levine & Crumrine, 1975; Pfost & Fiore, 1990; Piedmont, 1988). The social stigma resulting from trespassing into occupational fields traditionally perceived as gendered manifested as FOS.

Environments that reinforce gender roles and emphasize achievement and success as male qualities may be more conducive to the emergence of IP among women (Gibson-Beverly & Schwartz, 2008; Hoang, 2013). Women from underrepresented groups may be even more susceptible because they deal with family and gender role expectations, augmented by the stress associated with being members of historically oppressed classes (Clance et al., 1995). According to Gardner (2013), IP is widespread among women and students of color due to feelings of otherness or of not belonging. Accompanying those feelings of otherness is the dreaded fear of discovery that others will validate the impostors' secret fear that, in fact, they do not belong (Gardner, 2013).

Peteet et al. (2015) noted that first-generation students experience IP more often and more intensely than traditional students. First-generation students deal with minority stress, low socioeconomic status, lower self-esteem, lower self-efficacy, and higher fears of academic failure and so may be more "predisposed to higher levels of impostor phenomenon" (Peteet et al., 2015, p. 177). The researchers contend that students from underrepresented populations incorrectly attribute their perceived deficiencies to a lack of academic ability, but that the real cause of those feelings is the environment in higher education described as "covert institutional systemic networks that cultivate impostor phenomenon" (Cope Watson & Smith Betts, 2010, p. 1).

New and first-time experiences such as attending college, working in an unfamiliar environment, being a first-generation student, or being the first or one of a few in a field all contribute to the emergence of IP (Cope Watson & Smith Betts, 2010; Jarrett, 2010; Parkman, 2016). Sanford et al. (2015) reported that participants who experienced IP "lacked experience or age" and those who did not experience IP claimed that "experience helped them gain confidence" (p. 39). Doctoral students reported that experiences of IP decreased as time in the doctoral program increased (Craddock et al., 2011).

In this context, IP in first-time doctoral students might be a natural response to a "stressful and unknown environment" (Craddock et al., 2011, p. 439). Although more nontraditional students are enrolling and pursuing advanced degrees, the experiences of first-generation students who "persist to graduate school" and who experience IP are not extensively researched (Gardner & Holley, 2011, p. 79).

In other studies, participants revealed they originated from families where high academic achievement was expected and where failure was not an option (Sakulku & Alexander, 2011). Meeting the standards imposed by their families with the resultant fear of failure also contributed to impostor feelings. When examined in a situational context, impostor feelings may be a normal part of the student experience, so it is important to understand how doctoral students experience IP (Craddock et al., 2011; Fujie, 2010; Lovitts, 2001).

Fujie (2010) developed the State Impostor Phenomenon Scale (SIPS) to measure IP as a state. Based on research, Fujie concluded that feelings of fraudulence emerge and disappear situationally. The SIPS was created to measure impostor feelings as an emergent reaction or a state because of having a new experience, receiving evaluation, or facing an unexpected experience (Fujie, 2010).

Instruments used to detect IP, including the Harvey Impostor Scale, the Clance Impostor Scale, and the Perceived Fraudulence Scale, all measure IP as a trait and not as a state (Fujie, 2010). It is important to mention the SIPS (Fujie, 2010) because the literature suggests that IP may be a situationally constructed response (Cope Watson & Smith Betts, 2010; Jarrett, 2010; Zorn, 2005).

Several researchers, including Kolligian and Sternberg (1991), Ferrari and Thompson (2006), and McElwee and Yurak (2007), have questioned the existence of IP. The researchers proposed that IP is a self-presentational strategy generated from a need to protect one's ego. Kolligian and Sternberg found that students with self-perceptions of fraudulence were highly critical of themselves and closely monitored the impression they made on others to avoid discovery. Their studies also revealed a relationship between IP, perfectionism, and self-handicapping. Individuals experiencing IP are obsessed with maintaining an image of intellectual ability, so after a poor performance they claim a handicap to save face. Self-handicapping was not an issue when saving face was not warranted (Ferrari & Thompson, 2006).

McElwee and Yurak (2007) questioned if IP was a personality attribute or a self-presentational behavior or style. Self-presentation can be an intentional manipulative strategy, but it can also be an automatic unintentional response. If IP is not deliberate impression management, is it an automatic self-presentational response generated to protect the self from the negative emotions triggered by failure (McElwee & Yurak, 2007)? To quote the researchers, "How ironic that 'impostors' may be merely pretending to be impostors" (McElwee & Yurak, 2007, p. 218).

In studies where IP was detected among underrepresented students including Hispanics, underrepresented students were the minority population. Overt detection of IP in an HSI may be difficult to discern because the population primarily consists of underrepresented students. Based on the literature, impostor feelings may present among new and first-generation doctoral students, female doctoral students, doctoral students from underrepresented groups, and doctoral students majoring in academic disciplines traditionally occupied by women or men, all demographics found in HSIs.

METHOD

This study utilized an explanatory sequential mixed-methods design in which the quantitative and qualitative phases of the study are procedurally predetermined (Creswell, 2012; Creswell & Plano Clark, 2018; Plano Clark & Creswell, 2008). Seven hypotheses guided the quantitative phase of this study. The first three hypotheses assessed whether differences existed between or among the demographic groups by observing participants' self-perceptions of IP as part of their doctoral experience. The other four hypotheses explored more complex ways of observing IP levels between groups. The qualitative inquiry produced real-world knowledge about IP by exploring the experiences of doctoral students enrolled in the HSI. The mixed-methods question explored IP quantitative results from a more nuanced perspective generated from the qualitative findings.

Hypotheses and Questions

Quantitative Hypotheses

H_1: Female doctoral students will report higher levels of IP.

H_2: First-generation doctoral students will report higher levels of IP.

H_3: Doctoral students in social sciences programs will report higher levels of IP.

H_4: There is a first-order interaction between gender and generational status in relation to IP.

H_5: There is a first-order interaction between gender and type of program in relation to IP.

H_6: There is a first-order interaction between generational status and type of program in relation to IP.

H_7: There is a second-order interaction among gender, generational status, and type of program in relation to IP.

Qualitative Questions

1. How is IP revealed in doctoral students?
2. How do doctoral students describe and explain IP?

Mixed-Methods Question

1. How do the observed group level differences help to explain qualitative responses in regard to IP among doctoral students?

Sampling Procedure

The quantitative data collection phase was modeled after studies conducted by Cokley et al. (2013) and Peteet et al. (2015) that explored relationships between IP and student traits, including gender, generational status, and ethnicity. Stratified random sampling based on type of doctoral program, STEM (science, technology, engineering, and mathematics) or social sciences, was utilized to identify participants. STEM programs included disciplines in science, engineering, and mathematics, whereas social sciences programs included social sciences and humanities (Gardner, 2008, 2009; Golde, 2005; Lovitts, 2001; Sowell et al., 2008, 2015). Email invitations served to recruit participants enrolled in 19 doctoral programs categorized as STEM or social sciences. The email invitation contained a link to a 26-item survey that consisted of six demographic questions and the 20-item Clance Impostor Phenomenon Scale (CIPS). An additional link was embedded in the survey to recruit participants for the study's qualitative phase.

Purposeful sampling was used to identify participants for the qualitative data collection phase based on CIPS scores. Participants who experienced few impostor feelings, scoring 40 or less, and those who experienced intense impostor feelings, scoring 81 or higher—the two extremes of the CIPS—were specifically targeted for this study. Eligible participants were grouped by CIPS scores then by gender, type of program, and finally generational status. Individual semistructured interviews served to collect qualitative data. The interviews were audio recorded and transcribed after which a thematic analysis was conducted. Adherence to institutional review board protocols ensured the anonymity of participants and the confidentiality of responses. The COVID-19 outbreak severely limited the number of qualitative interviews.

Quantitative Analysis

A three-way factorial analysis of covariance served to explore the existence of a three-way interaction effect between gender, type of program, generational status, and IP. The dependent variable was IP, and the independent variables were gender, type of program, and generational status. Age was utilized as a covariate. Due to the expectation that the dominant population enrolled at the HSI would identify as Hispanic, therefore limiting the variability of the population, race/ethnicity was not a factor in this study.

Categorization of participants was based on self-reported responses. Participants' responses placed them into one of the three independent variable categories: female or male, STEM or social sciences program, and first- or second-generation student. For this study, a first-generation student was defined as one whose parents did not have a graduate degree. Age was used as the control factor to adjust for the differences that existed between doctoral students that could influence CIPS scores.

Qualitative Analysis

A constructivist grounded theory perspective served to analyze, explore, and interpret qualitative data. The purpose of the qualitative analysis was to connect back to the mixed-methods research questions, resulting in the development of a theory to explain IP experiences among doctoral student participants. Categorization of qualitative responses revealed thematic relationships linked to the quantitative variables of gender, type of program, and generational status.

RESULTS

The data did not provide statistically significant evidence to indicate that IP has more presence in the sample of doctoral students enrolled in the HSI. The hypotheses were tested through analysis of covariance using a p value of .005. Although the hypotheses were not significant, several observations can be made based on resulting effect sizes.

1. Female doctoral students reported higher levels of IP. Of participants who identified as male, 14% reported intense impostor feelings, having scored 81 or higher on the CIPS. Of participants who identified as female, 23% reported intense IP feelings, having scored 81 or higher on the CIPS. These results indicate that at the HSI, IP is not gender specific but that more female students reported higher levels of IP.
2. No significant difference in mean IP scores between first- and second-generation students were observed. Mean IP scores for first-generation students were 62.61 (SD = 18.88) and 62.27 (SD = 16.22) for second-generation students. This finding indicates that at the HSI, generational status has no effect on IP scores, conveying that first-generation doctoral students do not feel any more isolated or othered than second-generation students.
3. No significant difference in mean IP scores between STEM and social sciences programs were observed. The means were 63.31 (SD = 18.78) and 61.75 (SD = 17.51), respectively. Based on mean IP scores, participants in both STEM and social sciences experienced frequent episodes of IP. This indicates that program of study did not contribute to the emergence of intense IP experiences.
4. Gender and generational status were not statistically significant at $p > .05$. The main effect of gender yielded an effect size of .017, indicating that 1.7% of the variance in IP was explained by gender with F (1, 171) = 2.982, p = .086. The main effect of generational status yielded an effect size of .000, indicating that none of the variance in IP was explained by generational status with F (1, 171) = 0.010, p = .920. IP scores reported by first- and second-generation female doctoral students were 65.70 (SD = 17.48), whereas mean IP scores reported for first- and second-generation male doctoral students were 58.35 (SD = 18.18). First-generation female doctoral students' mean IP scores were 66.96 (SD = 17.80), whereas second-generation female doctoral students' mean IP scores were 63.06 (SD = 16.74). The reverse was observed for second-generation male doctoral students. Mean IP scores for second-generation male doctoral students were 60.89 (SD = 15.61), whereas mean IP scores for first-generation male doctoral students were 57.53 (SD = 18.98). Unlike first-generation students, who set the standard of what constitutes academic success, second-generation students enter higher education with a preexisting concept of academic success, a standard established by a prior generation that second-generation students are expected to meet if not surpass.
5. Gender and type of program were statistically insignificant at $p > .05$. The main effect of gender yielded an effect size of .017, indicating that only 1.7% of the variance in IP was explained by gender with F (1, 171) = 2.982,

$p = .086$. The main effect of type of program yielded an effect size of .001, indicating that 0.1% of the variance in IP was explained by type of program with $F (1, 171) = 0.105, p = .746$. The interaction effect was not significant, $F (1, 171) = 1.053, p = .306$, indicating that there was no combined effect for gender and type of program on IP. Although statistically insignificant, mean IP scores reported by female doctoral students in STEM and social sciences programs were 65.70 ($SD = 17.48$) and were 58.35 ($SD = 18.18$) for male doctoral students in the same programs. Mean IP scores for female doctoral students in STEM programs were 68.65 ($SD = 17.12$) and were 63.54 ($SD = 17.56$) for female doctoral students in social sciences programs. Mean IP scores for male doctoral students in STEM programs were 58.20 ($SD = 19.05$) and were 58.55 ($SD = 17.21$) for those in social sciences programs. Traditionally STEM programs have been viewed as male domains and social sciences programs as female domains. This may help to explain the difference in mean IP scores between female doctoral students in hard and social sciences programs and between male doctoral students in the same programs.

6. Generational status and type of program were not statistically significant at $p > .05$. The main effect of generational status yielded an effect size of .000, indicating that none of the variance in IP was explained by generational status with $F (1, 171) = 0.010, p = .920$. The main effect of type of program yielded an effect size of .001, indicating that 0.1% of the variance in IP was explained by type of program with $F (1, 171) = 0.105, p = .746$. Furthermore, the interaction effect was not significant, $F (1, 171) = 0.001, p = .971$, indicating that there was no combined effect for generational status and type of program on IP. First-generation doctoral students in STEM and social sciences programs reported higher mean IP scores than second-generation doctoral students in the same programs. Although statistically insignificant, mean IP scores for first-generation students in STEM and social sciences programs were 62.61 ($SD = 18.88$) whereas mean IP scores for second-generation students in the same programs were 62.27 ($SD = 16.21$). This finding aligns with the literature that indicates first-generation students are more likely to experience IP.

7. The second-order interaction between gender, generational status, and type of program was not statistically significant at $p > .05$. The second-order interaction effect between gender, generational status, and type of program was not significant, $F (1, 171) = 0.017, p = .898$, indicating that there was no combined effect for gender, generational status, and type of program on IP. Mean IP scores for first- and second-generation female doctoral students in STEM programs were 68.65 ($SD = 17.12$) and were 58.20 ($SD = 19.05$)

for first- and second-generation male doctoral students in the same program. The type of program may also help to explain the mean IP scores for female doctoral students. STEM programs have traditionally been male domains, so female students pursuing degrees in those fields may be more susceptible to IP. A reversal occurred for male doctoral students in STEM programs. Reported mean IP scores for second-generation male doctoral students in STEM programs were 61.00 (SD = 16.29), whereas first-generation male doctoral students in the same program reported a mean IP score of 56.94 (SD = 20.30). At the HSI, second-generation male doctoral students may feel more pressured to succeed academically due to imposed standards, set by the previous generation, the family, or the students themselves. This pressure may find expression as IP.

See Tables 9.1 and 9.2 for sample composition and summary of IP scores. Quantitative results indicated that IP was not statistically significantly different across participants' gender, program, and generational status. However, qualitative findings suggest that gender, generational status, and program of study influence IP experiences. Participants' responses contained elements of fakeness, discounting, and luck, themes associated with the three subscales of the CIPS (Chrisman et al., 1995; French et al., 2008; Fujie, 2010; Holmes et al., 1993; Langford & Clance, 1993). Other emergent themes included feelings of otherness/isolation, self-handicapping, self-presentation, mentorship, family support, and fear of evaluation.

Responses revealed the discounting of talents and skills. For example, admission to a doctoral program was attributed to factors such as a glitch, lowered admission standards, or timing:

> I expected to get in only because of the requirements being so low. I felt like had I applied to a different school that doesn't have a one hundred percent

TABLE 9.1. Race/Ethnicity of the Hispanic-Serving Institution

Race/ethnicity	N	%
Mexican/Hispanic/Latino/a/Chicano/a	118	65%
Black/African American	3	2%
Asian/Pacific Islander	9	5%
Native American	0	0%
White	38	21%
Biracial/multiracial	6	3%
International	8	4%
Total	182	100%

A Mixed-Methods Study of Impostor Phenomenon in a Hispanic-Serving Institution • 213

TABLE 9.2. Gender and IP Scores

Gender	Little IP	%	Moderate IP	%	Frequent IP	%	Intense IP	%	Total	%
Female	12	12%	26	25%	41	40%	24	23%	103	57%
Male	15	19%	29	37%	24	30%	11	14%	79	43%
Total	27	15%	55	30%	65	36%	35	19%	182	100%

Note. IP = impostor phenomenon.

> acceptance rate or had I applied to somebody who had some guidelines, some restrictions then I probably wouldn't have made it but I just happened to be in the right place, right time. You know the administrative staff was only requiring so much and I did it, I got it so I got in. (Participant 200225-0427)

Other participants believed that they did not possess the qualities to succeed in their program or did not fit in: "Engineering is for smart people, it's not for me. I should go to another field or something, you know?" (Participant 200225-0427).

> I've been accepted in the program. Yeah, I probably will finish, okay? I don't know that that means that I really belong. I don't know if that means it really, you know, I'm looking at all the people in the program. And we got a bunch of smart kids and a bunch of smart people. And I'm not sure that I am of the caliber that belong with this kind of behavior. (Participant 200226-0204)

Outwardly, participants accepted accolades from faculty and peers, but internally, they believed the praise was unmerited. They did not think their contribution was exceptional in any manner. When praised, some participants reacted with suspicion, especially when praised by faculty. These same participants felt that faculty lowered their expectations and so were disingenuous in their praise or evaluation. This suspicion materialized as doubt and insecurity that emerged as a mistrust of faculty. Paradoxically, despite these feelings, participants emphasized the importance of faculty mentorship:

> So far nobody's failed me. I think they have a minimum and a higher and yeah, they accommodate. What does that mean? I don't know, is he overestimating our ability or what? He's willing to accept whatever he has to work with. (Participant 200226-0204)

> So it's usually after we've met or something and somebody like praises me for some work, they're like, "Okay, thanks for this, thanks for all the hard work XXX's done and this and this." And I'm like well, all I did is basically updated a couple of spreadsheets and stuff. I mean—what I mean, I didn't do anything terribly interesting. Yeah. I mean, I just did this couple of minor pieces of work and it seems like they're praising me for it or they're giving me a lot of credit for what I feel is very low-effort work. It might have just been tedious and they didn't

want to do it but it's nothing, nothing that I saw as particularly useful. Useful or helpful to anything we were doing overall. (Participant 1 200303-0203)

Indirect comments regarding gender, ethnicity, and generational status also served to mask participants' insecurity regarding their standing in the doctoral program. One female participant was convinced that her presence in the program was continually questioned by male colleagues: "You know, it felt good, but at the same time, I did see the double takes that they would make. Like, 'What? Shouldn't you be cleaning a bathroom or something?' You know?" (Participant 200225-0427).

Another participant, who identified as a second-generation student, struggled reconciling challenges because she believed that in comparison to first-generation peers, she should be better equipped to handle adversity: "But I'm at a doctorate level, you know, I'm so—you know, I should know all of this by now" (Participant 190312-0130). Another participant claimed that gender issues did not exist but were only used as an excuse to cover unsatisfactory performance: "And I do think that sometimes we can hide under those expectations without even realizing that it is just that we're struggling with a particular task" (Participant 200225-008).

DISCUSSION

Participants' mean IP scores indicated frequent and shared IP experiences. However, qualitative responses offered a greater variance that pointed to an individually unique IP experience. Results suggested a conflict in the identity of doctoral student participants, which manifested as IP. Underneath the façade of competence is a student who is unable to acknowledge success on a personal level, perhaps revealing that participants possess a dual external/internal identity—one for show and one for safekeeping. Differing conclusions may be derived given the richness and complexity of the responses, but because this study focused on gender, program of study, and generational status, interpretation is limited to these three variables.

To conduct the study, several decisions had to be made. The study sample did not include students pursuing professional doctorates, such as those in physical or occupational therapy, pharmacy, and nursing. Moreover, participants who experienced moderate impostor feelings, with CIPS scores ranging between 41 and 60, and those who experienced frequent impostor feelings, with CIPS scores ranging between 61 and 80, were not considered for the qualitative sample. The qualitative study was limited to participants with few impostor feelings, who scored 40 or less on the CIPS, and those who experienced intense impostor feelings, who scored 81 or higher on the CIPS. It was expected that the contrast in responses from participants experiencing few and intense impostor feelings would provide a more comprehensive description of IP in the HSI.

The rationale used to categorize a program as STEM or social sciences was loosely based on the Council of Graduate School's definition of science, engineering, and mathematics fields and social sciences and humanities fields, as noted in the *PhD Completion and Attrition: Analysis of Baseline Demographic Data From the PhD Completion Project* (Sowell et al., 2008) publication. This study focused on gender, program of study, and generational status, although other variables, such as ethnicity, socioeconomic status, and grade point average, could have been considered. Finally, this study utilized the CIPS, so results are specific to the CIPS. Results could possibly differ using other IP instruments.

Because the selection of participants for the qualitative phase of this study cannot be considered random, generalization of results is limited. The sample was selected from doctoral students enrolled in an HSI geographically located on the United States/Mexico border, so the findings may not generalize to other populations. The race/ethnicity of participants is also a limitation, as most people surveyed are members of one race/ethnicity group given the setting of the study. As there was no control on the type of elicited response or on the response rate of participants, the demographic survey as a self-reported measure was a limitation. The lack of time to collect qualitative data was severely limited due to the COVID-19 outbreak. Greater in-depth interviews could have resulted in more nuanced responses and interpretations. In their present condition, the data from this study were rich and complex to analyze from a single theoretical framework.

A future study should explore the effect and interaction between age and IP. This recommendation is based on results that indicated that age was statistically significant at $p < .05$. The main effect of age yielded an effect size of .043, indicating that 4.3% of the variance in IP was explained by age with $F (1, 171) = 7.649, p = .006$. The interaction and effect of age and IP was not a topic of this study, as age served as a covariate. At least three participants mentioned age in their responses regarding IP experiences. Age may be a factor that predicts IP among doctoral students enrolled in an HSI.

Based on both quantitative and qualitative data, IP among second-generation male doctoral students should be further investigated. The literature on IP and generational status focuses on first-generation students. We did not locate any literature that references second-generation male doctoral students and IP. Further studies may determine if this is a common occurrence or an experience unique to male doctoral students enrolled in the HSI.

216 • Caudillo and Rincones

Although not a topic of research in this study, IP in relation to race/ethnicity at the HSI should also be further investigated. Studies show that IP is present among underrepresented groups in PWIs. A study should investigate if the same finding holds true among underrepresented students at the HSI where the predominant student population is Hispanic.

Recommendations for University Administrators

The literature recommends the incorporation of discussions on IP throughout a student's academic career. Based on comments made by participants, knowledge of IP is lacking at the HSI. Students need to know that IP is part of the doctoral student experience and that most will experience IP at some point in their academic career.

At the HSI, the institution should implement well-being checks in a safe, judgment-free setting with licensed professionals. In such a setting students can express their concerns, fears, and insecurities. The well-being check is to provide IP sufferers an opportunity to vent and allow licensed professionals to mediate in cases where students may require further assistance. The biggest fear IP sufferers face is the fear of discovery, so a safe environment is of utmost importance where, if only for a moment, the impostor can relax the exhausting impostor façade.

It is important to note that IP is an internal experience, so individuals experiencing IP cannot be identified by outward appearance. That is the insidious nature of IP and why more attention should be given to IP. Unless a student cries out for help, it is impossible to fathom the internal conflict of students with IP. The well-being of doctoral students must be of utmost importance, especially at institutions that cater to the educational advancement of underrepresented students.

CONCLUSION

Higher education at the HSI remains uncharted territory for many nontraditional students. One participant said, "We opened the door and stepped in, but now what?" Some nontraditional students continue to feel that they navigate those uncharted spaces "on a boat without a map." Traditional students find themselves in a similar dilemma, also needing a map but unable to acknowledge or recognize that need. The navigation is made more difficult for the student experiencing IP not necessarily because of the lack of institutional resources but because of the overwhelming fear of discovery.

Results at the HSI corroborated previous findings on IP that determined IP is not gender specific and more women than men experience IP. IP was more discernable in participants' responses, which reiterated findings from other studies on IP. Combined, these findings reinforce that at the HSI, IP is both a shared external experience and a very personal internal experience.

This study demonstrated that, despite impostor experiences, doctoral students at the HSI are resilient and persistent in their academic endeavors. Always under the pressure of maintaining a successful image, they exist in a paradox craving and repelling success. Although their time in higher education is a complex roller coaster of emotions triggered by IP, they remain academically successful. Whether the attainment of that PhD or EdD degree constitutes or satisfies personal success remains undetermined.

REFERENCES

Bremer, T. H., & Wittig, M. A. (1980). Fear of success: A personality trait or a response to occupational deviance and role overload? *Sex Roles*, *6*(1), 27–46. https://doi.org/10.1007/BF00288359

Brems, C., Baldwin, M. R., Davis, L., & Namyniuk, L. (1994). The imposter syndrome as related to teaching evaluations and advising relationships of university faculty members. *The Journal of Higher Education*, *65*(2), 183–193. https://doi.org/10.2307/2943923

Caballero, C. M., Giles, P., & Shaver, P. (1975). Sex-role traditionalism and fear of success. *Sex Roles*, *1*(4), 319–326. https://doi.org/10.1007/BF00287223

Cherry, F., & Deaux, K. (1978). Fear of success versus fear of gender-inappropriate behavior. *Sex Roles*, *4*(1), 97–101. https://doi.org/10.1007/BF00288380

Chrisman, S. M., Pieper, W., Clance, P. R., Holland, C., & Glickauf-Hughes, C. (1995). Validation of the Clance Imposter Scale. *Journal of Personality Assessment*, *65*(3), 456–467. https://doi.org/10.1207/s15327752jpa6503_6

Clance, P. R., Dingman, D., Reviere, S. L., & Stober, D. R. (1995). Imposter phenomenon in an interpersonal/social context: Origins and treatment. *Women & Therapy*, *16*(4), 79–96. https://doi.org/10.1300/J015v16n04_07

Clark, M., Verdeman, K., & Barba, S. (2014). Perceived inadequacy: A study of the imposter phenomenon among college and research librarians. *College & Research Libraries*, *75*(3), 255–271. https://doi.org/10.5860/crl12-423

Cokley, K., McClain, S., Enciso, A., & Martinez, M. (2013, April). An examination of the impact of minority status stress and imposter feelings on the mental health of diverse ethnic minority college students. *Journal of Multicultural Counseling and Development*, *41*(2), 82–95. https://doi.org/10.1002/j.2161-1912.2013.00029.x

Cope Watson, G., & Smith Betts, A. (2010). Confronting otherness: An e-conversation between doctoral students living with the imposter syndrome. *Canadian Journal for New Scholars in Education*, *3*(1), 1–13. https://journalhosting.ucalgary.ca/index.php/cjnse/article/view/30474

Craddock, S., Birnbaum, M., Rodriguez, K., Cobb, C., & Zeeh, S. (2011). Doctoral students and the impostor phenomenon: Am I smart enough to be here? *Journal of Student Affairs Research and Practice, 48*(4), 429–442. https://doi.org/10.2202/1949-6605.6321

Creswell, J. W. (2012). *Educational research: Planning, conducting, and evaluating quantitative and qualitative research* (4th ed.). Pearson.

Creswell, J. W., & Plano Clark, V. L. (2018). *Designing and conducting mixed methods research*. SAGE Publications.

Ferrari, J. R. and Thompson, T. (2006). Imposter fears: Links with self-presentational concerns and self-handicapping behaviours. *Personality and Individual Differences, 40*(2), 341–353. https://doi.org/10.1016/j.paid.2005.07.012

Flores, S. M., & Park, T. J. (2015). The effect of enrolling in a minority-serving institution for Black and Hispanic students in Texas. *Research in Higher Education, 56*(3), 247–276. https://doi.org/10.1007/s11162-014-9342-y

French, B. F., Ullrich-French, S. C., & Follman, D. (2008). The psychometric properties of the Clance Imposter Scale. *Personality and Individual Differences, 44*(5), 1270–1278. https://doi.org/10.1016/j.paid.2007.11.023

Fried-Buchalter, S. (1997). Fear of success, fear of failure, and the imposter phenomenon among male and female marketing managers. *Sex Roles, 37*(11–12), 847–859. https://doi.org/10.1007/BF02936343

Fujie, R. (2010). Development of the state imposter phenomenon scale. *Japanese Psychological Research, 52*(1), 1–11. https://doi.org/10.1111/j.1468-5884.2009.00417.x

Gardner, S. K. (2008). Fitting the mold of graduate school: A qualitative study of socialization in doctoral education. *Innovative Higher Education, 33*(2), 125–138. https://doi.org/10.1007/s10755-008-9068-x

Gardner, S. K. (2009). Conceptualizing success in doctoral education: Perspectives of faculty in seven disciplines. *The Review of Higher Education, 32*(3), 383–406. https://doi.org/10.1353/rhe.0.0075

Gardner, S. K. (2013). The challenges of first-generation doctoral students. *New Directions for Higher Education, 2013*(163), 43–54. https://doi.org/10.1002/he.20064

Gardner, S. K., & Holley, K. A. (2011). "Those invisible barriers are real": The progression of first-generation students through doctoral education. *Equity & Excellence in Education, 44*(1), 77–92. https://doi.org/10.1080/10665684.2011.529791

Gibson-Beverly, G., & Schwartz, J. P. (2008). Attachment, entitlement, and the imposter phenomenon in female graduate students. *Journal of College Counseling, 11*(2), 119–132. https://doi.org/10.1002/j.2161-1882.2008.tb00029.x

Golde, C. M. (1998). Beginning graduate school: Explaining first-year doctoral attrition. *New Directions for Higher Education, 1998*(101), 55–64. https://doi.org/10.1002/he.10105

Golde, C. M. (2005). The role of the department and discipline in doctoral student attrition: Lessons from four departments. *The Journal of Higher Education, 76*(6), 669–700. https://doi.org/10.1353/jhe.2005.0039

Hoang, Q. (2013). The imposter phenomenon: Overcoming internalized barriers and recognizing achievements. *The Vermont Connection, 34*(6), 42 – 51. https://scholarworks.uvm.edu/tvc/vol34/iss1/6/

Holmes, S. W., Kertay, L., Adamson, L. B., Holland, C. L., & Clance, P. R. (1993). Measuring the imposter phenomenon: A comparison of Clance's IP Scale and Harvey's I-P Scale. *Journal of Personality Assessment, 60*(1), 48–59. https://doi.org/10.1207/s15327752jpa6001_3

Horner, M. S. (1973). *Success avoidant motivation and behavior: Its developmental correlates and situational determinants: Final report.* https://files.eric.ed.gov/fulltext/ED101221.pdf

Jarrett, C. (2010). Feeling like a fraud. *The Psychologist, 23*(5), 380–383. https://www.bps.org.uk/psychologist/feeling-fraud

Kolligian, J., Jr., & Sternberg, R. J. (1991). Perceived fraudulence in young adults: Is there an "imposter syndrome"? *Journal of Personality Assessment, 56*(2), 308–326. https://doi.org/10.1207/s15327752jpa5602_10

Langford, J., & Clance, P. R. (1993). The imposter phenomenon: Recent research findings regarding dynamics, personality and family patterns and their implications for treatment. *Psychotherapy: Theory, Research, Practice, Training, 30*(3), 495–501. https://doi.org/10.1037/0033-3204.30.3.495

Lentz, M. E. (1982). Fear of success as a situational phenomenon. *Sex Roles, 8*(9), 987–997. https://doi.org/10.1007/BF00290023

Levine, A., & Crumrine, J. (1975). Women and the fear of success: A problem in replication. *American Journal of Sociology, 80*(4), 964–974. https://doi.org/10.1086/225902

Lovitts, B. E. (2001). *Leaving the ivory tower: The causes and consequences of departure from doctoral study.* Rowman and Littlefield Publishers.

McElwee, R. O., & Yurak, T. J. (2007). Feeling versus acting like an imposter: Real feelings of fraudulence or self-presentation? *Individual Differences Research, 5*(3), 201–220.

Parkman, A. (2016). The imposter phenomenon in higher education: Incidence and impact. *Journal of Higher Education Theory and Practice, 16*(1), 51–60. http://www.m.www.na-businesspress.com/JHETP/ParkmanA_Web16_1_.pdf

Peteet, B. J., Montgomery, L., & Weekes, J. C. (2015). Predictors of imposter phenomenon among talented ethnic minority undergraduate students. *The Journal of Negro Education, 84*(2), 175–186. https://doi.org/10.7709/jnegroeducation.84.2.0175

Pfost, K. S., & Fiore, M. (1990). Pursuit of nontraditional occupations: Fear of success or fear of not being chosen? *Sex Roles, 23*(1–2), 15–24. https://doi.org/10.1007/BF00289875

Piedmont, R. L. (1988). An interactional model of achievement motivation and fear of success. *Sex Roles, 19*(7–8), 467–490. https://doi.org/10.1007/BF00289719

Plano Clark, V. L., & Creswell, J. W. (2008). *The mixed methods reader.* SAGE Publications.

Sakulku, J., & Alexander, J. (2011). The imposter phenomenon. *International Journal of Behavioral Science, 6*(1), 73–92. https://www.sciencetheearth.com/uploads/2/4/6/5/24658156/2011_sakulku_the_impostor_phenomenon.pdf

Sanford, A. A., Ross, E. M., Blake, S. J., & Cambiano, R. L. (2015). Finding courage and confirmation: Resisting imposter feelings through relationships with mentors, romantic partners, and other women in leadership. *Advancing Women in Leadership, 35*, 31–41. https://doi.org/10.21423/awlj-v35.a140

Sowell, R., Allum, J., & Okahana, H. (2015). *Doctoral initiative on minority attrition and completion*. Council of Graduate Schools. https://cgsnet.org/wp-content/uploads/2022/09/Doctoral_Initiative_on_Minority_Attrition_and_Completion-2015.pdf

Sowell, R., Zhang, T., & Redd, K. (2008). *PhD completion and attrition: Analysis of baseline demographic data from the PhD completion project*. Council of Graduate Schools. https://cgsnet.org/wp-content/uploads/2022/01/phd_completion_and_attrition_analysis_of_baseline_demographic_data-2.pdf

Zorn, D. (2005). Academic culture feeds the imposter phenomenon. *Academic Leadership, 21*(8), 1–8.

10 IMPOSTOR PHENOMENON IN SCIENCE, TECHNOLOGY, ENGINEERING, AND MATHEMATICS

DEVASMITA CHAKRAVERTY

I did not anticipate going to graduate school at all because graduate school is for smart people, not me. I didn't even consider going to top schools since I'm not smart like that even though I had a 4.0 in all my engineering coursework.

—Student quoted in Chakraverty (2019, p. 10)

The impostor phenomenon (IP) is experienced widely in science, technology, engineering, and mathematics (STEM) fields. It correlates with a number of outcomes, not restricted to poor belonging and lower self-efficacy, with statistically significant gender differences that are even larger among individuals in STEM fields (Muradoglu et al., 2022). Women and BIPOC (Black, Indigenous, People of Color) individuals are disproportionately underrepresented in STEM at all levels of education and employment. The same groups (especially women) also report impostor feelings more frequently. STEM fields emphasize academic brilliance or raw intellectual talent as a precursor to success, which could make these groups vulnerable to IP. This chapter summarizes literature on IP specifically in STEM fields. It starts with an overview of the demographic characteristics of STEM fields. Then the chapter examines the psychometric properties of a popular scale on IP used specifically in STEM samples. The discussion next moves to IP across academic ranks, among BIPOC individuals, and among other underrepresented groups in STEM. The discussion then shifts to

https://doi.org/10.1037/0000397-011
The Impostor Phenomenon: Psychological Research, Theory, and Interventions,
K. Cokley (Editor)
Copyright © 2024 by the American Psychological Association. All rights reserved.

222 • *Devasmita Chakraverty*

IP occurring as a personality trait as well as a result of environmental influence. IP is discussed in relation to literature on othering as well as belonging. The chapter ends with strategies to manage or overcome IP as well as future directions of research.

DEMOGRAPHIC CHARACTERISTICS OF STEM FIELDS

The National Science Foundation (NSF) uses the term "STEM" to broadly include core sciences (physics, chemistry, and math), engineering, technology, psychology, and even the social sciences (anthropology, political science, and economics; Gonzalez & Kuenzi, 2012). The overall demographic characteristics in STEM, when compared with the U.S. population, highlights interesting disparities. In 2018, the U.S. population comprised 60.11% White, 12.54% Black, 5.76% Asian, 2.22% multiracial, 0.74% American Indian or Alaska Native, and 0.18% Native Hawaiian or other Pacific Islander (overall, 81.55% "not Hispanic or Latino") people. The remaining 18.45%, or 61.5 million, of the population was Hispanic or Latinx (NSF & National Center for Science and Engineering Statistics [NCSES], 2021).

Although 56.9% of U.S. citizens and permanent residents enrolled in science and engineering programs in 2018 were female, they earned only about 50% of bachelor's degrees, 44.7% of master's degrees, and 41.2% of doctoral degrees, forming 38.7% of the postdoctoral population (NSF & NCSES, 2021). These disparate numbers have been fairly consistent over the past decade. In 2019, more men than women were employed full time (13.3 million men vs. 10.7 million women), whereas women were about 1.9 times more likely to be employed part time (3 million women vs. 1.6 million men), as scientists and engineers. There are demographic variations even within science and engineering. Female degree recipients are overrepresented in psychology (70% at each level: bachelor's, master's, and doctoral), biological sciences (over 60% in bachelor's and master's, respectively, and over 50% in doctoral), and agricultural sciences (50% at each level: bachelor's, master's, and doctoral; NSF & NCSES, 2021). However, they are underrepresented as degree recipients in other fields like computer sciences (20% bachelor's, thereby affecting graduate enrollment, 32% master's, and 22% doctoral); engineering (22% bachelor's, 26% master's, and 25% doctoral); mathematics and statistics (42% bachelor's, 43% master's, and 28% doctoral), and worst of all, physics (21% bachelor's, 23% master's, and 21% doctoral).

Gender disparity occurs even in STEM fields where women are well-represented, posing challenges to retention and upward mobility in academia.

Although women outnumber men as PhD degree recipients in biomedical sciences, fewer women (including BIPOC women) take interest in tenure-track positions at research institutions (Gibbs et al., 2014). In college biology, there are gender gaps in academic achievement and participation in whole-class discussions; female underperformance on introductory biology exams (Eddy et al., 2014); and favoritism among men by male peers for being perceived as knowledgeable about course content (Grunspan et al., 2016). These factors and others make women perceive their learning environment as hostile. Among PhDs in science and engineering employed in universities and 4-year colleges in 2019, women were underrepresented across all academic positions and only 38% of them were tenured. Further, among faculty the ratio of men to women was 1.42 (president, provost, and chancellor), 1.78 (dean, department head, chair), 1.81 (research faculty), 1.72 (teaching faculty), 1.34 (adjunct faculty), 1.35 (postdoctorates), and 1.62 (research assistants; NSF & NCSES, 2021).

Similarly, BIPOC individuals are underrepresented in science and engineering at all levels compared with the U.S. population. In 2018, they received only 24%, 22%, and 13.6% of all bachelor's, master's, and doctoral degrees, respectively (NSF & NCSES, 2021). Bachelor's degree recipients were 58% White, 15.1% Hispanic or Latinx, 10.7% Asian, 8.5% Black, and 0.4% American Indian or Alaska Native individuals in 2018, with greater representation of minorities in science compared with engineering. Minority populations are better represented in psychology (20% Hispanic or Latinx, 12% Black), biological and agricultural sciences (13.6% Hispanic or Latinx), and computer science (8.9% Black). Hispanic or Latinx, Black, and Native American PhD recipients made up 7%, 3.5%, and 0.3% of individuals, respectively, and 1.6% of postdoctorates were Black (NSF, 2017). Additionally, White individuals constituted about 70% of full-time employees as compared with 8.6% full-time, 8.3% part-time, and 24.7% unemployed Hispanic or Latinx individuals (Hamrick, 2019). Hispanic women are most poorly represented, holding only 1.7% of all jobs in STEM (compared with 5.3% for Hispanic men; Martínez & Gayfield, 2019).

PSYCHOMETRIC PROPERTIES OF THE CLANCE IMPOSTOR PHENOMENON SCALE WITH STEM SAMPLES

The Clance Impostor Phenomenon Scale (CIPS; Clance, 1985) is a popular scale measuring IP (Rosenstein et al., 2020; Simon, 2020). This 20-item scale (item scores from 1–5) has total possible scores from 20 to 100 (40 or less: *few*, 41–60: *moderate*, 61–80: *frequent*, higher than 80: *intense IP*). Higher scores indicate intense and more frequent impostor experiences. Several STEM-based studies have examined the psychometric properties of the CIPS. Results showed satisfactory internal consistency reliability among 1,271 engineering students (French et al., 2008). Simon and Choi (2018) examined the factor structure of the CIPS with 211 STEM PhD students, showing a one-factor model with correlated residuals that best fit the data. Consequently, Lee and colleagues (2022) examined the psychometric properties of the CIPS for graduate students and professionals in STEM and found three factors: Self-Doubt, Luck, and Fear of Evaluation. Additionally, those with high Fear and high/low Self-Doubt experienced more IP and evaluated themselves less positively than those with low Fear and high/low Self-Doubt, showing that Fear superseded Self-Doubt as a defining feature of IP. Older participants, those currently not in training, and men had lower IP compared with their counterparts. The following sections review IP research with respect to academic stage, discipline, and demographic differences.

IMPOSTOR PHENOMENON ACROSS ACADEMIC RANKS IN STEM

> I feel [I am] not achieving as much as my colleagues of the same rank, and that I lack sufficient training in methods as well as in other areas of academic professionalism. I feel like everyone else seems to know things that I've never heard of before. I have to always go out and find information for myself and then wonder if I'm performing my research methodologies correctly. I just doubt myself all the time. (quoted from a faculty member in Chakraverty, 2022b, p. 8)

IP is experienced by individuals in STEM across academic ranks, including high school students, undergraduate students, doctoral scholars, postdoctoral scholars, and faculty members, as described next.

Undergraduate Education

IP has been studied early on among high school adolescents (e.g., Caselman et al., 2006; Hellman & Caselman, 2004), but the studies have not focused on STEM. However, these studies show that planned interventions to alleviate impostor feelings can be implemented as early as during adolescence. Among undergraduates in STEM, psychology students have been most extensively studied, followed by students in science, engineering, and pharmacy. These studies are predominantly correlational and U.S.-based (with some research in Australia and the United Kingdom), primarily employing cross-sectional surveys with predominantly White and female samples. Most of the findings are not specific to the field of STEM itself; the participants being in STEM was incidental. There is significant correlation between IP, fear of failure, self-doubt,

Impostor Phenomenon in Science, Technology, Engineering, and Mathematics • 225

and self-efficacy. These factors, especially fear of failure, significantly contributed to the decision of majoring in STEM (Nelson et al., 2019).

Psychology

Surveys with psychology students in the United States, United Kingdom, and Australia have measured correlation between IP and a variety of factors. These include greater family achievement orientation, higher grade-point average (GPA; King & Cooley, 1995), perfectionism, externalizing success, higher standards for self-evaluation, self-criticalness, intolerance toward failure in meeting high standards, greater negative emotions, attributing failure to self, overgeneralizing a single failure to overall self-concepts, anxiety, depression, dissatisfaction, and humiliation (Thompson et al., 1998). Other factors correlated with IP are greater perfectionistic concern over mistakes, overestimating the number of mistakes made, less performance satisfaction, lower self-rating of success, poor confidence in one's performance, greater negative affect, lower perceptions of control (Thompson et al., 2000), greater perceived parental control or overprotection, lower self-care, poor mental health (Sonnak & Towell, 2001), shame or guilt (Cowman & Ferrari, 2002), higher self-handicapping behaviors (Ferrari & Thompson, 2006), fear of success or failure, low self-esteem, low motivation, and negative effect on career planning and career striving (Neureiter & Traut-Mattausch, 2016). There is some evidence that IP is positively correlated with GPA (especially for women) among 491 students of educational psychology from one U.S. institution (Cokley et al., 2015). Although IP was historically believed to be a personality trait, it could be an emotional feeling or response to an external situation (McElwee & Yurak, 2010). This necessitates understanding systematic inequities that could evoke such responses.

STEM

A large proportion of undergraduates in STEM (McWilliams et al., 2023), as large as 87% according to one study, are prone to moderate to higher IP (Johnson, 2022). Contrary to findings from Cokley and colleagues (2015), low IP is strongly correlated with higher GPA and math self-efficacy, which are unrelated for those with high IP (Blondeau, 2014). Many students feel unwelcome and invalidated in STEM disciplines, especially due to stereotypical assumptions about their race and a lack of belonging (worsened by family, friends, and peers) that affects their self-esteem and self-perceptions. There is strong association between perfectionism, psychological distress, and impostor feelings for pharmacy students (Henning et al., 1998). Higher IP is correlated with lower ability confidence and lower self-acceptance (September et al., 2001). Math undergraduates with higher impostor feelings may have lower future

226 • *Devasmita Chakraverty*

expectations and are less likely to expect to attend graduate school or work in a STEM field irrespective of gender (Blondeau, 2014). Further, there are gender differences for IP, career interest, and self-efficacy as related to the future intention of pursuing math-related work and/or a career in STEM (Blondeau & Awad, 2018), as seen among majors in computer science, biochemistry, and mechanical engineering. Research shows that IP hinders adaptive coping and promotes maladaptive coping, also increasing difficulties in making decisions related to one's career and decreasing career planning and occupational self-efficacy (Neureiter & Traut-Mattausch, 2017). These findings are based on survey studies conducted in Canada and the United States. Most of the participants were science and engineering majors, unless specified otherwise.

Doctoral and Postdoctoral Education

Doctoral students are increasingly experiencing IP that could sabotage career advancement. However, not all studies exclusively focus on STEM. Many studies have only subsamples of participants from STEM, and the findings are not specific to STEM fields (e.g., Cohen & McConnell, 2019; Fraenza, 2016; Jöstl et al., 2012).

STEM

A survey with doctoral students in Austria revealed that one third of them reported moderate or high IP (Jöstl et al., 2012). One of the more comprehensive studies interviewed 90 doctoral students across the United States and found many aspects in doctoral training related to IP. As students progressed in their program, gained public recognition (e.g., through awards), compared themselves with their peers, communicated their research at conferences and in peer-reviewed journals, and applied research knowledge, they felt like impostors (Chakraverty, 2020c). Among postdoctorates, those feeling like impostors hesitated to pursue newer areas of research, make social connections, and apply for new positions; felt undeserving and unqualified; procrastinated; experienced mental health issues; and struggled with scientific communication (Chakraverty, 2020b). Participants across multiple STEM fields shared that they first experienced IP as early as while applying to or immediately after being admitted to a PhD program. Impostor feelings continued throughout the length of doctoral training. Many attributed their success to professional connections, good luck, pretense, and gender or racial identity, further intensifying IP (Chakraverty, 2019).

Astronomy and Astrophysics

Graduate students in astronomy or astrophysics who receive adequate mentorship are less likely to show impostor traits. Female astronomy students are more likely to experience IP than their male peers, also feeling poorly mentored and unwelcome in the program. The longer students stay in the program, the more likely they are to experience traits of IP, which is also correlated with feeling less likely to be mentored (Ivie & Ephraim, 2009). Ivie et al. (2016) surveyed 837 graduate students in astronomy and astrophysics (2012–2013) and found that although IP and lack of mentoring affected thoughts of leaving the field, it did not directly lead to attrition from the field. For each point increase in the IP average score, a participant was 1.74 times more likely to think of leaving the field (due to poor sense of belonging). Overall, those who scored the most on the scale were 9.13 times more likely to have considered leaving the field compared with those who scored the least. Those who scored higher had also considered changing advisors or working outside the field. Also, women (who felt like impostors more than men; were mentored poorly; and experienced the two-body problem, i.e., difficulty finding a job in the same geographic location as their partner or spouse) were more likely to change advisors and eventually choose a field other than physics or astronomy.

Engineering

Studies where engineering students are a subsample of a larger STEM sample pay little attention to the environment in engineering that fosters IP (Chakraverty, 2019, 2020a, 2020b, 2020c; Lee et al., 2022; Lige et al., 2017; Simon, 2020; Simon & Choi, 2018). So far, only four studies have specifically examined IP in engineering and computer science (Burt et al., 2017; McGee et al., 2019, 2022; Rosenstein et al., 2020), focusing on cultural identity, acculturation process (Burt et al., 2017), and engineering identity participants develop during training (McGee et al., 2019). Only one study has examined IP among engineering education researchers, who experienced high to intense IP and othering. Engineering fields were perceived to be culturally disparate and superior to engineering education. The communication style and vocabulary were different; people valued different research paradigms and methodologies and held different identities. Engineering educators felt that their research was not rigorous or impactful. Additionally, women were subjected to gendered experiences, lack of recognition, and invisibility (Chakraverty, 2021).

Faculty

We have limited understanding about IP among STEM faculty because most studies do not specifically focus on either faculty or STEM. Few studies in STEM have included faculty as a subsample (Chakraverty, 2020a, 2021; Lee et al., 2022). Alternatively, Vázquez (2022) interviewed tenure-track and tenured faculty from one U.S. university (with only a subsample in STEM) and found that many faculty members across genders, disciplines, and professional ranks experienced IP, isolation, and depression not only after becoming faculty members but also right from graduate school.

Survey studies with self-selected samples show that faculty from STEM and non-STEM fields experience moderate, high, or intense impostor feelings that correlate with faculty rank, lower self-esteem, anxiety, and burnout (e.g., Hutchins, 2015). IP among faculty is related to emotional exhaustion; distress; maladaptive coping skills; fear of not earning tenure; and other undesirable outcomes related to research, teaching, and administration (e.g., lower ability to teach, produce research output, and get grant funding; Hutchins, 2015). Faculty members experienced moderate to intense IP, more so when untenured. This was further exacerbated by hypercompetitive work cultures that glorify a "publish or perish" narrative; make training time undefined; leave achievement goals open-ended and subjective; and have faculty struggling with securing research funding, long publication times, and sparse support systems.

Additionally, faculty members could experience IP when questioned about expertise, during unfavorable peer comparisons, due to concerns about academic productivity, when internalizing negative feedback about one's research writing, when experiencing difficulty normalizing success, and when fearing rejections (Hutchins & Rainbolt, 2017). However, timely academic support and positive self-talk helped faculty cope with impostor fears. Only one study has examined faculty experiences in STEM (Chakraverty, 2022b). Impostor fears were related to both research and teaching activities and intensified through peer comparisons, fear of faculty evaluation, fear of public recognition, anticipatory fear of not knowing enough about one's domain of expertise, and perceived lack of research or teaching competencies. Faculty across all ranks and experience levels harbored such fears.

In academia, STEM is predominantly male and White, especially in higher positions and at research-intensive institutions, with an oversupply of graduate students and postdoctorates and few available faculty positions. Thus STEM faculty from marginalized groups, such as women and/or underrepresented minorities (e.g., BIPOC individuals, sexual minorities, first-generation learners, those with disabilities), may question their place in academia even more and experience intense IP, especially due to their underrepresentation in higher ranks in the professoriate.

In summary, common antecedents of IP include fear of recognition or evaluation (e.g., awards), unfavorable comparison with peers, fear of public speaking and publishing research, not exploring new areas of research, anticipatory fear of not knowing, perceived poor competency, and feeling undeserving or unqualified when compared across doctoral students, postdoctorates, and faculty in STEM. Assuming such fears persist long term and could negatively affect academic identity development, it is essential that IP is addressed early on, especially as doctoral students and postdoctorates will eventually become faculty members.

IMPOSTOR PHENOMENON AMONG BIPOC INDIVIDUALS IN STEM

> I've really benefited unequally by looking white and by having a white last name. I haven't really felt a lot of the microaggressions about race. When talking to friends who have felt those, my impostor syndrome comes in cuz it feels like I'm faking it. If they knew that I was Hispanic, I wouldn't have gotten as far. (quoted in Chakraverty, 2022c, p. 7)

Some of the more recent research about IP in STEM has focused on BIPOC individuals. Their underrepresentation in STEM, especially in higher ranks, could make them question their success, have a poor sense of belonging, and experience IP. For women of color, IP could also be linked to stereotype threat and the challenges of thriving in a chilly climate in fields that are White- and male-dominated. This could lead to eventual departure from STEM and affect larger level efforts of making STEM fields more equitable, diverse, and culturally competent (Chakraverty, 2013; Collins et al., 2020). It would be important to shift from a White paradigm and examine impostor experiences through a culturally relevant lens.

Black Individuals

Black students experience IP due to a multitude of reasons (not limited to racism, bias, and microaggressions) leading to exclusion or underrepresentation in STEM (Burt et al., 2017). Although Black women are slightly better represented than Black men, they additionally face gender-based bias, sexism, and exclusion (Chakraverty, 2020a; NSF & NCSES, 2021). This makes them prone to isolation and invisibility and puts them at-risk for not receiving adequate mentorship, especially from mentors who belong to the same background. For undergraduate Black students in STEM, IP is associated with higher psychological distress and lower self-esteem, which in turn could affect academic achievement (Peteet et al., 2015). Self-esteem mediates the relationship between IP and racial identity (Lige et al., 2017). Finally, academic self-efficacy significantly predicts persistence in STEM, with a significant negative correlation between academic self-efficacy and IP (Walker, 2018).

The literature is more extensive among Black doctoral students and postdoctorates, both in terms of the number of studies and methodological variety. Many of the findings are based on interview data. Race-based impostor experience is related to stress; burnout; poor confidence; performance anxiety; emotional instability; and poor sense of belonging in classrooms, engineering departments, universities, the engineering field, and the Black community among foreign-born, Black, and male PhD students in STEM (Burt et al., 2017). This highlights racialized experiences both during and outside classroom interactions and explains racial underrepresentation in engineering. Racialized IP can be attributed to the poor representation of Black early-career researchers (PhD students and postdoctorates) in engineering and computing, where marginalized individuals struggle to fit in STEM programs culturally (McGee et al., 2019). IP among Black scholars in STEM is related to being a racial minority in predominantly White spaces; poor belonging in the department, university, or field; experiencing judgment, racial microaggressions, and stereotyping; external appearances such as skin tone, looks, accent, and clothes; being mistaken as someone outside academia due to skin color; being treated as diversity enhancers of the program; and intersecting identities of gender, race (including being biracial), country of birth, and membership in model minority groups (Chakraverty, 2020a). Other contributors include family background (e.g., first-generation status, lack of family support), doubting one's ability to complete doctoral training, and intersecting race and gender identities that shape doctoral experiences and cause anxiety and procrastination (Simon, 2020). Those with low or moderate IP have fewer negative experiences than those with frequent or intense IP (Simon, 2021).

A few survey studies have shown mixed results: Black individuals experienced moderate to intense IP (Chakraverty, 2020a) and had no statistically significant difference in their CIPS scores when compared with non-Black students from a U.S.-based research university (Simon, 2020). None of these findings are generalizable to the larger Black population due to a small sample size restricted to one or few institutions, sampled conveniently or selectively and not probabilistically.

Recent research has highlighted an interesting aspect: Interviews and focus groups with Black individuals in engineering and computing schools found that all participants had experienced racism, IP, social exclusion, and poor mental health. However, campus administrators often positioned institutional and structural racism (an environmental stressor) as IP (an irrational individual-level psychological disorder), putting the burden of developing the right mindset and overcoming IP on individual behavior change (McGee et al., 2022). This completely negates the role of power and privilege in STEM. The authors argued that if racism were eradicated, racial minorities would possibly not experience IP or struggle to overcome it through self-efforts. This underscores the need to understand environmental contributors of IP rather than viewing it as a personality trait alone, as has mostly been done.

Hispanic or Latinx Individuals

Hispanic or Latinx individuals experience moderate, high, or intense IP due to their family background, their first-generation status, being a nonnative English speaker (where English is the language of research communication), and an incongruence between their looks and their racial/ethnic identity. They are often positioned as diversity enhancers and lack critical mass in STEM, leading to underrepresentation and isolation. Specifically, those from mixed backgrounds identifying as Hispanic or Latinx who were perceived to be White (e.g., blonde, with lighter skin tone, specific last names) were questioned about their racial/ethnic authenticity (Chakraverty, 2022c). So far, no other study has specifically focused on Hispanic/Latinx experiences in STEM (Chakraverty, 2022c, 2022d).

Native American Individuals

IP research among Native Americans in STEM is sparse. Only one study showed that Native Americans experienced high to intense IP that related to minority identity. Influencing factors included cultural differences with White peers, poor understanding of Indigenous culture or knowledge by others, lack of critical mass, fear of standing out, chilly academic environment, lack of family background or understanding of STEM, first-generation status, family upbringing, and one's looks and diversity status (Chakraverty, 2022a). Native Americans experienced a dissonance between their cultural values (e.g., communal goals, community-based beliefs, inclusivity) and the dominant culture of higher education, especially in STEM (e.g., individualistic, anthropocentric, focused on competition instead of collaboration, exclusionary, hierarchical, valuing independence, focused on meritocracy, marginalizing culturally informed pedagogies and practices). Integrating and succeeding in STEM meant giving up one's personal and cultural values to fit in.

In summary, commonalities among BIPOC individuals' impostor experiences include a dissonance between cultural, personal, and STEM identity; racism and microaggressions; and the fear of standing out due to lack of critical mass. However, there are certain interesting nuances. Multiracial people, and/or those who appeared White, felt that others found it hard to make sense of the incongruity in looks and diversity status, often questioning them. More research should explore these nuances of IP in the future.

IMPOSTOR PHENOMENON AMONG OTHER UNDERREPRESENTED GROUPS IN STEM

> As a first-generation college student, I was shocked when I was accepted to [name of Ivy League institution] for undergraduate studies, and suffered from significant self-doubt while there, to the extent that I did not challenge myself in my coursework, and continually avoided academic involvement in study groups, lab groups, and extra-help tutoring sessions. I was afraid of asking stupid questions or seeming unqualified to be there. (quoted in Chakraverty, 2019, p. 9)

The hypercompetitive nature of STEM classrooms makes first-generation students 2 to 3 times more likely to experience impostor feelings and negative course outcomes on a daily basis compared with their continuing-generation peers. This may be detrimental to their persistence and success in STEM. First-generation students are more likely to value communality and collaboration compared with their peers (Canning et al., 2020; Mason et al., 2022). Higher impostor feelings correlate with negative course outcomes, such as lower end-of-term course engagement, lower attendance, higher intentions of dropping the course, and lower grades (Canning et al., 2020). This contradicts a prior study that found that higher IP is correlated with higher GPA, especially among female undergraduates (Cokley et al., 2015). First-generation female learners are even more underrepresented in STEM. In undergraduate studies, they feel like impostors due to a lack of belonging in STEM, negative stereotypes about women that externally invalidate their membership in STEM (through family, peers, teachers, and the society), and lack of psychological well-being (owing to maladaptive coping methods and ineffective work habits; Trefts, 2019). Strategies such as positive interactions with STEM faculty and better peer support can manage and reduce impostor feelings. Additionally, stereotype threat significantly and positively predicted burnout and IP among lesbian, gay, and bisexual students in STEM, where IP mediated the relationship between stereotype threat and STEM identity in undergraduate students (Bastnagel, 2021).

PERSONALITY TRAIT VERSUS ENVIRONMENTAL INFLUENCE

> He [her male mentor] told me that I shouldn't share my opinion in meetings. He said that's not something that we should do here. I'm constantly getting those types of messages at work, that I shouldn't be speaking up. . . . We are never included in the conversation. My inner impostor is growing. It is a beast now. I constantly am doubting accomplishments. Part of me is like, I don't want to share my ideas because I am terrified that they will never give me credit for anything that I put effort into. . . . There's not a great diversity, and there's not

a lot of females in leadership roles. The environment makes you more prone to impostor syndrome. (quoted in Chakraverty, 2021, p. 768)

Most research on IP focused on individual-level correlates, including personality traits (e.g., maladaptive perfectionism), mental health issues (e.g., anxiety, depression, distress, burnout, suicidal ideation), and internal traits. This unidimensional view of IP is problematic because it puts the onus of managing and overcoming self-sabotaging beliefs on the individual (McGee et al., 2022). Higher IP is correlated negatively with transformational leadership style and positively with transactional and passive leadership styles, irrespective of gender. Therefore, impostor experience is correlated with less effective leadership traits (Domínguez-Soto et al., 2023).

Recent research has focused on the environmental factors of IP, more so for women and people of color. In STEM, these include a hypercompetitive environment (Canning et al., 2020); the collective underrepresentation of women, first-generation learners, and people of color (Canning et al., 2020; Chakraverty, 2022a, 2022c, 2022d); race-based and gender-based discrimination (Burt et al., 2017; Chakraverty, 2020a; Simon, 2020, 2021); unsupportive mentors (Simon, 2020); and workplace harassment (Aycock et al., 2019). Toxic STEM environments can affect persistence in STEM, especially for women (Tao & Gloria, 2019) and persons of color (Chakraverty, 2020a). It is especially important to understand the role of workplace violence in propagating IP.

Women and BIPOC individuals are disadvantaged at multiple levels. In STEM, they are fewer in number and tend to be underrepresented in higher positions of power, such as among faculty members, chairs, and deans (NSF & NCSES, 2021). Women and BIPOC individuals also experience a disproportionately higher incidence of workplace violence compared with men (National Academies of Sciences, Engineering, and Medicine, 2018). A large proportion of undergraduate women in physics will experience at least one form of sexual harassment (more specifically, gender harassment), which also correlates with heightened IP and a negative sense of belonging in physics (Aycock et al., 2019). IP is pervasive across several disciplines in STEM where women experience harassment. In doctoral education, these include disciplines with fieldwork (e.g., geology), disciplines that are historically dominated by men (e.g., physics), and disciplines that are more gender-diverse (e.g., biology), dispelling notions that gender equity could predict safer work environments (Chakraverty & Rishi, 2022). Forms of workplace violence include "non-physical abusive behavior (including verbal abuse), gender-based harassment, incivility, unwanted sexual attention, abusive supervision, and microaggressions, including unverified biological connections between gender and superiority/inferiority and uncomfortable questions/sexual comments from peers and older persons in power" (Chakraverty & Rishi, 2022, p. 26–27). Those perpetrating violence could belong to all genders and positions: male or female advisors, instructors, and peers.

People of color also report harassment in relation to impostor experiences. Black doctorates and postdoctorates reported stereotyping and tokenism (symbolic inclusion without any real integration); microaggressions and judgment; microassaults, microinsults, and microinvalidations; and IP due to race-based othering (Chakraverty, 2020a). Black individuals are judged based on looks, accent, and clothes and regarded as diversity enhancers who occupy educational positions without real merit; one person was even called "good Black" by a White faculty member to distinguish African first-generation immigrants ("good Black") from African Americans (Chakraverty, 2020a, p. 448).

Similarly, Latinas can experience moderate to intense impostor feelings attributed to their age, gender, and race/ethnicity and to gendered harassment, bias, and microaggressions (Acosta, 2020). Additionally, Hispanic or Latinx individuals report IP in relation to identity-based microaggressions from faculty members, peers, and the academic community in general. Overall, BIPOC individuals (especially women) are at a greater risk of experiencing harassment and unsafe work environments because of their racial and gender identity in a double bind effect. They are vulnerable to impostor feelings due to many reasons: internalizing workplace violence as something they deserve; feeling invisible and voiceless; feeling less trustful of others; feeling unable to develop a sense of belonging; feeling defeminized in fields dominated by older, upper-class men in power; questioning one's success in STEM and attributing it to luck and/or minority status; and feeling less deserving of their success. It is not uncommon for those experiencing impostor feelings and workplace harassment to tolerate such harassment just to fit in (Chakraverty, 2022d).

OTHERING IN STEM, SENSE OF BELONGING, AND IMPOSTOR PHENOMENON

> I feel I'm not one of them. My accent gets in the way of getting the message I want in a presentation. People look at me as, oh, she doesn't know what she's talkin' about—that impostor is there—it creates this environment where you are more anxious and maybe overdo it. The accent, that's part of, "Oh, the tiny little Mexican is here." (quoted in Chakraverty, 2022c, p. 9)

Othering is a "process which serves to mark and name those thought to be different from oneself" (Weis, 1995, p. 17). The contradiction of feeling like an impostor despite one's achievements can be understood from hierarchies and dominant identities in STEM fields. STEM fields have been historically dominated by upper-class, White and male, continuing-generation learners, who are also native English speakers, highlighting the hierarchical and exclusionary nature of the field that helps the dominant groups to persist and succeed in STEM while marginalizing others. Even research and teaching in STEM follows Western, positivistic paradigms of knowledge making, devoid of practices and pedagogies that are culturally informed and Indigenous (Chakraverty, 2022a). This disadvantages people of color and puts the burden of integrating, assimilating, belonging, thriving, and succeeding in STEM on those who fall outside the realm of these power structures. Such inequity also creates poor sense of belonging and heightened impostor feelings (Chakraverty, 2021). Therefore, women and BIPOC communities continue to be underrepresented or excluded in spaces of STEM learning often dominated by White men, especially in higher positions of power (NSF & NCSES, 2021). Those who do not fit the dominant demographic often fear being stereotyped negatively (e.g., as being lazy, less meritorious, or angry) and are cautious about how they represent their group and work harder to counter group-based negative perceptions (e.g., women cannot excel at math, Hispanic women are fiery or angry, nonnative English speakers cannot write well in English). Othering can also happen through gender harassment, race-based harassment, and microaggressions (Chakraverty, 2022d; Chakraverty & Rishi, 2022). Faculty members and doctoral advisors, peers, and other academic persons, both men and women, could contribute to such harassment by questioning someone's belonging in academia, showing lack of cultural awareness, harboring low academic expectations, making stereotypical assumptions about one's race and life choices, gaslighting behavior, and attributing success to their race rather than achievement.

STRATEGIES TO MANAGE OR OVERCOME IMPOSTOR PHENOMENON

> Since the workshop, I am better able to identify and acknowledge when I am feeling like an impostor. (quoted in Chang et al., 2022, p. 4)

Recommendations to manage IP include early intervention, especially from faculty mentors and preceptors. Faculty mentors are advised to familiarize their students with IP, share their own struggles, provide constructive feedback, and offer mentorship (Gresham-Dolby, 2022). Workshops that address IP and strengthen career resilience should be offered, such as one on IP and mindset for students in a summer research experience program that helped them develop coping strategies (Chang et al., 2022). The workshop focused on strategies to manage IP by activating a growth mindset. Mindfulness training programs are also highly recommended. In an intervention study, a mindfulness foundation was developed to help female graduate students in STEM manage IP through enhanced mindfulness and self-authorship (Lausch, 2021). *Self-authorship* refers to how individuals internalize information and advice they receive from others, navigate negative feedback or stereotypes, and use personal reasoning based on one's understanding of the self. Mindfulness foundation included self-awareness, self-compassion, and emotion regulation. Additionally, strengthening one's science identity could help individuals integrate better and foster a sense of belonging in STEM. Science identity develops early in life and involves substantial parental or family involvement (Chakraverty et al., 2018).

CONCLUSION AND FUTURE RESEARCH

Women, racial/ethnic minority individuals, first-generation learners, and sexual minority individuals (including those identifying as lesbian, gay, or bisexual) are historically underrepresented in STEM. Many of them also experience frequent and intense IP. We need more focused studies in many areas to understand this phenomenon better. IP in STEM has focused mostly on academia and not on those in the industry. Very little research has focused on first-generation learners and sexual minorities. Asian experiences are also largely undocumented, although Asian students and professionals are a rapidly growing group in STEM and are often subjected to racial bias, microaggressions, stereotyping, and harassment (Castro & Collins, 2021; Nicholson & Mei, 2020). We also need more studies comparing men and women and specifically studying men. Gender-based research often documents antecedents of IP specific to women; it would be interesting to see if specific situations make men vulnerable to IP.

Other than studying specific demographics in STEM, research should focus on refining the instruments to measure IP. The CIPS is one of the most widely used scales along with the lesser used Harvey Impostor Phenomenon Scale (Harvey, 1981). These scales are several decades old. The CIPS was developed after interviewing White women who experienced IP. These scales may not be suitable when used in other demographic or cultural contexts. Similarly, although there is some research from other countries, most of the studies in STEM are U.S.-centric (followed by some in Australia and the United Kingdom). Research from other countries could highlight cultural differences in our understanding of IP. Also, most of the research is in English, which makes it accessible to only the part of the world population that understands and speaks English. Language shapes our thoughts, our perceptions of the world, and the way we act (Boroditsky, 2011). Yet there is no apt contextual translation of the term "impostor phenomenon" in other languages.

In terms of study design, most of the studies use cross-sectional, correlational surveys. Data were collected from one or few (usually predominantly White) institutions by convenience sampling. Findings are not generalizable to a larger population. There are very few longitudinal studies (Clark et al., 2021; Ivie & Ephraim, 2009), although they could potentially explain the long-term impact of experiencing IP and whether it decreases with age and experience. Similarly, only one study used an experimental design (Thompson et al., 2000), although experimental designs could establish causal relationships between IP and other variables. Qualitative and mixed-methods studies are more recent and increasingly gaining prominence; these designs could potentially enhance our understanding of the phenomenon in new directions.

Finally, we need more research that examines environmental conditions that aggravate IP. IP was understood as a personality trait for a long time, and research has neglected the role of the environment. Overreliance on individual-level improvement measures also puts the onus of addressing this phenomenon on the person rather than looking at the micro- and macroenvironments in STEM. Addressing this phenomenon at a larger level will include deep work, from questioning the demographics of STEM to better sensitization against racism, sexism, stereotyping, bias, and microaggressions. Individuals are less likely to feel like an impostor in a nurturing, inclusive environment where their identity, experiences, and skills are valued. Safe academic spaces and workplaces can help individuals develop a better sense of belonging and not feel like impostors.

REFERENCES

Acosta, I. (2020). *You made it, are you still facing it? Educated Latinas experiencing impostor phenomenon and multiple microaggressions in the professional world* [Doctoral dissertation, California State University]. CSU Institutional Repository. https://dspace.calstate.edu/bitstream/handle/10211.3/216265/Final%20Dissertation%2C%20I.%20Acosta.pdf?sequence=1

Aycock, L. M., Hazari, Z., Brewe, E., Clancy, K. B., Hodapp, T., & Goertzen, R. M. (2019). Sexual harassment reported by undergraduate female physicists. *Physical Review: Physics Education Research*, *15*(1), Article 010121. https://doi.org/10.1103/PhysRevPhysEducRes.15.010121

Bastnagel, A. E. (2021). *Factors influencing LGB STEM majors' underrepresentation in STEM fields* [Doctoral dissertation, Purdue University Graduate School]. Hammer Research Repository.

Blondeau, L. A. (2014). *The impact of the impostor phenomenon on the math self-efficacy of males and females in STEM majors* [Doctoral dissertation, The University of Texas at Austin]. UT Electronic Theses and Dissertations. https://repositories.lib.utexas.edu/handle/2152/26007

Blondeau, L. A., & Awad, G. H. (2018). The relation of the impostor phenomenon to future intentions of mathematics-related school and work. *Journal of Career Development, 45*(3), 253–267. https://doi.org/10.1177/0894845316680769

Boroditsky, L. (2011). How language shapes thought. *Scientific American, 304*(2), 62–65. https://doi.org/10.1038/scientificamerican0211-62

Burt, B. A., Knight, A., & Roberson, J. (2017). Racializing experiences of foreign-born and ethnically diverse Black male engineering graduate students: Implications for student affairs practice, policy, and research. *Journal of International Students, 7*(4), 925–943. https://doi.org/10.32674/jis.v7i4.182

Canning, E. A., LaCosse, J., Kroeper, K. M., & Murphy, M. C. (2020). Feeling like an imposter: The effect of perceived classroom competition on the daily psychological experiences of first-generation college students. *Social Psychological and Personality Science, 11*(5), 647–657. https://doi.org/10.1177/1948550619882032

Caselman, T. D., Self, P. A., & Self, A. L. (2006). Adolescent attributes contributing to the imposter phenomenon. *Journal of Adolescence, 29*(3), 395–405. https://doi.org/10.1016/j.adolescence.2005.07.003

Castro, A. R., & Collins, C. S. (2021). Asian American women in STEM in the lab with "White Men Named John." *Science Education, 105*(1), 33–61. https://doi.org/10.1002/sce.21598

Chakraverty, D. (2013). *An examination of how women and underrepresented racial/ethnic minorities experience barriers in biomedical research and medical programs* [Doctoral dissertation, University of Virginia]. DigitalCommons. https://digitalcommons.unl.edu/dberspeakers/43

Chakraverty, D. (2019). Impostor phenomenon in STEM: Occurrence, attribution, and identity. *Studies in Graduate and Postdoctoral Education, 10*(1), 2–20. https://doi.org/10.1108/SGPE-D-18-00014

Chakraverty, D. (2020a). The impostor phenomenon among Black doctoral and postdoctoral scholars in STEM. *International Journal of Doctoral Studies, 15*, 433–460. https://doi.org/10.28945/4613

Chakraverty, D. (2020b). The impostor phenomenon among postdoctoral trainees in STEM: A U.S.-based mixed-methods study. *International Journal of Doctoral Studies, 15*, 329–352. https://doi.org/10.28945/4589

Chakraverty, D. (2020c). PhD student experiences with the impostor phenomenon in STEM. *International Journal of Doctoral Studies, 15*, 159–179. https://doi.org/10.28945/4513

Chakraverty, D. (2021). Impostor phenomenon among engineering education researchers: An exploratory study. *International Journal of Doctoral Studies, 16*, 757–776. https://doi.org/10.28945/4883

Chakraverty, D. (2022a). A cultural impostor? Native American experiences of impostor phenomenon in STEM. *CBE Life Sciences Education, 21*(1), Article ar15. https://doi.org/10.1187/cbe.21-08-0204

Chakraverty, D. (2022b). Faculty experiences of the impostor phenomenon in STEM fields. *CBE Life Sciences Education, 21*(4), Article ar84. https://doi.org/10.1187/cbe.21-10-0307

Chakraverty, D. (2022c). Impostor phenomenon among Hispanic/Latino early career researchers in STEM fields. *Journal of Latinos and Education.* Advance online publication. https://doi.org/10.1080/15348431.2022.2125394

Chakraverty, D. (2022d). Impostor phenomenon and identity-based microaggression among Hispanic/Latinx individuals in science, technology, engineering, and mathematics: A qualitative exploration. *Violence and Gender, 9*(3), 135–141. https://doi.org/10.1089/vio.2021.0061

Chakraverty, D., Newcomer, S. N., Puzio, K., & Tai, R. H. (2018). It runs in the family: The role of family and extended social networks in developing early science interest. *Bulletin of Science, Technology & Society, 38*(3–4), 27–38. https://doi.org/10.1177/0270467620911589

Chakraverty, D., & Rishi, M. (2022). Impostor phenomenon and discipline-specific experiences of violence in science, technology, engineering, and mathematics. *Violence and Gender, 9*(1), 22–29. https://doi.org/10.1089/vio.2021.0025

Chang, S., Lee, H. Y., Anderson, C. B., Kewis, K., Chakraverty, D., & Yates, M. S. (2022). Intervening on impostor phenomenon: Prospective evaluation of a workshop for health science students using a mixed-method design. *BMC Medical Education, 22,* Article 802. https://doi.org/10.1186/s12909-022-03824-7

Clance, P. R. (1985). *Clance Impostor Phenomenon Scale (CIPS)* [Database record]. APA PsycTests. https://doi.org/10.1037/t11274-000

Clark, S. L., Dyar, C., Inman, E. M., Maung, N., & London, B. (2021). Women's career confidence in a fixed, sexist STEM environment. *International Journal of STEM Education, 8*(1), Article 56. https://doi.org/10.1186/s40594-021-00313-z

Cohen, E. D., & McConnell, W. R. (2019). Fear of fraudulence: Graduate school program environments and the impostor phenomenon. *The Sociological Quarterly, 60*(3), 457–478. https://doi.org/10.1080/00380253.2019.1580552

Cokley, K., Awad, G., Smith, L., Jackson, S., Awosogba, O., Hurst, A., Stone, S., Blondeau, L., & Roberts, D. (2015). The roles of gender stigma consciousness, impostor phenomenon and academic self-concept in the academic outcomes of women and men. *Sex Roles, 73*(9–10), 414–426. https://doi.org/10.1007/s11199-015-0516-7

Collins, K. H., Price, E. F., Hanson, L., & Neaves, D. (2020). Consequences of stereotype threat and imposter syndrome: The personal journey from STEM-practitioner to STEM-educator for four women of color. *Taboo: The Journal of Culture and Education, 19*(4), 61–80. https://digitalscholarship.unlv.edu/taboo/vol19/iss4/10

Cowman, S. E., & Ferrari, J. R. (2002). "Am I for real?": Predicting impostor tendencies from self-handicapping and affective components. *Social Behavior and Personality, 30*(2), 119–125. https://doi.org/10.2224/sbp.2002.30.2.119

Domínguez-Soto, C., Labajo, V., & Labrador-Fernández, J. (2023). The relationship between impostor phenomenon and transformational leadership among students in STEM. *Current Psychology, 42,* 11195–11206. https://doi.org/10.1007/s12144-021-02358-3

Eddy, S. L., Brownell, S. E., & Wenderoth, M. P. (2014). Gender gaps in achievement and participation in multiple introductory biology classrooms. *CBE Life Sciences Education, 13*(3), 478–492. https://doi.org/10.1187/cbe.13-10-0204

Ferrari, J. R., & Thompson, T. (2006). Impostor fears: Links with self-presentational concerns and self-handicapping behaviours. *Personality and Individual Differences, 40*(2), 341–352. https://doi.org/10.1016/j.paid.2005.07.012

Fraenza, C. B. (2016). The role of social influence in anxiety and the imposter phenomenon. *Online Learning, 20*(2), 230–243. https://doi.org/10.24059/olj.v20i2.618

French, B. F., Ullrich-French, S. C., & Follman, D. (2008). The psychometric properties of the Clance Impostor Scale. *Personality and Individual Differences, 44*(5), 1270–1278. https://doi.org/10.1016/j.paid.2007.11.023

Gibbs, K. D., Jr., McGready, J., Bennett, J. C., & Griffin, K. (2014). Biomedical science PhD career interest patterns by race/ethnicity and gender. *PLOS ONE, 9*(12), Article e114736. https://doi.org/10.1371/journal.pone.0114736

Gonzalez, H. B., & Kuenzi, J. J. (2012). *Science, technology, engineering, and mathematics (STEM) education: A primer*. Congressional Research Service, Library of Congress.

Gresham-Dolby, C. (2022). Imposter syndrome: An opportunity to positively influence mentees. *Currents in Pharmacy Teaching & Learning, 14*(2), 130–132. https://doi.org/10.1016/j.cptl.2021.11.019

Grunspan, D. Z., Eddy, S. L., Brownell, S. E., Wiggins, B. L., Crowe, A. J., & Goodreau, S. M. (2016). Males under-estimate academic performance of their female peers in undergraduate biology classrooms. *PLOS ONE, 11*(2), Article e0148405. https://doi.org/10.1371/journal.pone.0148405

Hamrick, K. (2019). *Women, minorities, and persons with disabilities in science and engineering* (Special Report NSF 19-304). National Science Foundation, National Center for Science and Engineering Statistics. https://ncses.nsf.gov/pubs/nsf19304/digest/field-of-degree-minorities

Harvey, J. C. (1981). *The impostor phenomenon and achievement: A failure to internalize success* [Doctoral dissertation, Temple University]. ProQuest Dissertations Publishing. https://www.proquest.com/openview/af73692323572e8a3c1a4cda93ae39dd/1?pq-origsite=gscholar&cbl=18750&diss=y

Hellman, C. M., & Caselman, T. D. (2004). A psychometric evaluation of the Harvey Imposter Phenomenon Scale. *Journal of Personality Assessment, 83*(2), 161–166. https://doi.org/10.1207/s15327752jpa8302_10

Henning, K., Ey, S., & Shaw, D. (1998). Perfectionism, the impostor phenomenon and psychological adjustment in medical, dental, nursing and pharmacy students. *Medical Education, 32*(5), 456–464. https://doi.org/10.1046/j.1365-2923.1998.00234.x

Hutchins, H. M. (2015). Outing the imposter: A study exploring imposter phenomenon among higher education faculty. *New Horizons in Adult Education and Human Resource Development, 27*(2), 3–12. https://doi.org/10.1002/nha3.20098

Hutchins, H. M., & Rainbolt, H. (2017). What triggers imposter phenomenon among academic faculty? A critical incident study exploring antecedents, coping, and development opportunities. *Human Resource Development International, 20*(3), 194–214. https://doi.org/10.1080/13678868.2016.1248205

Ivie, R., & Ephraim, A. (2009). Mentoring and the imposter syndrome in astronomy graduate students. In A. L. Kinney, D. Khachadourian, P. S. Millar, & C. N. Hartman (Eds.), *Women in astronomy and space science: Meeting the challenges of an increasingly diverse workforce* (pp. 25–33). National Aeronautics and Space Administration. https://aas.org/sites/default/files/2019-09/WomeninAstroProceedings.pdf

Ivie, R., White, S., & Chu, R. Y. (2016). Women's and men's career choices in astronomy and astrophysics. *Physical Review: Physics Education Research, 12*(2), Article 020109. https://doi.org/10.1103/PhysRevPhysEducRes.12.020109

Johnson, E. (2022). *Imposter phenomenon among students in STEM education: A case study* [Doctoral dissertation, Wilmington University]. ProQuest Dissertations Publishing. https://www.proquest.com/openview/d7b86a9faf0bd9c0d02a60ee40f5fbf9/1?pq-origsite=gscholar&cbl=18750&diss=y

Jöstl, G., Bergsmann, E., Lüftenegger, M., Schober, B., & Spiel, C. (2012). When will they blow my cover? The impostor phenomenon among Austrian doctoral students. *Zeitschrift für Psychologie, 220*(2), 109–120. https://doi.org/10.1027/2151-2604/a000102

King, J. E., & Cooley, E. L. (1995). Achievement orientation and the impostor phenomenon among college students. *Contemporary Educational Psychology, 20*(3), 304–312. https://doi.org/10.1006/ceps.1995.1019

Lausch, S. (2021). *I will not stand in my way: Exploring the effects of mindfulness on impostor feelings through self-authorship in female STEM graduate students* [Doctoral dissertation, Boise State University]. Boise State University Theses and Dissertations. https://scholarworks.boisestate.edu/td/1805/

Lee, H. Y., Anderson, C. B., Yates, M. S., Chang, S., & Chakraverty, D. (2022). Insights into the complexity of the impostor phenomenon among trainees and professionals in STEM and medicine. *Current Psychology, 41*, 5913–5924. https://doi.org/10.1007/s12144-020-01089-1

Lige, Q. M., Peteet, B. J., & Brown, C. M. (2017). Racial identity, self-esteem, and the impostor phenomenon among African American college students. *The Journal of Black Psychology, 43*(4), 345–357. https://doi.org/10.1177/0095798416648787

Martínez, A., & Gayfield, A. (2019). *The intersectionality of sex, race, and Hispanic origin in the STEM workforce* (SEHSD Working Paper Number 2018-27). U.S. Census Bureau. https://www.census.gov/content/dam/Census/library/working-papers/2019/demo/sehsd-wp2018-27.pdf

Mason, H. R., Ata, A., Nguyen, M., Nakae, S., Chakraverty, D., Eggan, B., Martinez, S., & Jeffe, D. B. (2022). First-generation and continuing-generation college graduates' application, acceptance, and matriculation to U.S. medical schools: A national cohort study. *Medical Education Online, 27*(1), Article 2010291. https://doi.org/10.1080/10872981.2021.2010291

McElwee, R. O., & Yurak, T. J. (2010). The phenomenology of the impostor phenomenon. *Individual Differences Research, 8*(3), 184–197.

McGee, E. O., Botchway, P. K., Naphan-Kingery, D. E., Brockman, A. J., Houston, S., & White, D. T. (2022). Racism camouflaged as impostorism and the impact on Black STEM doctoral students. *Race Ethnicity and Education, 25*(4), 487–507. https://doi.org/10.1080/13613324.2021.1924137

McGee, E. O., Griffith, D. M., & Houston, S. L. (2019). "I know I have to work twice as hard and hope that makes me good enough": Exploring the stress and strain of Black doctoral students in engineering and computing. *Teachers College Record, 121*(4), 1–38. https://doi.org/10.1177/016146811912100407

McWilliams, D., Block, M., Hinson, J., & Kier, K. L. (2023). Impostor phenomenon in undergraduates and pharmacy students at a small private university. *American*

Journal of Pharmaceutical Education, 87(1), Article AJPE8728. https://doi.org/10.5688/ajpe8728

Muradoglu, M., Horne, Z., Hammond, M. D., Leslie, S. J., & Cimpian, A. (2022). Women—particularly underrepresented minority women—and early-career academics feel like impostors in fields that value brilliance. *Journal of Educational Psychology, 114*(5), 1086–1100. https://doi.org/10.1037/edu0000669

National Academies of Sciences, Engineering, and Medicine. (2018). *Sexual harassment of women: Climate, culture, and consequences in academic sciences, engineering, and medicine.* National Academies Press. https://doi.org/10.17226/24994

National Science Foundation. (2017). *Survey of graduate students and postdoctorates in science and engineering.* https://ncsesdata.nsf.gov/gradpostdoc/2017/

National Science Foundation & National Center for Science and Engineering Statistics. (2021). *Women, minorities, and persons with disabilities in science and engineering: 2021* (Special Report NSF 21–321). https://ncses.nsf.gov/pubs/nsf21321/

Nelson, K., McDaniel, J., & Tackett, S. (2019). Majoring in STEM: How the factors of fear of failure, impostor phenomenon, and self-efficacy impact decision-making. *National Social Science Journal, 52*(1), 76–87.

Neureiter, M., & Traut-Mattausch, E. (2016). An inner barrier to career development: Preconditions of the impostor phenomenon and consequences for career development. *Frontiers in Psychology, 7*, Article 48. https://doi.org/10.3389/fpsyg.2016.00048

Neureiter, M., & Traut-Mattausch, E. (2017). Two sides of the career resources coin: Career adaptability resources and the impostor phenomenon. *Journal of Vocational Behavior, 98*, 56–69. https://doi.org/10.1016/j.jvb.2016.10.002

Nicholson, H. L., & Mei, D. (2020). Racial microaggressions and self-rated health among Asians and Asian Americans. *Race and Social Problems, 12*(3), 209–218. https://doi.org/10.1007/s12552-020-09293-1

Peteet, B. J., Brown, C. M., Lige, Q. M., & Lanaway, D. A. (2015). Impostorism is associated with greater psychological distress and lower self-esteem for African American students. *Current Psychology, 34*(1), 154–163. https://doi.org/10.1007/s12144-014-9248-z

Rosenstein, A., Raghu, A., & Porter, L. (2020). Identifying the prevalence of the impostor phenomenon among computer science students. *Proceedings of the 51st Association for Computing Machinery Technical Symposium on Computer Science Education, Portland, Oregon* (pp. 30–36). Association for Computing Machinery. https://doi.org/10.1145/3328778.3366815

September, A. N., McCarrey, M., Baranowsky, A., Parent, C., & Schindler, D. (2001). The relation between well-being, impostor feelings, and gender role orientation among Canadian university students. *The Journal of Social Psychology, 141*(2), 218–232. https://doi.org/10.1080/00224540109600548

Simon, M. (2020). STEMming within a double minority: How the impostor syndrome affects Black women PhD students. *International Journal of Multiple Research Approaches, 12*(2), 185–201. https://doi.org/10.29034/ijmra.v12n2a2

Simon, M. (2021). Negotiating doctoral STEM studies: An in-depth look at the Black woman impostor. *Journal of African American Women and Girls in Education, 1*(2), 94–118. https://doi.org/10.21423/jaawge-v1i2a89

Simon, M., & Choi, Y. J. (2018). Using factor analysis to validate the Clance Impostor Phenomenon Scale in sample of science, technology, engineering and mathematics doctoral students. *Personality and Individual Differences, 121*, 173–175. https://doi.org/10.1016/j.paid.2017.09.039

Sonnak, C., & Towell, T. (2001). The impostor phenomenon in British university students: Relationships between self-esteem, mental health, parental rearing style and socioeconomic status. *Personality and Individual Differences, 31*(6), 863–874. https://doi.org/10.1016/S0191-8869(00)00184-7

Tao, K. W., & Gloria, A. M. (2019). Should I stay or should I go? The role of impostorism in STEM persistence. *Psychology of Women Quarterly, 43*(2), 151–164. https://doi.org/10.1177/0361684318802333

Thompson, T., Davis, H., & Davidson, J. (1998). Attributional and affective responses of impostors to academic success and failure outcomes. *Personality and Individual Differences, 25*(2), 381–396. https://doi.org/10.1016/S0191-8869(98)00065-8

Thompson, T., Foreman, P., & Martin, F. (2000). Impostor fears and perfectionistic concern over mistakes. *Personality and Individual Differences, 29*(4), 629–647. https://doi.org/10.1016/S0191-8869(99)00218-4

Trefts, S. (2019). *The imposter phenomenon in female, first-generation STEM majors* [Doctoral dissertation, California Lutheran University]. ProQuest Dissertations Publishing. https://www.proquest.com/openview/a8fbda808f0e0ea1c145c1092a94e7d2/1.pdf?pq-origsite=gscholar&cbl=18750&diss=y

Vázquez, E. (2022). Negative emotions, social isolation, and impostor syndrome in the pursuit of professional mastery in research universities. *The International Journal for Academic Development*. Advance online publication. https://doi.org/10.1080/1360144X.2022.2072848

Walker, C. A. 2018. *Impostor phenomenon, academic self-efficacy, and persistence among African-American female undergraduate STEM majors* [Doctoral dissertation, Northeastern University]. Digital Repository Service. https://doi.org/10.17760/D20316441

Weis, L. (1995). Identity formation and the processes of "othering": Unraveling sexual threads. *The Journal of Educational Foundations, 9*(1), 17–33.

11 IMPOSTOR PHENOMENON IN MEDICINE

DEVASMITA CHAKRAVERTY

Many of my colleagues and I often talk about the imposter syndrome and we feel like someone's really going to find out that I have absolutely no idea what I'm doing. I still think someone is going to send me a letter saying "actually it was a mistake. You weren't supposed to get into medical school, therefore, we're taking it all away." And yet you go on and you pass all your exams with flying colors, but it's this "who am I and am I really capable of doing this?"

—Physician quoted in LaDonna et al. (2018, p. 7)

The impostor phenomenon (IP) is widely experienced among students, physicians, physician–scientists, and faculty members, including those who are well advanced in their career. Those with impostor feelings, either episodically or more frequently, feel incompetent, question their success, and feel like a fraud. It is correlated with lower self-compassion, lower self-esteem, burnout, and stress. Although the term "impostor syndrome" is used commonly in popular literature, social media, podcasts, and opinion articles, the accurate term is "impostor phenomenon" (Clance & Imes, 1978), as the word "syndrome" has stigma and judgment associated with it (email communication with Dr. Clance, as cited in Chakraverty, 2019). Despite its association with many negative outcomes, IP is not an official clinical diagnosis of a psychiatric disorder (Fowler & Villanueva, 2023). However, whether it must be considered

https://doi.org/10.1037/0000397-012
The Impostor Phenomenon: Psychological Research, Theory, and Interventions,
K. Cokley (Editor)
Copyright © 2024 by the American Psychological Association. All rights reserved.

as a personality trait, fixed trait, individual trait, or temporary state that can be overcome through interventions (e.g., counseling, mentoring, therapy, group discussions) is not clear (Paladugu et al., 2021). The cultural or environmental aspects of impostor experiences are less understood (Franchi & Russell-Sewell, 2023; Seritan & Mehta, 2016).

Medicine is predominantly a White, male profession in the United States or North America, especially in higher ranks of position and power. This could make other individuals with marginalized identities even more vulnerable to IP. IP is more than a personality trait; it can be evoked by systemic inequities and other environmental factors. In medicine, systemic inequities disadvantage women when they are appreciated less, paid less, viewed as less competent, mistaken to be someone else based on gender stereotype, gaslit, patronized, and sexually harassed (Chakraverty, 2013; Mullangi & Jagsi, 2019). Most research in medicine has examined correlations between IP and other variables, including demographic variables.

This chapter reviews extant research on IP in medicine. First, the chapter presents an overview of the demographic characteristics of medicine, especially in the United States or North American context. Then the chapter examines popular scales used to measure IP in medicine. The discussion then shifts to IP among students (medical, graduate, and MD-PhD), professionals (residents, physicians, physician assistants, and veterinarians), and mixed samples. Lastly, the chapter points to evidence-based strategies to manage or overcome IP as well as several directions of future research.

DEMOGRAPHIC CHARACTERISTICS OF MEDICINE

As the U.S. population gets more diverse, it is important that the population of those providing patient care and furthering medical research matches the patient population. Unlike in STEM, women are not underrepresented in medicine at many levels. In U.S. medical schools in 2022 to 2023, women constituted 56.5% of applicants, 58% of first-time applicants, 55.7% of acceptances, and 55.6% of matriculants (Association of American Medical Colleges [AAMC], 2022). In 2018 to 2019, women constituted 50.9% of applicants and 47.9% of graduates but only 41.4% of faculty (their numbers declining at the associate professor and professor ranks) and 35.9% of most active physicians in medical schools (AAMC, 2019). In terms of racial/ethnic diversity (2018–2019), the pool is 46.8% White, 21.3% Asian, 8.4% Black, and 6.2% Hispanic or Latinx applicants; 49.8% White, 22% Asian, 7.1% Black, and 6.2% Hispanic or Latinx acceptances; 49.9% White, 22.1% Asian, 9.5% multiracial/multiethnic, 7.1%

Black, 6.2% Hispanic or Latinx, 0.2% American Indian or Alaska Native, and 0.1% Native Hawaiian or other Pacific Islander matriculants; and 54.6% White, 21.6% Asian, 8% multiracial/multiethnic, 6.2% Black, and 5.3% Hispanic or Latinx graduates. Full-time faculty continued to be predominantly White (63.9%) overall, especially at the professor and associate professor ranks, followed by 19.2% Asian, 5.5% Hispanic or Latinx, and 3.6% Black faculty (AAMC, 2018). Women and racial/ethnic minorities are underrepresented in faculty positions. The active physician pool is 56.2% White, 17.1% Asian, 5.8% Hispanic or Latinx, and 5% Black (AAMC, 2019). Additionally, first-generation college graduates are less likely to apply and get accepted to medical school versus their continuing-generation peers, although both groups are equally likely to matriculate (Mason et al., 2022).

Medicine is a highly regarded but also a high-stakes, demanding, and competitive field where people are perceived as high achievers and expected to be competent, confident, and accurate in patient diagnoses, with little room for errors or failures (LaDonna et al., 2018). This exposes medical professionals to stress, anxiety, self-doubt, and feelings of inadequacy. They tend to question and assess themselves harshly, especially in stressful environments. Medicine also places heavy importance on talent and brilliance, which could make students and professionals (especially women) experience poor sense of belonging, low self-efficacy, and frequent or intense IP, as seen in at least 37 fields in medicine and health sciences (Muradoglu et al., 2022).

MEASURING IMPOSTOR PHENOMENON IN MEDICINE

The Clance Impostor Phenomenon Scale (CIPS; Clance, 1985) is popularly used in medicine (e.g., Addae-Konadu et al., 2022; Bhama et al., 2021; Campos et al., 2022; Egwurugwu et al., 2018; Holliday et al., 2020; Houseknecht et al., 2019; Landry et al., 2022; Leach et al., 2019; Levant et al., 2020b; Maqsood et al., 2018; Mascarenhas et al., 2019; Neufeld et al., 2023; Rosenthal et al., 2021; Shreffler et al., 2021; Sullivan & Ryba, 2020; Swope et al., 2017). In many of these studies, participants are considered to be "impostors" or in the clinical range of IP when they score 62 or higher out of 100 on the CIPS (Henning et al., 1998; Ikbaal & Musa, 2018; Kogan et al., 2020; Mattie et al., 2008). Thus, 62 is considered as a cutoff score in differentiating between those experiencing high/intense IP and low/moderate IP. A less frequently used scale in medicine is the Young Impostor Scale (Qureshi et al., 2017; Schmulian et al., 2020; Shill-Russell et al., 2022), with eight dichotomous, yes/no questions to evaluate the presence or absence of IP. A

248 • *Devasmita Chakraverty*

yes response for five or more out of eight questions indicates IP (Villwock at al., 2016). One study used both scales (Appleby et al., 2020).

IMPOSTOR PHENOMENON AMONG STUDENTS

A larger portion of IP literature in medicine has focused on medical students. Additionally, there is limited literature examining IP among graduate students and MD-PhD dual degree students. This section summarizes IP among all three groups.

Medical Students

Medical education and training varies in different countries. In general, entry to medical schools in the United States and Canada requires a 4-year bachelor's degree with premed courses prior to entry. Training is typically 4 years long (2 years of preclinical and 2 years of clinical training), leading up to a doctor of medicine or doctor of osteopathic medicine degree (Levant et al., 2020b). However, in India, Iran, Pakistan, and other countries, medical school entry occurs right after completing high school. Training is longer, varying between 5.5 to 7 years of undergraduate studies, leading to a bachelor of medicine and bachelor of surgery degree (Couper, 2004; Supe & Burdick, 2006). Thus, the mean age of medical students varies by 4 to 5 years at the time of entry, and "medical students" may refer to undergraduate or graduate students depending on the country. This is important because research shows mixed results about the relationship between impostor experiences and age (Bravata et al., 2020) and students could first experience IP during undergraduate studies or even earlier (Chakraverty, 2019).

Survey studies show interesting correlations among medical students across countries. IP was prevalent in about 47.5% of the medical students in the final year of training (mean age: 24 years) in one medical school in Pakistan, with about 53.3% of women experiencing it (Qureshi et al., 2017). In another sample in Pakistan, 97% of medical students experienced moderate, high, or intense IP, with 3rd-year students experiencing it more severely and frequently (Maqsood et al., 2018). IP was negatively and significantly correlated to lack of self-esteem and control over utilization of emotional intelligence among medical students in Iran and Armenia (Ghorbanshirodi, 2012). However, the study disregarded the role of the environment in fostering impostor feelings. In India, 40% to 45% of medical students experienced moderate or higher IP, with significant associations with poor self-esteem, lack of adequate hours of sleep, and age (Mascarenhas et al., 2019). One study in Malaysia found no significant differences between genders among 4th-year medical students; IP positively correlated with psychological distress, poor self-esteem, depression, anxiety, stronger intentions of quitting medical school without completing training, and feeling unprepared to transition to internship after graduating from medical school, also known as housemanship (Ikbaal & Musa, 2018). One study in Nigeria found that IP correlated negatively with age and self-esteem among undergraduate medical students (Egwurugwu et al., 2018). In Brazil, 89% of the undergraduate medical students in one study experienced moderate, high, or intense IP (Campos et al., 2022). Additionally, high or intense IP was related to marital status (being unmarried); low physical activity; prior diagnoses of depression, anxiety, or other mental health issues; use of antidepressants; burnout (emotional exhaustion and cynicism); and not contributing to family income. This study identified new, unexamined factors that may have cultural relevance, such as marital status and contribution to family income, and also confirmed prior research that correlated IP and mental health issues (Campos et al., 2022). Medical students at one institution in the United Kingdom experienced frequent to clinically significant IP, with female students scoring higher than their male peers, on average (Franchi & Russell-Sewell, 2023). These studies collected data from one or two institutions, and the findings may not be generalizable.

In Canada, 73% of medical students across three institutions reported moderate to intense IP. Female students reported more IP than male students, and the severity of IP varied significantly by gender (Neufeld et al., 2023). IP was positively correlated with impersonal general causality orientation (orientation toward obstacles preventing goal attainment), controlled motivation to attend medical school (orientation toward rewards, gains, and approvals rather than inherent interest and autonomy toward attending medical school), and lower need psychological satisfaction (need for autonomy, competence, and relatedness) in medical school. This suggests that more self-determined students (in general and in medical school) whose basic psychological needs are fulfilled in medical school will experience less severe and fewer episodes of IP (Neufeld et al., 2023).

In the United States, several studies have surveyed one or more medical schools. Findings showed that IP is positively correlated with neuroticism, internal locus of control, and family control among MD students. There were significant differences across genders. For example, IP in men is positively correlated with internal locus of control and neuroticism, with significant associations with family control. Among women, IP was only positively correlated with neuroticism and not related to any of the other variables (Casselman, 1991).

250 • *Devasmita Chakraverty*

Gender-based findings were corroborated in another study in which more than twice the number of women experienced IP compared with men; female gender was significantly associated with IP for medical students across all years. IP was particularly intense in the 4th year of training and also significantly associated with burnout, cynicism, emotional exhaustion, and depersonalization (Villwock at al., 2016). In line with these findings, 89.7% of medical students at another school experienced moderate, frequent, or intense IP. There were no clear associations between IP scores and the United States Medical Licensing Examination Step 1 scores across those experiencing few, moderate, frequent, or intense IP feelings. This suggested that student experiences of IP may not always be related to academic achievement (Shreffler et al., 2021). Impostor phenomenon is also significantly positively associated with maladaptive perfectionism (a dysfunctional mindset of excessive self-criticism) and suicidal ideation; IP mediated the relationship between both. This study recommended holding interventions to improve resilience for those with maladaptive perfectionism to reduce suicidal ideation as well as bringing about systemic change to address the culture of perfection in medicine (Brennan-Wydra et al., 2021).

Only one U.S. study has examined IP among osteopathic medical students across nine institutions. Gender-based findings showed that female osteopathic students experienced IP at a higher rate than male students. IP was not related to previous success on their Medical College Admission Test scores or undergraduate grade-point average in science. IP is not dependent on the male-to-female ratio in medical school. This means that the number of female peers does not affect impostor experiences (Shill-Russell et al., 2022).

These cross-sectional survey studies sampled participants across one medical school (except Shill-Russell et al., 2022), had a predominantly White sample, and measured IP only once. Interestingly, two longitudinal studies have measured IP across multiple time points. Houseknecht et al. (2019) measured the following parameters among medical students from one institution in the United States at three different time points: professional identity, IP, calling to serve in medicine, and wellness. The study found a significant decrease in physician identity from preclinical to clinical years but no statistically significant changes in wellness, calling to medicine, or IP. However, between the 1st and the 4th year, impostor experiences increased and wellness and physician identity decreased. The study had a small sample size of 21 students but shows the need for more longitudinal studies to understand time-based nuances and whether IP increases, decreases, or becomes stable with time. In another longitudinal study, IP was measured across two time points: immediately before starting medical school and at the end of the 1st year. In this study, 87% of the medical students experienced high or very high IP at the beginning of medical school that increased significantly, both in frequency and intensity, at the end of the year. IP was related to low self-compassion, sociability, self-esteem, alienation from peers, neuroticism, anxiety, and loneliness; women experienced frequent and intense IP compared with men (Rosenthal et al., 2021). Both these studies recruited participants from a single medical school, which could be a limitation to making broad generalizations about a larger medical student population.

Transition points are critical in medical training and represent times when students are more likely to face challenges, experience IP, and drop out (Chakraverty et al., 2018, 2020). At least three studies have specifically examined transition points during medical training with respect to IP. In one study, 93% of the students experienced moderate, frequent, or intense IP during their 3rd year (transition from preclinical to clinical training). Students also hesitated to acknowledge recognition, considered themselves less capable than their peers (especially for women), remembered failures more than successes, and worried about success (especially for women). Those who reported burnout and unreal perceptions about self also feared and avoided evaluation and showed wellness concerns. Such fears and perceptions were prevalent while transitioning from the preclinical to clinical phase of medical training (Levant et al., 2020b). Additionally, IP scores and stress scores were around 9% and 17% for men and women, respectively, with women being 59% of the sample. IP was correlated with stress for students of all genders and negatively correlated with the United States Medical Licensing Examination Step 1 scores for men but not women (Levant et al., 2020a). In another study, 95.8% of 163 students had moderate, frequent, or intense IP, particularly during the transition to medical school and from preclinical to clinical training (Swope et al., 2017). Women had higher average IP scores compared with men and so did 2nd-year students compared with 1st-year students.

Graduate Students and MD-PhD Students

Research among graduate students in allied health disciplines such as audiology, occupational therapy, and chiropractic shows that 37% to 40% experience IP, and women are many times more likely to experience IP than men (Kimball et al., 2021; Schmulian et al., 2020). Students are also at risk for compassion fatigue (Schmulian et al., 2020). These cross-sectional survey studies were conducted across one or few departments from one school in Australia and the United States.

MD-PhD students may experience moderate, high, or intense IP related to several factors: professional identity formation as physician–scientists, which is different from physician identity or scientist identity; fear of evaluation; minority status, especially for racial/ethnic minorities; and transitions between the MD and PhD phases of the program (Chakraverty et al., 2022). MD-PhD students in this study struggled to develop a physician–scientist identity and lacked a sense of belonging in medicine or research. Other studies have also indicated that MD-PhD participants struggle to consider themselves as both physician and scientist and face challenges in developing a sense of belonging and/or transitioning between the various phases of the program (Chakraverty et al., 2018, 2020).

IMPOSTOR PHENOMENON AMONG MEDICAL PROFESSIONALS

Other than studies of students, research on IP in medicine has largely focused on physicians and residents. There is limited literature examining IP among physician assistants and veterinarians. This section summarizes literature on IP in each of these populations.

Residents

Prevalence of IP ranges anywhere between 43% and 94% among the resident population. It is related to a number of factors: lack of resident wellness, burnout, psychological distress, depression, anxiety, and poor well-being (Baumann et al., 2020). About 76% of residents from six general surgery residency programs in one U.S. study experienced significant or severe IP (Bhama et al., 2021). No statistically significant difference was found across gender and years of practice for general surgery residents (Bhama et al., 2021; Leach et al., 2019). Trainees also experienced higher levels of IP than faculty. The authors urged future research to examine if the training culture for residents worsened IP. Other studies have found that female residents experience higher incidents of IP than male residents in family medicine (Oriel et al., 2004). Female residents perceived themselves to be less competent, less intelligent, and less ready to practice family medicine after graduation. The study with the largest sample size, 720 pharmacy residents, found that about 60% of them experienced frequent and intense IP that was significantly predicted by previous diagnoses of mental health issues and increased work hours (especially > 80 hours/week; Sullivan & Ryba, 2020). IP was significantly correlated with poor resident well-being that further worsened with age, previous mental health diagnosis, and increased work hours. One Canadian study measured IP among foreign-trained residents in internal medicine and found that they were almost

11 times more likely to experience IP than domestic residents (Legassie et al., 2008). About half of the internal medicine residents experienced IP that correlated with burnout. Senior residents were almost 16.5 times more likely to experience burnout, and female residents were more likely to experience IP than male residents. Overall, these were all survey studies based on one or few institutions and varied in sample size and gender proportion, from 30% women (Leach et al., 2019) to 78% women (Sullivan & Ryba, 2020). Participants were predominantly White (91%; Leach et al., 2019).

Physicians

Multiple studies have examined IP among physicians using cross-sectional surveys and convenience sampling, with a wide range of sample size from 30 (Deshmukh et al., 2022) to 3,116 (Shanafelt et al., 2022). However, one Iranian study randomly sampled 65 physicians from one city and found a significant inverse correlation between IP and self-esteem. There were no significant gender differences (Kamarzarrin et al., 2013). Physicians who experience moderate, frequent, or intense IP are between 1.28 and 2.13 times more likely to experience burnout (Shanafelt et al., 2022). IP was also correlated with suicidal ideation, lower sense of professional fulfilment, and disappointment with accomplishments. Although interventions to overcome IP are important, one study showed that years of experience, exposure to mentorship, and gender had no difference in the prevalence of IP and could not predict who would feel like an impostor and who would not (Paladugu et al., 2021). The prevalence of IP (sometimes, often, or always) was as high as 83% among 30 clinical radiologists, with significant correlation with burnout. About 57% of them had more than 10 years of work experience. A majority had experienced IP as an attending and during medical training (as a student, intern, or resident; Deshmukh et al., 2022).

In one of the very few interview studies conducted with 28 midcareer or mid-to-late-career physicians at a Canadian medical school, many, even with advanced careers, questioned their achievements, considering their successes and career advancement in contrast to their perceived incompetence. Those experiencing IP severely doubted themselves, felt insecure, and could not internalize positive feedback. They kept their insecurities private, did not talk to peers and colleagues, and felt like a fraud in a white coat. Frequent career transitions and new professional challenges worsened IP. Some viewed their impostor experiences positively, protecting them from overconfidence and making them humble and grounded (LaDonna et al., 2018). Survey studies have not uncovered these nuances before.

Similarly, in a case study with three physicians in palliative care, physicians with impostor feelings experienced burnout, inadequacy, self-doubt, and fear of being discovered as unskilled and fraudulent (Lawton et al., 2020). Physicians struggled with clinical decision making and IP, feeling less knowledgeable when explaining their clinical decisions to trainees and colleagues, teaching trainees from other specialties and backgrounds, working with an expert, and experiencing a lack of collaboration between a teacher and learner.

Experiencing IP shapes professional identity formation, as early-career physicians with 5 or fewer years of experience since residency training question their competence and decision-making abilities and experience burnout (Stelling et al., 2023). This study interviewed 11 faculty physicians from one U.S.-based medical school and reiterated the need to provide support during transition from structured residency training to unsupervised practice.

Physician Assistants

In the United States, physician assistants complete a 2-year, full-time program and are supervised by physicians. A survey study among physician assistants with an average of 4.9 years in practice (range: 0–35 years) showed that about one third of 269 individuals experienced IP (Mattie et al., 2008). There were no statistically significant gender differences. Those with more years of practice experienced lower IP; higher IP correlated with anxiety and depression. In another study, 39% of 83 physician assistants (both current students and graduates) experienced IP (Prata & Gietzen, 2007b). Female physician assistants experienced higher IP and were more likely to experience impostor feelings than their male peers. Similar to Mattie and colleagues' (2008) findings, rate of impostorism decreased with increasing age, clinical experience, and number of years since graduation. Therefore, older or more experienced physician assistants could be less likely to experience IP (Prata & Gietzen, 2007b). Impostor feelings also declined significantly after 1 or 2 years of professional practice and after 4 or more years of graduation.

Veterinarians

Similar to other groups in medicine, 50% to 70% of veterinarians across different countries were found to experience impostor feelings. One study with 941 veterinarians across the United States, the United Kingdom, New Zealand, and other countries showed that women, new practitioners (5 or fewer years of practice), and those living in the United Kingdom or New Zealand were more likely to feel like impostors in their professional but not personal lives (Kogan et al., 2020). Another survey study with 300 students, interns, residents, and faculty in veterinary medicine showed that 45% to 50% of the students, 60% to 68% of the house officers (interns and residents), and 26% to 34% of the faculty members experienced IP (Appleby et al., 2020). Both studies surveyed convenience samples overrepresented by women and White individuals, with broad age ranges (18–75 years) and vast experience levels (0–21 years; Appleby et al., 2020).

IMPOSTOR PHENOMENON AMONG MIXED SAMPLES

Many studies have included both students and professionals. Among mental health professionals, IP is positively related with compassion fatigue and burnout and inversely related with compassion satisfaction (Clark et al., 2022). Among more than 1,000 students and practitioners in nutrition and dietetics, the average score on the CIPS showed high IP (Landry et al., 2022). About 65% of the sample experienced frequent or intense IP. IP was lower among older people, those with educational and professional achievements, and members of professional groups (Academy Dietetic Practice Groups and Member Interest Groups). Further, higher IP was related to more time spent on social media, lower job satisfaction, and poor well-being. The finding that gender and race/ethnicity did not predict higher IP should be treated with caution because of a nonrepresentative, convenience sample (Landry et al., 2022). In both studies, women and non-Hispanic, White participants were disproportionately overrepresented.

A mixed group of 477 medical, dental, nursing, and pharmacy students from one school showed strong associations between psychological distress, perfectionism, and IP that predicted psychological adjustment more than demographic characteristics among those undergoing distress. About 30% of the sample showed clinical symptoms of IP, whereas 27.5% of students experienced psychiatric levels of distress. Additionally, 37.8% of women versus 22% of men showed clinical symptoms of IP; the mean impostor score in the sample was significantly higher for women than for men. The overall sample was 53% women, who were overrepresented in pharmacy and nursing (78% for each fields) and underrepresented in medicine (47%) and dentistry (26.7%). Women in pharmacy and nursing were more likely to have been treated for mental health issues prior to starting their program compared with women in medicine and dentistry. Also, 85% of the participants were White. Overall, medical and dental students were more at risk for psychological distress earlier in training that related to IP and socially prescribed perfectionism. IP strongly correlated with distress for nursing students and socially prescribed perfectionism for pharmacy students (Henning et al., 1998).

Three components of IP were uncovered in a study with a subsample of medical students, MD-PhD students, residents, physicians, and physician faculty: Luck, Self-Doubt, and Fear of Evaluation. In fact, Fear of Evaluation superseded Self-Doubt when shaping impostor experiences. Being older, not in training, and male contributed to lower IP (Lee et al., 2022). In another study, undergraduate medical and dental students, predominantly from Year 1 and 2, scored high on IP scale, on average. Overall, 15% of 485 participants (18% female, 11% male) experienced intense IP that was predicted by age, female sex, and time off prior to starting medical school. Female sex posed a twofold higher risk to IP and was the only significant predictor of intense impostor experiences (Holliday et al., 2020).

More recently, a sample of medical students, residents, fellows, and attendings in OB/GYN experienced frequent IP on average (Addae-Konadu et al., 2022). Overall, 92% of the 139 participants experienced moderate, frequent, or intense IP, with no differences based on gender or race. IP was related to anxiety and also significantly associated with the training status in medicine, with trainees experiencing higher IP than experienced physicians.

STRATEGIES TO MANAGE OR OVERCOME IMPOSTOR PHENOMENON

Strategies offered to manage or overcome IP focus mostly at the individual level by fostering confidence, resilience (Holliday et al., 2020), and self-awareness about IP and related behaviors; journaling about struggles to success; keeping a record of positive assessment, feedback, or evaluation; celebrating success; accepting compliments; seeking mentors and sponsors; questioning the inner voices deeming oneself as fraudulent; seeking coaching or therapy; focusing on one's strengths; and celebrating successes and normalizing failures (Seritan & Mehta, 2016). In an editorial, experts recommended the five Rs: recognition, rational thinking, reframing, readiness, and repetition upon recurrence (Arleo et al., 2021). Similarly, a review article for women in neurology suggested many personal strategies to overcome IP: naming it, acknowledging that it is common and normalizing it, admitting imperfection, removing the focus on oneself, reframing self-criticism, focusing on strengths and achievements, decoupling self-worth and achievement, acting confident, keeping a learning mindset, and identifying key mentors (Armstrong & Shulman, 2019). Other strategies to address IP include recognition through increased self-awareness, discussing one's insecurities with trusted colleagues to normalize and validate them, maintaining a log of success, sensitizing colleagues to IP, and seeking professional mental health care (Lawton et al., 2020).

These recommendations put the onus of managing and overcoming IP on the self or individual and overlook systemic and environmental factors that could cause it (McGee et al., 2022). Institutional strategies include workshops; counseling sessions to normalize impostor feelings, especially during academic transition (Prata & Gietzen, 2007a); mentorship programs, including targeted mentorship for underrepresented groups; additional support for international students or professionals; leadership training; and fostering a culture where mistakes are not penalized (Lazarus, 2021; Seritan & Mehta, 2016). One such workshop (around 45 minutes) for internal medicine residents from all 3 years of training included small- and large-group discussions, think-pair-share activities, and individual reflections (Baumann et al., 2020). A postworkshop survey indicated that the majority of the participants found the workshop effective for improving resident wellness and resilience. They could self-identify signs of IP and manage it. Another informational and interactive workshop conducted to raise awareness in a radiology department (around 60 minutes) found that a majority of the participants exhibited frequent or intense IP on the CIPS. However, no follow-up assessment was conducted to measure the effectiveness of the workshop (Deshmukh et al., 2022).

Other interventions have been implemented. Metz and colleagues (2020a) designed an online module to raise awareness, provide coping mechanisms, and measure intervention efficacy for IP among 1st-year doctor of dental medicine students in one school. Participants watched a 14-minute video (that included six coping mechanisms) during the 2nd week of the first semester, took the CIPS survey immediately after, and then took the same survey after 18 weeks. The average IP scores decreased in 18 weeks, as did the percentage of students experiencing intense IP (13.6% to 4.9%) during the same time. Women scored higher than men (indicating more frequent IP), but there were no statistically significant differences across different race/ethnicity or age groups. Coping mechanisms included decreasing time spent on nonessential tasks and scheduling essential tasks to avoid procrastination (Metz et al., 2020b). There are at least two limitations of this study. First, no data were collected before participants watched the video. Second, the absence of a control group (those who did not watch the video at all) makes it difficult to establish causality and claim that the online training module caused impostor feelings to decrease.

In another intervention study, 203 students at the beginning of their 1st year of dental school participated in a mandatory Mind–Body Wellness Course that included a lecture on understanding IP. They attended a second lecture on IP and mindfulness 6 months later. Students completed the CIPS scale before the second lecture; afterward, they completed a survey about whether the mindfulness practices they learned influenced their perceptions of coping with IP. In this sample, 90% experienced moderate, frequent, or intense IP. Half of them (51%) were able to predict their CIPS classification correctly, whereas 43% underestimated their scores, that is, they scored higher than they thought. After the second lecture, 93% were more aware of how IP could influence their thoughts, behaviors, and actions; 86% felt confident that they could recognize their impostor feelings; 86% felt that the mindfulness exercise was useful in building habits to manage IP; and 83% felt confident in utilizing mindfulness practices to mitigate IP (Pastan et al., 2022). Once again, participants did not take a survey before watching the first lecture. Additionally, there was no control group (a group that did not attend any of the lectures). Thus, it is difficult to establish causality and claim that the mindfulness lectures impacted participants' ability to manage IP.

CONCLUSION AND FUTURE DIRECTIONS

IP afflicts people across all ranks: students, residents, physicians, and faculty. In medicine, more than in STEM, most studies use the term "impostor syndrome" and not "impostor phenomenon," despite IP not being an official clinical diagnosis of a syndrome or psychiatric disorder (Fowler & Villanueva, 2023). Dr. Pauline R. Clance recommended the term "phenomenon" because of the stigma and judgment associated with a syndrome (email communication, as cited in Chakraverty, 2019). The two terms have different meanings, and it would be prudent to mindfully use the recommended term. Additionally, most studies use a cutoff score of 62 out of 100 on the CIPS. Those who score above it are termed as "impostors" (Ikbaal & Musa, 2018; Paladugu et al., 2021; Prata & Gietzen, 2007a) rather than "someone who experiences impostor phenomenon." Other terms used are "true impostors" (those who persist despite continuous success, positive experience, or positive reinforcement), "strategic impostors," and "transient impostors" (a lesser, more temporary form in which IP lessens as a person gains more self-confidence about their ability over time; Leonhardt et al., 2017; Prata & Gietzen, 2007b). Most studies use the CIPS to diagnose and measure IP, and the Young Impostor Scale is less frequently used. The CIPS was first developed after interviewing majority White women experiencing IP (Clance, 1985) and may not accurately reflect impostor experiences in other countries and/or cultural contexts. There is a need to refine the instrument of measurement based on the cultural context.

Further, most of the studies are cross-sectional and correlational, with conveniently sampled participants across one or few (predominantly White) medical institutions (Ghorbanshirodi, 2012; Ikbaal & Musa, 2018; Maqsood et al., 2018; Mascarenhas et al., 2019; Qureshi et al., 2017). Few studies used random sampling (Ghorbanshirodi, 2012; Kamarzarrin et al., 2013; Maqsood et al., 2018). Thus most studies may have participation bias (only those experiencing IP or familiar with the term participated). Although it still helps us to establish relationships between IP and several other demographic (e.g., sex, race, ethnicity) and psychological variables, mental health (e.g., anxiety, depression), and personality traits (e.g., introversion), the findings are not generalizable to the larger population and do not accurately highlight cultural and contextual nuances in the understanding of IP. Our understanding could improve from more qualitative studies, mixed-methods studies (by collecting and analyzing data in different ways; Chang et al., 2022), longitudinal studies (to understand IP's evolution with time), and experimental studies (to isolate causal factors).

Most research has surveyed participants in English, which makes articulating impostor experiences less accessible to people not fluent in or familiar with English. Language shapes our behavior, interactions, thoughts, perceptions, and articulation (Boroditsky, 2011). A contextual translation of the term "impostor phenomenon" in other languages could enhance a shared understanding of the term itself and help determine if the phenomenon is universal.

Little research has focused on first-generation learners, sexual minorities, or persons with disability. We need more studies that highlight identity-based experiences of IP in medicine, for example, for members of the BIPOC (Black, Indigenous, People of Color) community, who often report race-based bias, harassment, microaggressions, judgment, and stereotyping (National Academies of Sciences, Engineering, and Medicine, 2018). The connections between these experiences and IP is not clearly understood. Further, many studies show gender-based trends of impostor experiences (e.g., Neufeld et al., 2023). We need to understand how people of different genders experience IP.

Most importantly, we need to explore new lines of research that examine academic and work environments that make one susceptible to IP. Although most of the suggested strategies to manage IP have been at the individual level, these interventions may only be short term. Instead, we need to better understand what kinds of environments trigger impostor feelings and what safe learning environments in medicine could look like (Franchi & Russell-Sewell, 2023). This can help those with IP develop a strong sense of identity and belonging, irrespective of their demographic background.

REFERENCES

Addae-Konadu, K., Carlson, S., Janes, J., Gecsi, K., & Stephenson-Famy, A. B. (2022). Am I really qualified to be here: Exploring the impact of impostor phenomenon on training and careers in OB/GYN medical education. *Journal of Surgical Education*, *79*(1), 102–106. https://doi.org/10.1016/j.jsurg.2021.08.013

Appleby, R., Evola, M., & Royal, K. (2020). Impostor phenomenon in veterinary medicine. *Education in the Health Professions*, *3*(3), 105–109. https://doi.org/10.4103/EHP.EHP_17_20

Arleo, E. K., Wagner-Schulman, M., McGinty, G., Salazar, G., & Mayr, N. A. (2021). Tackling impostor syndrome: A multidisciplinary approach. *Clinical Imaging*, *74*, 170–172. https://doi.org/10.1016/j.clinimag.2020.12.035

Armstrong, M. J., & Shulman, L. M. (2019). Tackling the imposter phenomenon to advance women in neurology. *Neurology: Clinical Practice*, *9*(2), 155–159. https://doi.org/10.1212/CPJ.0000000000000607

Association of American Medical Colleges. (2018). *Faculty roster: U.S. medical school faculty*. https://www.aamc.org/data-reports/faculty-institutions/interactive-data/2016-us-medical-school-faculty

Association of American Medical Colleges. (2019). *Diversity in medicine: Facts and figures 2019*. https://www.aamc.org/data-reports/workforce/report/diversity-medicine-facts-and-figures-2019

Association of American Medical Colleges. (2022). *2022 facts: Applicants and matriculants data*. https://www.aamc.org/data-reports/students-residents/interactive-data/2022-facts-applicants-and-matriculants-data

Baumann, N., Faulk, C., Vanderlan, J., Chen, J., & Bhayani, R. K. (2020). Small-group discussion sessions on imposter syndrome. *MedEdPORTAL: The Journal of Teaching and Learning Resources*, *16*, Article 11004. https://doi.org/10.15766/mep_2374-8265.11004

Bhama, A. R., Ritz, E. M., Anand, R. J., Auyang, E. D., Lipman, J., Greenberg, J. A., & Kapadia, M. R. (2021). Imposter syndrome in surgical trainees: Clance Imposter Phenomenon Scale assessment in general surgery residents. *Journal of the American College of Surgeons*, *233*(5), 633–638. https://doi.org/10.1016/j.jamcollsurg.2021.07.681

Boroditsky, L. (2011). How language shapes thought. *Scientific American*, *304*(2), 62–65. https://doi.org/10.1038/scientificamerican0211-62

Bravata, D. M., Watts, S. A., Keefer, A. L., Madhusudhan, D. K., Taylor, K. T., Clark, D. M., Nelson, R. S., Cokley, K. O., & Hagg, H. K. (2020). Prevalence, predictors, and treatment of impostor syndrome: A systematic review. *Journal of General Internal Medicine*, *35*(4), 1252–1275. https://doi.org/10.1007/s11606-019-05364-1

Brennan-Wydra, E., Chung, H. W., Angoff, N., ChenFeng, J., Phillips, A., Schreiber, J., Young, C., & Wilkins, K. (2021). Maladaptive perfectionism, impostor phenomenon, and suicidal ideation among medical students. *Academic Psychiatry*, *45*, 708–715. https://doi.org/10.1007/s40596-021-01503-1

Campos, I. F. D. S., Camara, G. F., Carneiro, A. G., Kubrusly, M., Peixoto, R. A. C., & Peixoto, A. A., Junior. (2022). Impostor Syndrome and its association with depression and burnout among medical students. *Revista Brasileira de Educação Médica*, *46*(2), Article e068. https://doi.org/10.1590/1981-5271v46.2-20200491.ING

Casselman, S. E. (1991). *The imposter phenomenon in medical students: Personality correlates and developmental issues* [Doctoral dissertation, Old Dominion University, Virginia Consortium for Professional Psychology]. ProQuest Dissertations Publishing. https://www.proquest.com/openview/bc12f782b83911eb5921bed621554960/1?pq-origsite=gscholar&cbl=18750&diss=y

Chakraverty, D. (2013). *An examination of how women and underrepresented racial/ethnic minorities experience barriers in biomedical research and medical programs* [Doctoral dissertation, University of Virginia]. DigitalCommons. https://digitalcommons.unl.edu/dberspeakers/43

Chakraverty, D. (2019). Impostor phenomenon in STEM: Occurrence, attribution, and identity. *Studies in Graduate and Postdoctoral Education, 10*(1), 2–20. https://doi.org/10.1108/SGPE-D-18-00014

Chakraverty, D., Cavazos, J. E., & Jeffe, D. B. (2022). Exploring reasons for MD-PhD trainees' experience of impostor phenomenon. *BMC Medical Education, 22*(1), Article 333. https://doi.org/10.1186/s12909-022-03396-6

Chakraverty, D., Jeffe, D. B., Dabney, K. P., & Tai, R. H. (2020). Exploring reasons that U.S. MD-PhD students enter and leave their dual-degree programs. *International Journal of Doctoral Studies, 15*, 461–483. https://doi.org/10.28945/4622

Chakraverty, D., Jeffe, D. B., & Tai, R. H. (2018). Transition experiences in MD-PhD programs. *CBE Life Sciences Education, 17*(3), Article ar41. https://doi.org/10.1187/cbe.17-08-0187

Chang, S., Lee, H. Y., Anderson, C. B., Kewis, K., Chakraverty, D., & Yates, M. S. (2022). Intervening on impostor phenomenon: Prospective evaluation of a workshop for health science students using a mixed-method design. *BMC Medical Education, 22*(1), Article 802. https://doi.org/10.1186/s12909-022-03824-7

Clance, P. R. (1985). *Clance Impostor Phenomenon Scale (CIPS)* [Database record]. APA PsycTests. https://doi.org/10.1037/t11274-000

Clance, P. R., & Imes, S. A. (1978). The imposter phenomenon in high achieving women: Dynamics and therapeutic intervention. *Psychotherapy: Theory, Research, & Practice, 15*(3), 241–247. https://doi.org/10.1037/h0086006

Clark, P., Holden, C., Russell, M., & Downs, H. (2022). The impostor phenomenon in mental health professionals: Relationships among compassion fatigue, burnout, and compassion satisfaction. *Contemporary Family Therapy, 44*(2), 185–197. https://doi.org/10.1007/s10591-021-09580-y

Couper, I. D. (2004). Medicine in Iran: A brief overview. *South African Family Practice, 46*(5), 5–7. https://doi.org/10.1080/20786204.2004.10873077

Deshmukh, S., Shmelev, K., Vassiliades, L., Kurumety, S., Agarwal, G., & Horowitz, J. M. (2022). Imposter phenomenon in radiology: Incidence, intervention, and impact on wellness. *Clinical Imaging, 82*, 94–99. https://doi.org/10.1016/j.clinimag.2021.11.009

Egwurugwu, J. N., Ugwuezumba, P. C., Ohamaeme, M. C., Dike, E. I., Eberendu, I., Egwurugwu, E. N., Ohamaeme, R. C., & Egwurugwu, U. F. (2018). Relationship between self-esteem and impostor syndrome among undergraduate medical students in a Nigerian university. *International Journal of Brain and Cognitive Sciences, 7*(1), 9–16.

Fowler, K. R., & Villanueva, L. (2023). From the bedside to the boardroom: Imposter syndrome in nursing leadership. *Nurse Leader, 21*(3), E7–E10. https://doi.org/10.1016/j.mnl.2022.10.003

Franchi, T., & Russell-Sewell, N. (2023). Medical students and the impostor phenomenon: A coexistence precipitated and perpetuated by the educational environment? *Medical Science Educator, 33*, 27–38. https://doi.org/10.1007/s40670-022-01675-x

Ghorbanshirodi, S. (2012). The relationship between self-esteem and emotional intelligence with imposter syndrome among medical students of Guilan and Heratsi Universities. *Journal of Basic and Applied Scientific Research, 2*(2), 1793–1802.

Henning, K., Ey, S., & Shaw, D. (1998). Perfectionism, the impostor phenomenon and psychological adjustment in medical, dental, nursing and pharmacy students. *Medical Education, 32*(5), 456–464. https://doi.org/10.1046/j.1365-2923.1998.00234.x

Holliday, A. M., Gheihman, G., Cooper, C., Sullivan, A., Ohyama, H., Leaf, D. E., & Leaf, R. K. (2020). High prevalence of imposterism among female Harvard medical and dental students. *Journal of General Internal Medicine, 35*(8), 2499–2501. https://doi.org/10.1007/s11606-019-05441-5

Houseknecht, V. E., Roman, B., Stolfi, A., & Borges, N. J. (2019). A longitudinal assessment of professional identity, wellness, imposter phenomenon, and calling to medicine among medical students. *Medical Science Educator, 29*(2), 493–497. https://doi.org/10.1007/s40670-019-00718-0

Ikbaal, M. Y., & Musa, N. A. S. (2018). Prevalence of impostor phenomenon among medical students in a Malaysian private medical school. *International Journal of Medical Students, 6*(2), 66–70. https://doi.org/10.5195/ijms.2018.10

Kamarzarrin, H., Khaledian, M., Shooshtari, M., Yousefi, E., & Ahrami, R. (2013). A study of the relationship between self-esteem and the imposter phenomenon in the physicians of Rasht city. *European Journal of Experimental Biology, 3*(2), 363–366.

Kimball, K. A., Roecker, C. B., & Hoyt, K. (2021). Impostor phenomenon among U.S. chiropractic students. *The Journal of Chiropractic Education, 35*(2), 209–214. https://doi.org/10.7899/JCE-19-10

Kogan, L. R., Schoenfeld-Tacher, R., Hellyer, P., Grigg, E. K., & Kramer, E. (2020). Veterinarians and impostor syndrome: An exploratory study. *Veterinary Record, 187*(7), 271–278. https://doi.org/10.1136/vr.105914

LaDonna, K. A., Ginsburg, S., & Watling, C. (2018). "Rising to the level of your incompetence": What physicians' self-assessment of their performance reveals about the imposter syndrome in medicine. *Academic Medicine, 93*(5), 763–768. https://doi.org/10.1097/ACM.0000000000002046

Landry, M. J., Bailey, D. A., Lee, M., Van Gundy, S., & Ervin, A. (2022). The impostor phenomenon in the nutrition and dietetics profession: An online cross-sectional survey. *International Journal of Environmental Research and Public Health, 19*(9), Article 5558. https://doi.org/10.3390/ijerph19095558

Lawton, A. J., Lawton, C. W., Dietz, S. S. B., Stevens, E. E., & Weis, J. M. (2020). Exploring and managing the impostor phenomenon in palliative care: A case series. *Journal of Palliative Medicine, 23*(4), 586–590. https://doi.org/10.1089/jpm.2019.0094

Lazarus, A. (2021). Impact of imposter syndrome on physicians' practice and leadership development. *The Journal of Medical Practice Management, 37*(1), 367–372.

Leach, P. K., Nygaard, R. M., Chipman, J. G., Brunsvold, M. E., & Marek, A. P. (2019). Impostor phenomenon and burnout in general surgeons and general surgery residents. *Journal of Surgical Education, 76*(1), 99–106. https://doi.org/10.1016/j.jsurg.2018.06.025

Lee, H. Y., Anderson, C. B., Yates, M. S., Chang, S., & Chakraverty, D. (2022). Insights into the complexity of the impostor phenomenon among trainees and professionals in STEM and medicine. *Current Psychology, 41*, 5913–5924. https://doi.org/10.1007/s12144-020-01089-1

Legassie, J., Zibrowski, E. M., & Goldszmidt, M. A. (2008). Measuring resident well-being: Impostorism and burnout syndrome in residency. *Journal of General Internal Medicine, 23*(7), 1090–1094. https://doi.org/10.1007/s11606-008-0536-x

Leonhardt, M., Bechtoldt, M. N., & Rohrmann, S. (2017). All impostors aren't alike—Differentiating the impostor phenomenon. *Frontiers in Psychology, 8*, Article 1505. https://doi.org/10.3389/fpsyg.2017.01505

Levant, B., Villwock, J. A., & Manzardo, A. M. (2020a). Impostorism in American medical students during early clinical training: Gender differences and inter-correlating factors. *International Journal of Medical Education, 11*, 90–96. https://doi.org/10.5116/ijme.5e99.7aa2

Levant, B., Villwock, J. A., & Manzardo, A. M. (2020b). Impostorism in third-year medical students: An item analysis using the Clance Impostor Phenomenon Scale. *Perspectives on Medical Education, 9*(2), 83–91. https://doi.org/10.1007/S40037-020-00562-8

Maqsood, H., Shakeel, H. A., Hussain, H., Khan, A. R., Ali, B., Ishaq, A., & Shah, S. A. Y. (2018). The descriptive study of imposter syndrome in medical students. *International Journal of Research in Medical Sciences, 6*(10), 3431–3434. https://doi.org/10.18203/2320-6012.ijrms20184031

Mascarenhas, V. R., D'Souza, D., & Bicholkar, A. (2019). Prevalence of impostor phenomenon and its association with self-esteem among medical interns in Goa, India. *International Journal of Community Medicine and Public Health, 6*(1), 355–359. https://doi.org/10.18203/2394-6040.ijcmph20185272

Mason, H. R., Ata, A., Nguyen, M., Nakae, S., Chakraverty, D., Eggan, B., Martinez, S., & Jeffe, D. B. (2022). First-generation and continuing-generation college graduates' application, acceptance, and matriculation to U.S. medical schools: A national cohort study. *Medical Education Online, 27*(1), Article 2010291. https://doi.org/10.1080/10872981.2021.2010291

Mattie, C., Gietzen, J., Davis, S., & Prata, J. (2008). The imposter phenomenon: Self-assessment and competency to perform as a physician assistant in the United States. *The Journal of Physician Assistant Education, 19*(1), 5–12. https://doi.org/10.1097/01367895-200819010-00002

McGee, E. O., Botchway, P. K., Naphan-Kingery, D. E., Brockman, A. J., Houston, S., & White, D. T. (2022). Racism camouflaged as impostorism and the impact on Black STEM doctoral students. *Race, Ethnicity and Education, 25*(4), 487–507. https://doi.org/10.1080/13613324.2021.1924137

Metz, C. J., Ballard, E., & Metz, M. J. (2020a). The stress of success: An online module to help first-year dental students cope with the impostor phenomenon. *Journal of Dental Education, 84*(9), 1016–1024. https://doi.org/10.1002/jdd.12181

Metz, C. J., Ballard, E., & Metz, M. J. (2020b). The stress of success: An online module to help first-year DMD students cope with the impostor phenomenon. *The FASEB Journal, 34*(S1), Article 1. https://doi.org/10.1096/fasebj.2020.34.s1.03311

Mullangi, S., & Jagsi, R. (2019). Imposter syndrome: Treat the cause, not the symptom. *JAMA, 322*(5), 403–404. https://doi.org/10.1001/jama.2019.9788

Muradoglu, M., Horne, Z., Hammond, M. D., Leslie, S. J., & Cimpian, A. (2022). Women—particularly underrepresented minority women—and early-career academics feel like impostors in fields that value brilliance. *Journal of Educational Psychology, 114*(5), 1086–1100. https://doi.org/10.1037/edu0000669

National Academies of Sciences, Engineering, and Medicine. (2018). *Sexual harassment of women: Climate, culture, and consequences in academic sciences, engineering, and medicine.* National Academies Press.

Neufeld, A., Babenko, O., Lai, H., Svrcek, C., & Malin, G. (2023). Why do we feel like intellectual frauds? A self-determination theory perspective on the impostor phenomenon in medical students. *Teaching and Learning in Medicine, 35*(2), 180–192. https://doi.org/10.1080/10401334.2022.2056741

Oriel, K., Plane, M. B., & Mundt, M. (2004). Family medicine residents and the impostor phenomenon. *Family Medicine, 36*(4), 248–252.

Paladugu, S., Wasser, T., & Donato, A. (2021). Impostor syndrome in hospitalists: A cross-sectional study. *Journal of Community Hospital Internal Medicine Perspectives, 11*(2), 212–215. https://doi.org/10.1080/20009666.2021.1877891

Pastan, C. D., Mc Donough, A. L., Finkelman, M., & Daniels, J. C. (2022). Evaluation of mindfulness practice in mitigating impostor feelings in dental students. *Journal of Dental Education, 86*(11), 1513–1520. https://doi.org/10.1002/jdd.12965

Prata, J., & Gietzen, J. W. (2007a). Imposter phenomenon in physician assistant education. *Journal of the American Academy of PAs, 20*(7), 32–33. https://doi.org/10.1097/01720610-200707000-00047

Prata, J., & Gietzen, J. W. (2007b). The imposter phenomenon in physician assistant graduates. *The Journal of Physician Assistant Education, 18*(4), 33–36. https://doi.org/10.1097/01367895-200718040-00007

Qureshi, M. A., Taj, J., Latif, M. Z., Zia, S., Rafique, M., & Chaudhry, M. A. (2017). Imposter syndrome among Pakistani medical students. *Annals of King Edward Medical University, 23*(2), 107–111. https://doi.org/10.21649/akemu.v23i2.1647

Rosenthal, S., Schlussel, Y., Yaden, M., DeSantis, J., Trayes, K., Pohl, C., & Hojat, M. (2021). Persistent impostor phenomenon is associated with distress in medical students. *Family Medicine, 53*(2), 118–122. https://doi.org/10.22454/FamMed.2021.799997

Schmulian, D. L., Redgen, W., & Fleming, J. (2020). Impostor syndrome and compassion fatigue among graduate allied health students: A pilot study. *Focus on Health Professional Education: A Multi-Professional Journal, 21*(3), 1–14. https://doi.org/10.11157/fohpe.v21i3.388

Seritan, A. L., & Mehta, M. M. (2016). Thorny laurels: The impostor phenomenon in academic psychiatry. *Academic Psychiatry, 40*(3), 418–421. https://doi.org/10.1007/s40596-015-0392-z

Shanafelt, T. D., Dyrbye, L. N., Sinsky, C., Trockel, M., Makowski, M. S., Tutty, M., & West, C. P. (2022). Imposter phenomenon in U.S. physicians relative to the U.S. working population. *Mayo Clinic Proceedings, 97*(11), 1981–1993. https://doi.org/10.1016/j.mayocp.2022.06.021

Shill-Russell, C., Russell, R. C., Daines, B., Clement, G., Carlson, J., Zapata, I., & Henderson, M. (2022). Imposter syndrome relation to gender across osteopathic medical schools. *Medical Science Educator, 32*(1), 157–163. https://doi.org/10.1007/s40670-021-01489-3

Shreffler, J., Weingartner, L., Huecker, M., Shaw, M. A., Ziegler, C., Simms, T., Martin, L., & Sawning, S. (2021). Association between characteristics of impostor phenomenon in medical students and step 1 performance. *Teaching and Learning in Medicine, 33*(1), 36–48. https://doi.org/10.1080/10401334.2020.1784741

Stelling, B. E. V., Andersen, C. A., Suarez, D. A., Nordhues, H. C., Hafferty, F. W., Beckman, T. J., & Sawatsky, A. P. (2023). Fitting in while standing out: Professional identity formation, imposter syndrome, and burnout in early career faculty physicians. *Academic Medicine, 98*(4), 514–520. https://doi.org/10.1097/ACM. 0000000000005049

Sullivan, J. B., & Ryba, N. L. (2020). Prevalence of impostor phenomenon and assessment of well-being in pharmacy residents. *American Journal of Health-System Pharmacy, 77*(9), 690–696. https://doi.org/10.1093/ajhp/zxaa041

Supe, A., & Burdick, W. P. (2006). Challenges and issues in medical education in India. *Academic Medicine, 81*(12), 1076–1080. https://doi.org/10.1097/01.ACM. 0000246699.94234.ab

Swope, K., Thompson, B. M., & Haidet, P. (2017). Imposter phenomenon across the span of medical training. *Journal of General Internal Medicine, 32*, Article S223.

Villwock, J. A., Sobin, L. B., Koester, L. A., & Harris, T. M. (2016). Impostor syndrome and burnout among American medical students: A pilot study. *International Journal of Medical Education, 7*, 364–369. https://doi.org/10.5116/ijme.5801.eac4

PART **III** INTERVENTIONS AND TRENDS

12

CRITICAL ISSUES OF THE IMPOSTOR PHENOMENON AND INTERVENTIONS FOR HISTORICALLY MARGINALIZED PEOPLE

LISA ORBÉ-AUSTIN AND RICHARD ORBÉ-AUSTIN

Although the impostor phenomenon (IP) can have a significant impact across populations, it is important to consider the unique ways that IP impacts historically marginalized people. IP can affect individuals' perception of their competence, prevent them from internalizing skills, and lead them to view their experience and expertise in a deficit-oriented manner as well as affect how they function and behave in the face of that perceived inadequacy (e.g., N. S. Bernard et al., 2002; Clance & Imes, 1978; Neureiter & Traut-Mattausch, 2016b; Want & Kleitman, 2006). Therefore, this IP experience needs to be noted in how we treat, engage, and support historically marginalized individuals who experience IP or how we address it ourselves when we are from a marginalized community. IP, by its very nature, instills behaviors, thoughts, and feelings that are very dangerous for historically marginalized people (e.g., people of color, women, first-generation students), especially when that community is victim to stereotypes and discrimination connected to success, intelligence, capability, competence, or the lack thereof. Cokley et al. (2017) found that, for African Americans, higher levels of impostor feelings increased the impact of perceived discrimination and feelings of depression. This reinforcement in oppressive environments validates that impostor feelings may be accurate, especially when we perceive them as inherent flaws in ourselves rather

https://doi.org/10.1037/0000397-013
The Impostor Phenomenon: Psychological Research, Theory, and Interventions,
K. Cokley (Editor)
Copyright © 2024 by the American Psychological Association. All rights reserved.

than the result of dysfunction, brutality, and oppression of discriminatory systems. Discrimination and systemic oppression can affect our ability to reach the levels that we aspire to. IP can prevent us from finding our own agency and the connection to what we want and desire. It can also deprive us of the knowledge and understanding that we deserve what we desire and should empower ourselves to fight for it.

For historically marginalized communities, the experiences of not belonging, feeling othered, and having to "work twice as hard to get half as much" are often a reality due to systemic oppression evidenced through prejudice, discrimination, and microaggressions. This creates an environment rife with the additional triggering factors for IP beyond those that are normative and common (e.g., new experiences, making a mistake). These additional experiences serve to further embed and reinforce IP and make it that much more difficult to overcome. The cycle of IP and the deeply grooved path that it creates leads people to betray themselves (i.e., their dreams, their agency, their boundaries) consistently and to follow what others want or need from them as the central and often only voices that they listen to (e.g., Cowman & Ferrari, 2002; Thompson et al., 2000; Vergauwe et al., 2015). Oppressive environments and leaders benefit from these dynamics as those with IP work harder, feel more insecure, and constantly attempt to prove themselves in service of these systems with greater loyalty to the organization than to themselves (Neureiter & Traut-Mattausch, 2016a). In addition, the concept of success, which is so integral to IP, can be complicated for those from historically marginalized groups because our success can be very weighty and have implications for others in our family or community, such as providing access, opportunities, and models for community members, which may not have the same importance and value for privileged groups. Not succeeding in ways that familial and communal kin are counting on can have severe implications (e.g., resources, opportunity, modeling, access), which can be far worse when you are from a marginalized community. The cost of not dealing with one's IP may have reverberating consequences. What if instead people could live in their greatness and pursue all the things that matter to them without overworking or feeling insecure, creating a belonging to the right communities of people who have their aligned values and perspectives?

In this chapter, we discuss critical issues and concerns related to IP experienced by marginalized groups. We explore the additive issues that occur and the ways it may be experienced differently by distinct marginalized groups. We also discuss some of the interventions that may be particularly useful for historically marginalized people and how it may need to be thought about from different perspectives by coaches, therapists, and the individuals themselves when they are working to change and overcome the experience of IP.

THE DOUBLE IMPACT OF IMPOSTOR PHENOMENON

For marginalized communities, IP is not solely an intrapersonal experience. Individuals often experience it both internally and externally. That critical and unrelenting voice that those with IP hear internally is echoed by external voices steeped in racism, misogyny, xenophobia, and any other form of identity-based hate that seeks to oppress them. In *The Souls of Black Folk*, W. E. B. Du Bois (2008) discussed the double consciousness that Black people experience in the United States. Du Bois utilized the phrase "double consciousness" to refer to the requirement for Black people to have both an internal view of themselves and also another perspective based on how they were being interpreted through a White lens. This concept can be further extrapolated to refer to the experience that any member of a marginalized group can have when they view themselves by two different perspectives: their own self-concept and the perception of themselves from the majority and privileged group's point of view. When that internal sense of self is distorted and feels not good enough, a majority group's discriminatory perspective can reinforce these unhealthy narratives and make it difficult to experience one's true capability, competence, and even real tangible accomplishments.

With IP, Orbé-Austin and Orbé-Austin (2020) called this experience the *double impact*, when you experience IP internally and simultaneously experience the same messages from discriminatory environments, cultures, and people, who communicate to you that you are a fraud, you are not good enough, and you are in your position undeservedly because of your identity (e.g., "affirmative action candidate," "diversity candidate"). This external messaging can make it extremely hard for historically marginalized people with IP to believe that they are actually not an impostor, especially when they are isolated from their community and not sharing this experience with others. This double impact can make IP more difficult to overcome because it is being reinforced by external environments, including majority culture bosses, work environments, and peers.

The isolating nature of IP often makes it challenging to build community because when a person struggles with IP, the fear of being exposed as a fraud can make it uncomfortable and anxiety-provoking to share vulnerabilities, challenges, and one's whole self with others (e.g., Clance et al., 1995). Yet research shows that a powerful intervention against IP can be building community, especially with peers and more experienced colleagues, to help dispel some of the notions that you should not be internalizing that come from external sources and reinforce IP (Vergauwe et al., 2015). Ironically, with IP, individuals are more likely to internalize these external, even discriminatory, messages reinforcing impostor feelings over the ones that reinforce one's strengths, skills, and accomplishments, which are more accurate, because they match up with internal notions that we are not good enough, which have been instilled since early in our lives (Want & Kleitman, 2006).

Systemically, leaders need to recognize the deleterious effects of work cultures that allow their employees to engage in behaviors that are discriminatory and preserve the power of privileged groups. Ignoring such behaviors, not addressing them in a significant manner, or primarily considering how to protect the organization first makes leaders complicit in creating unsafe environments for marginalized people where they benefit from the hard work, organizational commitment, and poor self-care habits that are foundational for IP. This reveals a blatant disregard for the consequences of these behaviors, including burnout, depression, and anxiety, which are completely destructive for a company's marginalized employees.

THE ADDITIVE AND DISCRIMINATORY TRIGGERS FOR MARGINALIZED GROUPS

IP is not experienced at every moment of every day. It is typically experienced when an individual is triggered. Some of the most common triggers are a new job or assignment (where a person may feel novice and not certain about their skill), a complex project (in which there are many places to go wrong), publicly visible tasks (in which one may fear important eyes on their work), punitive work cultures (where there is not a lot of space for mistake making), and a toxic boss (one that particularly challenges an individual's competence in one way or another). When you are from a marginalized community, the mere experience of this identity in oppressive systems can lead us to feel that we are less than, not capable, and frauds, thoughts that are triggered by acts of discrimination, microaggressions, feelings of isolation, inequitable treatment or access, and gaslighting of the oppressive experiences around one's identity. These additional triggers support oppressive systems and simultaneously reinforce the internal IP narrative that says you don't belong here, you are not good enough, and people around you know and are communicating that. When one struggles with IP, it is hard, if not nearly impossible, to externalize these discriminatory behaviors and see them as separate from you and belonging to privileged and oppressive systems, which makes them easier to fight. IP stands in the way of seeing these triggers for what they are (i.e., attempts to oppress, minimize, and invalidate), and instead they become confirmation that IP thoughts and behaviors are valid.

When people experience a blatantly discriminatory act (i.e., that involves behaviors intended to diminish them, such as harassment or unfavorable treatment), it indicates they are being targeted in an environment that perceives them as less than. If they are not protected from that incident, it further communicates that the environment, whether passively or actively, agrees with this behavior. This can make these additional discriminatory triggers even more powerful because they become a communication not just from the individual committing the act but from the entire system. Therefore, if individuals experience a trigger like this, they can feel like not only does one person believe they are a fraud but that this notion is completely backed by the institution. For example, if a coworker calls you a "diversity hire," it suggests not only that they think you did not earn your position fairly or without assistance but also that the entire organization, in this example, human resources, your hiring manager, and your hiring committee, has potentially conspired to assist you because you are incapable of acquiring a position like this on your own. You can see in this example that if you struggle to externalize a message like "You are a diversity hire," then you can feel like this opinion is held by more than the person communicating it with you.

Although it may seem clear why these experiences may trigger people from marginalized groups, let us take a closer look at how they operate. Microaggressions (i.e., statements, actions, or incidents of subtle or unintentional discrimination) are like death by a thousand cuts where each incident serves as proof that a person is not welcome or included like everyone else. The isolation can leave individuals feeling that they are not part of a system or organization and are apart and separate. In situations where individuals lack mentorship or sponsorship, they may feel like they have no advocates or are on their own. Even in situations when people from marginalized groups have been assigned a mentor, if that mentor appears to be acting as their mentor solely out of duty or to be doing the minimum, the marginalized employee may receive clear messages about how the organization may not have committed to them. When persons from a historically marginalized group are being treated differently than those from privileged groups and they can see the benefits are clearly inequitable, they may feel less than or overlooked. Finally, when individuals from historically marginalized groups raise concerns about what they believe is occurring regarding these behaviors connected to their identity but they are gaslit; the response is reactive, quick, or defensive; or they are made to feel like their experience is incorrect, normative, or impossible, without sincere attempts at exploration, it further highlights a disregard and dismissal of their value that can make them feel not good enough, a fraud, or that they do not belong.

Because these discriminatory triggers for historically marginalized people are connected to their identity, the very root of who they are, it may be hard to disconnect from those triggers, especially when their internal IP narrative matches up with these communications. These additional discriminatory triggers can affect how often one is triggered, which can equate to a greater frequency of IP experiences. This can translate to experiencing the impact and consequences of the IP cycle, which includes overworking and self-sabotaging more often, making one more prone to burnout, anxiety, and depression (N. S. Bernard et al., 2002). Understanding the additional discriminatory triggers that people from historically marginalized groups may be susceptible to is important as they consider the types of environments, bosses, and cultures they want to engage with. Such understanding may also help with processing how IP may be affecting them in ways in which they were not aware. Environments that do not support them in discriminatory ways are more likely to reinforce their IP, which increases the likelihood that they will engage in the IP cycle of overworking (and thus chronic burnout) or self-sabotaging, which will definitely influence their ability to succeed, sustain, and excel in these environments.

IMPACT OF FIRST-GENERATIONAL EXPERIENCES

One historically marginalized group that warrants special consideration when examining IP is those individuals with first-generational experiences (e.g., first to go to college, first to pursue a specific profession). IP has been studied in first-generation college students and has been found to contribute to poor mental health and academic outcomes. Canning and colleagues (2019) found that impostor feelings were heightened for first-generation college students in a science, technology, engineering, and mathematics course when they perceived the classroom to be highly competitive. Such increased impostor feelings resulted in greater dropout intentions, lower engagement, lower attendance, and lower grades. The first-generational experiences of individuals can trigger impostor feelings in a variety of ways. First, because they may not have any role models to emulate, first-generation individuals may find they lack knowledge about how to navigate systems such as higher education or the workplace. Therefore, they may feel like they do not belong and are impostors due to their lack of knowledge regarding college or work cultures. Unable to speak to anyone about these feelings of not belonging and being an impostor, they often suffer in silence, not seeking the support they need that would confirm their experiences are normative and also provide support for how to navigate these competitive environments in more successful ways (e.g., by developing community and not doing things in isolation).

Further, individuals with first-generational experiences may also feel the responsibility of succeeding as a means to benefit their families, creating increased pressure to quickly master the intricacies of college or work life, including academically, professionally, and socially. If they are unable to do so immediately or meet some adverse circumstances (e.g., a poor grade, a less than stellar performance review), it may confirm their impostor narrative, creating more stressors. Holden and colleagues (2021) found that as compared with continuing-generation students, impostor phenomenon is more strongly correlated with stress among first-generation students.

Another way that IP adversely affects first-generation populations is through their notion that hard work may be considered the only way to succeed when this is not necessarily accurate. They may assume that in order to not be exposed as a fraud, they must overwork and never make a mistake, which can cause adverse physical and mental health outcomes. In this perspective, first-generation individuals believe that mistake making is a sign of their fraudulence, which may trigger a loss of confidence and diminish their belief that they belong in an academic institution or a company, increasing their impostor feelings.

Interventions that normalize transitional experiences at work or in college, acknowledge mistake making as normative, and provide support for individuals with first-generational experiences to discuss their challenges can help to decrease impostor feelings and improve academic and work outcomes.

The 3Cs (Clarify, Choose, Create) model that Orbé-Austin and Orbé-Austin (2020) developed to help individuals overcome IP can be a helpful intervention tool for first-generation individuals. In the first part of the model, Clarify, individuals explore their IP origin story; understand their triggers (e.g., a new class or job, a high-profile assignment); and change their thin, inaccurate narratives about themselves. For example, oftentimes first-generation individuals feel that they do not have any skills or talents and are just lucky to have any success in an academic or professional setting. This is a thin narrative. Thickening one's narrative means being able to internalize one's skills and deepen the story which you tell yourself about your journey. Thus, rather than attributing success to luck, first-generation individuals would own their unique skills (e.g., communication, interpersonal, leadership), and understand how they contribute to their achievements.

In Choose, the second phase of the model, first-generation individuals speak their truth, that is, they work to not feel embarrassed to discuss their IP experience as well as their distinct talents. Unfortunately, many individuals experiencing IP suffer in silence, fearful of being ridiculed or dismissed if they explore their feelings of being a fraud. In the second step of the Choose phase, individuals work to silence automatic negative thoughts (ANTs) that sustain false beliefs about their impostorism. Typical ANTs are mindreading, wherein individuals believe they know what others are thinking about them, usually something negative (e.g., "She is not intelligent enough to be in this college"); catastrophizing, wherein one thinks about the worst-case scenarios (e.g., "If I failed this test, I will need to drop out of college"); and fortune-telling, wherein one believes she can predict an event (e.g., "If I do not complete this project on time, my manager will demote me"). By silencing ANTs and replacing them with more positive statements, first-generation individuals can reduce impostor feelings. In the final stage of Choose, individuals focus on valuing and caring about themselves, centering self-care activities (e.g., exercise, meditation, rest) as key strategies to counter overwork, which is often a hallmark of those individuals dealing with IP.

In the last phase of the 3Cs model, Create, individuals (a) experiment with new roles, such as the help seeker, someone who asks for help, or the collaborator, one who shares responsibilities, instead of attempting to do everything on their own; (b) build their dream team, a group of supporters to help them counter impostor phenomenon, such as a mentor, an impostor phenomenon expert, and the cheerleader, an individual who is always present to provide emotional support; and (c) explore conditions for optimal performance by understanding which previous areas of the model (e.g., silencing ANTs, identifying triggers) should be the focus of their efforts to conquer impostor phenomenon (Orbé-Austin & Orbé-Austin, 2020). The 3Cs model is a great tool to help first-generation individuals overcome impostor phenomenon and thrive in their career and academic pursuits, and it can be used by academic institutions through various student services (e.g., first-year seminar, counseling, career services) to support them in this endeavor. It can also be utilized in work settings by managers, senior leaders, and human resources professionals to help historically marginalized individuals counter the double impact and excel in achieving their career goals.

WOMEN AND THE IMPACT OF IMPOSTOR PHENOMENON

Although it has often been erroneously reported that women experience IP in greater numbers, no research to date conclusively supports that assertion. What we do know is that in a world of work where women make significantly less than men, have less access to executive and board positions, and decrease in numbers as positions of power increase, the impact of IP cannot be underestimated. A piece of the work that needs to be done in the area of IP and gender is to not perpetuate these ideas that IP is a women's issue because research suggests that the effect of IP is wide reaching and does stretch across gender experiences (e.g., Badawy et al., 2018).

Although the prevalence of IP is not determined by gender, we have begun to understand that coping strategies across genders may differ. When IP is experienced by women, they have been shown to work harder, perform at higher standards, and be more engaged (Orbé-Austin & Orbé-Austin, 2022). These may appear to be beneficial outcomes; however, they can also render the struggle, pain, and distress invisible, and women commonly minimize or dismiss IP as not affecting them. Meanwhile, the negative impacts are significant and can impede career advancement, promotion, and compensation.

We do not see the beneficial performance outcomes for women with IP in environments where gender stigma or bias is prevalent. One such environment is male-dominated work systems (e.g., sciences, technology, mathematics). In these arenas, women become acutely aware of the negative manner in which they are perceived and experience gender stigma consciousness (GSC). GSC occurs when you experience your gender as more salient and visible than your performance (Pinel, 1999). It becomes very important in these types of environments to be aware of how IP and GSC are affecting performance. Isolation needs to be mitigated by female mentors and female professional communities that can provide a counterbalance and support in developing strategies for coping with the actual experiences of discrimination and microaggressions in their environments. In terms of systemic interventions, attention, resources, and training need to be devoted to creating environments focused on reducing gender-based bias and creating safe cultures that support the growth and development of women. The topic of gender and IP is discussed more thoroughly in Chapter 7.

RACE, RACIAL IDENTITY, AND IMPOSTOR PHENOMENON

When evaluating the impact of IP on historically marginalized populations, it is critical to also examine the roles of race and racial identity. Cokley and colleagues (2017) found that among African American college students, high levels of impostor feelings had a significant impact on perceived discrimination and anxiety. Among Asian American college students, impostor feelings mediated the relationship between perceived discrimination and both anxiety and depression (Cokley et al., 2017). Another study found that, for African Americans, IP is highly correlated with depression, survivor's guilt, low self-esteem, and high psychological distress (Austin et al., 2009). A study by Peteet and colleagues (2015) also demonstrated that higher levels of IP predicted higher levels of psychological distress and lower levels of self-esteem among African American college students.

Sellers and his colleagues (1997) defined *racial identity* as the thoughts and beliefs about what it means to be of a certain race and the level of importance and affect that an individual places on this identity. D. L. Bernard et al. (2018) found differences among Black students with various racial ideologies, with individuals who had a multiculturalist racial identity reporting the lowest IP scores and individuals with a humanist racial identity reporting the highest IP scores, indicating that racial identity can serve as a protective resilience factor. This same study found that racial discrimination experiences led to increased levels of IP. Lige et al. (2017) also found that in a sample of African American college students, those who felt positively about their race and their membership in it were more likely to report higher self-esteem and lower levels of IP. More research on the impact of racial identity on IP is needed to better understand how to create more suitable interventions that suit the needs of historically marginalized populations. The topic of race and IP is discussed more thoroughly in Chapters 8 and 9.

DIFFERENTIAL CAREER IMPACTS

When examining the career impact of impostor phenomenon on marginalized populations, as previously discussed, the double impact may contribute to differential career outcomes. Individuals who struggle with IP tend to report lower job satisfaction and may be less likely to pursue career advancement opportunities due to a lower motivation to lead (Neureiter & Traut-Mattausch, 2017). They may also be less inclined to pursue opportunities in professions where they may feel they do not belong. Therefore, when considering the needs of historically marginalized groups, understanding differential career impacts as a result of IP will be critical in developing tailored interventions unique to the concerns of this population. Such interventions can be useful in also addressing IP in oppressive environments (e.g., academic, work settings).

THE IMPORTANCE OF ADDRESSING IMPOSTOR PHENOMENON IN OPPRESSIVE ENVIRONMENTS

Although interventions focused on helping individuals build awareness of their impostor feelings are crucial to overcome IP, it is also critical to engage and develop systems-level interventions because oppressive environments can trigger and sustain IP. Toxic workplaces have been found to exacerbate impostor feelings and contribute to negative outcomes, such as lower job productivity and burnout (Anjum et al., 2018; Guan et al., 2017). Systems-level interventions, such as organizational support, can create healthier work environments, which help neutralize impostor feelings and produce more positive outcomes, such as greater job satisfaction and better organizational citizenship behavior, or behaviors that increase the efficiency and effectiveness of an organization, such as helping colleagues with their projects (Vergauwe et al., 2015).

When individuals overcome impostor phenomenon, they feel more able to internalize their skills and accomplishments, do not feel the need to overwork or be perfectionistic, and can focus on their life and career goals. However, when these individuals return to an oppressive environment, their impostor feelings may be triggered, and organizational pressures may make them harder to reverse or use intrapersonal skills to defeat, possibly jeopardizing progress on keeping IP vanquished.

Oppressive or toxic work environments are ones in which discriminatory behavior such as racism, misogyny, transphobia, and homophobia are pervasive and tolerated by the leaders of the organization. They also are characterized by bullying and workplace harassment (Guan et al., 2017). These types of environments are consistently triggering to those dealing with IP, as the message being sent to marginalized populations is that "you don't belong here and you will constantly need to prove that you are worthy." Such messages and discrimination can increase impostor feelings for individuals (D. L. Bernard et al., 2018). Therefore, systems-level interventions that not only describe IP and its common triggers but also explore the double impact on marginalized populations will be essential in addressing IP in oppressive environments. Further, organizational environments that prioritize psychological safety, have zero tolerance policies for discriminatory or bullying behaviors (no matter the seniority of the committer of the violation), thoughtfully train their leaders and managers not to reinforce IP behaviors, and value the health and well-being of their employees through action are the types of organizational interventions that will matter in helping people from historically marginalized groups reduce their IP.

HOW LEADERS, MANAGERS, AND MENTORS ARE CRUCIAL IN REDUCING IMPOSTOR PHENOMENON

In addition to systems-level interventions, the support of leaders, managers, and mentors will be crucial to helping historically marginalized groups conquer IP. Orbé-Austin and Orbé-Austin (2020) discussed the importance of a dream team to help individuals overcome impostor phenomenon. The dream team should include members such as a mentor, a cheerleader, a grounder, and an action planner. According to Johnson and Smith (2019), a mentor can help an individual overcome IP by

- normalizing impostor feelings by pointing out that 70% of people have indicated an experience with impostor feelings,
- sharing one's own experiences with IP,
- affirming the mentee's skills and talents,
- countering negative self-talk of the mentee, and
- not allowing the mentee to give the mentor all of the credit for the mentee's success.

It is helpful to have more than one mentor. Guidance from more than one person can provide different perspectives and reduce the tendency to rely on a mentor for external validation, which is a hallmark for those who struggle with IP. However, such mentorship should be focused on the needs of the mentee and healthy exchange between mentor and mentee, rather than as a means for the mentor to provide rigid direction to the mentee. Toxic mentors can add to impostor feelings if they trigger the mentee to constantly prove they are worthy of mentorship.

Historically marginalized populations face unique challenges in the workplace and are impacted by bias and other forms of discrimination, which can negatively affect their career development. For instance, a report by McKinsey and the Lean In Foundation (Krivkovich et al., 2022) found that Black women are significantly less likely than women of other races to say that a manager shows interest in their career development. A lack of support from supervisors or mentors has been found to exacerbate impostor feelings (Pervez et al., 2021), whereas positive support can reduce such feelings. It becomes critical for supervisors and mentors to acknowledge the experiences of IP and provide proactive support for their direct reports and mentees by offering environments that are not toxically competitive (e.g., where there are scapegoats and stars or no room for learning or making mistakes); creating psychologically safe teams (i.e., where people feel safe to dissent or be their full selves); providing guidance and support for healthy collaboration (e.g., intervening when there is tension, conflict, or inaction); not promoting, supporting, or ignoring factions that evolve on their teams that exclude others; addressing self-sabotaging behavior like procrastination with direction and concrete feedback; not promoting perfectionism or people-pleasing; and most importantly, making sure that they are working as needed on their own IP experiences and any tendencies to trigger or encourage them.

It is important for managers to understand that IP affects a person not only intrapersonally (i.e., within themselves) but also interpersonally (i.e., in their behavior with others). Not addressing their own IP experiences as a manager can lead to micromanaging; modeling overworking tendencies; being highly perfectionistic and anxious about performance and work product, especially when it is public; having trouble with mistake making in themselves and others; and not leveraging opportunities when awards, accolades, or recognition occur for the team. These behaviors can have a detrimental effect on their team and require managers to do their own work in resolving these issues.

In addition, it is incumbent upon managers to interrogate the ways in which their leadership may support privileged and noninclusive perspectives that may further enforce the marginalization and disconnection of marginalized groups from the system. It may be necessary for managers who are devoted to the reduction of IP, especially for marginalized people in their organization, to explore and address questions like the following:

- How does my leadership style create exclusive experiences? Do I give voice to some and silence others? Do I behave in authoritarian ways that do not allow others to develop their decision-making power? How do I engage in more inclusive leadership?
- Who do I promote or advocate for promotion? Do I look for certain characteristics that may exclude diverse candidates? Do I make it seem like there is only one way to get ahead or to be successful? How do I address this in my review process?
- How do I promote support for members of my teams from historically marginalized groups? Do I expect them to do it all on their own? Do I provide and support their use of resources within and outside of the organization? What am I doing to increase their retention in the organization or field?
- How might the ways that I lead or what I expect from team members be culturally encapsulated (i.e., ignoring or lacking knowledge about others' worldviews and not recognizing the significance of culture on their perspectives, behaviors, or desires) or supporting cultural hegemony (i.e., supporting the dominance of one cultural perspective and ignoring or neglecting the relevance of others)?
- Whom do I mentor? Are they similar to me? How can I change that?

The relevance of senior leaders, mentors, and supervisors in the course of addressing and conquering IP is significant and requires both introspection and action to create more inclusive and supportive spaces where employees can discuss the impact of IP on their work and how it is triggered by the current environment. The ability to address the changes in leadership and culture become incredibly important to their endeavor and vital to the retention and advancement of historically marginalized people in these organizations.

CONCLUSION

Although more attention has been paid to IP in recent years, more exploration is needed to better understand its unique impact on historically marginalized communities. Whether discussing first-generation students, women, people of color, or other historically marginalized groups, the double impact of IP is a critical element to consider when planning interventions. This experience of both feeling like an impostor internally and then also receiving signals from the environment that you do not belong can adversely affect the academic and career aspirations of individuals from historically marginalized populations, resulting in greater dropout intentions; less inclination to take on leadership roles; and higher rates of continuance commitment, meaning the intention to remain at a job, which may influence compensation over the long term (Canning et al., 2020; Vergauwe et al., 2015). Interventions such as the 3Cs model (Orbé-Austin & Orbé-Austin, 2020), which help historically marginalized populations understand their triggers (e.g., a new job, an unfamiliar project), silence their ANTs (e.g., mindreading: "Everyone thinks I don't belong here because I am not smart enough"), create a more accurate narrative for their success (e.g., "I have skills and knowledge which have enabled me to succeed in this role"), and find a dream team of support, will enable them to conquer their IP and thrive in their academic and professional pursuits.

REFERENCES

Anjum, A., Ming, X., Siddiqi, A. F., & Rasool, S. F. (2018). An empirical study analyzing job productivity in toxic workplace environments. *International Journal of Environmental Research and Public Health, 15*(5), Article 1035. https://doi.org/10.3390/ijerph15051035

Austin, C. C., Clark, E. M., Ross, M. J., & Taylor, M. J. (2009). Impostorism as a mediator between survivor guilt and depression in a sample of African American college students. *College Student Journal, 43*(4, Pt. A), 1094–1109.

Badawy, R. L., Gazdag, B. A., Bentley, J. R., & Brouer, R. L. (2018). Are all impostors created equal? Exploring gender differences in the impostor phenomenon–performance link. *Personality and Individual Differences, 131,* 156–163. https://doi.org/10.1016/j.paid.2018.04.044

Bernard, D. L., Hoggard, L. S., & Neblett, E. W. (2018). Racial discrimination, racial identity, and impostor phenomenon: A profile approach. *Cultural Diversity and Ethnic Minority Psychology, 24*(1), 51–61. https://doi.org/10.1037/cdp0000161

Bernard, N. S., Dollinger, S. J., & Ramaniah, N. V. (2002). Applying the Big Five personality factors to the impostor phenomenon. *Journal of Personality Assessment, 78*(2), 321–333. https://doi.org/10.1207/S15327752JPA7802_07

Canning, E. A., LaCosse, J., Kroeper, K. M., & Murphy, M. C. (2020). Feeling like an impostor: The effect of perceived classroom competition on the daily psychological experiences of first-generation college students. *Social Psychological and Personality Science, 11*(5), 647–657. https://doi.org/10.1177/1948550619882032

Clance, P. R., Dingman, D., Reviere, S. L., & Stober, D. R. (1995). Impostor phenomenon in an interpersonal/social context: Origins and treatment. *Women & Therapy, 16*(4), 79–96. https://doi.org/10.1300/J015v16n04_07

Clance, P. R., & Imes, S. A. (1978). The impostor phenomenon in high achieving women: Dynamics and therapeutic intervention. *Psychotherapy: Theory, Research, & Practice, 15*(3), 241–247. https://doi.org/10.1037/h0086006

Cokley, K., Smith, L., Bernard, D., Hurst, A., Jackson, S., Stone, S., Awosogba, O., Saucer, C., Bailey, M., & Roberts, D. (2017). Impostor feelings as a moderator and mediator of the relationship between perceived discrimination and mental health among racial/ethnic minority college students. *Journal of Counseling Psychology, 64*(2), 141–154. https://doi.org/10.1037/cou0000198

Cowman, S. E., & Ferrari, J. R. (2002). "Am I for real?": Predicting impostor tendencies from self-handicapping and affective components. *Social Behavior and Personality, 30*(2), 119–125. https://doi.org/10.2224/sbp.2002.30.2.119

Du Bois, W. E. B. (2008). *The souls of Black folk* (B. H. Edwards, Ed.). Oxford University Press.

Guan, S., Xiaerfuding, X., Ning, L., Lian, Y., Jiang, Y., Liu, J., & Ng, T. B. (2017). Effect of job strain on job burnout, mental fatigue and chronic diseases among civil servants in the Xinjiang Uygur autonomous region of China. *International Journal of Environmental Research and Public Health, 14*(8), Article 872. https://doi.org/10.3390/ijerph14080872

Holden, C. L., Wright, L. E., Herring, A. M., & Sims, P. L. (2021). Impostor phenomenon among first- and continuing-generation college students: The roles of perfectionism and stress. *Journal of College Student Retention.* Advance online publication. https://doi.org/10.1177/15210251211019379

Johnson, W., & Smith, D. (2019). Mentoring someone with impostor phenomenon. *Harvard Business Review.* https://hbr.org/2019/02/mentoring-someone-with-imposter-phenomenon

Krivkovich, A., Liu, W. W., Nguyen, H., Rambachan, I., Robinson, N., Williams, M., & Yee, L. (2022, October 18). *Women in the workplace 2022.* https://www.mckinsey.com/featured-insights/diversity-and-inclusion/women-in-the-workplace-archive

Lige, Q., Peteet, B., & Brown, C. (2017). Racial identity, self-esteem, and the impostor phenomenon among African American college students. *The Journal of Black Psychology, 43*(4), 345–357. https://doi.org/10.1177/0095798416648787

Neureiter, M., & Traut-Mattausch, E. (2016a). An inner barrier to career development: Preconditions of the impostor phenomenon and consequences for career development. *Frontiers in Psychology, 7*, Article 48. https://doi.org/10.3389/fpsyg.2016.00048

Neureiter, M., & Traut-Mattausch, E. (2016b). Inspecting the dangers of feeling like a fake: An empirical investigation of the impostor phenomenon in the world of work. *Frontiers in Psychology, 7*, Article 1445. https://doi.org/10.3389/fpsyg.2016.01445

Neureiter, M., & Traut-Mattausch, E. (2017). Two sides of the career resources coin: Career adaptability resources and the impostor phenomenon. *Journal of Vocational Behavior, 98*, 56–69. https://doi.org/10.1016/j.jvb.2016.10.002

Orbé-Austin, L., & Orbé-Austin, R. (2020). *Own your greatness: Overcome impostor phenomenon, beat self-doubt, and succeed in life.* Ulysses Press.

Orbé-Austin, L., & Orbé-Austin, R. (2022). *Your unstoppable greatness: Break free from impostor phenomenon, cultivate your agency, and achieve your ultimate career goals.* Ulysses Press.

Pervez, A., Brady, L. L., Mullane, K., Lo, K. D., Bennett, A. A., & Nelson, T. A. (2021). An empirical investigation of mental illness, impostor phenomenon, and social support in management doctoral programs. *Journal of Management Education, 45*(1), 126–158. https://doi.org/10.1177/1052562920953195

Peteet, B., Brown, C., Lige, Q., & Lanaway, D. (2015). Impostorism is associated with greater psychological distress and lower self-esteem for African American students. *Current Psychology, 34*(1), 154. https://doi.org/10.1007/s12144-014-9248-z

Pinel, E. C. (1999). Stigma consciousness: The psychological legacy of social stereotypes. *Journal of Personality and Social Psychology, 76*(1), 114–128. https://doi.org/10.1037/0022-3514.76.1.114

Sellers, R. M., Rowley, S. A. J., Chavous, T. M., Shelton, J. N., & Smith, M. A. (1997). Multidimensional inventory of Black identity: A preliminary investigation of reliability and construct validity. *Journal of Personality and Social Psychology, 73*(4), 805–815. https://doi.org/10.1037/0022-3514.73.4.805

Thompson, T., Foreman, P., & Martin, F. (2000). Impostor fears and perfectionistic concern over mistakes. *Personality and Individual Differences, 29*(4), 629–647. https://doi.org/10.1016/S0191-8869(99)00218-4

Vergauwe, J., Wille, B., Feys, M., De Fruyt, F., & Anseel, F. (2015). Fear of being exposed: The trait-relatedness of the impostor phenomenon and its relevance in the work context. *Journal of Business and Psychology, 30*(3), 565–581. https://doi.org/10.1007/s10869-014-9382-5

Want, J., & Kleitman, S. (2006). Impostor phenomenon and self-handicapping: Links with parenting styles and self-confidence. *Personality and Individual Differences, 40*(5), 961–971. https://doi.org/10.1016/j.paid.2005.10.005

13

AN EVOLVING ANALYSIS OF IMPOSTOR SYNDROME FROM 1983 TO THE PRESENT

Implications for Clinicians and Researchers

VALERIE YOUNG

An increasing number of organizations are offering educational programming on impostor phenomenon/syndrome (IP/IS). However, these and other education-based efforts have been largely overlooked in the academic and therapeutic communities. The purpose of this chapter is to share the origins, evolution, and resulting analysis of a long-standing and widely used educational intervention to IP/IS. Conclusions are expected to be of primary value to clinicians, academic advisors, executive coaches, and others who work directly with individuals. Secondary beneficiaries include researchers seeking uncharted areas of inquiry; university and corporate learning and development practitioners responsible for professional development; organizational culture specialists tasked with fostering psychological safety in the workplace;

https://doi.org/10.1037/0000397-014
The Impostor Phenomenon: Psychological Research, Theory, and Interventions,
K. Cokley (Editor)
Copyright © 2024 by the American Psychological Association. All rights reserved.

286 • *Valerie Young*

and professionals whose job it is to attract, retain, and advance diverse populations in achievement settings.[1]

AN EDUCATIONAL INTERVENTION TO IP/IS

Unlike the other 27 contributors to this volume, I am neither an academic researcher nor a psychologist. I am an educator and practitioner, who, in 1983, used the findings from my doctoral research to design the first educational intervention to IP/IS—an intervention that would go on to be experienced by half a million people worldwide. This outlier status merits mention for two reasons. First, some may consider analysis communicated in a more accessible manner to be less serious or significant. Second, there is the widely recognized bias in academia against qualitative research. Analysis based on observation alone is deemed even less valid. This is ironic considering the very concept of IP came not from empirical study but entirely from psychologists Pauline Rose Clance and Suzanne Imes's (1978) observations.

Clance and Imes's (1978) initial analysis was informed by their academic training in clinical psychology as well as Imes's (1979) doctoral research on gender differences in attribution. Similarly, the analysis and subsequent approach to addressing IP/IS described here has been informed by my academic training in education and doctoral research on internal barriers to

---

[1]Within a few years, the same experience Clance and Imes described in 1978 as *impostor phenomenon* would be referred to by some as *impostor syndrome*. The Library of Congress found the earliest searchable use of the latter term in a 1981 abstract for a report by the Center for Research on Women in Science at Morris Brown College on factors influencing the persistence/achievement of Black high school and college women in the sciences and health professions. That same year, it appeared in several popular women's magazines. Impostor "syndrome" would quickly prevail in popular discourse. The explanation for this linguistic shift may come down to one's literal source of reference. For clinicians, that would be the *Diagnostic and Statistical Manual of Mental Disorders*, where "syndrome" describes a mental disease or disorder. Outside of this world however, the defining source is not the *Diagnostic and Statistical Manual of Mental Disorders* but rather the dictionary. *Merriam-Webster's Dictionary* cites two definitions of "syndrome." The first clinical usage contains terms like "symptoms," "abnormality," and "condition." However, the second—and equally valid—meaning of syndrome is "a set of concurrent things (such as emotions and actions) that usually form an identifiable pattern" (Merriam-Webster, n.d.). It is therefore reasonable to assume the term "syndrome" emerged in the popular culture not to imply a psychological disorder but as a valid alternative to describe the thoughts, feelings, and behaviors associated with the impostor experience. For this reason, it would be disingenuous for me to stray from the less siloed term "impostor syndrome" that I and others have used responsibly for over 4 decades. That said, out of courtesy to the intended readership of this book, the abbreviation IP/IS will be used throughout.

women's occupational achievement (Young, 1985).[2] In keeping with her position as an academic, Clance followed her and Imes's detailed examination of their observational findings with extensive empirical research. Likewise, in keeping with my position as an independent educator, my analysis began with qualitative research and was followed by detailed examination of extensive observational findings.

One third of the women in Clance and Imes's (1978) sample were therapy clients. The rest were in growth-oriented groups or classes they facilitated. Observations occurred largely in a therapeutic context with women who did not yet have a name for their feelings of intellectual phoniness. In contrast, the observations and analysis described here occurred in an educational context with men and women who both self-identify and self-selected to participate in an interactive educational program on "impostor syndrome." Collectively these participants constitute a considerably larger and broader pool. Of the 178 women in Clance and Imes's sample, 136 were students (110 undergraduate, 20 graduate, six medical); 20 were untenured faculty; and 22 were nonuniversity affiliated professional women, none of whom held management roles.

In contrast, an estimated 40,000 students have participated in the IP/IS intervention program over a span of 4 decades. Initial participants were largely undergraduate women in engineering. Since 2010 however, participants have been primarily male and female doctoral and medical students; postdocs; and to a lesser extent, pharmaceutical fellows and law students. During this same period, a similar professional development program was conducted for early career and tenured faculty, deans, and nonacademic administrators at a dozen R-1 institutions.

Comparatively few studies on IP/IS have been conducted in business settings. The analyses presented here are informed by training sessions delivered to tens of thousands of professionals, managers, and senior leaders at such

---

[2]My work has been influenced to a significant degree by my graduate experience in the college of education at the University of Massachusetts, Amherst, in the late 1970s and early 1980s—a department which, in 1968, established the elimination of institutional racism as a core commitment. Specifically, my views on social factors impacting IP/IS stem from my academic concentration in what can be described as oppression awareness. Key influencers were course instructor Judith Katz's (1978) work on racism awareness training, faculty advisor Bailey Jackson III (1976) and fellow students Rita Hardiman (1982) and Jean Kim's (1981) work on racial identity development theory, and Jackson and Hardiman's (1988) conceptualizations of the dynamics of oppression and their application to the effective design and facilitation of what would later be known as diversity and social justice training (Hardiman & Jackson, 1997). Extensive course work in group dynamics, psychological education, and what is now referred to as social–emotional and psychodynamic aspects provided learning on important frameworks for how education could be used to guide individuals in the exploration of dysfunctional patterns in a nontherapeutic context.

diverse organizations as Pfizer, P&G, Intel, Moody's, Boeing, the National Cancer Institute, Diageo, the National Aeronautics and Space Administration, and the National Basketball Association, among many others. This work has been further informed by programs delivered to members of professional associations in such dissimilar fields as banking, trucking, and commercial real estate and with participants representing a wide spectrum of occupations, including nurses, physicists, speech pathologists, financial planners, chemists, optometrists, librarians, microbiologists, executive assistants, accountants, scientists, clinical psychologists, marriage and family therapists, engineers, physicians, fiction writers, jewelers, and entrepreneurs.

The analysis is also informed by considerable interaction with diverse populations. Initially, requests for educational programming came almost exclusively either from or for women. However, since 2009, groups have been mostly mixed and, in a few cases, majority male. Participant ages have ranged from high schoolers and traditionally aged undergraduate students to early-, mid-, and late-career professionals. Interactive sessions have been conducted as part of university programming for first-generation students; Native American and Hispanic undergraduates in engineering; and Black and Hispanic doctoral students in engineering, chemistry, and physics, as well as programs initiated by Asian and women's corporate employee resource groups. From a larger culture perspective, this educational intervention has been attended by participants from every continent except Antarctica.

Evidence suggesting the effectiveness of this intervention is inferred from five sources commonly considered in the entrepreneurial world: (a) anonymous participant evaluations indicating increased awareness of IP/IS, including what it is, where it comes from, how it manifests in the form of common coping and protecting behaviors, practical tools to address it, and anticipated increase in confidence; (b) unsolicited progress reports from past attendees; (c) unsolicited referrals from past clients to potential future clients; (d) repeat invitations to deliver this intervention—in some cases, as many as six times—at numerous organizations including Stanford, MIT, University of Pennsylvania, Cornell, Meharry Medical College, University of Texas, University of Michigan, Columbia, Cornell, Harvard, Yale, Google, Microsoft, IBM, Hello Fresh, JP Morgan, Vanguard, YUM!, and Society of Women Engineers; (e) use of my findings in educational programming at numerous corporations and universities, including by three contributors to this book.

Despite evidence of the effectiveness of this educational intervention as well as the significant growth in educational programming on IP/IS, there has been scant interest in academia in examining education-based interventions. One exception is a study by Austrian psychologists comparing the effectiveness of coaching and training (Zanchetta et al., 2020). The study, which sought to lower IP scores by fostering a growth mindset, found coaching most effective. From an educational point of view, it is notable that neither intervention used the term "impostor phenomenon" or "impostor syndrome" explicitly, nor were subjects aware of the connection between the training/coaching and this topic. Thus, issues being measured, such as IP-related "concern about mistakes (tendency to cover up errors) and their fear of negative evaluation" were addressed only in the abstract (Zanchetta et al., 2020, p. 5). This is in stark contrast to humanistic education, which centers the learner in the change process.

In a review of the IP/IS literature, Bravata et al. (2020) recommended "a prospective evaluation of the use of individual and group cognitive behavioral therapy focused on addressing impostor feelings on clinical and workplace outcomes for employed populations across a range of professions" (p. 1272). The breadth of experience described here offers a jumping-off point for clinicians to explore how key concepts presented here may increase clinical and workplace outcomes for employed populations across a range of professions as well as for students.

Finally, working directly with significant numbers of individuals who self-identify with IP/IS in an educational capacity has provided the unparalleled opportunity to observe patterns and trends for which no data currently exist. For example, since the global COVID-19 pandemic began in 2020, an increasing number of educational programs are being delivered virtually. Of the over 100 virtual programs delivered between 2017 and 2022, there is one audience who can be predictively expected not to share publicly. This is associates who work in large, 500- to 3,000-attorney law firms. One could infer that people who go into law tend toward introversion. Or one could infer, as I have, that in highly competitive environments, where in this case, everyone is vying for partner, the public admission of impostor feelings at worst is professionally risky and at best could be an understudied contributing factor to IP/IS. Clinicians using cognitive behavioral therapy and others who counsel law associates might use this finding to help this population better contextualize IP/IS feelings they assume are unique to them. Organizational psychologists seeking to test this theory might partner with state or provincial bar associations to compare the rates and intensity of IP/IS among associates in large global law firms to those of early-career attorneys working in small practices or as sole practitioners.

SUMMARY OF EARLY RESEARCH AND FINDINGS

The purpose of my 1985 study was to develop a descriptive model of internal barriers to women's occupational achievement with the goal of informing

290 • *Valerie Young*

educational strategies for teachers, trainers, and career counselors. The study was exploratory and drew from related research and theories from psychology, sociology, women's studies/feminist writings, business management, organizational literature, and career-related literature.

In-depth interviews were conducted with 15 professional women whose work involved addressing female advancement in some capacity that was learning-directed. Subjects worked in management and nonmanagement positions in corporate settings; social services; a trade school for adult women; and community, state, and private colleges. More than half (eight) were women of color (six Black, one Latina, one Asian). In addition, all were chosen based on their likelihood to work with women who were racially diverse and from varied class backgrounds. Three major areas were found to be central to understanding and addressing internal barriers to women's achievement: (a) other directedness, (b) sociocultural expectations and realities, and (c) issues related to performance. The following is a brief overview of how each area was understood by subjects and extrapolated from the relevant research at that time.

Other Directedness Dimension

The other directedness component of the model describes the central nature of relationships in women's lives, their capacity to care for and about others, and their sense of connectedness and responsibility to those around them.[3] Subjects cited this as a salient factor in many aspects of women's achievement experiences. For example, women's role as caregiver in the private world of the family was thought to put the needs of others in conflict with their own. Subjects also observed in women a higher need for affiliation. This was consistent with findings that girls are more concerned with being liked and more vulnerable to criticism (Rosenberg & Simmons, 1975) and that women may have a higher need for approval (Baruch et al., 1983). Women's desire to preserve interpersonal relationships in the workplace and their need to be liked and accepted were seen as frequently coming at the expense of efficacy.

Other directedness was also reflected in the interpretation of success itself. If measured by the attainment of money, status, and power, then women were considered less successful and more cautious. However, in the private realm of

---

[3]The term "other directedness" was inspired by social psychologist Carol Gilligan, whose 1982 book, *In a Different Voice*, broke new ground when she challenged the prevailing theory of developmental psychology that said girls were largely incapable of achieving the same level of moral reasoning as boys. Rather than being lesser, she argued, women's moral reasoning is simply different and has at its core an "obligation to exercise care and avoid hurt" and to avoid isolation (1982, p. 73).

relationships, women were thought to both excel and take risks. But because these arenas are less valued, skills and achievements related to care, concern, and connectedness were said to go unrecognized by society and often by women themselves. A related pattern was a tendency for women to define success in less individualistic terms to include the quality of relationships, being of service, and making a meaningful contribution. This communal orientation was also cited as more typical of Asian and Black populations.

Sociocultural Expectations and Realities Dimension

The largest of the three categories to emerge from the data was that which addressed sociocultural factors. Study subjects described external factors as either causal or compounding women's inner obstacles. These fell into two overlapping areas: (a) sociocultural expectations, which referred to the prevailing expectations regarding appropriate gender roles and behaviors held by society generally as well as by specific social groups, socioeconomic classes, families, and ultimately women themselves, and (b) sociocultural realities, which spoke to the challenges of striving in a male-oriented work culture as well as structural impediments related to systemic sexism, racism, classism, and age discrimination. As other researchers argued at the time, the oppression of Black (Joseph & Lewis, 1981), Asian (Fujutomi & Wong, 1973), Native American (Kidwell, 1976), and Latina (Nieto-Gomez, 1973) women must be viewed within a context that incorporates race and class inequities.

Performance Dimension

The performance component of the model encompassed how women experience themselves relative to success, failure, and competence. Subjects described women's definition of competence as guided by exceedingly high standards. This in turn was thought to cause them to equate competence with unaided achievement, expertise, perfectionism, and absence of failure. The expectation, too, is that to be considered competent, women must demonstrate expertise in all endeavors and in multiple roles. These responses were thought to leave women particularly vulnerable to IP/IS.

Fast-forward to today, we see IP/IS increasingly being dismissed as a "white-lady thing" (Jamison, 2023, para. 24). This narrative stems largely from the pool of women who signed up to work with either Clance or Imes in therapy or in growth groups and therefore on whom their 1978 conclusions were based. However, as I found in my own early literature review (Young, 1985), Asian American researchers had reported evidence of impostor feelings in Asian women 2 years earlier. Throughout their interviews with first- and second-generation Chinese American women, as well as women in Japan, Lilly Wong Fillmore, then associate dean of the Graduate School of Education at the University of California Berkley, and doctoral student in school psychology Jacqueline Leon Cheong uncovered a countervailing pattern of acknowledged competence on the one hand and self-doubt and negative self-evaluation on the other. The result, they wrote, was a strong fear of being "intellectual frauds" and that "what individual success is achieved tends to be attributed to luck and hard work rather than ability" (Fillmore & Cheong, 1976, p. 165).

EVOLUTION AND APPLICATION OF THE MODEL

The most all-encompassing shift since 1985 was the surprising discovery that an educational application of a model intended to describe internal barriers specifically to female achievement would prove useful for anyone with IP/IS. What follows is a brief overview of evolution of the original analyses as well as how two of the three categories have been further developed to be used in educational interventions.

Evolution of the Other Directedness Dimension

The emphasis on care, concern, and connection continues to matter because of its potential to complicate the achievement experience for people with IP/IS. After all, the road to success is nothing if not a series of choices, such as whether and where to attend college or relocate for work, choice of major and then career path, whether to negotiate salary or ask for a raise, and whether to share accomplishments or keep them to yourself. Not coincidentally, these are also the very decision points where impostor feelings most often get triggered—especially for women.

From a young age, girls learn from their mothers to sacrifice themselves by putting others' needs first. As Gilligan (1982, p. 138) wrote, "This obligation between selfishness and responsibility complicates for women the issue of choice, leaving them suspended between an ideal of selflessness and the truth of their own agency and needs." Participants often speak of the real or perceived potential for their achievement choices to affect others in one of two ways. The first is the sense that "if I win, someone else has to lose." In an aptly titled paper, *In Danger of Winning*, Lee Anne Bell (1996) documented a 3-year project working with girls in an urban elementary school in the United States that found girls routinely suppressed pride or excitement about their achievement to spare others' feelings. For adult women, career advancement that requires spending more time at work can trigger concerns about the impact of one's success on family. If moving up in the organization also entails a physical move, it can mean disrupting your partner's career or children's education or being away from aging parents. These decisions are difficult enough. Feeling like a fraud can make it harder to parse whether hesitation to advance is due to relationship considerations or to perceived inadequacies.

Other directedness also speaks to the real or perceived potential of success to affect relationships between ourselves and others. When connection is paramount in your life, any decision that holds the potential to lessen the connection can be disconcerting. As Gilligan (1982, p. 42) observed, in achievement women recognize "the danger [of] isolation, a fear that in standing out or being set apart by success, they will be left alone." Subsequent research confirms female concerns about being liked are well-founded. In mock job interviews, observers noted that angry male candidates not only deserved more status and a higher salary but could be expected to do better at the job than angry women. Irritability in men is accepted as a sign of status, but when women lost their temper, they were viewed as less competent.

Girls and women continue to express concerns about being too smart or bossy. In a survey by the Girl Scouts of the USA (2008), a third of girls aged 8 to 17 who indicated a desire to be leaders worried about making people mad at them, being laughed at, not being liked, or coming across as bossy. Given the strong social pressure to fit in, it is easy to see why many girls learn to downplay or devalue their abilities to avoid ostracism—a lesson that is often carried into adulthood. Clinical and educational interventions should be mindful of the difference between minimizing achievement to guard against bragging backlash and believing one is not actually responsible for success.

Concerns about the isolating effects of success apply to all women irrespective of race and to men of color. White women and people of color, including men, are keenly aware that the higher up the organizational chart they climb, the less diverse the landscape becomes. The isolation is even more profound if you are expected to leave your racial identity at the door. You do not have to occupy the executive suite to know that a promotion can incur jealousy and even resentment from people who were once your peers and often friends. For first-generation students and professionals, success may alienate them from the people they grew up with. The loss of connection may be so intolerable that some people deliberately choose a job below their training or capabilities. In one example, a participant with a PhD in business was working as a bookkeeper. IP/IS certainly contributed to lowering the occupational bar, but as she explained, her position was also a way to close the connection gap: "When

294 • *Valerie Young*

people find out I have a PhD, I feel a gulf widening between us." Being forced to decide between career advancement and potential isolation can make it harder for individuals with IP/IS and clinicians and educators alike to separate impostor-related fears from legitimate misgivings.

Finally, subjects in the 1985 study portrayed women as often having a more layered definition of success. Forty years later, the pace of organizational life has accelerated to the point where everyone is operating in a state of perpetual overwhelm, creating a reality where the hunger for meaning, satisfaction, and balance is less gendered. As a consequence, clinicians should be mindful that when faced with the decision to pursue a promotion, stay in a doctoral program, scale a business, or otherwise achieve in ways that may result in less balance, meaning, or contribution, it can be harder for someone with impostor feelings to parse out, "Am I afraid or hesitant because I don't think I can do it?"—which is IP/IS talking—or "Do I not want it?" The answer may not be either one or the other, but it does tend to be more one than the other.

Evolution and Application of the Sociocultural Expectations and Realities Dimension

The sociocultural expectations and realities in the model originally spoke, in part, to what had been prevailing expectations regarding appropriate gender roles and behaviors for women at that time. Subsequent experience has found that early messages and expectations, not only from family but also from teachers, coaches, school counselors, and other influential adults, can lay the groundwork for impostor feelings in anyone. Discouraging messages especially can linger for years. If the only response to a report card with all As and one B is, "What's that B doing there?" the child quickly learns that only perfection is acceptable. There are of course many reasons why parents might push their children to earn top grades. For example, participants who grew up with highly educated parents report being expected to follow suit. Notably, there can be a social context. In some immigrant communities, for example, education is seen as the path to their children's success, even survival. And because of systemic racism, the message many Black participants received as children was, "You have to be better to be seen as equal." Other children may have earned excellent grades yet received no praise at all. Still others may have grown up being told everything they did was remarkable. Another potential scenario is Clance and Imes's (1978) observation that in families with multiple siblings or close relatives, another child may have been designated the intelligent one: "One part of her believes the family myth; another part wants to disprove it" (p. 243).

To be effective, educational interventions must address the potential role family dynamics may play in fostering IP/IS. At the same time, a deep dive into childhood messaging has not been found to be a prerequisite for diminishing impostor feelings. Even if everyone had the desire, access, or means to take advantage of therapy, framing the alleviation of impostor feelings as contingent on discovering childhood wounds or another single origin has the potential to delay or even derail the search for solutions. A 44-year-old Brit named Adam posting on my blog spoke of wrestling with "low self-esteem and a lack of belief for as long as I can remember." For years, Adam said, he thought he "was constantly 'faking it,' or 'getting away with it,' fearing that I would be one day found out for not being as good as people thought I was, or as how I portrayed myself to be." To learn there is a name for these feelings and other people feel the same was, he said, "a revelation." However, Adam was also struggling to find the source of these feelings:

> Having seen a few counsellors over the last 20 years, the focus has always seemingly been on trying to get to the bottom of some "emotional trauma," which has led to the sense of being an imposter. In truth, I have led a relatively charmed, lucky life and I consider myself lucky and blessed in so many ways—I grew up in a loving home, had great opportunities, was relatively bright at school, good at sport, popular with friends and girls, went to university, travelled etc. Would understanding where my sense of inadequacy, and constantly (negatively) comparing my skills with others, has come from, help in really getting over it once and for all and then being the confident self I long to be?

It would of course help Adam to understand why he and countless millions of people around the world feel like impostors. But such understanding does not always come through the singular lens of emotional trauma, family originated or otherwise. I question, too, the narrative that posits impostor feelings as indicative of unworthiness. I have never had the honor to speak to Michelle Obama about her professed "impostor syndrome," but evidence, including her autobiography and highly pressured status as the first Black first lady of the United States, makes it unlikely it stems only from feeling unworthy. If feeling unworthy or, for that matter, childhood wounds were the core source of impostor feelings, then by extension populations often found to have higher rates of IP/IS, including those in STEM (science, technology, engineering, and mathematics) and doctoral students, would be presumed to have more problematic parenting messages or feel less worthy.

IP/IS is, of course, a psychological phenomenon that involves thoughts, feelings, and behaviors—all of which can and should be addressed in an educational intervention. Research has shown IP/IS is associated with higher levels of anxiety and depression (see Chapter 3). I have certainly encountered participants experiencing clinical depression and/or anxiety who were referred to counseling. At the same time, in important ways, IP/IS has been overpsychologized. Most people who self-identify with IP/IS are not necessarily depressed, anxious, or struggling with low self-esteem. Rather they are relatively well-adjusted people who, for a host of reasons that are both understandable and unrelated to psychology, have difficulty internalizing their accomplishments and came to believe they have fooled others into thinking they are more capable and competent than they believe themselves to be. To be effective, clinical and educational interventions should raise awareness of sources that are not familial, trauma-related, or linked to self-worth.

This includes the need to understand the connection between impostor feelings and social group membership not only as it relates to gender, race, and class but to include disability, language, and age. It can help to think of IP/IS as being more likely to occur among individuals from any group who (a) face stereotypes related to competence and intelligence; (b) are more likely to be achieving in settings where they are one of the few, the only, or the first member of their group; and (c) experience pressure to represent not only themselves but their entire social group.

In 2008, a fourth dimension was added to the original model to include the need to evoke awareness of the extent to which a sense of belonging fosters confidence. The more we see people who look like us, the more confident we likely feel. Conversely, when fewer people in a setting look like us, it can, and for many people does, influence how confident we feel. For example, psychologists seeking to understand the possible effects of gender-imbalanced settings on advanced math, science, and engineering students had them watch videos portraying a summer leadership conference (Murphy, 2007). One video showed a conference where men outnumbered women three to one, and another portrayed a conference with equal numbers of men and women. The women who watched the first video reported a lower sense of belonging and less desire to participate. Significantly, just watching the gender-imbalanced video caused these elite female students to experience faster heart rates, perspire more, and be more easily distracted—all indicators of stress.

Similarly, the more we *hear* people who sound like us, the more confident we might be expected to feel. The on-site version of the educational intervention has been delivered at over 100 universities across the United States and Canada as well as in the United Kingdom, Denmark, and Japan and to doctoral student members of Visibility STEM Africa. The largest contingency to attend are international students. This may reflect their relatively large numbers on campus, especially in PhD programs. However, it could also point to variables like the added stress of navigating the doctoral process in a different culture and language, stereotypes based on language fluency (Paladino et al., 2009), a lack of belonging, and difficulty reconciling the internalization of accomplishments with external cultural expectations of modesty. In addition to bringing awareness of these factors in clinical and educational interventions, such attendance points to areas for future research.

The empirical connection between belonging, stereotypes, and vulnerability to IP/IS can be extrapolated from Claude Steele and Jason Aronson's concept of stereotype threat (Steele & Aronson, 1995). They found the fear of confirming a negative stereotype can induce stress, which in turn affects performance. Further, the more accomplished one is, the more the effect shows up. Relevant findings include how the addition of a checkbox to indicate gender prior to taking a math exam caused the scores of female students to go down. When a box was added to indicate race, scores of the Asian American students went down. When students with a physical disability were told their performance on a logic test would be evaluated by students without a disability, they performed worse than those who were told the evaluator would also have a disability (Desombre et al., 2018).

Clinical interventions that evoke awareness of the intersection between IP/IS and the lived experiences of people in marginalized groups validate that experience. When done as part of an educational intervention, they also serve to provide all participants with important social context. At the same time, an emerging narrative in the public arena suggests that IP/IS is solely a function of sexism, racism, or other forms of oppression and therefore should not be addressed by individuals. In fact, there are situational, occupational, and organizational sources of IP/IS largely unrelated to systemic bias. These sources have been found for some to be equally or more consequential than social group membership. Anecdotally, clinicians and others know that just making people aware that there is a name for these nebulous feelings of impostorism and they are not alone can itself be liberating. By the same token, clinical and educational interventions that evoke awareness of the "perfectly good reasons" why IP/IS is common among others who operate in a similar situational, occupational, or organizational context can have a similar releasing effect.

There are many ways to normalize IP/IS among students. A plausible reason for this group having the highest rates of IP/IS is that they are in the position of having their knowledge and intellect tested, graded, and often compared with others over a period of years, which constitutes a situation presumed to be highly conducive to impostor feelings. IP/IS can be further contextualized for international students by pointing out that constant evaluation is even more challenging when performing in another language. After all, we all feel smarter communicating in our first language.

Frequently students report only experiencing impostor feelings upon entering a doctoral program. Situationally this makes sense. As doctoral students they are expected to not only master course work but pass qualifying examinations and do original research as well. The uniquely pressured experience of earning a doctorate is so high it may trump other triggers. Not surprisingly, researchers examining IP/IS among Black female PhD students in STEM uncovered a heightened awareness of lack of role models, stereotyping, and isolation. But in terms of IP/IS, there were no significant differences in rates between these and non-Black students. (Simon, 2020). Postdocs may have the expectation that attaining a doctorate will confer a level of expertise sufficient to quiet IP/IS, yet Cisco (2020) found that despite all that training, postdocs still feel academically unprepared, which in turn reinforces the belief that they are an intellectual impostor. Instead of feeling like an impostor despite having a PhD, postdocs and others may feel like an impostor because they have a PhD. Now people look at them differently. They see them as someone who is smart. They may lead them to wonder: How will I ever measure up?

All students—formal or otherwise—would be well-served by understanding that every field, from law to psychology to art, has its own specialized and often unnecessary convoluted language. To be deemed sufficiently knowledgeable or scholarly, you are required to elevate concepts that could just as easily be described in everyday language. At times, the language of scholarly writing can be so dense that even when relatively well versed in an area, students must reread passages multiple times to comprehend what is being said. Whether the reader eventually deciphers it or not, the fact that they had to struggle in the first place can set off impostor alarms when in fact, if more experts communicated with the goal of making their work accessible to a larger population, everyone, including students, would feel a lot smarter and be more informed.

Another situational context for IP/IS is the experience of working alone. Unlike employees, people who are self-employed or solo practitioners do not get regular performance reviews. Left on their own they are apt to take a more critical eye to their performance. With no one to bounce ideas off or problem solve with, the pressure to succeed is singular. You do not have to work alone to feel like you are in it alone. Results of a coaching intervention done with 46 Israeli executives—half women, half men—found that the explicit reason for wanting coaching was to increase knowledge and skill as leaders. However, the indirect catalyst was executive loneliness and feelings of impostorism (Kuna, 2019).

Occupational considerations offer another potentially helpful context for IP/IS. Several achievement arenas warrant context and thus the opportunity for clinicians and educators to normalize impostor feelings for those who work in them. One is information-dense, rapidly changing fields like technology, science, and medicine. Higher observed rates of IP/IS here may be due, in part, to the false belief that a competent person would be able to keep up when no one possibly could. In STEM fields where health and safety are paramount, the understandable demand for functional perfectionism can morph into unhealthy perfectionism and IP/IS. Workplaces that revolve around science and medicine have large numbers of highly educated people, a scenario that itself can give rise to unhealthy comparisons between those who are highly credentialed as well as those who are not.

IP/IS is also considered highly common among people who work in creative fields. This is unsurprising given writers, actors, musicians, designers, and advertisers/marketers do work that is highly subjective. When that work is also open to public critique, there is a real or imagined belief that one is only as good as their last performance or creation. Another population observed to be at risk of IP/IS is typically highly paid management consultants who must navigate the reality of being a relative novice in their client's world and the client's expectation that the consultant has all the answers (Bourgoin & Harvey, 2018).

A final context worthy of consideration is work culture. This can mean the culture of a specific workplace, whether that be a department, division, or entire organization. A survey of 10,400 tech workers conducted by an anonymous workplace social network used primarily by tech workers posed the question, "Do you suffer from impostor syndrome?" (Blind Staff Writer, 2018). Rates of self-reported impostor feelings across 17 large tech companies ranged from a high of 73% to a low of 47%. This finding suggests something may be happening on the organizational level, which merits further inquiry and contextualizing.

In other cases, organization culture refers to entire sectors or industries where core aspects of the overarching sector are relatively consistent from one individual workplace to another. Case in point is higher education, where IP/IS is rampant. Like science and medicine, this may again be a function of being surrounded by highly educated people. However, even administrators who hold an advanced degree are keenly aware they may never be as well regarded as faculty. Faculty are held to high intellectual standards measured by their ability to have their research consistently published in scholarly journals, secure grants, and survive a grueling tenure process. Scholarly debate and rigorous investigation motivate many people to pursue a tenure track in the first place; however, York University philosophy professor Cael Cohen (formerly Cael Diane Zorn) insists that the less desirable elements of academic culture—aggressive competitiveness, scholarly isolation, nationalism among and between disciplines, and lack of mentoring—is the main reason IP/IS is rampant in higher education.

Just as academia fosters a culture of constant critique for faculty, doctoral students, and postdocs alike, medical culture—and medical education especially—can be characterized as a culture of shaming. This includes medical residents being subjected to the anxiety-producing and potentially demoralizing teaching method known as pimping, whereby attending physicians and residents ask students on-the-spot medical questions in front of patients and fellow students. Like those in the United States, medical students in the United Kingdom talk of being discouraged by a notable lack of praise, where the highest assessment that can be earned on the final qualifying exam is "No concern."

Clinical and educational interventions should pay attention to how non-psychological sources of impostor feelings are framed. This means explicitly presenting the act of normalizing as an effective cognitive tool in mitigating impostor feelings. Helping individuals see how their internal experience may, in part, be an understandable response to external factors serves two purposes. First, contextualizing can reduce the initial pressure to resolve what is often viewed entirely as a personal problem. When, for example, early-career faculty or medical students and residents are helped to see that the critical or shaming environment may not be the culture they thought they were signing up for but it is the culture they—and others—are in, they can contextualize their impostor feelings more and personalize them less.

Second, normalizing IP/IS flips the individual and collective narrative from "Why do I feel like an impostor?" to "How could I not?" For individuals in marginalized groups, contextualizing IP/IS also helps interrupt the false belief that if they were truly competent, they would not be unnerved being, for example, the only Indigenous medical student, one of a few female analysts, or the first blind division head. The explicit message needs to be that you can be perfectly competent and still experience normal stress in these situations.

Evolution and Application of the Performance Dimension

Analysis of the performance dimension has evolved in four significant ways. First is heightened awareness of how the value placed on honesty as it relates to disclosure of lack of knowledge or experience may make women more reluctant to heed the advice to act as if they feel more confident than they do (Young, 2023). Second, it is now clear that the link between IP/IS and exaggerated notions of competence first made in 1985 is not unique to women. Third, although for people in marginalized groups this high internal bar must still be viewed, at least in part, in relation to social realities, it is now clear that if oppression were to disappear tomorrow but the same cognitive distortions regarding competence, failure, mistakes, criticism, and fear remained, IP/IS would remain as well.

The fourth and most significant expansion of the original model involves the understanding of how people who self-identify with IP/IS interpret what it takes to be competent. To test the working theory that IP/IS is the result of our unrealistic, unsustainable notions of competence, I designed an educational exercise to bring individual and collective attention to what are often unconscious rules regarding competence. Participants were first asked to complete three sentence stems on their own: "If I were 'really' smart, talented, qualified, and competent, I *should* . . . I'd *never* . . . and I'd *always* . . ." These personal reflections were then shared in small groups, and a compilation list was reported out to the entire group. Rules commonly reflected beliefs like I *should* be perfect, excel at everything I do, and know the answer when asked; I'd *never* make a mistake, fail, be confused, or need help; and I'd *always* get it right the first try, feel confident, come up with original theories or ideas, and succeed.

This exercise has since been conducted with tens of thousands of participants. Women continue to cite more societal expectations like "I should be able to anticipate and meet other people's needs, always apologize, and never brag." Overall, however, participants uniformly hold themselves to idealistic and unmaintainable standards, a bar perhaps best reflected by the male doctoral student at Stanford university who said, "I feel I should already know what I came here to learn."

Despite ample research linking IP/IS with perfectionism, when applied in the field, repeated application of this experience revealed this link does not ring true for everyone. Instead a pattern emerged: Although everyone who self-identified with IP/IS was found to hold exaggerated notions of competence, not everyone shared the same version of what this means. A thematic analysis of thousands of responses to the exercise revealed four additional and underresearched cognitive distortions specific to competence. Although they have come to be known as the five types of IP/IS, they are, in fact, five ways people who experience IP/IS measure their competence. They are described as the perfectionist, soloist, natural genius, expert, and superhuman.

Briefly, the *perfectionist's* primary concern is on how things are done. Which is to say, they expect to perform and produce flawlessly 100% of the time. Falling short, even a little, triggers fraud feelings. The *expert* is essentially the knowledge version of the perfectionist. Here the emphasis is on what and how much they know. Because they expect to understand and retain everything, even a minor gap of knowledge feels like failure. Someone who ascribes to the *soloist* view of competence cares mostly about who completes the task. Because they think they should be able to do everything on their own, needing help, tutoring, or coaching is taken as proof of inadequacy. The soloist may think of ideas the same way. As a graduate student, scholar, or budding entrepreneur, they expect to come up with ideas that are totally new and original. If someone else got there first, they are crushed. Competence for the *natural genius* is measured based on ease and speed. The fact that they must study, struggle to master a subject or skill, or do not nail it on the first attempt is taken as failure. The *superhuman* gauges their competence on how many roles they can perform masterfully. Falling short in any role inside or, as is more often the case for women, outside of work feels like failure. The common denominator for all five orientations is that failure to consistently attain the idealized notion of competence confirms their impostorism. Some individuals identify strongly with one type, others associate with more than one.

These five competence distortions are currently undergoing validation and are expected to occur on a continuum. Even without validation, actual experience coupled with widespread usage of these five competence distortions by others who have authored books on IP/IS, including two psychologists (Hibberd, 2019; Mann, 2019) and a physician who has trained, supervised, and mentored hundreds of physicians (Hunt, 2020), as well as by psychology and other faculty and administrators at numerous universities, including three contributors to this book, suggests a high degree of resonance and merits qualitative and quantitative inquiry.

Clinical and educational interventions must help people with IP/IS reframe these specific forms of competence distortion. This includes understanding the ways people with IP/IS experience failure, mistakes, setbacks, self-doubt, and critical feedback (not addressed here). Moreover, reframing begins with once again flipping the entire narrative around IP/IS. After all, if up to 82% of people tested experience some degree of IP/IS (Bravata et al., 2020), that begs the questions, what is going on with the other 18% and, as importantly, why are we not studying them? Some undoubtedly suffer from the irrational self-confidence known as the Dunning–Kruger effect (Dunning, 2011). But there is a minority within that minority whom clinicians, educators, and researchers need to better understand. These are capable people who are genuinely humble but have never felt like impostors—people I refer to as *humble realists*™. The cognitive container of a humble realist offers an alternative point of reference that is more aspirational than "nonimpostor" and more attainable than trying to cure IP/IS.

To be clear, reframing is not the same as interventions aimed at countering negative self-talk. For one, the emphasis on positive affirmations and recommendations to "talk to yourself like you would your best friend" or "challenge your inner critic" frames the self-judgments associated with IP/IS in purely individual terms rather than as a collective misinterpretation of competence. Shifting the task to adopting a realistic understanding of competence alleviates, at least in part, the arguably more daunting challenge of trying to fix oneself.

Additionally, interventions that stress positive self-talk fail to consider the extent to which those who experience IP/IS conflate competence and confidence. For many, the fact that they even engage in negative self-talk proves they must in fact be an impostor. The thinking here is, "If I were truly competent, I'd always be confident." This is unsurprising considering the prevalence of solutions that promise to "banish your inner critic forever" and "achieve unshakable confidence in yourself."

In a similar vein, people with IP/IS are often encouraged to make a list of achievements. The exercise is meant to yield a tangible reminder of how well the person has done in the past and therefore can reasonably expect to do in the future. A related recommendation is to maintain an ongoing success file to review when impostor feelings strike. These exercises no doubt have value for students and early-career individuals whose achievement journey is just beginning. A success file also serves as a helpful memory jog for anyone who must update their resume or CV or write an annual self-appraisal or a professional biography. However, as an antidote to IP/IS, these techniques have not been found to have lasting value.

One reason may be that the problem for people with IP/IS is not that they forgot they earned top grades, landed the big account, or won a Grammy. The problem is seeing success as largely due to external factors like luck, timing, and the supposed simplicity of the task and with those the beliefs that "If I can do it, anyone can"; "It's just because they like me"; or success is due to the efforts, pity, or low standards of others. Here again, the solution is to instill an individual and collective awareness that, rather than being excuses for our success, factors like luck, timing, connections, and personality play a legitimate role in success. It is what you do with them that counts (Young, 2023).

Second, the problem is less one of being unaware of wins as it is the disproportionate identification with losses and critical feedback. It is unlikely that reflecting on past accomplishments would help the doctoral student who took the fact that he had failed his qualifying exam at a previous institution as proof he really was a fraud. Nor would it help the NASA engineer who, in her words, was "depressed for weeks" following a performance review in which her manager cited five areas where she had excelled along with one remarkably minor recommendation for improvement, which she experienced as criticism. In other words, attempts to counter IP/IS by emphasizing strengths alone will not help when confronted with inevitable and equally valid evidence of failure and deficits.

Reframing should not be confused with the kinds of pep talks frequently given to people with IP/IS: "You've got this! You can do it! You deserve to be here!" Although presumably true, these are not enough to move the impostor needle in any lasting way. That is because people who are humble but do not feel like impostors think differently in three ways: They (a) have a realistic view of competence that includes not only awareness of and appreciation for their knowledge and abilities but respect for the humanness of their limitations; (b) have a healthy response to failure, mistakes, setbacks, and negative feedback; and (c) understand that a certain amount of fear and self-doubt goes with the achievement territory.

For these reasons, effective clinical and educational interventions should help individuals with IP/IS to fundamentally change their relationship with competence. If they truly understood—as humble realists do—that they have just as much right as the next person to make a mistake, have an "off day," not know the answer, struggle to understand a topic, ask for help, be better at some skills than others, be in the midst of a learning curve, learn from constructive feedback, or fall flat on their face, then there would be nothing to feel like an impostor about.

Contrary to what people with IP/IS presume, people who do not feel like impostors are not inherently more intelligent, capable, competent, talented, qualified, or even confident than they are. Rather, the only difference is that in the exact same situation where they feel like an impostor, humble realists are thinking different thoughts. This means the way to stop feeling like an impostor is to stop thinking like an impostor. Clinical or educational interventions that utilize general cognitive behavioral therapy are not enough. What is required is an in-depth understanding of the contextual sources of IP/IS and the specific competence distortions at the core of IP/IS.

The *Peanuts* cartoon character Linus once said, "I am burdened by a great potential." This sentiment applies to the impostor experience as well. Deep down, people who self-identify with IP/IS know they are no impostor. When pressed, participants acknowledge that they really do know they have the capacity to achieve most goals they will set for themselves in life, not quickly, easily, perfectly, or masterfully or without help, mistakes, setbacks, or failure. But they really do know they can succeed. It is just that the debris of impostor thinking coupled with a lack of the broader context for IP/IS gets in their way.

CONCLUSION

Educational interventions represent an underexplored approach to IP/IS. In addition to prompting self-reflection and pattern exploration, clinical and educational interventions can provide pragmatic tools that have been observed to be effective in helping people with IP/IS talk themselves down off the impostor ledge more quickly.

REFERENCES

Baruch, G., Barnett, R., & Rivers, C. (1983). *Lifeprints: New patterns of love and work for today's women*. McGraw-Hill.

Bell, L. A. (1996). In danger of winning: Consciousness raising strategies for empowering girls in the United States. *Women's Studies International Forum, 19*(4), 419–427. https://doi.org/10.1016/0277-5395(96)00025-8

Blind Staff Writer. (2018). 58 percent of tech workers feel like impostors. *Blind Blog—Workplace Insights*. https://www.teamblind.com/blog/index.php/2018/09/05/58-percent-of-tech-workers-feel-like-impostors/

Bourgoin, A., & Harvey, J.-F. (2018). Professional image under threat: Dealing with learning–credibility tension. *Human Relations, 71*(12), 1611–1639. https://doi.org/10.1177/0018726718756168

Bravata, D. M., Watts, S. A., Keefer, A. L., Madhusudhan, D. K., Taylor, K. T., Clark, D. M., Nelson, R. S., Cokley, K. O., & Hagg, H. K. (2020). Prevalence, predictors, and treatment of impostor syndrome: A systematic review. *Journal of General Internal Medicine, 35*(4), 1252–1275. https://doi.org/10.1007/s11606-019-05364-1

Cisco, J. (2020). Exploring the connection between impostor phenomenon and post-graduate students feeling academically unprepared. *Higher Education Research & Development, 39*(2), 200–214. https://doi.org/10.1080/07294360.2019.1676198

Clance, P. R., & Imes, S. A. (1978). The imposter phenomenon in high achieving women: Dynamics and therapeutic intervention. *Psychotherapy: Theory, Research, & Practice, 15*(3), 241–247. https://doi.org/10.1037/h0086006

Desombre, C., Anegmar, S., & Delelis, G. (2018). Stereotype threat among students with disabilities: The importance of the evaluative context on their cognitive performance. *European Journal of Psychology of Education, 33*, 201–214. https://doi.org/10.1007/s10212-016-0327-4

Dunning, D. (2011). The Dunning–Kruger effect: On being ignorant of one's own ignorance. In J. M. Olson & M. P. Zanna (Eds.), *Advances in experimental social psychology* (Vol. 44, pp. 247–296). Academic Press. https://doi.org/10.1016/B978-0-12-385522-0.00005-6

Fillmore, L. W., & Cheong, J. L. (1976). The early socialization of Asian-American female children. In S. M. Hufstedler, S. A. Minter, F. J. Rutherford, M. Timpane, L. Datta, & S. Chipman (Eds.), *Proceedings of a conference on the educational and occupational needs of Asian-Pacific-American Women* (pp. 237–253). U.S. Department of Education.

Fujutomi, I., & Wong, D. (1973). The new Asian American woman. In S. Sue & N. Wagner (Eds.), *Asian Americans: Psychological perspectives*. Science and Behavior Books Inc.

Gilligan, C. (1982). *In a different voice: Psychological theory and women's development*. Harvard University Press.

Girl Scouts of USA. (2008). *Change it up! What girls say about redefining leadership.* https://www.girlscouts.org/content/dam/girlscouts-gsusa/forms-and-documents/about-girl-scouts/research/change_it_up_executive_summary_english.pdf

Hardiman, R. (1982). White identity development: A process-oriented model for describing the racial consciousness of White Americans. *Dissertation Abstracts International Section A: Humanities and Social Sciences, 43*(1–A), Article 104.

Hardiman, R., & Jackson, B. W. (1997). Conceptual foundations for social justice courses. In M. Adams, L. A. Bell, & P. Griffin (Eds.), *Teaching for diversity and social justice: A sourcebook* (pp. 16–29). Routledge.

Hibberd, J. (2019). *The imposter cure: Escape the mind-trap of imposter syndrome.* Hatchette Book Group.

Hunt, J. L. (2020). *Unlocking your authentic self: Overcoming impostor syndrome, enhancing self-confidence, and banishing self-doubt.* Jennifer Hunt MD.

Imes, S. (1979). *The impostor phenomenon as a function of attribution patterns and internalized femininity/masculinity in high achieving women and men* [Doctoral dissertation, Georgia State University]. ProQuest Dissertations Publishing.

Jackson, B. W. (1976). Black identity development. In L. Golubschick & B. Persky (Eds.), *Urban social and educational issues* (pp. 158–164). Kendall/Hunt.

Jackson, B. W., & Hardiman, R. (1988). Oppression: Conceptual and developmental analysis. In M. Adams & L. S. Marchesani (Eds.), *Racial and cultural diversity, curricular content and classroom dynamics: A manual for college teachers.* University of Massachusetts.

Jamison, L. (2023, February 6). Why everyone feels like they're faking it. *The New Yorker.* https://www.newyorker.com/magazine/2023/02/13/the-dubious-rise-of-impostor-syndrome

Joseph, G. L., & Lewis, J. (1981). *Conflicts in Black and White feminist perspectives.* Doubleday & Company.

Katz, J. (1978). *White awareness: A handbook for anti-racism training* (3rd ed.). University of Oklahoma Press.

Kidwell, C. S. (1976). *The status of American Indian women in higher education* [Paper presentation]. The Conference on the Educational and Occupational Needs of American Indian Women, Albuquerque, NM, United States.

Kim, J. (1981). Processes of Asian American identity development: A study of Japanese American women's perceptions of their struggle to achieve positive identities as Americans of Asian ancestry. *Dissertation Abstracts International Section A: Humanities and Social Sciences, 42*(4–A), Article 1551.

Kuna, S. (2019). Executives' impostor phenomenon and loneliness as catalysts for executive coaching with management consultants. *The Journal of Applied Behavioral Science, 55*(3), 306–326. https://doi.org/10.1177/0021886319832009

Mann, S. (2019). *Why do I feel like an imposter? How to understand and cope with imposter syndrome.* Watkins.

Merriam-Webster. (n.d.). Syndrome. In *Merriam-Webster.com dictionary*. Retrieved September 3, 2023, from https://www.merriam-webster.com/dictionary/syndrome

Murphy, M. C., Steele, C. M., & Gross, J. J. (2007). Signaling threat: How situational cues affect women in math, science, and engineering settings. *Psychological Science, 18*(10), 879–885. https://doi.org/10.1111/j.1467-9280.2007.01995.x

Nieto-Gomez, A. (1973). La feminista. *Encuentro Femenil, 1*, 34–47.

Paladino, M. P., Poddesu, L., Rauzi, M., Vaes, J., Cadinu, M., & Forer, D. (2009). Second language competence in the Italian-speaking population of Alto-Adige/Südtirol: Evidence for linguistic stereotype threat. *Journal of Language and Social Psychology, 28*(3), 222–243. https://doi.org/10.1177/0261927X09335333

Rosenberg, F. R., & Simmons, R. G. (1975). Sex differences in the self-concept in adolescence. *Sex Roles, 1*(2), 147–159. https://doi.org/10.1007/BF00288008

Simon, M. (2020). STEMming within a double minority: How the impostor syndrome affects Black women Ph.D. students. *International Journal of Multiple Research Approaches, 12*(2), 185–201. https://doi.org/10.29034/ijmra.v12n2a2

Steele, C. M., & Aronson, J. (1995). Stereotype threat and the intellectual test performance of African Americans. *Journal of Personality and Social Psychology, 69*(5), 797–811. https://doi.org/10.1037/0022-3514.69.5.797

Young, V. (1985). *A model of internal barriers to women's occupational achievement* [Doctoral dissertation, University of Massachusetts Amherst]. ScholarWorks. https://scholarworks.umass.edu/dissertations_1/4055

Young, V. (2023). *The secret thoughts of successful women: And men: Why capable people suffer from impostor syndrome and how to thrive in spite of it* (2nd ed.). Crown Business.

Zanchetta, M., Junker, S., Wolf, A. M., & Traut-Mattausch, E. (2020). Overcoming the fear that haunts your success: The effectiveness of interventions for reducing the impostor phenomenon. *Frontiers in Psychology, 11*, Article 405. https://doi.org/10.3389/fpsyg.2020.00405

14

RESEARCH-BASED STRATEGIES FOR COMBATING THE IMPOSTOR PHENOMENON IN HIGHER EDUCATION

DANIELLE ROSENSCRUGGS AND
LAURA SCHRAM

When Dr. Kevin Cokley first approached us to write this chapter on applied strategies for managing impostor experiences in higher education contexts, we were honored and thrilled to contribute to such an important project. However, as we began writing, our own impostor feelings started to creep in. We wondered, separately and together, who we were to speak with authority on this topic. Despite Laura's years of experience developing and facilitating impostor phenomenon (IP) workshops in her role at Rackham Graduate School at the University of Michigan and Danielle's research agenda focusing on strategies for mitigating the impacts of IP among graduate students as a PhD candidate in developmental psychology, both of us fell into the trappings of our impostor cycles. Even as scholars knowledgeable on the topic of IP, we were not immune to the common maladaptive thought patterns (e.g., doubting our place in this edition) that emerged, ignoring the evidence that we belonged in the collection and were up to the task (the least of which was the invitation from a preeminent IP scholar).

Upon reflection, we realized we were perfect examples of the insidious and toxic nature of IP. It was a humbling reminder that everyone is susceptible to negative self-talk and self-doubt, particularly when we allow ourselves to suffer in isolation. Although it would be understandable to feel defeated by the

https://doi.org/10.1037/0000397-015
The Impostor Phenomenon: Psychological Research, Theory, and Interventions,
K. Cokley (Editor)
Copyright © 2024 by the American Psychological Association. All rights reserved.

ubiquity of these experiences or the ease with which impostor cycles are triggered, we chose to reframe our experience as support for the pressing need for this important collection. Managing IP is a nonlinear process. Some days will be great, and others will be challenging. But the only way any of us can expect to make progress is by staying committed to the ongoing process of combating IP.

Accordingly, we are thrilled to contribute to this critical conversation about IP within higher education contexts. In this chapter, we invite you to explore how higher education institutions (HEIs) can effectively and efficiently balance empirical evidence and practical limitations to conceptualize and deliver student-facing IP interventions while working toward institutional-level changes to address systemic factors that foster IP. The content and strategies we share are drawn from findings from an extensive literature review and our work designing and facilitating IP workshops. We acknowledge that more research is needed and, as a result, do not claim to have all of the answers or act as infallible guides. Instead, we hope this chapter serves as a call to action for social science scholars. Although the scholarship on the existence of IP is not new, applied research is still in its infancy. As a result, there is a wide gap in the extant research related to evidence-based IP strategies and interventions, particularly within higher education contexts. This gap must be filled if HEIs hope to effectively support students in interrupting their impostor cycles.

However, despite the literature limitations, we believe the information we present is helpful for higher education administrators, faculty, or staff educators looking to minimize students' experiences of IP. With that said, we welcome you into this critical conversation!

COAUTHOR POSITIONALITY STATEMENT

Given that this chapter provides information on interventions we share with students in our collaborative work as scholar-practitioners facilitating IP workshops, it is appropriate to describe our positionality and summarize our identities. Both coauthors are White, cisgender women whose undergraduate and graduate studies occurred at predominantly White institutions (PWIs) in the United States. We do not have lived experiences at minority-serving institutions and therefore do not have direct experience working with students in those contexts. Both coauthors are social scientists (political science and developmental psychology) who conducted their doctoral studies at the University of Michigan, Ann Arbor, where we currently collaboratively lead psychoeducational workshops and guest lectures on IP. We both dealt with IP during our time as doctoral students, which led to our shared interest in providing support for graduate students struggling with impostor thinking. Scientific objectivity is a matter of degrees, and we acknowledge our identities as women in quantitatively oriented social science fields and lived experiences of IP at PWIs influence our interest in IP interventions in higher education.

IMPOSTOR PHENOMENON MANIFESTATIONS IN HIGHER EDUCATION

IP manifestations within HEIs have been discussed throughout this collection; therefore, we do not provide an in-depth review here. However, we give a brief overview to set up our chapter. Readers interested in a more detailed discussion of this topic are encouraged to (re)visit Chapters 5, 7, 8, 9, 10, and 11.

IP is prevalent on college campuses (Bravata et al., 2020; Vaughn et al., 2020), and the empirical literature has demonstrated that students of all types (e.g., traditional, nontraditional, first-generation) from all disciplines (e.g., science, technology, engineering, mathematics, humanities) and levels of study (e.g., undergraduate, graduate, professional) are vulnerable to impostor thoughts and feelings (McWilliams et al., 2023; Parkman, 2016; Pervez et al., 2021). Across student groups, IP has also been shown to be correlated with a variety of academic (e.g., test anxiety, academic success, achievement orientation, academic self-efficacy) and psychological (e.g., perfectionism, self-esteem, neuroticism) factors and has been established as a reliable predictor of student mental health (Parkman, 2016). IP triggers have been shown to vary by context, identity, and personality characteristics; however, research across education levels has found that common triggers include progress evaluations, public recognition, peer comparisons, academic and professional skill development, applied learning, and help seeking (Chakraverty, 2020; S. Chang et al., 2022; Cisco, 2020). Additionally, among medical students, IP is associated with burnout and depression (Villwock et al., 2016), along with mediating the relationship between maladaptive perfectionism and suicidal ideation (Brennan-Wydra et al., 2021).

Various identity and social characteristics (e.g., gender, race, socioeconomic status, parenting styles) have also been discussed in relation to students' IP experiences. However, the most commonly explored are gender, race, and ethnicity, and research has shown that many students feel that the status of these identities contributes to their feelings of impostorism (Chakraverty, 2019; McGee et al., 2022). It should not be surprising that gender is often explored in the context of IP, as the foundational research by Clance and Imes (1978) identified IP as a phenomenon among high-achieving women. Since then, multiple studies have confirmed the connection between gender and IP, with most finding female students are more susceptible than their male peers (Cusack et al., 2013; Metz et al., 2020; Villwock et al., 2016). However, findings from systematic reviews have caused some to question gendered patterns, as more recently, IP has been shown to be common among both women and men (Bravata et al., 2020; Gottlieb et al., 2020). Furthermore, while interrogating the documented gender differences, Cokley et al. (2015) found that, among undergraduate students, gender stigma consciousness (i.e., awareness of the stigmatized status of one's gender) positively predicted IP for both male and female students, although IP only positively predicted grade-point average for women. Although effects were greater for female students, these findings indicate that a combination of internalized gender socialization and stigma consciousness could be driving documented gender differences in IP rather than innate gender-based differences (Cokley et al., 2015).

Racial and ethnic identities have also been explored in relation to students' IP experiences. Research has found that students who identify with minoritized groups may be more susceptible to IP, particularly at PWIs (Parkman, 2016). As a result, these students suffer from greater psychological distress and reduced mental well-being (Peteet, Brown, et al., 2015; Peteet, Montgomery, & Weeks, 2015). For example, among African, Asian, and Latin American students, impostor feelings were stronger predictors of mental health (e.g., anxiety, depression, loss of behavioral control, positive affect) than minority status stress (Cokley et al., 2013). Additionally, among minoritized graduate students, experiences of microaggressions and racism were connected to impostor feelings (Chakraverty et al., 2022; McGee et al., 2022). However, the intensity of these connections and the underlying mechanisms are not homogenous across all minoritized groups (Cokley et al., 2017). Triggers, correlates, and manifestations of IP are incredibly nuanced, so more work is needed to understand IP in higher education through culturally informed frameworks (Stone et al., 2018).

ADDRESSING THE IMPOSTOR PHENOMENON IN HIGHER EDUCATION

Given the prevalence of IP in higher education, there is a growing demand for efforts to support students in reducing their impostor experiences. It is no longer acceptable to assume that IP will naturally dissipate with time, as multiple studies have found that academic advancement and achievement are insufficient in combating impostor feelings. For example, one study of 1st-year medical students found that IP scores were significantly higher at the end of the year compared with the beginning (Rosenthal et al., 2021), and another found that the 4th year of medical school was associated with the highest levels of IP (Villwock et al., 2016).

However, although many HEIs have begun to recognize the epidemic levels of IP, most are unsure how to tackle the issue. In attempts to minimize students' IP experiences, many have created resources and programs (Parkman, 2016), including online resource hubs, single-session workshops, psychoeducational minicourses, and curriculum integration (e.g., orientations, proseminars). Unfortunately, in most cases, the provided content is designed primarily based on mass media/pop psychology resources. This reliance on unsubstantiated resources is understandable, given the imbalance between the scholarly and lay literature related to IP. Although only a handful of empirical studies have explored higher education IP interventions (Cisco, 2020), thousands of popular media publications have discussed the topic (Bravata et al., 2020; Holt et al., 2023).

Nevertheless, despite the IP intervention scholarship's limitations, HEIs that focus their IP combating approaches on student-facing programs must resist the urge to implement untested methods as an overreliance on lay resources, which could exacerbate IP experiences. For example, a plethora of pop psychology pieces based on select empirical studies (e.g., Tewfik, 2022) have promoted the supposed upsides of IP. However, most have been written for corporate audiences with explicit or implied goals of maximizing profits, prompting team harmony, and minimizing turnover. Additionally, they have stopped short of full-person considerations, often downplaying or ignoring psychological costs (e.g., diminished mental health). Therefore, by promoting the benefits of maladaptive coping strategies (e.g., fear of failure, perfectionism), HEIs could inadvertently perpetuate students' impostor cycles, particularly among high-achieving students.

Furthermore, much of the lay IP literature frames strategies as cures rather than management techniques, which many publicly available university resources and programs mimic. In their materials, these programs present workshops, minicourses, and the like as cures that will eliminate IP. However, it is unreasonable to expect that impostor thoughts and feelings, like any maladaptive patterns, can be entirely eliminated within a short intervention or single-session workshop. Therefore, creators of these resources must be mindful of the language used when promoting and delivering IP content. Instead of promising cures, which could further exacerbate feelings of failure or fraudulence when that unrealistic goal is not met, it would be better to let students know that the intended purpose is to minimize or manage their impostor experiences. For example, Dr. Valerie Young, a prominent IP scholar, explained that rather than trying to overcome impostorism, it is more realistic to develop reframing and coping skills that will allow individuals to move away from living impostor lives and instead experience fleeting impostor moments (Young, 2017).

Individual-Level Impostor Phenomenon Interventions

Individual-level interventions are considered the gold standard for IP management on many campuses, despite the scarcity of empirically validated interventions and a growing movement among scholars to reject pathologizing conceptualizations. Furthermore, due to the lack of IP-specific scholarship, many administrators and faculty interested in evidence-based, individual-level approaches must be creative in developing IP curricula, workshops, and interventions, drawing mainly from the peripheral literature. In some respects, this solution makes sense, as multiple systematic reviews and empirical studies have established critical correlates of IP, including depression, anxiety, low self-esteem, low efficacy, heightened neuroticism, perfectionism, somatic symptoms, and social dysfunction (Bravata et al., 2020; Dudău, 2014; Fleischhauer et al., 2021; Schubert & Bowker, 2019; Thompson et al., 2000; Tigranyan et al., 2021). As a result, some scholars have suggested the extension of evidence-based strategies for established correlates in treating IP while practitioners wait for the maturation of the IP scholarship (Bravata et al., 2020; Jacobs & Sasser, 2021).

Providing students with individual-level evidence-based strategies can empower them to interrupt their impostor cycles. To be most effective, these strategies should be actionable, allowing for independent implementation following formal training. Although there are many design elements to consider when creating IP interventions and workshops, research has shown that the most effective programs incorporate some type of skill-oriented content along with cognitive behavioral or mindfulness-based strategies (Conley et al., 2013). We have chosen to highlight several interpersonal and intrapersonal strategies that may effectively minimize IP by interrupting impostor cycles, addressing maladaptive coping strategies, and mitigating related adverse effects.

A range of evidence-based IP interventions could be offered depending on the context. Fortunately, IP research has shown that using any evidence-based strategy is more effective than no strategy (Barr-Walker et al., 2020). However, whenever possible, it is best to provide a variety of IP management strategies, even as postintervention resources, as broader intervention research has shown that multistrategy approaches may hold the most promise. For example, multicomponent positive psychology interventions, which incorporate the development of multiple facets of well-being, are more effective than single strategy designs at promoting long-term change (Morgan & Simmons, 2021; Myers et al., 2017; Rusk et al., 2018).

Student-level IP interventions are just one piece of the puzzle and should not be considered sufficient to address campus-wide IP crises. However, we believe implementing individual-level evidence-based programs is a critical first step. Thus, we have provided a brief discussion of promising designs and management strategies that have been shown to reduce IP. This section should not be considered an exhaustive review but a curated selection of approaches with the most empirical support.

Psychoeducational and Skill-Oriented Approaches

Initially used in clinical settings to treat mental illness, psychoeducational approaches may effectively support students' social and emotional well-being (J. A. Brown et al., 2020), including managing impostor thoughts and feelings. Although diverse in their specific application, these approaches typically utilize evidence-based, didactic designs that provide condition-specific, systematic, structured information (Ekhtiari et al., 2017) that considers whole-person experiences (Motlova et al., 2017). By integrating informational, emotional, motivational, behavioral, and cognitive elements, these approaches can empower participants through increased topic literacy and self-efficacy (Ekhtiari et al., 2017). One of the advantages of use in higher education settings is the flexibility of application (Lukens & McFarlane, 2004), which allows programs to be tailored to meet the needs of specific student populations and department structures. In the case of IP, psychoeducational group experiences may provide great value and opportunities for group discussions, social learning, and support, which can reduce feelings of isolation, self-blame, and shame (N. W. Brown, 2018; Hutchins & Flores, 2021; Lukens & McFarlane, 2004). Additionally, systematic reviews of higher education well-being interventions have shown that psychoeducational programs are most effective when delivered in multisession modules incorporating didactic sessions, skill-oriented training, supervised practice, or individual coaching (Conley et al., 2013).

Most of the publicly available higher education IP programs we reviewed were delivered as single or multisession informational or psychoeducational workshops led by external facilitators or, more often, in-house staff educators or faculty. A core practice used in nearly all instances was an early establishment of a shared understanding of the IP construct, including common manifestations. Approaches included introducing students to the psychological construct (e.g., defining IP elements), helping them identify typical manifestations of IP (e.g., how and when IP may show up), and recognizing IP in themselves (e.g., their IP thought patterns). An overview of common maladaptive coping strategies and their associated long-term negative consequences was also typical, as was the informal administration of the Clance Impostor Phenomenon Scale (Clance, 1985), which was used to provide students with insights into their IP levels. Although many of these elements are simple in design, the literature supports their use. For example, qualitative research has shown that by simply learning how to name their experiences and recognize that they are not alone in their feelings, students experience some immediate relief from IP (Haney et al., 2018). Additionally, by participating in group discussions, students can appreciate the universal nature of IP, which can normalize their own experiences and reduce solitary suffering (Haney et al., 2018; Hutchins & Flores, 2021).

Intrapersonal Strategies

The most empirically supported individual-focused interventions rely on cognitive reframing and retraining strategies to address maladaptive, self-critical cognitive distortions. Cognitive behavioral approaches are commonly utilized in clinical settings and can include a variety of therapeutic models (e.g., cognitive behavioral therapy [CBT], cognitive process therapy, mindfulness-based CBT). These models have been proposed as effective strategies for combating impostor thinking (Clance & Imes, 1978; Playforth, 2021), and nonclinical adaptations have been studied for use within higher education settings. Although specific content and delivery vary across methods and settings, the goal of reprogramming maladaptive cognitive processes using reframing, deidentification, and interrupting maladaptive cognitive cycles is constant. Therefore, it can be expected that, when incorporated into IP interventions, these cognitive reframing strategies may effectively reduce impostor thoughts by interrupting students' impostor cycles. Over time this could lead to the retraining of automatic, persistent negative self-talk patterns and maladaptive cognitive distortions (e.g., thinking they are frauds), particularly if students are given a chance to rehearse in safe settings, even before the new patterns feel authentic (Lukens & McFarlane, 2004).

The few empirically validated IP-specific interventions conducted using these strategies have shown promise. For example, Hutchins and Flores (2021) investigated the potential benefits of a multisession psychoeducational IP workshop based on an adaptation of the 12-step cognitive processing therapy process. By incorporating commonly used cognitive processing tools and interactive exercises (e.g., ABC Theory, Challenging Questions, Problematic Thinking Patterns), the intervention reduced feelings of impostorism and increased core self-evaluation beliefs (i.e., self-esteem, generalized self-efficacy, neuroticism, locus of control). Additionally, qualitative responses indicated that participants' improved ability to recognize "stuck points" (i.e., moments when one gets stuck in IP thoughts) was a necessary first step in managing IP and that relating to fellow participants' IP examples helped normalize their own experiences, leading to greater levels of acceptance (Hutchins & Flores, 2021). Although this intervention was studied in nonacademic settings, similar outcomes could be expected for students.

Several scholars have also identified a positive relationship between IP and fixed mindsets (Kumar & Jagacinski, 2006). Mindset theory suggests that those with a so-called fixed mindset attribute intelligence to innate ability, compared with those with a growth mindset who believe that effort and practice are the best predictors of learning and that intelligence is expandable (Dweck, 1986, 2017). Zanchetta et al. (2020) posited that IP is associated with a fixed mindset (i.e., intelligence is considered a stable trait) rather than a growth mindset (i.e., mistakes are viewed as opportunities for learning). These scholars found that coaching and training interventions aimed at promoting growth mindsets reduced IP, with the coaching intervention having the most substantial impact on IP levels (Zanchetta et al., 2020). S. Chang et al. (2022) found similar success for mindset-oriented IP interventions in higher education settings. Following a summer research program that included a workshop on IP and growth mindset, students reported increased endorsements of growth mindset related to academic ability and reductions in impostor feelings, specifically fears of being exposed as lacking knowledge (S. Chang et al., 2022). Therefore, growth mindset strategies, which encourage growth and learning from constructive feedback, particularly those that include one-on-one coaching, could be helpful for students who avoid input out of fear of negative appraisals (a common IP characteristic).

Another approach to address students' maladaptive thought patterns and cognitive distortions is the integration of mindfulness-based strategies. Like other cognitive approaches, mindfulness-based strategies may buffer students against the trappings of the impostor cycle by reducing emotion dysregulation, rumination, and overidentification with state emotions (Hofmann et al., 2010; Suh et al., 2019). Multiple systematic reviews and meta-analyses (e.g., Bamber & Schneider, 2016; Dawson et al., 2020; Gu et al., 2015) have substantiated the positive mental well-being impacts of mindfulness-based interventions (MBIs), and the proposed psychological mechanisms underlying their effectiveness (e.g., cognitive and emotional reactivity, mindfulness, rumination, worry) provide compelling support for IP management applications.

Although there has been limited direct investigation of MBIs' impact on IP, promising evidence indicates their effectiveness in reducing various predictors and adverse outcomes associated with IP in higher education settings. Multiple studies have demonstrated that MBIs can enhance students' well-being (Wingert et al., 2022) and decrease psychological distress (Barbosa et al., 2013; Falsafi, 2016; Finkelstein et al., 2007; Huberty et al., 2019; Lampe & Müller-Hilke, 2021; Rosenzweig et al., 2003), both of which are significant predictors and outcomes of IP (Peteet, Montgomery, & Weeks, 2015; Wei et al., 2020). Moreover, MBIs have been shown to reduce forms of behavioral self-handicapping, including avoidance-focused coping (de Vibe et al., 2018). These strategies (e.g., procrastination, avoidance), which are commonly employed by IP sufferers to avoid negative self-evaluation, as well as shame, a maladaptive response that often leads to rumination and negative self-evaluation, have both been shown to predict impostor thinking (Cowman & Ferrari, 2002). Furthermore, shame has been found to mediate the relationship between students' impostor feelings and psychological distress (Wei et al., 2020). Therefore, MBIs may also be beneficial in the treatment of IP stemming from students' ability to reduce both behavioral self-handicapping (Blouin-Hudon et al., 2017; Dionne, 2016; Rad et al., 2023) and shame (for a review, see Goffnett et al., 2020). Lastly, MBIs have demonstrated efficacy in reducing students' perfectionist tendencies (James & Rimes, 2018; Wimberley et al., 2016), which are established predictors of IP (Dudău, 2014; Pannhausen et al., 2022; Wang et al., 2019). However, further research is needed to confirm the potential benefits of MBIs in directly addressing IP.

As typical manifestations of IP include critical self-talk, isolation, and rumination, mindfulness-based approaches that increase self-compassion could be especially beneficial, as they could bolster students' ability to resist the trappings of their impostor cycles. Self-compassion scholar Kristin Neff (2003) proposed a three-element mindful self-compassion model that expands upon the core tenets of mindfulness. These elements are self-kindness versus self-criticism (in times of stress, being warm and loving toward oneself instead of being critical or judgmental), common humanity versus isolation (recognizing mistakes and suffering are part of the human experience), and mindfulness versus overidentification (taking a balanced view of oneself and avoiding rumination or overidentification with emotions). Multiple correlational studies have established a negative relationship between students' self-compassion and IP (e.g., Patzak et al., 2017; Rosenthal et al., 2021) as well as common IP correlates, including maladaptive perfectionism (Mehr & Adams, 2016), rumination (Smeets et al., 2014), depression, and burnout (Richardson et al., 2020) among both undergraduate and graduate students. Self-compassion has also been shown to moderate the relationship between IP and psychological distress among Asian American university students, such that greater self-compassion weakened the association between IP and psychological distress (Wei et al., 2020). However, more experimental research is needed to fully understand the causal relationship between self-compassion and IP, as one correlational study found a positive association between self-compassion and IP among psychology doctoral students (Tigranyan et al., 2021). Fortunately, a growing number of experimental studies are exploring these relationships; however, at the moment, most are in the context of master's theses and doctoral dissertations. Although not yet published in peer-reviewed journals, their findings are promising. For example, Liu (2022) found that following a brief self-compassion intervention, undergraduate students experienced significant decreases in IP and maladaptive perfectionism, along with increases in overall psychological well-being.

However, all mindfulness-based approaches are not created equal, so evidence-based strategies should be utilized rather than relying on oversimplified techniques. Just as "think differently" would not be sufficient instruction for CBT-style cognitive reframing techniques, to be effective, mindfulness-based strategies must go beyond "just breathe." Additionally, care should be taken to manage students' expectations appropriately and avoid perpetuating feelings of fraud or failure. It is critical to ensure that students understand that delayed benefits are normal and not a reflection of the quality of their efforts. As with any cognitive retraining approach, mindfulness and self-compassion practices should be titrated and done regularly to realize the full benefits.

Unfortunately, the recent surge in superficial mindfulness interventions (e.g., very brief breath work) and commercialization of mindfulness products (e.g., mindfulness apps) has led some to be quick in their dismissal of all mindfulness-based approaches, despite growing empirical support. Often relying on straw man arguments, many dismissals are based on mischaracterizations that suggest mindfulness is just about breathing away problems. Critics have also challenged the individual-level focus of many IP strategies, including mindfulness-based techniques. For example, McGee et al. (2022) argued that individualized IP strategies that ask students to "breathe, yoga pose, meditate, and affirm their own ways to cope" can be harmful to Black and other marginalized students, as they perpetuate the myth that internal, individual-level changes are sufficient for addressing inequitable systems of power (p. 488). We concur that, for many students, IP is often the product of structural and interactional racism and traditional conceptualizations of impostor syndrome fail to account for critical social and environmental issues. However, we disagree that individual-level strategies, including mindfulness-based approaches, should summarily be dismissed. We realize that more IP-specific research is needed in this area, and we encourage scholars to continue investigating these approaches. However, in the meantime, we believe if thoughtfully designed and responsibly delivered (e.g., accounting for the legacy of White supremacy in HEIs), these intrapersonal strategies can be valuable tools to help students manage their IP experiences, especially in the context of inequitable or racist educational settings.

In addition to the variety of cognitive strategies designed to reframe maladaptive thought patterns, research has also found that supporting the development of academic or professional skills can reduce IP and improve student well-being. For example, skill-oriented programs, particularly those that included supervised practice, have been shown to reduce students' emotional distress (e.g., depression, anxiety, stress) while promoting self-confidence, social and emotional skills, and prosocial behavior (Conley et al., 2013). Furthermore, research has shown that, among college students, there is a negative relationship between IP and conscientiousness (Bernard et al., 2002). Therefore, interventions that incorporate academic and professional skill training (e.g., time management, study skills) and support discipline-specific competence development (e.g., scholarship literacy) may be especially beneficial for combating IP (Bernard et al., 2002; Cisco, 2020).

Cisco (2020) incorporated academic skills training into his postgraduate student IP intervention, which was based on an adaptation of previously validated clinical interventions. Like the psychoeducational models previously discussed, he began by introducing students to the IP construct and allowing them to identify their own IP experiences; recognize the associated adverse effects; and consider their use of standard, maladaptive coping strategies (e.g., avoidance, procrastination). Following the didactic content, students were guided through strategies for developing academic literacy and field-specific skills based on literacy pedagogy research. In total, the intervention consisted of four literacy-based workshops held over 1 month. Although all the workshops utilized a group support model, only the first workshop included content and discussions explicitly dedicated to IP. Workshops 2 through 4 focused on disciplinary and academic literacy using various literacy paradigms (e.g., content area reading and writing, disciplinary literacy, academic literacy, discourse theory). After the program, participants in the experimental condition experienced a 23% reduction in IP scores compared with the control group. However, although these findings are promising, some aspects warrant additional study. For example, there was a greater reduction in IP scores among the PhD students compared with the master's students, as well as differential rates of IP reduction by gender, with male students experiencing more significant drops. Therefore, although the intervention appeared to be successful overall, the effects of the treatment may not have been universally beneficial across all students, as program level and identity characteristics seemed to affect outcomes.

Metz and colleagues (2020) also developed a promising academic skill-based IP intervention. They explored the impacts of an online IP intervention embedded as a module in a course for first-year dental doctoral students and found it effectively reduced students' IP levels. As part of this coping skills intervention, students watched an informational video on IP, which included testimonials from former students related to their IP experiences. The video also reviewed evidence-based strategies for dealing with common maladaptive coping practices (e.g., procrastination, overpreparing). Most participants felt that the workshop increased awareness of IP and provided practical strategies for interrupting their impostor cycles. In postintervention follow-ups, the two most utilized coping strategies were scheduling techniques to reduce procrastination and overpreparing for nonessential tasks (Metz et al., 2020). As there was no control group, it is possible IP reductions were due to acclimation to graduate school; however, as discussed earlier, research has shown that program progress alone does not serve as an effective buffer against the development or perpetuation of IP (Rosenthal et al., 2021; Villwock et al., 2016).

Interpersonal Strategies

In addition to intrapersonal strategies, various interpersonal strategies (i.e., social strategies) are related to fewer experiences of impostor thoughts and feelings (Barr-Walker et al., 2020). Social strategies are still utilized at the individual level, but rather than relying exclusively on introspection and self-reflection, they seek to reduce IP experiences by encouraging reliance on social support through diverse mentor networks, affinity groups, and peer support. By utilizing social strategies, students can build upon their individual-level IP management skills while improving their understanding of their IP experiences in the context of sociocultural factors, such as stereotype threat, experiences of racism, and microaggressions (Joshi & Mangette, 2018).

One social strategy proposed to reduce the adverse effects of IP is the cultivation of a robust and diverse mentor network. Although not explicitly investigating student experiences, Manongsong and Ghosh (2021) explored the potential benefits of diversified developmental support for minoritized women working in higher education. Based on their findings, they proposed that diverse mentor networks could effectively combat impostor thoughts and feelings. Given the structure of the U.S. education system, this strategy may be most accessible to graduate students due to the commonly utilized mentor–mentee structure. Posselt (2018a) highlighted the critical role of faculty mentors in supporting doctoral students, including their ability to normalize struggle and failure and encourage adaptive coping strategies, which are crucial for managing students' IP experiences.

Although robust and diversified mentor networks would likely serve all students, there is reason to believe it could be most effective for students who identify with historically marginalized or excluded groups within the academy or their discipline (e.g., women, ethnically/racially minoritized students, queer students, first-generation students). For example, research has shown that first-generation students, compared with their continuing-generation counterparts, are less likely to utilize campus support resources or seek help when they are struggling (J. Chang et al., 2020). However, much of this research has relied on deficit-based models that are fixated on the shortcomings of these students in higher education settings (T. Payne et al., 2021), including lack of academic engagement, low self-esteem, lower grade-point average, and higher attrition rates (Macias, 2013; Schwartz et al., 2018). In contrast, T. Payne et al. (2021) took a strengths-based approach and discovered that first-generation students did engage in help-seeking behaviors; they were just more reliant on their personal networks when deciding whether to seek help and plan the appropriate course of action. Therefore, departments must ensure that these students have access to and are encouraged to develop a diverse set of mentors to help them navigate hidden curricula and recognize the impacts of inequitable systems and institutions on their mental health and academic success.

There has also been extensive research on the benefits of peer mentorship in higher education contexts, which could extend to combating IP. For mentees, participation in peer-mentoring programs provided psychosocial and instrumental support (Grant-Vallone & Ensher, 2000), which led to increases in retention rates (Ward et al., 2010), campus integration (Collings et al., 2014), academic performance (Asgari & Carter, 2016), sense of community (Paolucci et al., 2021), feelings of belonging (Dennehy & Dasgupta, 2017), and strengthened social bonds (Fávero et al., 2018). Student mentors have also been shown to benefit from peer-mentoring relationships through increased opportunities for self-development (Paolucci et al., 2021) and experiences of personal satisfaction (Kalpazidou Schmidt & Faber, 2016). Although there is little empirical research on peer mentorship related to IP, numerous scholars have suggested that it could be an effective strategy for combating feelings associated with IP (Fowler & Villanueva, 2023), such as isolation (Sattler et al., 2012), and increasing program diversity (Fraiman et al., 2022). Additionally, the few studies that have explored the connection between peer mentorship and IP have provided promising results. For example, Graham and McClain (2019) found that Black college students at PWIs who received peer mentorship experienced lower levels of IP and an increased sense of belonging and college adjustment compared with their peers who did not have peer mentors. Sattler et al. (2012) also found that participation in peer-led mentoring groups increased students' academic identity development and self-affirmation while decreasing their impostor feelings. So, although much more work is needed, particularly related to the characteristics of mentor relationships that are most effective in combating IP, it appears to be a worthwhile strategy.

Similar to formal peer-mentorship models, participation in affinity groups has also been proposed to deal with IP experiences. Research has shown that when students sought social support from individuals outside their program, they often reported greater improvements in their impostorism feelings than those who sought help from department peers (Gardner et al., 2019). This difference indicates that having a broad network of peers beyond department area cohorts, such as those found through affinity groups, could provide the best support for students as they work to manage their IP. Additionally, the benefits of peer support may be multidirectional, with those offering support gaining as much from the interaction as those seeking it. For example, students experiencing IP reported that providing social support to their struggling peers helped them reframe and reduce their own feelings of impostorism (Gardner et al., 2019). However, for some, reaching out to peers for support fueled feelings of impostorism (Gardner et al., 2019), possibly due to maladaptive social comparisons, so it may not be a strategy that works for everyone.

Although not all affinity groups are designed around racial or ethnic group identity, much of the IP and broader student well-being research has focused on these identity characteristics. Research has established a connection between racial/ethnic group identity and mental health among minoritized students, with group identity positively predicting psychological empowerment and well-being (McClain et al., 2016; Molix & Bettencourt, 2010). Furthermore, minority stress and impostor feelings are negative predictors of mental health for Black college students in the United States (McClain et al., 2016). Therefore, participation in affinity groups may serve as a buffer against developing impostor thoughts and feelings, particularly for historically marginalized students attending PWIs. For example, as part of their development of a culturally informed model of IP for Black graduate students attending PWIs, Stone et al. (2018) identified awareness of low racial representation and feelings of otherness as factors contributing to students' impostor experiences and feelings of emotional isolation. They recommend participation in affinity groups as one potential strategy for targeting IP. T. Payne et al. (2021) also highlighted the critical role of solid peer networks in bolstering help-seeking behavior and well-being among ethnic minority first-generation students. For example, many students viewed help-seeking behavior as a sign of weakness, noting stereotype threat as a compounding factor (T. Payne et al., 2021). Those willing to seek support preferred to rely on peers rather than faculty and, through the development of these networks, were able to increase their social capital and experience greater levels of support (T. Payne et al., 2021). Social capital benefits become collective by improving individual and, by extension, group levels. In the context of IP interventions, those collective benefits could be realized if members of an affinity group attend IP trainings and share coping strategies with group members. This knowledge sharing could also help normalize IP experiences and increase the likelihood of IP strategies being practiced beyond the formal training period. Therefore, to support these students in mitigating IP and associated adverse effects, IP interventions must discuss and encourage the importance of peer-based affinity groups.

However, it is not enough to promote participation in affinity groups, as the relationship between racial/ethnic identity and IP has been shown to be mediated by self-esteem. Therefore, for affinity groups to be effective, it is imperative that these groups, and by extension, their members, feel supported, included, and empowered by their institutions (Lige et al., 2017).

Institution-Level Strategies

Although individual-focused interventions can provide temporary symptom relief from the adverse outcomes of IP and associated maladaptive coping mechanisms, as discussed in earlier chapters, IP does not occur in a vacuum. Various cultural and systemic factors influence it. Therefore, individual-level strategies are band-aids and will not effectively treat the causal issues at the core of our institutions. The long-term goal should be to move beyond individual approaches to develop institutional-level interventions aimed at thwarting inciting incidents that trigger students' impostor cycles. Signaling the need for these types of changes, scholars have begun to advocate for a shift from considering impostorism as an individual issue (i.e., impostor syndrome) and instead conceptualizing it within the context of environmental and cultural factors that contribute to impostor feelings (Cokley et al., 2017; Feenstra et al., 2020; McClain et al., 2016; McGee et al., 2022).

Interestingly, this is not a new concept, even though contemporary IP scholarship has been nearly exclusively dedicated to exploring the construct through an individual lens. For example, Clance et al. (1995) discussed the role of social and interpersonal context in developing IP, highlighting the impact of familial and social messaging on gender-role socialization. Cokley et al. (2017) also found that among ethnic minority students, there was a positive relationship between experiences of racial discrimination on campus and impostor thoughts and feelings. If IP interventions continue to exclusively focus on person-based messaging and approaches that ignore the impact of social context on the development and manifestations of IP, they run the risk of perpetuating the dangerous myth that IP is an individual issue that must be solely resolved by the individual (Feenstra et al., 2020; McGee et al., 2022).

Much of the IP scholarship has come from psychology, leading to an understandable imbalanced attention to individual factors and mitigation strategies. However, the more we learn about the phenomenon, the more we understand that it is not an individual issue that originates within the individual but rather a (maladaptive) coping response to inequitable and exclusionary systems and power structures. Therefore, if HEIs want to create meaningful change in reducing toxic IP experiences, they must accept their role in creating the environments, policies, and situations that contribute to the flourishing of IP. Simply providing life preservers to drowning students while ignoring the system-level factors that are pushing them into the dangerous water is, at best, ignorant short-sightedness and, at worst, willful indifference. Institutions genuinely committed to supporting the well-being of their students must stop placing the entire burden on the individual and work toward high-level structural change.

Hidden Curricula

As we have discussed, societal, institutional, and interpersonal factors play significant roles in developing and manifesting impostorism on college and university campuses (Feenstra et al., 2020). The hidden curriculum of higher education, both at the undergraduate and graduate levels, creates institutional barriers that foster students' perceived fraudulence and self-doubt, particularly among first-generation college students and students from historically marginalized backgrounds. Jack (2019) argued that the unwritten rules of higher education constitute a hidden curriculum that tests students' ability to navigate complex and exclusionary institutions rather than rewarding academic achievements. He noted that undergraduate institutions rarely offer any formal curriculum on the importance of developing relationships with faculty, attending office hours, and creating connections with staff to access institutional resources. He explains that some of the most commonly used words in undergraduate education are rarely described to students (e.g., syllabus, fellowship), and graduate school is no different. Similarly, in her model of graduate education, Posselt (2018b) included impostorism as one of the primary challenges faced in doctoral education. She asserted that impostor syndrome is fostered by the emphasis on rigor in doctoral education and is triggered by experiences of isolation, insufficient mentoring, and competition with peers (Posselt, 2018b).

Drawing on a survey of graduate students across all programs at a large midwestern university, Cohen and McConnell (2019) found that controlling for other factors, perceptions of insufficient mentorship, competition for funding, and isolation in graduate school are associated with higher IP among postgraduate students. Similarly, in her field guide to graduate school, Calarco (2020) argued that the hidden curriculum of graduate school contributes to impostor thoughts; there is a lack of formal education on discipline-specific jargon, academic writing, publishing, or how and where to present one's research (e.g., how to give a conference presentation; Calarco, 2020; Cisco, 2020). In addition, heavy reading loads (and the unspoken assumption that graduate students should know that no one is expected to read everything), as well as the significant gaps in formal research methodological training, can also lead to students feeling that they do not measure up intellectually, fostering students' feelings of impostorism (Calarco, 2020).

IP interventions must extend beyond student-focused psychoeducational workshops to include institution-level responses to address these hidden curricula, which permeate all higher education levels (Feenstra et al., 2020). Departments, schools, and colleges must work to uncover their hidden curricula and provide formal instruction on the unwritten norms and rules of higher education. These efforts should happen at the start of undergraduate training, perhaps incorporated into required first-year student orientations. Additionally, students could be assigned first-year academic advisors who provide one-to-one coaching and support, including explicit discussion of norms and definitions of educational jargon. First-year writing seminars, required by many colleges, could also be a vehicle for formal curriculum on topics such as navigating institutional support resources, deciphering and defining higher education terminology, academic writing, and the role of faculty in supporting students.

At the graduate level, these efforts could include reducing departmental hierarchies to empower students as active participants in their development as scholars-in-training. Metz et al. (2020) solicited suggestions from doctoral students regarding institutional-level changes that could support their efforts to reduce IP, particularly during critical transition periods. Students suggested curriculum and environmental changes, including the elimination of class ranks, reductions in course load, more welcoming orientations, and pass/fail grading (Metz et al., 2020). Graduate proseminars could also be a space to normalize IP and generate open discussion among peers about impostor feelings. Graduate advisors should also explicitly decode the hidden graduate curriculum during one-to-one advising appointments, especially during the first year when students are adjusting to the new expectations of graduate school.

Curricular Integration
For HEIs that choose to offer individual-level IP interventions, some changes can also be made at the institutional or departmental level to bolster the impact.

For example, incorporating IP interventions or content into curricular activities would reduce barriers to entry associated with free-standing programs. Several studies have found that identity characteristics (e.g., gender, race, religion, socioeconomic status), perceived barriers (e.g., access, usability), and academic level (e.g., undergraduate, graduate) affect students' understanding of mental health issues, perceptions of public stigma, and self-stigma toward help-seeking behavior (e.g., Clement et al., 2015; Dunley & Papadopoulos, 2019; Eisenberg et al., 2009; Pedersen & Paves, 2014). Others have found that many students struggle to find or justify the time to prioritize mental health and well-being (Broglia et al., 2021; Czyz et al., 2013; Givens & Tjia, 2002). Furthermore, Clance and Imes (1978) argued that individuals' experiences of IP are not necessarily recognized or readily admitted. So, by incorporating IP interventions into the required curriculum, more students in need of IP support could be exposed to the materials and resources.

Beyond removing real and perceived barriers, a systematic review of universal well-being promotion interventions in higher education showed that interventions incorporated into the curriculum were more effective than cocurricular small-group formats (Conley et al., 2013). Although not empirically explored, scholars speculate that the effect of curriculum integration might be due to a combination of students' familiarity with the classroom as a space for learning as well as getting more time to understand and internalize the new content, as course-based approaches tend to be longer in duration than free-standing workshops or small-group trainings (Conley et al., 2013). In the case of IP, S. Chang et al. (2022) similarly found that students appreciated the opportunity to participate in IP workshops during orientation, noting the usefulness of starting the semester off on the right foot and understanding its integration as an endorsement from the department of the importance of the content. Furthermore, class-based programs may also be less stigmatized than interventions that may be viewed as similar to therapy (H. Payne, 2022). Additionally, by removing the "elective" status, institutions signal to students that they view well-being and whole-person development as integral to students' experiences and success.

Institutional-level strategies are crucial for optimally supporting historically marginalized students in minimizing their IP experiences. For example, Stone et al. (2018) identified institution-level factors, including lack of representation and discrimination, that contribute to creating and perpetuating IP among Black students at PWIs. They argued for campus-wide initiatives that affirm Black students' presence and intellectual contributions rather than relying exclusively on individual-level resilience initiatives. One recommendation they provided was to develop psychoeducational programs and trainings for non-Black students and faculty aimed at reducing negative biases related to Black intelligence and increasing cultural competence (Stone et al., 2018). In addition, to protect against the incorporation of harmful biases or assumptions, diverse groups of people, including students, should be included in developing and facilitating program content. By involving students, content is also more likely to be delivered in a relatable manner (e.g., cultural references, language, style; Benton et al., 2020; Hudson et al., 2014), leading participants to be more willing to express vulnerability (Djohari & Higham, 2020), which is critical when dealing with a sensitive topic like IP.

Faculty and Impostor Phenomenon

Another consideration relates to the ability of the faculty to support students as they work to manage their impostor thoughts and feelings. First, it is essential to acknowledge that most faculty are not experts on IP. Second, extensive research highlights the prevalence of IP among faculty at all levels (Hutchins, 2015; Hutchins & Rainbolt, 2017; Parkman, 2016), and scholars have argued that those who enter their professional roles with unresolved impostor issues may pass along maladaptive thought patterns or coping strategies to their trainees (Dancy & Brown, 2011). Therefore, it may be unrealistic to expect faculty mentors and advisors to effectively promote and model healthy behaviors if they, too, are suffering. Third, the prevalence of IP among faculty could negatively affect the effectiveness of student-centered IP interventions. For example, doctoral students who participated in a first-year IP intervention reported that they felt that consistent reinforcement (e.g., repeated content exposure, reminders from faculty) would be critical to their success in managing their impostor thoughts following the intervention (Metz et al., 2020). This type of continued reinforcement would not be possible if faculty could not recognize IP in themselves or their students or if they were unaware of adaptive coping strategies.

Consequently, institutions should take a two-pronged approach to combat IP, empowering both students and faculty. On the faculty side, this could be accomplished by creating faculty development programs to cultivate institutional cultures that address and prevent IP at all levels. These programs could educate faculty about evidence-based interventions and strategies that can be used by faculty and also embedded in their courses or shared with their mentees. To alleviate the burden on faculty, institutions can invite higher education staff with expertise in IP, such as educators in the counseling center or teaching and learning center, to provide guest lectures and resources for embedding interventions in their courses and advising. Furthermore, given that perceptions of low-quality mentorship are associated with higher IP among graduate

Strategies for Combating the Impostor Phenomenon in Higher Education • 329

students, graduate programs should also provide formal faculty mentorship training to ensure high-quality relationships between advisors and advisees (Cohen & McConnell, 2019).

FUTURE DIRECTIONS

No doubt remains concerning the prevalence of IP on our campuses. What is left to discover is how institutions and departments can effectively drive higher level change while still directly supporting students as they navigate their IP experiences. In light of the field's growing understanding of the roles that systems of power and campus climate play in the development and perpetuation of IP, it may be tempting to dismiss individual-level IP interventions summarily. However, we believe they can still provide great value when developed using culturally informed frameworks, considering the unique impacts of identity and social status factors, and thoughtfully delivered as part of larger campus-wide efforts. Just as we encourage our students to let go of perfectionist tendencies that freeze progress, we should not let the perfect be the enemy of the good when supporting them. While we wait for the fruits of our labors to manifest at the institutional level, we have a responsibility to arm our students with tools that can empower them to minimize the frequency and impact of their impostor thoughts and feelings. Demanding or driving institution-level change does not require the wholesale rejection of individual approaches that have been demonstrated to alleviate student suffering.

Therefore, we hope this chapter serves as a call to action for social science scholars and higher education administrators. There is still much progress to be made when it comes to identifying and implementing effective evidence-based strategies for mitigating students' IP experiences. More research is needed in areas related to individual protective mechanisms; institutional interventions; and strategies for dealing with the social, cultural, and environmental factors contributing to student suffering. In the meantime, commitment is needed across all levels of HEIs to shift the focus away from individual conceptualizations of IP (i.e., impostor syndrome) and instead recognize IP as a consequence of inequitable and discriminatory environments.

REFERENCES

Asgari, S., & Carter, F., Jr. (2016). Peer mentors can improve academic performance: A quasi-experimental study of peer mentorship in introductory courses. *Teaching of Psychology, 43*(2), 131–135. https://doi.org/10.1177/0098628316636288

Bamber, M. D., & Schneider, J. K. (2016). Mindfulness-based meditation to decrease stress and anxiety in college students: A narrative synthesis of the research. *Educational Research Review, 18*, 1–32. https://doi.org/10.1016/j.edurev.2015.12.004

Barbosa, P., Raymond, G., Zlotnick, C., Wilk, J., Toomey, R., III, & Mitchell, J., III. (2013). Mindfulness-based stress reduction training is associated with greater empathy and reduced anxiety for graduate healthcare students. *Education for Health, 26*(1), 9–14. https://doi.org/10.4103/1357-6283.112794

Barr-Walker, J., Werner, D. A., Kellermeyer, L., & Bass, M. B. (2020). Coping with impostor feelings: Evidence based recommendations from a mixed methods study. *Evidence Based Library and Information Practice, 15*(2), 24–41. https://doi.org/10.18438/eblip29706

Benton, A. D., Santana, A., Vinklarek, A. J., Lewis, C. M., Sorensen, J. M., & Hernandez, A. (2020). Peer-led sexual health education: Multiple perspectives on benefits for peer health educators. *Child & Adolescent Social Work Journal, 37*(5), 487–496. https://doi.org/10.1007/s10560-020-00661-9

Bernard, N. S., Dollinger, S. J., & Ramaniah, N. V. (2002). Applying the Big Five personality factors to the impostor phenomenon. *Journal of Personality Assessment, 78*(2), 321–333. https://doi.org/10.1207/S15327752JPA7802_07

Blouin-Hudon, E. M. C., & Pychyl, T. A. (2017). A mental imagery intervention to increase future self-continuity and reduce procrastination. *Applied Psychology, 66*(2), 326–352. https://doi.org/10.1111/apps.12088

Bravata, D. M., Watts, S. A., Keefer, A. L., Madhusudhan, D. K., Taylor, K. T., Clark, D. M., Nelson, R. S., Cokley, K. O., & Hagg, H. K. (2020). Prevalence, predictors, and treatment of impostor syndrome: A systematic review. *Journal of General Internal Medicine, 35*(4), 1252–1275. https://doi.org/10.1007/s11606-019-05364-1

Brennan-Wydra, E., Chung, H. W., Angoff, N., ChenFeng, J., Phillips, A., Schreiber, J., Young, C., & Wilkins, K. (2021). Maladaptive perfectionism, impostor phenomenon, and suicidal ideation among medical students. *Academic Psychiatry, 45*(6), 708–715. https://doi.org/10.1007/s40596-021-01503-1

Broglia, E., Millings, A., & Barkham, M. (2021). Student mental health profiles and barriers to help seeking: When and why students seek help for a mental health concern. *Counselling & Psychotherapy Research, 21*(4), 816–826. https://doi.org/10.1002/capr.12462

Brown, J. A., Russell, S., Hattouni, E., & Kincaid, A. (2020). Psychoeducation. In *Oxford Research Encyclopedia of Education*. https://doi.org/10.1093/acrefore/9780190264093.013.974

Brown, N. W. (2018). *Psychoeducational groups: Process and practice*. Routledge. https://doi.org/10.4324/9781315169590

Calarco, J. (2020). *A field guide to grad school: Uncovering the hidden curriculum*. Princeton University Press.

Chakraverty, D. (2019). Impostor phenomenon in STEM: Occurrence, attribution, and identity. *Studies in Graduate and Postdoctoral Education, 10*(1), 2–20. https://doi.org/10.1108/SGPE-D-18-00014

Chakraverty, D. (2020). PhD student experiences with the impostor phenomenon in STEM. *International Journal of Doctoral Studies, 15*, 159–179. https://doi.org/10.28945/4513

Strategies for Combating the Impostor Phenomenon in Higher Education • 331

Chakraverty, D., Cavazos, J. E., & Jeffe, D. B. (2022). Exploring reasons for MD-PhD trainees' experiences of impostor phenomenon. *BMC Medical Education, 22*(1), Article 333. https://doi.org/10.1186/s12909-022-03396-6

Chang, J., Wang, S. W., Mancini, C., McGrath-Mahrer, B., & Orama de Jesus, S. (2020). The complexity of cultural mismatch in higher education: Norms affecting first-generation college students' coping and help-seeking behaviors. *Cultural Diversity and Ethnic Minority Psychology, 26*(3), 280–294. https://doi.org/10.1037/cdp0000311

Chang, S., Lee, H. Y., Anderson, C., Lewis, K., Chakraverty, D., & Yates, M. (2022). Intervening on impostor phenomenon: Prospective evaluation of a workshop for health science students using a mixed-method design. *BMC Medical Education, 22*(1), Article 802. https://doi.org/10.1186/s12909-022-03824-7

Cisco, J. (2020). Using academic skill set interventions to reduce impostor phenomenon feelings in postgraduate students. *Journal of Further and Higher Education, 44*(3), 423–437. https://doi.org/10.1080/0309877X.2018.1564023

Clance, P. R. (1985). *Clance Impostor Phenomenon Scale (CIPS)* [Database record]. APA PsycTests. https://doi.org/10.1037/t11274-000

Clance, P. R., Dingman, D., Reviere, S. L., & Stober, D. R. (1995). Impostor phenomenon in an interpersonal/social context: Origins and treatment. *Women & Therapy, 16*(4), 79–96. https://doi.org/10.1300/J015v16n04_07

Clance, P. R., & Imes, S. A. (1978). The impostor phenomenon in high achieving women: Dynamics and therapeutic intervention. *Psychotherapy: Theory, Research, & Practice, 15*(3), 241–247. https://doi.org/10.1037/h0086006

Clement, S., Schauman, O., Graham, T., Maggioni, F., Evans-Lacko, S., Bezborodovs, N., Morgan, C., Rüsch, N., Brown, J. S. L., & Thornicroft, G. (2015). What is the impact of mental health-related stigma on help-seeking? A systematic review of quantitative and qualitative studies. *Psychological Medicine, 45*(1), 11–27. https://doi.org/10.1017/S0033291714000129

Cohen, E. D., & McConnell, W. R. (2019). Fear of fraudulence: Graduate school program environments and the impostor phenomenon. *The Sociological Quarterly, 60*(3), 457–478. https://doi.org/10.1080/00380253.2019.1580552

Cokley, K., Awad, G., Smith, L., Jackson, S., Awosogba, O., Hurst, A., Stone, S., Blondeau, L., & Roberts, D. (2015). The roles of gender stigma consciousness, impostor phenomenon and academic self-concept in the academic outcomes of women and men. *Sex Roles, 73*(9–10), 414–426. https://doi.org/10.1007/s11199-015-0516-7

Cokley, K., McClain, S., Enciso, A., & Martinez, M. (2013). An examination of the impact of minority status stress and impostor feelings on the mental health of diverse ethnic minority college students. *Journal of Multicultural Counseling and Development, 41*(2), 82–95. https://doi.org/10.1002/j.2161-1912.2013.00029.x

Cokley, K., Smith, L., Bernard, D., Hurst, A., Jackson, S., Stone, S., Awosogba, O., Saucer, C., Bailey, M., & Roberts, D. (2017). Impostor feelings as a moderator and mediator of the relationship between perceived discrimination and mental health among racial/ethnic minority college students. *Journal of Counseling Psychology, 64*(2), 141–154. https://doi.org/10.1037/cou0000198

Collings, R., Swanson, V., & Watkins, R. (2014). The impact of peer mentoring on levels of student well-being, integration and retention: A controlled comparative evaluation of residential students in U.K. higher education. *Higher Education, 68*(6), 927–942. https://doi.org/10.1007/s10734-014-9752-y

Conley, C. S., Durlak, J. A., & Dickson, D. A. (2013). An evaluative review of outcome research on universal mental health promotion and prevention programs for higher education students. *Journal of American College Health, 61*(5), 286–301. https://doi.org/10.1080/07448481.2013.802237

Cowman, S. E., & Ferrari, J. R. (2002). "Am I for real?": Predicting impostor tendencies from self-handicapping and affective components. *Social Behavior and Personality, 30*(2), 119–125. https://doi.org/10.2224/sbp.2002.30.2.119

Cusack, C. E., Hughes, J. L., & Nuhu, N. (2013). Connecting gender and mental health to imposter phenomenon feelings. *Psi Chi Journal of Psychological Research, 18*(2), 74–81. https://doi.org/10.24839/2164-8204.JN18.2.74

Czyz, E. K., Horwitz, A. G., Eisenberg, D., Kramer, A., & King, C. A. (2013). Self-reported barriers to professional help seeking among college students at elevated risk for suicide. *Journal of American College Health, 61*(7), 398–406. https://doi.org/10.1080/07448481.2013.820731

Dancy, T. E., & Brown, M. C. (2011). The mentoring and induction of educators of color: Addressing the impostor syndrome in academe. *Journal of School Leadership, 21*(4), 607–634. https://doi.org/10.1177/105268461102100405

Dawson, A. F., Brown, W. W., Anderson, J., Datta, B., Donald, J. N., Hong, K., Allan, S., Mole, T. B., Jones, P. B., & Galante, J. (2020). Mindfulness-based interventions for university students: A systematic review and meta-analysis of randomised controlled trials. *Applied Psychology: Health and Well-Being, 12*(2), 384–410. https://doi.org/10.1111/aphw.12188

Dennehy, T. C., & Dasgupta, N. (2017). Female peer mentors early in college increase women's positive academic experiences and retention in engineering. *Proceedings of the National Academy of Sciences of the United States of America, 114*(23), 5964–5969. https://doi.org/10.1073/pnas.1613117114

de Vibe, M., Solhaug, I., Rosenvinge, J. H., Tyssen, R., Hanley, A., & Garland, E. (2018). Six-year positive effects of a mindfulness-based intervention on mindfulness, coping and well-being in medical and psychology students; Results from a randomized controlled trial. *PLOS ONE, 13*(4), Article e0196053. https://doi.org/10.1371/journal.pone.0196053

Dionne, F. (2016). Using acceptance and mindfulness to reduce procrastination among university students: Results from a pilot study. *Revista Prâksis, 13*(1), 8–20. https://www.redalyc.org/journal/5255/525553723001/525553723001.pdf

Djohari, N., & Higham, R. (2020). Peer-led focus groups as "dialogic spaces" for exploring young people's evolving values. *Cambridge Journal of Education, 50*(5), 657–672. https://doi.org/10.1080/0305764X.2020.1754763

Dudău, D. P. (2014). The relation between perfectionism and impostor phenomenon. *Procedia: Social and Behavioral Sciences, 127*, 129–133. https://doi.org/10.1016/j.sbspro.2014.03.226

Dunley, P., & Papadopoulos, A. (2019). Why is it so hard to get help? Barriers to help-seeking in postsecondary students struggling with mental health issues: A scoping review. *International Journal of Mental Health and Addiction, 17*(3), 699–715. https://doi.org/10.1007/s11469-018-0029-z

Dweck, C. S. (1986). Motivational processes affecting learning. *American Psychologist, 41*(10), 1040–1048. https://doi.org/10.1037/0003-066X.41.10.1040

Dweck, C. S. (2017). From needs to goals and representations: Foundations for a unified theory of motivation, personality, and development. *Psychological Review, 124*(6), 689–719. https://doi.org/10.1037/rev0000082

Eisenberg, D., Downs, M. F., Golberstein, E., & Zivin, K. (2009). Stigma and help seeking for mental health among college students. *Medical Care Research and Review, 66*(5), 522–541. https://doi.org/10.1177/1077558709335173

Ekhtiari, H., Rezapour, T., Aupperle, R. L., & Paulus, M. P. (2017). Neuroscience-informed psychoeducation for addiction medicine: A neurocognitive perspective. *Progress in Brain Research, 235*, 239–264. https://doi.org/10.1016/bs.pbr.2017.08.013

Falsafi, N. (2016). A randomized controlled trial of mindfulness versus yoga: Effects on depression and/or anxiety in college students. *Journal of the American Psychiatric Nurses Association, 22*(6), 483–497. https://doi.org/10.1177/1078390316663307

Fávero, C. V. B., Moran, S., & Eniola-Adefeso, O. (2018). The power of peer mentoring in enabling a diverse and inclusive environment in a chemical engineering graduate program. *Chemical Engineering Education, 52*(2), 79–88. https://eric.ed.gov/?id=EJ1174638

Feenstra, S., Begeny, C. T., Ryan, M. K., Rink, F. A., Stoker, J. I., & Jordan, J. (2020). Contextualizing the impostor "syndrome." *Frontiers in Psychology, 11*, Article 575024. https://doi.org/10.3389/fpsyg.2020.575024

Finkelstein, C., Brownstein, A., Scott, C., & Lan, Y. L. (2007). Anxiety and stress reduction in medical education: An intervention. *Medical Education, 41*(3), 258–264. https://doi.org/10.1111/j.1365-2929.2007.02685.x

Fleischhauer, M., Wossidlo, J., Michael, L., & Enge, S. (2021). The impostor phenomenon: Toward a better understanding of the nomological network and gender differences. *Frontiers in Psychology, 12*, Article 764030. https://doi.org/10.3389/fpsyg.2021.764030

Fowler, K. R., & Villanueva, L. (2023). From the bedside to the boardroom: Imposter syndrome in nursing leadership. *Nurse Leader, 21*(3), E7–E10. https://doi.org/10.1016/j.mnl.2022.10.003

Fraiman, Y. S., Montoya-Williams, D., Ellis, J., Fadel, C. W., Bonachea, E. M., & Peña, M. M. (2022). Plugging the leaky pipeline: The role of peer mentorship for increasing diversity. *Pediatrics, 150*(4), Article e2021055925. https://doi.org/10.1542/peds.2021-055925

Gardner, R. G., Bednar, J. S., Stewart, B. W., Oldroyd, J. B., & Moore, J. (2019). "I must have slipped through the cracks somehow": An examination of coping with perceived impostorism and the role of social support. *Journal of Vocational Behavior, 115*, Article 103337. https://doi.org/10.1016/j.jvb.2019.103337

Givens, J. L., & Tjia, J. (2002). Depressed medical students' use of mental health services and barriers to use. *Academic Medicine, 77*(9), 918–921. https://doi.org/10.1097/00001888-200209000-00024

Goffnett, J., Liechty, J. M., & Kidder, E. (2020). Interventions to reduce shame: A systematic review. *Journal of Behavioral and Cognitive Therapy, 30*(2), 141–160. https://doi.org/10.1016/j.jbct.2020.03.001

Gottlieb, M., Chung, A., Battaglioli, N., Sebok-Syer, S. S., & Kalantari, A. (2020). Impostor syndrome among physicians and physicians in training: A scoping review. *Medical Education, 54*(2), 116–124. https://doi.org/10.1111/medu.13956

Graham, J., & McClain, S. (2019). A canonical correlational analysis examining the relationship between peer mentorship, belongingness, impostor feelings, and Black collegians' academic and psychosocial outcomes. *American Educational Research Journal, 56*(6), 2333–2367. https://doi.org/10.3102/0002831219842571

Grant-Vallone, E. J., & Ensher, E. A. (2000). Effects of peer mentoring on types of mentor support, program satisfaction and graduate student stress. *Journal of College Student Development, 41*(6), 637–642.

Gu, J., Strauss, C., Bond, R., & Cavanagh, K. (2015). How do mindfulness-based cognitive therapy and mindfulness-based stress reduction improve mental health and wellbeing? A systematic review and meta-analysis of mediation studies. *Clinical Psychology Review, 37*, 1–12. https://doi.org/10.1016/j.cpr.2015.01.006

Haney, T. S., Birkholz, L., & Rutledge, C. (2018). A workshop for addressing the impact of the imposter syndrome on clinical nurse specialists. *Clinical Nurse Specialist, 32*(4), 189–194. https://doi.org/10.1097/NUR.0000000000000386

Hofmann, S. G., Sawyer, A. T., Witt, A. A., & Oh, D. (2010). The effect of mindfulness-based therapy on anxiety and depression: A meta-analytic review. *Journal of Consulting and Clinical Psychology, 78*(2), 169–183. https://doi.org/10.1037/a0018555

Holt, J., Millear, P., Warren-James, M., & Kannis-Dymand, L (2023). Interventions to address impostor phenomenon: A scoping review protocol. *JBI Evidence Synthesis, 21*(5), 1051–1057 https://doi.org/10.11124/JBIES-22-00086

Huberty, J., Green, J., Glissmann, C., Larkey, L., Puzia, M., & Lee, C. (2019). Efficacy of the mindfulness meditation mobile app "Calm" to reduce stress among college students: Randomized controlled trial. *JMIR mHealth and uHealth, 7*(6), Article e14273. https://doi.org/10.2196/14273

Hudson, H. K., Bliss, K. R., Bice, M. R., Lodyga, M. G., & Ragon, B. M. (2014). Creating peer-led media to teach sensitive topics: Recommendations from practicing health educators. *Journal of Health Education Teaching, 5*(1), 28–35.

Hutchins, H. M. (2015). Outing the imposter: A study exploring imposter phenomenon among higher education faculty. *New Horizons in Adult Education and Human Resource Development, 27*(2), 3–12. https://doi.org/10.1002/nha3.20098

Hutchins, H. M., & Flores, J. (2021). Don't believe everything you think: Applying a cognitive processing therapy intervention to disrupting imposter phenomenon. *New Horizons in Adult Education and Human Resource Development, 33*(4), 33–47. https://doi.org/10.1002/nha3.20325

Hutchins, H. M., & Rainbolt, H. (2017). What triggers imposter phenomenon among academic faculty? A critical incident study exploring antecedents, coping, and development opportunities. *Human Resource Development International, 20*(3), 194–214. https://doi.org/10.1080/13678868.2016.1248205

Jack, A. (2019). *The privileged poor: How elite colleges are failing disadvantaged students.* Harvard University Press. https://doi.org/10.4159/9780674239647

Jacobs, M. D., & Sasser, J. T. (2021). Impostor phenomenon in undergraduate nursing students: A pilot study of prevalence and patterns. *The Journal of Nursing Education, 60*(6), 329–332. https://doi.org/10.3928/01484834-20210520-05

James, K., & Rimes, K. A. (2018). Mindfulness-based cognitive therapy versus pure cognitive behavioural self-help for perfectionism: A pilot randomised study. *Mindfulness, 9*, 801–814. https://doi.org/10.1007/s12671-017-0817-8

Joshi, A., & Mangette, H. (2018). Unmasking of impostor syndrome. *Journal of Research, Assessment, and Practice in Higher Education, 3*(1), Article 3.

Juberg, M., Spencer, S. D., Martin, T. J., Vibell, J., da Costa Ferro, A., Kam, B., & Masuda, A. (2019). A mindfulness-based intervention for college students, faculty, and staff: A preliminary investigation. *Clinical Case Studies, 18*(3), 185–199. https://doi.org/10.1177/1534650119836166

Kalpazidou Schmidt, E., & Faber, S. T. (2016). Benefits of peer mentoring to mentors, female mentees and higher education institutions. *Mentoring & Tutoring, 24*(2), 137–157. https://doi.org/10.1080/13611267.2016.1170560

Kumar, S., & Jagacinski, C. M. (2006). Imposters have goals too: The imposter phenomenon and its relationship to achievement goal theory. *Personality and Individual Differences, 40*(1), 147–157. https://doi.org/10.1016/j.paid.2005.05.014

Lampe, L. C., & Müller-Hilke, B. (2021). Mindfulness-based intervention helps preclinical medical students to contain stress, maintain mindfulness and improve academic success. *BMC Medical Education, 21*(1), Article 145. https://doi.org/10.1186/s12909-021-02578-y

Lige, Q. M., Peteet, B. J., & Brown, C. M. (2017). Racial identity, self-esteem, and the impostor phenomenon among African American college students. *The Journal of Black Psychology, 43*(4), 345–357. https://doi.org/10.1177/0095798416648787

Liu, S. (2022). *Effects of a brief self-compassion intervention for college students with impostor phenomenon* [Doctoral dissertation, Iowa State University]. ProQuest Dissertations Publishing.

Lukens, E. P., & McFarlane, W. R. (2004). Psychoeducation as evidence-based practice: Considerations for practice, research, and policy. *Brief Treatment and Crisis Intervention, 4*(3), 205–225. https://doi.org/10.1093/brief-treatment/mhh019

Macias, L. (2013). Choosing success: A paradigm for empowering first-generation college students. *About Campus: Enriching the Student Learning Experience, 18*(5), 17–21. https://doi.org/10.1002/abc.21133

Manongsong, A. M., & Ghosh, R. (2021). Developing the positive identity of minoritized women leaders in higher education: How can multiple and diverse developers help with overcoming the impostor phenomenon? *Human Resource Development Review, 20*(4), 436–485. https://doi.org/10.1177/15344843211040732

McClain, S., Beasley, S. T., Jones, B., Awosogba, O., Jackson, S., & Cokley, K. (2016). An examination of the impact of racial and ethnic identity, impostor feelings, and minority status stress on the mental health of Black college students. *Journal of Multicultural Counseling and Development, 44*(2), 101–117. https://doi.org/10.1002/jmcd.12040

McGee, E. O., Botchway, P. K., Naphan-Kingery, D. E., Brockman, A. J., Houston, I. I. S., & White, D. T. (2022). Racism camouflaged as impostorism and the impact on Black STEM doctoral students. *Race, Ethnicity and Education, 25*(4), 487–507. https://doi.org/10.1080/13613324.2021.1924137

McWilliams, D., Block, M., Hinson, J., & Kier, K. L. (2023). Impostor phenomenon in undergraduates and pharmacy students at a small private university. *American

Journal of Pharmaceutical Education, 87(1), Article AJPE8728. https://doi.org/10.5688/ajpe8728

Mehr, K. E., & Adams, A. C. (2016). Self-compassion as a mediator of maladaptive perfectionism and depressive symptoms in college students. *Journal of College Student Psychotherapy, 30*(2), 132–145. https://doi.org/10.1080/87568225.2016.1140991

Metz, C. J., Ballard, E., & Metz, M. J. (2020). The stress of success: An online module to help first-year dental students cope with the impostor phenomenon. *Journal of Dental Education, 84*(9), 1016–1024. https://doi.org/10.1002/jdd.12181

Molix, L., & Bettencourt, B. A. (2010). Predicting well-being among ethnic minorities: Psychological empowerment and group identity. *Journal of Applied Social Psychology, 40*(3), 513–533. https://doi.org/10.1111/j.1559-1816.2010.00585.x

Morgan, B., & Simmons, L. (2021). A "PERMA" response to the pandemic: An online positive education programme to promote well-being in university students. *Frontiers in Education, 6*, Article 642632. https://doi.org/10.3389/feduc.2021.642632

Motlova, L. B., Balon, R., Beresin, E. V., Brenner, A. M., Coverdale, J. H., Guerrero, A. P., Louie, A. K., & Roberts, L. W. (2017). Psychoeducation as an opportunity for patients, psychiatrists, and psychiatric educators: Why do we ignore it? *Academic Psychiatry, 41*(4), 447–451. https://doi.org/10.1007/s40596-017-0728-y

Myers, N. D., Prilleltensky, I., Prilleltensky, O., McMahon, A., Dietz, S., & Rubenstein, C. L. (2017). Efficacy of the Fun for Wellness online intervention to promote multidimensional well-being: A randomized controlled trial. *Prevention Science, 18*(8), 984–994. https://doi.org/10.1007/s11121-017-0779-z

Neff, K. D. (2003). Self-compassion: An alternative conceptualization of a healthy attitude toward oneself. *Self and Identity, 2*(2), 85–101. https://doi.org/10.1080/15298860309032

Pannhausen, S., Klug, K., & Rohrmann, S. (2022). Never good enough: The relation between the impostor phenomenon and multidimensional perfectionism. *Current Psychology, 41*, 888–901.

Paolucci, E. O., Jacobsen, M., Nowell, L., Freeman, G., Lorenzetti, L., Clancy, T., Paolucci, A., Pethrick, H., & Lorenzetti, D. L. (2021). An exploration of graduate student peer mentorship, social connectedness and well-being across four disciplines of study. *Studies in Graduate and Postdoctoral Education, 12*(1), 73–88. https://doi.org/10.1108/SGPE-07-2020-0041

Parkman, A. (2016). The imposter phenomenon in higher education: Incidence and impact. *Journal of Higher Education Theory & Practice, 16*(1), 51–60.

Patzak, A., Kollmayer, M., & Schober, B. (2017). Buffering impostor feelings with kindness: The mediating role of self-compassion between gender-role orientation and the impostor phenomenon. *Frontiers in Psychology, 8*, Article 1289. https://doi.org/10.3389/fpsyg.2017.01289

Payne, H. (2022). The BodyMind Approach® to support students in higher education: Relationships between student stress, medically unexplained physical symptoms and mental health. *Innovations in Education and Teaching International, 59*(4), 483–494. https://doi.org/10.1080/14703297.2021.1878052

Payne, T., Muenks, K., & Aguayo, E. (2021). "Just because I am first gen doesn't mean I'm not asking for help": A thematic analysis of first-generation college students' academic help-seeking behaviors. *Journal of Diversity in Higher Education*. Advance online publication. https://doi.org/10.1037/dhe0000382

Pedersen, E. R., & Paves, A. P. (2014). Comparing perceived public stigma and personal stigma of mental health treatment seeking in a young adult sample. *Psychiatry Research, 219*(1), 143–150. https://doi.org/10.1016/j.psychres.2014.05.017

Pervez, A., Brady, L. L., Mullane, K., Lo, K. D., Bennett, A. A., & Nelson, T. A. (2021). An empirical investigation of mental illness, impostor syndrome, and social support in management doctoral programs. *Journal of Management Education, 45*(1), 126–158. https://doi.org/10.1177/1052562920953195

Peteet, B. J., Brown, C. M., Lige, Q. M., & Lanaway, D. A. (2015). Impostorism is associated with greater psychological distress and lower self-esteem for African American students. *Current Psychology, 34*(1), 154–163. https://doi.org/10.1007/s12144-014-9248-z

Peteet, B. J., Montgomery, L., & Weekes, J. C. (2015). Predictors of imposter phenomenon among talented ethnic minority undergraduate students. *The Journal of Negro Education, 84*(2), 175–186. https://doi.org/10.7709/jnegroeducation.84.2.0175

Playforth, K. (2021). Impostor syndrome. In P. M. Garrett & K. Yoon-Flannery (Eds.), *A pediatrician's path* (pp. 219–225). Springer. https://doi.org/10.1007/978-3-030-75370-2_33

Posselt, J. (2018a). Normalizing struggle: Dimensions of faculty support for doctoral students and implications for persistence and well-being. *The Journal of Higher Education, 89*(6), 988–1013. https://doi.org/10.1080/00221546.2018.1449080

Posselt, J. R. (2018b). Rigor and support in racialized learning environments: The case of graduate education. *New Directions for Higher Education, 2018*(181), 59–70. https://doi.org/10.1002/he.20271

Rad, H. S., Samadi, S., Sirois, F. M., & Goodarzi, H. (2023). Mindfulness intervention for academic procrastination: A randomized control trial. *Learning and Individual Differences, 101*, Article 102244. https://doi.org/10.1016/j.lindif.2022.102244

Richardson, C. M., Trusty, W. T., & George, K. A. (2020). Trainee wellness: Self-critical perfectionism, self-compassion, depression, and burnout among doctoral trainees in psychology. *Counselling Psychology Quarterly, 33*(2), 187–198. https://doi.org/10.1080/09515070.2018.1509839

Rosenthal, S., Schlussel, Y., Yaden, M., DeSantis, J., Trayes, K., Pohl, C., & Hojat, M. (2021). Persistent impostor phenomenon is associated with distress in medical students. *Family Medicine, 53*(2), 118–122. https://doi.org/10.22454/FamMed.2021.799997

Rosenzweig, S., Reibel, D. K., Greeson, J. M., Brainard, G. C., & Hojat, M. (2003). Mindfulness-based stress reduction lowers psychological distress in medical students. *Teaching and Learning in Medicine, 15*(2), 88–92. https://doi.org/10.1207/S15328015TLM1502_03

Rusk, R. D., Vella-Brodrick, D. A., & Waters, L. (2018). A complex dynamic systems approach to lasting positive change: The synergistic change model. *The Journal of Positive Psychology, 13*(4), 406–418. https://doi.org/10.1080/17439760.2017.1291853

Sattler, B., Carberry, A., & Thomas, L. D. (2012). Peer mentoring: Linking the value of a reflective activity to graduate student development. In *2012 Frontiers in Education Conference Proceedings* (pp. 1–6). IEEE. https://doi.org/10.1109/FIE.2012.6462332

Schubert, N., & Bowker, A. (2019). Examining the impostor phenomenon in relation to self-esteem level and self-esteem instability. *Current Psychology, 38*(3), 749–755. https://doi.org/10.1007/s12144-017-9650-4

Schwartz, S. E. O., Kanchewa, S. S., Rhodes, J. E., Gowdy, G., Stark, A. M., Horn, J. P., Parnes, M., & Spencer, R. (2018). "I'm having a little struggle with this, can you help me out?": Examining impacts and processes of a social capital intervention for first-generation college students. *American Journal of Community Psychology, 61*(1–2), 166–178. https://doi.org/10.1002/ajcp.12206

Smeets, E., Neff, K., Alberts, H., & Peters, M. (2014). Meeting suffering with kindness: Effects of a brief self-compassion intervention for female college students. *Journal of Clinical Psychology, 70*(9), 794–807. https://doi.org/10.1002/jclp.22076

Stone, S., Saucer, C., Bailey, M., Garba, R., Hurst, A., Jackson, S. M., Krueger, N., & Cokley, K. (2018). Learning while Black: A culturally informed model of the impostor phenomenon for Black graduate students. *The Journal of Black Psychology, 44*(6), 491–531. https://doi.org/10.1177/0095798418786648

Suh, H., Sohn, H., Kim, T., & Lee, D. G. (2019). A review and meta-analysis of perfectionism interventions: Comparing face-to-face with online modalities. *Journal of Counseling Psychology, 66*(4), 473–486. https://doi.org/10.1037/cou0000355

Tewfik, B. A. (2022). The impostor phenomenon revisited: Examining the relationship between workplace impostor thoughts and interpersonal effectiveness at work. *Academy of Management Journal, 65*(3), 988–1018. https://doi.org/10.5465/amj.2020.1627

Thompson, T., Foreman, P., & Martin, F. (2000). Impostor fears and perfectionistic concern over mistakes. *Personality and Individual Differences, 29*(4), 629–647. https://doi.org/10.1016/S0191-8869(99)00218-4

Tigranyan, S., Byington, D. R., Liupakorn, D., Hicks, A., Lombardi, S., Mathis, M., & Rodolfa, E. (2021). Factors related to the impostor phenomenon in psychology doctoral students. *Training and Education in Professional Psychology, 15*(4), 298–305. https://doi.org/10.1037/tep0000321

Vaughn, A. R., Taasoobshirazi, G., & Johnson, M. L. (2020). Impostor phenomenon and motivation: Women in higher education. *Studies in Higher Education, 45*(4), 780–795. https://doi.org/10.1080/03075079.2019.1568976

Villwock, J. A., Sobin, L. B., Koester, L. A., & Harris, T. M. (2016). Impostor syndrome and burnout among American medical students: A pilot study. *International Journal of Medical Education, 7*, 364–369. https://doi.org/10.5116/ijme.5801.eac4

Wang, K. T., Sheveleva, M. S., & Permyakova, T. M. (2019). Imposter syndrome among Russian students: The link between perfectionism and psychological distress. *Personality and Individual Differences, 143*, 1–6. https://doi.org/10.1016/j.paid.2019.02.005

Ward, E. G., Thomas, E. E., Disch, W. B., & West Hartford, C. T. (2010). Goal attainment, retention, and peer mentoring. *Academic Exchange Quarterly, 14*(2), 170–176.

Wei, M., Liu, S., Ko, S. Y., Wang, C., & Du, Y. (2020). Impostor feelings and psychological distress among Asian Americans: Interpersonal shame and self-compassion. *The Counseling Psychologist, 48*(3), 432–458. https://doi.org/10.1177/0011000019891992

Wimberley, T. E., Mintz, L. B., & Suh, H. (2016). Perfectionism and mindfulness: Effectiveness of a bibliotherapy intervention. *Mindfulness, 7*, 433–444. https://doi.org/10.1007/s12671-015-0460-1

Wingert, J. R., Jones, J. C., Swoap, R. A., & Wingert, H. M. (2022). Mindfulness-based strengths practice improves well-being and retention in undergraduates: A preliminary randomized controlled trial. *Journal of American College Health, 70*(3), 783–790. https://doi.org/10.1080/07448481.2020.1764005

Young, V. (2017). *Thinking your way out of imposter syndrome* [Video]. TEDNYC Idea Search 2017. https://youtu.be/h7v-GG3SEWQ

Zanchetta, M., Junker, S., Wolf, A. M., & Traut-Mattausch, E. (2020). "Overcoming the fear that haunts your success": The effectiveness of interventions for reducing the impostor phenomenon. *Frontiers in Psychology, 11*, Article 405. https://doi.org/10.3389/fpsyg.2020.00405

15

TRENDS WITHIN THE IMPOSTOR PHENOMENON LITERATURE

STEVEN STONE-SABALI

The impostor phenomenon (IP) was conceived over 4 decades ago and is becoming an increasingly popular topic. Roughly 150 to 200 internet articles about IP or the impostor syndrome are published monthly (Bravata et al., 2020). Everyday conversations include someone mentioning their experience with impostor syndrome or feeling like a fraud. Millions have viewed viral TikTok videos of people discussing their experiences with IP (e.g., Sarfo, 2021). IP even appears in popular magazines that target various demographic segments of society, including *Women's Health*, *Men's Health*, *Essence Magazine*, *Black Enterprise*, *Asian Wealth Magazine*, *Gay Times*, *BeLatina*, *Time Magazine*, *Cosmopolitan*, and *People Magazine*.

Though the growing public acknowledgment and acceptance of IP as a common experience is relatively recent, empirical research and scholarly discourse about IP date back to 1978. This multidecade body of scholarship has experienced notable turning points and developments that are important for understanding the history and future trajectory of IP scholarship. However, documenting these broader trends within IP scholarship has received relatively less attention, as only a few systematic reviews of IP scholarship exist.

Paraphrasing Zupic and Čater (2015), synthesizing a scholarly body of literature and illuminating its latent trends are important tasks for advancing a

https://doi.org/10.1037/0000397-016
The Impostor Phenomenon: Psychological Research, Theory, and Interventions,
K. Cokley (Editor)
Copyright © 2024 by the American Psychological Association. All rights reserved.

topic of interest, reducing intellectual redundancy, and aiding a field's progression (Mukherjee et al., 2022). Moreover, systematically reviewing and analyzing trends within a body of literature can produce findings that allow scholars to expand and build on prior scholarship. On the other hand, failing to document the structures and contours of a body of scholarship can result in missed opportunities for research collaborations, overlook notable areas of scholarship and research trends, and hinder the advancement of IP's scientific trajectory and research impact. Thus, understanding the trends within IP scholarship may help scholars (a) contextualize and organize foundational IP literature, (b) navigate and reconcile historical tensions in the field, (c) illuminate current research trends and existing gaps, and (d) identify opportunities for collaboration and innovation.

To this end, the current chapter provides an overview of the publication and topical trends within the IP literature. A brief review of systematic reviews and bibliometric analyses is provided. Next, the chapter summarizes a bibliometric investigation of the IP literature and showcases its findings, such as the latent publication patterns (e.g., most cited authors, most cited articles) and topical trends (knowledge clusters) within the IP literature. The chapter concludes with a summary and implications for future directions.

SYSTEMATIC REVIEW AND BIBLIOMETRIC ANALYSIS

A *systematic review* is a form of research synthesis that describes the methodologies used to query, evaluate, and synthesize a body of literature. Reviewing literature in a systematic manner is particularly useful in consolidating and interpreting findings and trends from the whole range of independently conducted studies, not just the results from a handful of studies. By using an organized approach and explicating the research methodology, systematic reviews allow scholars to make sense of aggregate findings or trends, reproduce and verify other scholars' work, and improve the reliability and validity of prior investigative conclusions.

Bibliometric analysis (e.g., performance analysis and science mapping) is a specific type of systematic review that applies quantitative and statistical approaches to bibliographic data, such as citation patterns and the number of publications (Mukherjee et al., 2022). Bibliometrics includes essential techniques for evaluating academic research output (Cobo et al., 2015) and uncovering the genesis and trajectory of a body of scholarship (Hérubel, 1999). For example, bibliometrics allows scholars to statistically identify relevant authors in a particular field, geographical regions involved in the production of scholarship, highly cited articles of a specific field, and latent topical patterns or knowledge clusters that represent predominant schools of thought and intellectual focus. Other review techniques exist, such as content analysis, but tend to utilize qualitative discernment to synthesize the literature. In contrast, bibliometrics contributes to scientific knowledge by providing a quantitative and relatively objective understanding of publishing patterns and trends of scholarly activity for a given subject area (Donthu et al., 2021; Ellegaard & Wallin, 2015; Koskinen et al., 2008).

In a recent study by Stone-Sabali and colleagues (2023), bibliometric analyses were employed on a set of IP literature to understand the trends in IP literature. Three databases (Web of Science, Scopus, and PsycInfo) were used to locate peer-reviewed IP journal articles published before January 17, 2022. Search terms entered into the databases included common terms associated with IP, including "impostor phenomenon," "imposter phenomenon," "impostor syndrome," "imposter syndrome," "impostorism," "imposterism," and "perceived fraudulence." The database search returned 978 documents. After removing duplicates, irrelevant articles (i.e., articles that did not relate to the IP construct), and documents that were not peer-reviewed, the final data set consisted of 399 articles. An analysis of the bibliometric indicators followed and revealed publishing patterns and knowledge clusters (i.e., trends) within the IP literature. A summary of the findings is covered next as well as an expanded discussion of the topical trends.

PUBLISHING PATTERNS WITHIN THE IMPOSTOR PHENOMENON LITERATURE

Performance analysis was used to identify publishing patterns within the IP literature (Cobo et al., 2015). Broadly, this type of analysis uses performance indicators to identify notable pillars within a body of knowledge, including the number of citations, the most cited authors, the geographic distribution of papers, and the most relevant journal publications.

Impostor Phenomenon Citations

The data set of IP peer-reviewed journal articles has amassed more than 21,700 citations over 4 decades. In addition, it maintains an average of approximately 55 citations per article and has an h-index (a measure of scholarly footprint and impact) of 75 (Hirsch, 2005). The 10 most cited articles (see Table 15.1) have received approximately 7,400 citations, representing roughly one third (34%) of all citations.

344 • *Steven Stone-Sabali*

TABLE 15.1. Most Cited Impostor Phenomenon Articles

Article	Number of citations
Clance & Imes (1978)	2,304
Solorzano & Yosso (2001)	1,487
Henning, Ey, & Shaw (1998)	612
Clance & O'Toole (1987)	585
Striegel-Moore, Silberstein, & Rodin (1993)	389
Cokley, McClain, Enciso, & Martinez (2013)	361
Langford & Clance (1993)	353
Reis (1987)	351
Chrisman, Pieper, Clance, Holland, & Glickauf-Hughes (1995)	345
Sakulku & Alexander (2011)	281

Note. From "Mapping the Evolution of the Impostor Phenomenon Research: A Bibliometric Analysis," by S. Stone-Sabali, D. L. Bernard, K. J. Mills, and P. R. Osborn, 2023, *Current Psychology*, p. 7 (https://doi.org/10.1007/s12144-022-04201-9). Copyright 2023 by Springer Nature. Reprinted with permission.

Impostor Phenomenon Authors

Thousands of authors have contributed to the IP literature. The metric of number of authorship credits received can be used to identify the most relevant IP authors. Authorship credit is received whenever a scholar contributes to a published article, and first-author positions are assumed to reflect the lead author and superior authorship status. Across any authorship position (i.e., first author to the last author), there were 1,158 total author entries. Excluding duplicates, 1,019 unique authors contributed to IP scholarship.

Authors with the most authorship credit across any position (i.e., first author to the last author) include Chakraverty ($n = 7$ articles; Washington State University), Cokley ($n = 7$ articles; University of Michigan), Clance ($n = 6$ articles; Georgia State University), and Bernard ($n = 5$ articles; University of Missouri). Six authors were tied with four author positions: Neureiter (University of Salzburg), Hutchins (University of North Texas), Stone (Ohio State University), Traut-Mattausch (University of Salzburg), Hurst (Lanehurst Psychological Services), and Jackson (University of Wisconsin, Eau Claire).[1]

In the first-author position only, 357 nonduplicate authors contributed to IP articles, including Chakraverty ($n = 6$ articles), Bernard ($n = 4$ articles), Cokley ($n = 4$ articles), Hutchins ($n = 4$ articles), Clance ($n = 3$ articles),

---

[1]Note, Mirjam Neureiter is now recognized as Mirjam Zanchetta; Steven Stone is now recognized as Steven Stone-Sabali, and Ashley Hurst is now recognized as Ashley Lanehurst.

Neureiter ($n = 3$ articles), Brauer ($n = 3$ articles; Martin Luther University Halle-Wittenberg), and Yaffe ($n = 3$ articles; Tel-Hai Academic College).

Geographic Location of Publication

Identifying the geographic location of publications is a way to measure the dispersion of a topic and can be viewed as a proxy of a topic's popularity and expansion. Scholars with first-author positions were located across 41 countries. The top five countries with the most published articles accounted for approximately 80% of all articles. The majority of articles (63.1% or 252) were published in the United States, followed by the United Kingdom ($n = 27$ or 6.7%), Canada ($n = 16$ or 4.0%), Australia ($n = 14$ or 3.5%), Germany ($n = 11$ or 2.7%), India ($n = 8$ or 2.0%), Israel ($n = 8$ or 2.0%), Austria ($n = 6$ or 1.5%), and Brazil ($n = 4$ or 1.0%). A handful of countries published three articles each, including Scotland, Spain, Singapore, and France. Several countries published two articles each, including Saudi Arabia, Romania, Russia, Pakistan, the Netherlands, and Italy. More than half of all countries ($n = 22$ or 53.6%) published one IP article and collectively represented 5.4% of all documents. These countries included Wales, Scotland, Northern Ireland, Thailand, Switzerland, Sri Lanka, South Africa, Serbia, Poland, Peru, Nova Scotia, Nepal, Malaysia, Kazakhstan, Japan, Israel, Ireland, Grenada, Greece, Finland, Belgium, and Bangladesh.

Journal Publications

Examining the journals that published an IP article can be viewed as a proxy for its popularity and scholarly interests. In total, 277 scholarly journals published IP articles. The journals with the most IP articles include *Personality and Individual Differences* ($n = 18$), *Frontiers in Psychology* ($n = 13$), and *Current Psychology* ($n = 8$). Two journals published seven articles, including the *International Journal of Doctoral Studies* ($n = 7$) and the *Journal of Personality Assessment* ($n = 7$). Six articles were published in the *Medical Education* journal. A significant number of journals (79.7% or 221) published a single IP article, which accounted for approximately 55% of all IP articles.

KNOWLEDGE CLUSTERS AND TOPICAL TRENDS

The bibliometric technique of science mapping was used to identify latent knowledge clusters and topical trends within the IP literature. A coword or co-occurrence of terms method (i.e., an established algorithmic approach that uses an equivalence index and clustering) was used to reveal topical connections within a data corpus (Callon et al., 1991). A tab-delimited file containing each article's title and abstract was created and imported into VOSviewer, a text-mining tool (Van Eck & Waltman, 2010). Then, the following clustering criteria were selected to create a list of terms: title and abstract, full counting of all term occurrences, and a minimum of 10 occurrences per term, resulting in 250 terms. From there, VOSviewer's default setting was to select the most relevant terms ($n = 150$) by identifying all terms in the 60th percentile. VOSviewer then gave each term a relevance score, and terms with a relevance score of one or greater were retained for the subsequent cluster analysis. Next, VOSviewer mapped and visualized the co-occurrence of terms within the titles and abstracts of all documents. Five knowledge clusters or trends emerged and can be found in a map of connecting nodes in Figure 15.1. Cluster membership is indicated by a box surrounding the corresponding nodes. Further, the proximity of a node indicates its degree of relatedness to other terms and clusters. A discussion of the five clusters follows.

Cluster One: Initial Construct and Scale Development

Cluster One (the bottom left cluster) represented the early development of the IP construct, possible gender effects, and the psychometric development of the Clance Impostor Phenomenon Scale (CIPS; Chrisman et al., 1995). This period of IP literature was foundational to subsequent scholarship, given that it included Clance and Imes's (1978) original conceptualization of the construct.

FIGURE 15.1. Analysis of Common Terms

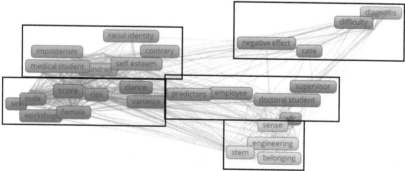

Note. cips = Clance Impostor Phenomenon Scale; wfc = work-family conflict; stem = science, technology, engineering, and mathematics. From "Mapping the Evolution of the Impostor Phenomenon Research: A Bibliometric Analysis," by S. Stone-Sabali, D. L. Bernard, K. J. Mills, and P. R. Osborn, 2023, *Current Psychology*, p. 8 (https://doi.org/10.1007/s12144-022-04201-9). Copyright 2023 by Springer Nature. Reprinted with permission.

According to Clance and Imes, "women who experience the impostor phenomenon maintain a strong belief that they are not intelligent . . . and they are convinced that they have fooled anyone who thinks otherwise" (p. 241). For instance, women graduate students strongly believed their high academic marks were due to luck, incorrect grading, or poor judgment by their professors. In addition, professional women (e.g., faculty members) who experienced IP believed they were unqualified to be in academia and that their colleagues overestimated their abilities.

Because Clance and Imes's (1978) conceptualization of IP was based on their clinical and teaching experiences with high-achieving women (i.e., professionals, college students), they reasoned that IP was experienced more frequently and more intensely among women than men. The notion that gender influenced the development of IP encouraged a swath of subsequent research examining gender differences. In a systematic review of IP research, Bravata and colleagues (2020) found 33 studies examining gender differences. Approximately half of the studies found that women reported higher levels of IP than men (e.g., Cokley et al., 2015), and half of the studies (e.g., Fried-Buchalter, 1997) found that men and women reported IP equally (i.e., no gender differences). Thus, evidence to support the notion that IP was more common for women than men was equivocal.

A final pillar in this initial wave of IP research included different attempts to design and psychometrically validate IP scales. Harvey's (1981) unpublished doctoral dissertation included the first IP scale, the 14-item Harvey Impostor Phenomenon Scale. This scale's suboptimal reliability was less than ideal (Harvey, 1981) and therefore inspired the development of the 20-item CIPS (Clance, 1985). The CIPS (Clance, 1985) assumed the IP experience included three subthemes: (a) feeling that one was an intellectual phony (Fake), (b) believing that one's success was due to luck (Luck), and (c) diminishing one's contributions to their success (Discount). Around the same time, Kolligian and Sternberg (1991) published a 51-item Perceived Fraudulence Scale (PFS) that represented an alternative conceptualization of IP that was primarily characterized by the experience of feeling fraudulent and unworthy of success. Thus, two competing scales existed.

Chrisman and colleagues (1995) published a pivotal psychometric investigation and comparison between the CIPS and PFS that examined the competing scales and resultantly shaped how IP would be measured for years to come. First, the PFS and the CIPS were found to be highly correlated and conceptually related, despite their differing conceptualizations (Chrisman et al., 1995). Second, the authors reported empirical evidence to support the existence of the three subscales (Fake, Luck, and Discount). Third, the CIPS used half as many items as the PFS (20 items vs. 51 items), which made using the CIPS more ideal and efficient. As a result, the CIPS became the most widely used scale to measure IP.

Despite the popularity of the CIPS, there are valid concerns regarding its true factor structure and item composition, particularly related to how prior scale validation studies inconsistently approached psychometric validation (cf. Brauer & Wolf, 2016; Chrisman et al., 1995; French et al., 2008; Kertay et al., 1992). In some instances, researchers have deleted two items prior to analyzing the factor structure, and in other instances, researchers have deleted four items. Further, the items selected for deletion have varied across studies. As a result, past findings offered mixed conclusions. That is, empirical support existed for a three-factor model (Brauer & Wolf, 2016; Chrisman et al., 1995; Kertay et al., 1992) and a theoretically inconsistent two-factor model (French et al., 2008). Ultimately, scholars were encouraged to use a total scale score due to concerns about factor instability (French et al., 2008).

Subsequent scale development efforts also examined the features and factor structure of IP. Leary and coresearchers (2000) noted that the CIPS included correlates of IP (e.g., worry) instead of core features (e.g., inauthenticity). This inspired them to create an ad hoc unidimensional seven-item IP scale. More recently, Ibrahim and colleagues (2022) advanced the debate surrounding the dimensionality of IP (i.e., unidimensional vs. multidimensional; e.g., Luck, Fake, Discount). Specifically, they validated the 31-item Impostor Phenomenon Profiler, a multidimensional measure of IP across six scales: Competence Doubt, Working Style, Alienation, Other-Self Divergence, Frugality, and Need for Sympathy. In summary, scale development for IP represents a significant area of scholarly attention that continues to develop as the field searches for a gold standard to measure IP (Mak et al., 2019).

Cluster Two: Contextual Stressors and Identities

Cluster Two (the top left cluster) captured IP's relationship to medical students, self-esteem, and racial identity. Given the educational and professional contexts for medical professionals and students (e.g., frequent evaluations, memorization of large amounts of information, peer competitiveness, pressure to be seen as experts), it is not surprising that this demographic group experiences significant stressors and psychological vulnerabilities, such as IP. Henning and colleagues' (1998) article was perhaps the first to consider IP among medical students and is the third most cited impostor article. Their study examined how perfectionism and IP impacted medical students' well-being. Unexpectedly, Henning and colleagues (1998) found that perfectionism levels were relatively normal compared with the wider population. On the other hand, scores for IP were significantly elevated among medical students (Henning et al., 1998) and were the strongest predictor of distress among the entire sample and across specific disciplines (e.g., dental, pharmacy, medical, nursing). Arguably, these groundbreaking findings thrust IP into the limelight within the medical profession and led to important subsequent findings. For instance, Thomas and Bigatti's (2020) systematic literature reported a high prevalence (e.g., > 50%) of IP among medical students and professionals and a robust relationship between poor mental health and IP. Moreover, Brennan-Wydra and colleagues' (2021) investigation found an association between IP and suicidal ideation among medical students.

Similarly, IP's relation to racial identity (one's attitudes about race and racial group) was shaped by the acknowledgment that Black college students experienced significant contextual stressors, such as racial isolation, racism, pressure to prove their character and academic merit, and pressure from being the first in their family to attend college or graduate school. Ewing and colleagues (1996) were among the first to explore these interrelations and found that racial identity predicted IP when one's academic self-concept was considered. Later research revealed that specific types of racial identities were associated with higher and lower levels of IP (Bernard et al., 2018) and that mental health was dependent on racial identity (via ethnic identity) more than IP (McClain et al., 2016). Together, the findings indicated that racial identity was an important factor when considering IP among African Americans. In addition, these prior studies reflected the broader trend of examining how IP intersected with marginalized groups and birthed a new area of IP scholarship. This includes how IP was more harmful to the well-being of college students of color than discrimination (Cokley et al., 2013), exacerbated the negative effects of discrimination (Bernard et al., 2017; Cokley et al., 2017), and was related to culturally salient factors for African American students (e.g., negative academic expectations, racial isolation; Bernard & Neblett, 2018; Stone et al., 2018).

Cluster Three: Careers and Professional Settings

Cluster Three (the center right cluster) contains terms such as doctoral students, employees, supervisors, and work–family conflict (WFC) theory. Thus, it is reasonable to presume that this cluster reflects the relationships between IP, career transition, and workplace professionals and settings. This trend echoes Bravata and colleagues' (2020) systematic review that highlighted a robust relationship between IP and job burnout, decreased job satisfaction, and reduced job performance. In retrospect, investigations of workplace impostor tendencies were expected, given that conceptualizations of IP were partially derived from the experiences of working professionals (Clance & Imes, 1978). Yet a sizable amount of IP literature has solely focused on student populations (Bravata et al., 2020) and omitted the experiences of working professionals. A focus on working professionals perhaps became more apparent following the Great Recession of 2008, which likely increased pressure for professionals to justify their employment and maintain job security by demonstrating superior workplace performance (Vergauwe et al., 2015). Given the current worrisome economic climate (e.g., historic inflation, central bank interest rate increases) and looming concerns of another global recession, an understanding of IP in the workplace may be particularly relevant.

Thus, scholars became curious about how fears of being exposed as a phony and the inability to internalize success (i.e., IP) were associated with stress and burnout in the workplace (Maslach & Leiter, 2014). In one of the first investigations, Vergauwe and colleagues (2015) revealed intriguing connections between IP and workplace outcomes. First, the researchers reported that higher IP scores were related to decreases in job satisfaction, a popular study variable given its connection to employee well-being (Faragher et al., 2005) and performance (Judge et al., 2001). Second, increased impostor scores were associated with decreases in ideal workplace behaviors (i.e., altruism, conscientiousness, civic virtue, courtesy, and sportsmanship; Vergauwe et al., 2015). Third, employees with higher impostor tendencies were less likely to leave their workplace for another organization (Vergauwe et al., 2015). In summary, IP was associated with decreased workplace satisfaction, but individuals with high impostorism were more likely to remain at their respective workplaces.

Subsequent research continued examining IP's connection to work and further illuminated associations to work- and career-related variables. This included negative associations between IP and how one perceived their professional success, their beliefs of having professional value, salary, and promotions (Neureiter & Traut-Mattausch, 2016). Furthermore, impostor tendencies were related to different career outcomes for students versus working professionals. On the one hand, students reported a stronger negative association between IP and career planning and striving. In contrast, impostor tendencies in working professionals had stronger negative associations with motivation for leadership positions (Neureiter & Traut-Mattausch, 2016).

Beyond negative career outcomes, IP was linked to detrimental effects on working professionals' personal lives. Indeed, multiple studies (e.g., Crawford et al., 2016) have used WFC to conceptualize experiencing IP in the workplace. WFC hypothesizes that workplace pressures may spill over and interfere with one's family roles. Supporting evidence was found by Crawford and colleagues

(2016), who reported that increased impostor tendencies related to increased emotional exhaustion, which was associated with a decreased ability to participate in family roles.

Examining IP in the work context has also contributed to promising findings for the larger field of IP scholarship. Several studies have reported significant mediational pathways that suggest other variables mitigate the negative impact of IP. For instance, individual dispositions and attributes (e.g., optimism, adaptability, knowledge of job markets) may mediate IP's relationship with career/job satisfaction and how one perceives their success or professional value. Perceived workplace social support was another mediating variable for the negative effects of IP (Crawford et al., 2016; Vergauwe et al., 2015), suggesting that contextual factors (not just individual traits) should be considered when examining impostor tendencies in the workplace. The culmination of mediational investigations was one of the first rigorous IP interventions. Specifically, Zanchetta and colleagues (2020) provided coaching to employees to address fears of negative evaluations and reported that the coaching program significantly reduced IP scores.

Cluster Four: STEM and Sense of Belonging

Cluster Four (the bottom right cluster) represented IP's relationship with one's sense of belonging and science, technology, engineering, and mathematics (STEM). IP and sense of belonging appear to have conceptual overlap. Key features of IP include believing that one's success is due to external factors (e.g., luck, leniency by others, aberrations) rather than internal attributes and believing that others will eventually discover their intellectual phoniness. Given this characterization, it is plausible to assume that individuals with impostor tendencies believe they are unqualified and do not belong in their respective workplaces or educational settings. Similarly, one's sense of belonging can be characterized as a person's perception of how much they are accepted and belong to a respective profession or academic discipline (Stachl & Baranger, 2020). A greater sense of belonging is associated with increased persistence, and a decreased sense of belonging (i.e., feeling like an outsider) is associated with changing disciplines (Aycock et al., 2019).

In STEM fields, individuals with an increased sense of belonging feel valued and respected by other community members and believe they are intellectually capable of fulfilling discipline-related roles and functions. White men constitute the majority in STEM fields, whereas individuals of color and women are often underrepresented, marginalized, or cast as outsiders. Several researchers recognize how these representational challenges in STEM fields may contribute to impostor tendencies and a decreased sense of belonging. Their work has resulted in important findings in STEM and the broader IP literature. Specifically, a notable theme throughout IP literature in the STEM field is how the social landscape or the environmental context, versus individual attributes, contributes to impostor feelings and decreased sense of belonging.

For example, Graham and McClain (2016) explicitly investigated sense of belonging and impostorism among Black college students. Their findings reported that students who felt more connected to the university tended to have higher belongingness scores while endorsing lower impostor feelings, concluding that the perceived social context for Black students relates to impostor tendencies. McGee and coresearchers (2019) interviewed Black STEM doctoral students and postdoctoral researchers. They suggested that the lack of Black faculty or the undiversified racial composition within academic departments contributed to or exacerbated impostor tendencies. Regarding women in STEM, increased impostor tendencies were associated with negative perceptions of the research training environment for women (Tao & Gloria, 2019). Furthermore, individuals with lower impostor feelings reported being more confident about completing their degree, and that feeling was strengthened as the numerical representation of women in a STEM program increased. Thus, a greater numerical representation of women in STEM weakened the effect of IP. Conversely, hostile and marginalizing environments toward women, via gender and sexual harassment, were associated with a decreased sense of belonging and increased impostor feelings for women in STEM (Aycock et al., 2019).

Finally, the work of Chakraverty added a layer of complexity to understanding impostor feelings among women and students of color (i.e., Black students) in STEM. Distinct themes emerged when investigating impostor experiences in White female students in STEM (Chakraverty, 2020b), compared with themes that emerged when investigating the impostor experiences in Black STEM students (Chakraverty, 2020a). For instance, impostor themes with White STEM female students included (a) progress and public recognition, (b) comparing oneself with others, (c) developing skills such as public speaking and scientific writing, (d) applying new knowledge, and (e) asking for help. Arguably, these themes represent expected or common worries among graduate students. On the other hand, impostor themes with Black STEM students reflected a racialized component, including (a) being the only Black student; (b) a lack of belonging; (c) stereotyping, microaggressions, and judgment; (d) worry about external appearances; (e) feeling like their achievements (e.g., graduate school admissions) were due to initiatives to enhance diversity and not their merit and intellect; and (f) complicated intersecting identities. The thematic divergences across the two groups ultimately reinforce notions that suggest racialized and environmental components influence the development and maintenance of IP (Stone et al., 2018).

Cluster Five: Conceptual and Diagnostic Challenges

Cluster Five (the top right cluster) has relatively less conceptual clarity than the other clusters. Salient terms within this cluster include phrases such as "difficulty" and "diagnosing," so it can be argued that the cluster reflects difficulties with conceptualizing or diagnosing IP. Multiple explanations may explain long-standing challenges with describing and categorizing IP. First, the wording used to describe feeling like a phony is inconsistently applied. That is, Clance and Imes (1978) coined the phrase "impostor phenomenon" and intentionally avoided using the term "impostor syndrome," due to concerns that the word "syndrome" ignored socially influenced causes of impostor tendencies (e.g., gender stereotypes, discrimination) and instead suggested women were the sole or primary cause (Kaplan, 2009). Yet the term "impostor syndrome" is routinely used on websites, blogs, and social media (i.e., lay literature). Second, though IP experience is commonly associated with distress and impairment (i.e., anxiety and depression), it does not represent a diagnosable set of symptoms or pervasive mental illness (Kolligian & Sternberg, 1991). For example, the current versions of the *Diagnostic and Statistical Manual of Mental Disorders* (American Psychiatric Association, 2013) and the *International Statistical Classification of Diseases and Related Health Problems* (World Health Organization, 2019) do not recognize IP as a clinical diagnosis. The result is uncertainty about classification. On the one hand, scholars and practitioners recognize that impostor tendencies are widely experienced phenomena associated with anxious and depressive symptoms. Conversely, IP is not a recognized medical category that scholars and health professionals can apply.

Third, theoretical explanations describing the origin of IP need to be further developed. Clance and Imes's (1978) original framework cited harmful gender and family-of-origin dynamics as causes of IP in women. However, a lack of evidence supporting impostor gender differences challenged those hypotheses. As a result, etiologies of IP via Clance and Imes's (1978) framework remained unclear, notwithstanding research that provided preliminary evidence of gender-related mechanisms, such as gender stigma consciousness (Cokley et al., 2015). Furthermore, the lack of theoretical clarity and difficulties conceptualizing IP likely relate to the measurement challenges mentioned in Cluster One. At best, evidence supporting the underlying dimensions of IP (e.g., Fake, Luck, Discount) is mixed. Multiple studies have found conflicting support for IP construct and dimensionality, including support for a one-factor, two-factor, three-factor, and six-factor model (Chrisman et al., 1995; French et al., 2008; Ibrahim et al., 2022; Leary et al., 2000). The contrasting findings imply that the IP construct is incompletely understood, which plausibly contributes to the conceptualization and diagnostic difficulties.

SUMMARY OF SYNTHESIS

This chapter discussed the latent publication and topical trends within the IP peer-reviewed literature. The publication trends indicate that IP is a widely popular and studied construct, as evidenced by increasing rates of publications and consumption in mainstream society. Over 1,000 scholars have written about IP experiences across 277 scholarly outlets. In addition, IP has expanded from its geographic origins in the United States to include over 40 countries internationally. Topical trends within the IP literature identified five knowledge clusters or trends:

- the IP construct, gender effects, and scale development;
- IP's relationship to medical students and racial identity;
- relationships between IP and career-related outcomes;
- IP, STEM, and sense of belonging; and
- difficulty with diagnosing and understanding IP.

The benefits of understanding these trends within IP scholarship are two-fold. First, existing and emerging scholars can quickly orient themselves to salient topical trends within IP research, perhaps reducing intellectual redundancy and promoting efficient intellectual inquiry. Second, understanding prominent IP authors and highly cited articles can aid scholars in conceptualizing new investigations that can potentially expand the extant scholarship. For example, leading authors Chakraverty, Bernard, and Cokley's respective work reflects growing areas of IP research that captures the experiences of racially marginalized or underrepresented groups. Scholars interested in the intersection of the socioracial context (e.g., racially homogenous academic settings) and impostor tendencies can use their work as a foundation to inform novel investigations.

WHAT TRENDS ARE MISSING?

A by-product of identifying topical trends within IP scholarship is an indirect illumination of potentially underexplored areas, such as theoretical frameworks and interventions. Repeated calls have been made to encourage more impostor prevention and intervention-based research (e.g., Bravata et al., 2020). Important components for advancing prevention efforts are frameworks that explain the etiologies and causal factors of IP. However, this is an underdeveloped area. As mentioned previously, Clance and Imes's (1978) framework has limitations, given that empirical findings do not support gender differences. In addition, IP frameworks tend not to address culturally salient factors, which is misaligned with research suggesting the salience of racialization experiences (e.g., Bernard et al., 2018; Cokley et al., 2013; Ewing et al., 1996; McClain et al., 2016).

To date, only Bernard and Neblett's (2018) novel framework has attempted to address this gap in the literature and is therefore worth mentioning. By utilizing empirically salient variables, Bernard and Neblett created a framework that explained the development of IP in African American adolescents. The scholars submitted five factors that promote or hinder psychological adjustment and self-perceptions of competence, including (a) *stratifying social position variables* such as race, gender, and socioeconomic status; (b) *parenting variables* that may influence adolescents' perceptions of their competence; (c) *racial discrimination* that could undermine competence and belonging; (d) *environmental or contextual factors* such as the academic setting that could influence healthy identity development; and (e) *learner characteristics* such as Afro-coping strategies and racial identity. Though empirically established variables from independent studies were used to inform this framework, additional investigations examining the complete framework are needed to strengthen the model. Ultimately, the model is promising given that it provides a framework of IP development that includes culturally specific variables rather than solely relying on the experiences of White samples. This contribution to the extant literature is especially needed given research highlighting the destructive relationship between impostor tendencies and negative well-being outcomes for individuals of color (e.g., Cokley et al., 2013).

Beyond prevention initiatives, another sorely needed area of investigation is interventions for IP as only a handful of articles describing interventions exist. Heinrich (1997) and Haney and colleagues (2018) provided workshops to address impostor feelings among nursing professionals and students. Though quantitative data were not collected, the researchers utilized participant feedback and determined that interventions successfully addressed impostor thoughts and feelings. Cisco (2020) is one of the first investigations that implemented a traditional design to assess intervention effectiveness. In particular, the researcher examined the effectiveness of a nonrandom, treatment-control group intervention among graduate students. The intervention was a skills workshop that included four components, which (a) identified IP and its consequences, (b) reviewed disciplinary and academic literacy strategies, (c) taught participants to read academic journal articles, and (d) implemented literacy strategies to write literature reviews. As a result of the intervention, the researcher reported that IP scores were significantly reduced for participants in the treatment group.

Similarly, Hutchins and Flores's (2021) intervention applied principles of cognitive processing therapy to address IP cognitions among professionals. The intervention utilized multiple workshops to help participants address maladaptive thoughts and beliefs and develop skills for building adaptive thinking patterns. According to the findings, the intervention was associated with significantly decreased IP scores 3 months after the intervention. Lastly, Zanchetta and colleagues (2020) employed a rigorous randomly assigned coaching intervention to reduce impostor thoughts and feelings among young working professionals. According to the findings, the coaching intervention's emphasis on fears of negative evaluations significantly reduced IP scores postintervention.

FUTURE DIRECTIONS

The possible directions of future research on IP are endless. Categories of future research likely will span the areas of refinement and expansion. *Refinement* addresses limitations pertaining to the theoretical conceptualization and measurement of IP. As mentioned previously, the field will likely benefit from sound theoretical frameworks that account for precipitating and moderating factors. Moreover, such theories will need to capture contextual elements, including broad or universal factors and salient cultural experiences for marginalized groups. Scales that measure IP may need to be refined to disaggregate core IP experiences (e.g., feeling like a phony) from common correlates such as anxiety (Leary et al., 2000). Alternatively, new conceptualizations of IP could emerge. For instance, instead of differentiating anxiety from the IP construct, scholars may explore how IP is subsumed under the umbrella of anxiety disorders, as is the case with social anxiety, general anxiety, and specific phobias.

The *expansion* of future IP research will likely consist of efforts to further illuminate populations that experience IP and factors that agitate and mitigate the effects of IP. That is, researchers will continue to identify moderators and mediators of IP across various professions and age groups (e.g., minors, older adults). New connections extending beyond IP's relation to mental health and career outcomes will also emerge. Though more difficult to foresee, this shift may include identifying associations between IP and interpersonal outcomes such as parenting, social relationships, and romantic relationships. Lastly, given the current literature's focus on college students and professionals and IP's impact on mental health and career satisfaction, it would not be unreasonable to expect clinical intervention research to emerge that provides guidance for treatments in university counseling centers and across employee assistance programs.

CONCLUSION

IP was once an isolating experience that was reluctantly acknowledged. Individuals who felt like an impostor suffered in silence and worried that others would discover their secret of being unqualified and incompetent. Thanks to over 4 decades of scholarship, IP has emerged as a more acceptable topic within everyday discourse. Similarly, bringing the latent trends within the IP literature to the surface is equally important for advancing the field, as doing so allows scholars to connect to the salient contours and structures that shape the IP literature. As a result, the topography of the IP literature (i.e., salient publication and topical trends) presented in this chapter helps reduce intellectual redundancy and propel future avenues of intellectual exploration. Furthermore, the findings presented in this chapter can guide researchers toward investigating less salient trends as potential additive avenues of new research and scholarship.

REFERENCES

American Psychiatric Association. (2013). *Diagnostic and statistical manual of mental disorders* (5th ed.). https://doi.org/10.1176/appi.books.9780890425596

Aycock, L. M., Hazari, Z., Brewe, E., Clancy, K. B. H., Hodapp, T., & Goertzen, R. M. (2019). Sexual harassment reported by undergraduate female physicists. *Physical Review: Physics Education Research, 15*(1), Article 010121. https://doi.org/10.1103/PhysRevPhysEducRes.15.010121

Bernard, D. L., Hoggard, L. S., & Neblett, E. W. (2018). Racial discrimination, racial identity, and impostor phenomenon: A profile approach. *Cultural Diversity and Ethnic Minority Psychology, 24*(1), 51–61. https://doi.org/10.1037/cdp0000161

Bernard, D. L., Lige, Q. M., Willis, H. A., Sosoo, E. E., & Neblett, E. W. (2017). Impostor phenomenon and mental health: The influence of racial discrimination and gender. *Journal of Counseling Psychology, 64*(2), 155–166. https://doi.org/10.1037/cou0000197

Bernard, D., & Neblett, E. (2018). A culturally informed model of the development of the impostor phenomenon among African American youth. *Adolescent Research Review, 3*(3), 279–300. https://doi.org/10.1007/s40894-017-0073-0

Brauer, K., & Wolf, A. (2016). Validation of the German-language Clance Impostor Phenomenon Scale (GCIPS). *Personality and Individual Differences, 102*, 153–158. https://doi.org/10.1016/j.paid.2016.06.071

Bravata, D. M., Watts, S. A., Keefer, A. L., Madhusudhan, D. K., Taylor, K. T., Clark, D. M., Nelson, R. S., Cokley, K. O., & Hagg, H. K. (2020). Prevalence, predictors, and treatment of impostor syndrome: A systematic review. *Journal of General Internal Medicine, 35*(4), 1252–1275. https://doi.org/10.1007/s11606-019-05364-1

Brennan-Wydra, E., Chung, H. W., Angoff, N., ChenFeng, J., Phillips, A., Schreiber, J., Young, C., & Wilkins, K. (2021). Maladaptive perfectionism, impostor phenomenon, and suicidal ideation among medical students. *Academic Psychiatry, 45*(6), 708–715. https://doi.org/10.1007/s40596-021-01503-1

Callon, M., Courtial, J. P., & Laville, F. (1991). Co-word analysis as a tool for describing the network of interactions between basic and technological research: The case of polymer chemistry. *Scientometrics, 22*(1), 155–205. https://doi.org/10.1007/BF02019280

Chakraverty, D. (2020a). The impostor phenomenon among Black doctoral and post-doctoral scholars in STEM. *International Journal of Doctoral Studies, 15*, 433–460. https://doi.org/10.28945/4613

Chakraverty, D. (2020b). PhD student experiences with the impostor phenomenon in STEM. *International Journal of Doctoral Studies, 15*, 159–179. https://doi.org/10.28945/4513

Chrisman, S. M., Pieper, W. A., Clance, P. R., Holland, C. L., & Glickauf-Hughes, C. (1995). Validation of the Clance Impostor Phenomenon Scale. *Journal of Personality Assessment, 65*(3), 456–467. https://doi.org/10.1207/s15327752jpa6503_6

Cisco, J. (2020). Using academic skill set interventions to reduce impostor phenomenon feelings in postgraduate students. *Journal of Further and Higher Education, 44*(3), 423–437. https://doi.org/10.1080/0309877X.2018.1564023

Clance, P. R. (1985). *The impostor phenomenon: When success makes you feel like a fake.* Bantam Books.

Clance, P. R., & Imes, S. A. (1978). The imposter phenomenon in high achieving women: Dynamics and therapeutic intervention. *Psychotherapy: Theory, Research, & Practice, 15*(3), 241–247. https://doi.org/10.1037/h0086006

Clance, P. R., & O'Toole, M. A. (1987). The imposter phenomenon. *Women & Therapy, 6*(3), 51–64. https://doi.org/10.1300/J015V06N03_05

Cobo, M. J., Martínez, M. A., Gutiérrez-Salcedo, M., Fujita, H., & Herrera-Viedma, E. (2015). 25 years at knowledge-based systems: A bibliometric analysis. *Knowledge-Based Systems, 80*, 3–13. https://doi.org/10.1016/j.knosys.2014.12.035

Cokley, K., Awad, G., Smith, L., Jackson, S., Awosogba, O., Hurst, A., & Roberts, D. (2015). The roles of gender stigma consciousness, impostor phenomenon and academic self-concept in the academic outcomes of women and men. *Sex Roles, 73*, 414–426. https://doi.org/10.1007/s11199-015-0516-7

Cokley, K., McClain, S., Enciso, A., & Martinez, M. (2013). An examination of the impact of minority status stress and impostor feelings on the mental health of diverse ethnic minority college students. *Journal of Multicultural Counseling and Development, 41*(2), 82–95. https://doi.org/10.1002/j.2161-1912.2013.00029.x

Cokley, K., Smith, L., Bernard, D., Hurst, A., Jackson, S., Stone, S., Awosogba, O., Saucer, C., Bailey, M., & Roberts, D. (2017). Impostor feelings as a moderator and mediator of the relationship between perceived discrimination and mental health among racial/ethnic minority college students. *Journal of Counseling Psychology, 64*(2), 141–154. https://doi.org/10.1037/cou0000198

Crawford, W. S., Shanine, K. K., Whitman, M. V., & Kacmar, K. M. (2016). Examining the impostor phenomenon and work–family conflict. *Journal of Managerial Psychology, 31*(2), 375–390. https://doi.org/10.1108/JMP-12-2013-0409

Donthu, N., Kumar, S., Mukherjee, D., Pandey, N., & Lim, W. M. (2021). How to conduct a bibliometric analysis: An overview and guidelines. *Journal of Business Research, 133*, 285–296. https://doi.org/10.1016/j.jbusres.2021.04.070

Ellegaard, O., & Wallin, J. A. (2015). The bibliometric analysis of scholarly production: How great is the impact? *Scientometrics, 105*(3), 1809–1831. https://doi.org/10.1007/s11192-015-1645-z

Ewing, K. M., Richardson, T. Q., James-Myers, L., & Russell, R. K. (1996). The relationship between racial identity attitudes, worldview, and African American graduate students' experience of the imposter phenomenon. *The Journal of Black Psychology, 22*(1), 53–66. https://doi.org/10.1177/00957984960221005

Faragher, E. B., Cass, M., & Cooper, C. L. (2005). The relationship between job satisfaction and health: A meta-analysis. *Occupational and Environmental Medicine, 62*(2), 105–112. https://doi.org/10.1136/oem.2002.006734

French, B. F., Ullrich-French, S. C., & Follman, D. (2008). The psychometric properties of the Clance Impostor Scale. *Personality and Individual Differences, 44*(5), 1270–1278. https://doi.org/10.1016/j.paid.2007.11.023

Fried-Buchalter, S. (1997). Fear of success, fear of failure, and the imposter phenomenon among male and female marketing managers. *Sex Roles, 37*(11–12), 847–859. https://doi.org/10.1007/BF02936343

Graham, J., & McClain, S. (2019). A canonical correlational analysis examining the relationship between peer mentorship, belongingness, impostor feelings, and Black collegians' academic and psychosocial outcomes. *American Educational Research Journal, 56*(6), 2333–2367. https://doi.org/10.3102/0002831219842571

Haney, T. S., Birkholz, L., & Rutledge, C. (2018). A workshop for addressing the impact of the imposter syndrome on clinical nurse specialists. *Clinical Nurse Specialist, 32*(4), 189–194. https://doi.org/10.1097/NUR.0000000000000386

Harvey, J. C. (1981). *The impostor phenomenon and achievement: A failure to internalize success* [Unpublished doctoral dissertation]. Temple University.

Heinrich, K. T. (1997). Transforming impostors into heroes: Metaphors for innovative nursing education. *Nurse Educator, 22*(3), 45–50. https://doi.org/10.1097/00006223-199705000-00018

Henning, K., Ey, S., & Shaw, D. (1998). Perfectionism, the impostor phenomenon and psychological adjustment in medical, dental, nursing and pharmacy students. *Medical Education, 32*(5), 456–464. https://doi.org/10.1046/j.1365-2923.1998.00234.x

Hérubel, J. (1999). Historical bibliometrics: Its purpose and significance to the history of disciplines. *Libraries & Culture, 34*(4), 380–388. https://www.jstor.org/stable/25548766

Hirsch, J. E. (2005). An index to quantify an individual's scientific research output. *Proceedings of the National Academy of Sciences of the United States of America, 102*(46), 16569–16572. https://doi.org/10.1073/pnas.0507655102

Hutchins, H. M., & Flores, J. (2021). Don't believe everything you think: Applying a cognitive processing therapy intervention to disrupting imposter phenomenon. *New Horizons in Adult Education and Human Resource Development, 33*(4), 33–47. https://doi.org/10.1002/nha3.20325

Ibrahim, F., Münscher, J. C., & Herzberg, P. Y. (2022). The facets of an impostor— Development and validation of the impostor-profile (IPP31) for measuring impostor phenomenon. *Current Psychology, 41*(6), 3916–3927. https://doi.org/10.1007/s12144-020-00895-x

Judge, T. A., Thoresen, C. J., Bono, J. E., & Patton, G. K. (2001). The job satisfaction–job performance relationship: A qualitative and quantitative review. *Psychological Bulletin, 127*(3), 376–407. https://doi.org/10.1037/0033-2909.127.3.376

Kaplan, K. (2009). Unmasking the impostor. *Nature, 459*(7245), 468–469. https://doi.org/10.1038/nj7245-468a

Kertay, L., Clance, P. R., & Holland, C. L. (1992). *A factor study of the Clance Impostor Phenomenon Scale* [Unpublished manuscript]. Georgia State University.

Kolligian, J., Jr., & Sternberg, R. J. (1991). Perceived fraudulence in young adults: Is there an "imposter syndrome"? *Journal of Personality Assessment, 56*(2), 308–326. https://doi.org/10.1207/s15327752jpa5602_10

Koskinen, J., Isohanni, M., Paajala, H., Jääskeläinen, E., Nieminen, P., Koponen, H., Tienari, P., & Miettunen, J. (2008). How to use bibliometric methods in evaluation of scientific research? An example from Finnish schizophrenia research. *Nordic Journal of Psychiatry, 62*(2), 136–143. https://doi.org/10.1080/08039480801961667

Langford, J., & Clance, P. R. (1993). The imposter phenomenon: Recent research findings regarding dynamics, personality and family patterns and their implications for treatment. *Psychotherapy: Theory, Research, & Practice, 30*(3), 495–501. https://doi.org/10.1037/0033-3204.30.3.495

Leary, M. R., Patton, K. M., Orlando, A. E., & Funk, W. W. (2000). The imposter phenomenon: Self perceptions, reflected appraisals, and interpersonal strategies. *Journal of Personality, 68*(4), 725–756. https://doi.org/10.1111/1467-6494.00114

Mak, K., Kleitman, S., & Abbott, M. J. (2019). Impostor phenomenon measurement scales: A systematic review. *Frontiers in Psychology, 10*, Article 671. https://doi.org/10.3389/fpsyg.2019.00671

Maslach, C., & Leiter, M. P. (2014). Burnout in the workplace: A global problem in need of solution. In S. Cooper & K. Ratele (Eds.), *Psychology serving humanity: Proceedings of the 30th International Congress of Psychology* (pp. 116–127). Psychology Press.

McClain, S., Beasley, S. T., Jones, B., Awosogba, O., Jackson, S., & Cokley, K. (2016). An examination of the impact of racial and ethnic identity, impostor feelings, and minority status stress on the mental health of Black college students. *Journal of Multicultural Counseling and Development, 44*(2), 101–117. https://doi.org/10.1002/jmcd.12040

McGee, E. O., Griffith, D. M., & Houston, S. L., II. (2019). "I know I have to work twice as hard and hope that makes me good enough": Exploring the stress and strain of Black doctoral students in engineering and computing. *Teachers College Record, 121*(4), 1–38. https://doi.org/10.1177/016146811912100407

Mukherjee, D., Lim, W. M., Kumar, S., & Donthu, N. (2022). Guidelines for advancing theory and practice through bibliometric research. *Journal of Business Research, 148*, 101–115. https://doi.org/10.1016/j.jbusres.2022.04.042

Neureiter, M., & Traut-Mattausch, E. (2016). Inspecting the dangers of feeling like a fake: An empirical investigation of the impostor phenomenon in the world of work. *Frontiers in Psychology, 7*, Article 1445. https://doi.org/10.3389/fpsyg.2016.01445

Reis, S. M. (1987). We can't change what we don't recognize: Understanding the special needs of gifted females. *Gifted Child Quarterly, 31*(2), 83–89. https://doi.org/10.1177/001698628703100208

Sakulku, J., & Alexander, J. (2011). The impostor phenomenon. *International Journal of Behavioral Science, 6*(1), 73–92.

Sarfo, K. [@dr.kojosarfo]. (2021, April 29). good news, we can fix this ♀ #imposter-syndrome #imposter #confidence #insecurities #anxiety [Video]. TikTok. https://www.tiktok.com/@dr.kojosarfo/video/6956697059487517957

Solorzano, D. G., & Yosso, T. J. (2001). Critical race and LatCrit theory and method: Counter-storytelling. *International Journal of Qualitative Studies in Education, 14*(4), 471–495. https://doi.org/10.1080/09518390110063365

Stachl, C. N., & Baranger, A. M. (2020). Sense of belonging within the graduate community of a research-focused STEM department: Quantitative assessment using a visual narrative and item response theory. *PLOS ONE, 15*(5), Article e0233431. https://doi.org/10.1371/journal.pone.0233431

Stone, S., Saucer, C., Bailey, M., Garba, R., Hurst, A., Jackson, S. M., Krueger, N., & Cokley, K. (2018). Learning while Black: A culturally informed model of the impostor phenomenon for Black graduate students. *The Journal of Black Psychology, 44*(6), 491–531. https://doi.org/10.1177/0095798418786648

Stone-Sabali, S., Bernard, D. L., Mills, K. J., & Osborn, P. R. (2023). Mapping the evolution of the impostor phenomenon research: A bibliometric analysis. *Current Psychology*. Advance online publication. https://doi.org/10.1007/s12144-022-04201-9

Striegel-Moore, R. H., Silberstein, L. R., & Rodin, J. (1993). The social self in bulimia nervosa: Public self-consciousness, social anxiety, and perceived fraudulence. *Journal of Abnormal Psychology, 102*(2), 297–303. https://doi.org/10.1037/0021-843X.102.2.297

Tao, K. W., & Gloria, A. M. (2019). Should I stay or should I go? The role of impostorism in STEM persistence. *Psychology of Women Quarterly, 43*(2), 151–164. https://doi.org/10.1177/0361684318802333

Thomas, M., & Bigatti, S. (2020). Perfectionism, impostor phenomenon, and mental health in medicine: A literature review. *International Journal of Medical Education, 11*, 201–213. https://doi.org/10.5116/ijme.5f54.c8f8

van Eck, N. J., & Waltman, L. (2010). Software survey: VOSviewer, a computer program for bibliometric mapping. *Scientometrics, 84*, 523–538. https://doi.org/10.1007/s11192-009-0146-3

Vergauwe, J., Wille, B., Feys, M., De Fruyt, F., & Anseel, F. (2015). Fear of being exposed: The trait-relatedness of the impostor phenomenon and its relevance in the work context. *Journal of Business and Psychology, 30*(3), 565–581. https://doi.org/10.1007/s10869-014-9382-5

World Health Organization. (2019). *International statistical classification of diseases and related health problems* (11th ed.). https://icd.who.int/

Zanchetta, M., Junker, S., Wolf, A. M., & Traut-Mattausch, E. (2020). "Overcoming the fear that haunts your success"—The effectiveness of interventions for reducing the impostor phenomenon. *Frontiers in Psychology, 11,* Article 405. https://doi.org/10.3389/fpsyg.2020.00405

Zupic, I., & Čater, T. (2015). Bibliometric methods in management and organization. *Organizational Research Methods, 18*(3), 429–472. https://doi.org/10.1177/1094428114562629

Index

A

AAMC (Association of American Medical Colleges), 246
Absenteeism, 90
Academia
  faculty support and, 228
  harassment in, 235
  impostor phenomenon (IP) and, 204, 228
  stress and, 71
  women and minority faculty in, 228
  women and tenure-track positions at research institutions, 223
Academic achievement
  Black students and, 230
  gender gaps in, 223
  medical students and, 250
  perfectionism and, 122
  self-discipline and, 124
Academic faculty. *See* Faculty
Academic literacy, 320
Academic malfunctioning, 71
Academic outcomes and racial discrimination, 191
Academic performance, 164
Academic skills training, 320, 321
Academic survivors' guilt, 184, 188
Accomplishments. *See* Achievement

Achievement, 112–117
  academic and perfectionism, 122
  academic environment and, 112, 113–114
  anxiety and, 120
  fear of failure and, 121
  gender and, 113
  lab environment and, 115–116
  list of, 303
  mediators of, 118–124
  medical students and, 250
  mental health and, 118–120
  perfectionism and, 121, 122
  personality and, 121–122
  self-efficacy and, 122–123
  self-regulation and, 123–124
  shame and, 120
  workplace environment and, 112, 114–115
Adolescents and suicidal ideation, 63
Affiliation and women, 290
Affinity groups, 323–324
  African American students and, 323
  institutional support for, 324
  racial identity and, 323
Affirmative Action, 194
  candidates, 271

363

364 • *Index*

African Americans, 349
  depression and, 277
  impostor phenomenon (IP) and, 47, 52, 269, 355
  psychological distress and, 278
  racial identity and, 349
  self-esteem and, 278
  survivor's guilt and, 277
African American students
  acting White and, 191
  affinity groups and, 323
  anti-intellectual stereotypes of, 188–189
  anxiety and, 277
  belongingness and, 189, 352
  campus underrepresentation and, 189
  college completion rates of, 181
  college enrollment rates of, 181
  community-level risk factors and, 189–190
  coping strategies and, 192–193
  cultural misalignment and, 190
  depression and, 277
  in engineering and computing schools, 230
  first-generation status and, 192
  impostor phenomenon (IP) and, 182–183, 183–184, 194
  individual-level risk factors and, 192–193
  inequitable access to college, 187–188
  ingroup expectations and, 191
  John Henryism and, 193
  otherness and, 189
  outgroup expectations and, 190
  perceptions of intellectual incompetence and, 185
  perfectionism and, 193
  racial identity and, 184
  racism and, 181–182, 190–191, 231, 277
  relational-level risk factors and, 190–191
  in science, technology, engineering, and mathematics (STEM), 229–231, 234, 352
  self-compassion and, 318
  self-efficacy and, 230
  self-esteem and, 230
  societal-level risk factors, 187–189
  socioecological analysis of, 186–193
  vulnerability of, 183
Afro-coping strategies, 355
Aggressive communication, 95

Alcohol and sleep, 103
Amazon Mechanical Turk, 147
American Psychological Association (APA), 61
  anxiety, definition of, 70
  depression, definition of, 67
  mental health, definition of, 61
  self-esteem, definition of, 68
Analogy tests, 116
Anti-intellectual stereotypes, 188–189
ANTs (automatic negative thoughts), 276
Anxiety, 112, 118, 119, 274. *See also* State anxiety; Trait anxiety
  achievement and, 120
  African American college students and, 277
  Asian American college students and, 277
  burnout and, 98
  definition of, 70
  faculty and, 228
  forms of, 70
  historically marginalized individuals and, 274
  impostor phenomenon (IP) and, 70–71, 112, 118, 119, 295
  mental health and, 63
  perfectionism and, 71, 72
  performance, 94–95
  physician assistants and, 254
  school and work successes and, 120
  test, 119
Anxious overconcern, 72
APA. *See* American Psychological Association (APA)
Asian students
  anxiety and, 277
  depression and, 277
  discrimination and, 277
  in science, technology, engineering, and mathematics (STEM), 236
Asian Wealth Magazine, 341
Assertive communication, 95
  burnout prevention and, 100
  self-advocacy and, 100
Assertiveness, 96–97
Association of American Medical Colleges (AAMC), 246
Astronomy students, 227–228
  women, 227
Astrophysics students, 227
  women, 227

Automatic negative thoughts (ANTs), 276
Avoidance, 320

B

Beck Depression Inventory, 63
BeLatina, 341
Belongingness, 189, 192
  African American college students and, 352
  African American students and, 189
  confidence and, 296
  First-generation college students (FGCSs) and, 192
  historically marginalized individuals and, 270
  in science, technology, engineering, and mathematics (STEM), 235–236, 351–353
Bias, 229
  participation, 259
Bibliometric analysis, 342–343
Bifactor modeling, 146
  Clance Impostor Phenomenon Scale (CIPS) and, 147
Black Enterprise, 341
Black, Indigenous, or person of color (BIPOC)
  marginalization and, 88
  in science, technology, engineering, and mathematics (STEM), 221, 223–224, 229–231, 233–234, 352
  workplace violence and, 233
Black students. *See* African American students
Boundaries
  burnout prevention and, 100–101
  enforcing, 101
  flexible, 100–101
  self-advocacy and, 100
  self-preservation and, 96–97
  situation-dependent, 100
  work–life imbalance and, 97
Bragging backlash, 293
Bullying, 279
Burnout, 250, 274, 318, 349, 350. *See also* Burnout prevention
  anxiety and, 98
  assertiveness and, 96–97
  boundaries and, 96–97, 97
  career and, 99
  causes and cures of, 83

character strengths and, 87
chronic stress and, 83
core self-evaluations and, 86
cynicism and, 99
definition of, 83
depression and, 98
disengagement from work and, 83
effort–reward imbalance and, 91
emotional exhaustion and, 84
faculty and, 228
family upbringing and, 85
historically marginalized individuals and, 274
impostor phenomenon (IP) and, 83–84
indecision and, 86
insomnia and, 98
interventions for, 84
job–person fit and, 89
job role-related stress and, 89–90
marginalization and, 88
medical students and, 250
mental health and, 98
mental health professionals and, 255
micromanagement and, 90
mistakes and, 99
negative consequences of, 97–99
negative self-evaluation and, 83
perfectionism and, 85
personal relationships and, 98
physical health and, 97
physicians and, 253
prevention, 101–102
professional inefficacy and, 84
psychological safety and, 90–91
rejection sensitivity and, 94
residents and, 252–253
self-doubt and, 83, 98
signs of, 83, 105
stress and, 83, 94
workaholism and, 86
work–life imbalance and, 91–92
workplace, 89–91, 350
Burnout–impostor syndrome cycle, 106
Burnout prevention, 100–106
  assertive communication and, 100
  boundaries and, 100–101
  executive coaching and, 104
  learning and development for, 104
  personal time off and, 101–102
  person-centered resources for, 103–104

366 • *Index*

Burnout prevention (*continued*)
  recommendations for individuals,
    99–103
  recommendations for organizations,
    103–106
  self-advocacy and, 100–101
  self-care and, 101–103
  workplace culture and, 104–106

C

Campus underrepresentation, 189
Capgras syndrome, 55
Career aspirations, 165
Career outcomes, 350
Career resilience workshops, 236
Careers
  burnout and, 99
  crisis and, 83
  guidance and, 172
  historically marginalized individuals
    and, 278
  impostor phenomenon (IP) and, 99
  in science, technology, engineering, and
    mathematics (STEM), 165
Caregiving, 290
Catastrophizing, 276
CBT (cognitive behavioral therapy), 316
Center for Research on Women in Science,
  286
CFA (confirmatory factor analysis), 134
CFI (comparative fit indices), 134
Character strengths, 87
Chi-square test, 134
Chronic fear, 82
Chronic stress, 83, 97, 99, 101
  burnout and, 83
CIPS. *See* Clance Impostor Phenomenon
  Scale (CIPS); 6-item CIPS (CIPS-6);
  10-item CIPS (CIPS-10)
Clance Impostor Phenomenon Scale
  (CIPS), 68, 133, 134, 139–141, 206,
  208, 223, 237, 258, 316, 346. *See
  also* 6-item CIPS (CIPS-6); 10-item
  CIPS (CIPS-10)
  bifactor model of, 147
  construct validity and, 139–141
  cutoff scores and, 141
  dimensionality and, 141, 348
  efficiency of, 348
  Japanese version of, 150
  for medical fields, 247

  Perceived Fraudulence Scale (PFS) vs.,
    141, 347
  psychometric properties of with
    science, technology, engineering,
    and mathematics (STEM) samples,
    223–224
  reliability of, 139
  subscales of, 347
  10-item CIPS vs., 148
  three-factor model of, 140
  20-item CIPS, 347
Clance, Pauline, 45, 161
Class-based programs, 327
Classmate support, 163
Climate gendered traits, 167–169
Clinical interventions, 297. *See
  also* Interventions
  competence distortions and, 301–302
  impostor phenomenon (IP) and,
    302–303
Coaching interventions, 356
Cognitive behavioral therapy (CBT), 316
Cognitive distortion, 316
Cognitive process therapy, 316
College
  African American students completion
    rates, 181
  African American students enrollment
    rates, 181
  inequitable access to, 187–188
  prevalence of Impostor phenomenon
    (IP) at, 63, 311–312
  underrepresentation and, 189
Common humanity, 318
Communication
  aggressive, 95
  anxiety, 71, 72
  assertive, 95, 100
  passive, 95
  passive-aggressive, 95
  styles, 95
Community building as impostor
  phenomenon (IP) intervention, 271
Community-level risk factors, 189–190
Comparative fit indices (CFI), 134
Compassion fatigue, 251
  mental health professionals and, 255
Competence, 291, 304
  confidence and, 303
  development of, 320
  distortions, 301–302
  humble realists and, 302

impostor phenomenon (IP) and, 52
measurement of, 301–302
performance dimension and, 300–301
realistic understanding of, 303
reframing, 302
women and, 300–301
Confidence, 256
belongingness and, 296
competence and, 303
impostor phenomenon (IP) and, 206
performance dimension and, 300
women and, 300
Confirmatory factor analysis (CFA), 134
Confrontation, healthy, 96
Conscientiousness, 123, 320
Conservation of resources theory, 82
Constant demands, 82
Construct validity, 133–134
Clance Impostor Phenomenon Scale
(CIPS) and, 139–141
Harvey Impostor Phenomenon Scale
(HIPS) and, 138
Ibrahim's Impostor Phenomenon Profile
(IPP30) and, 146
Leary Impostor Phenomenon scale and,
144
Perceived Fraudulence Scale (PFS) and,
142–143
10-item CIPS and, 148
Content validity, 133
Contextualizing, 300
Continuous demands, 82
Convergent validity, 133
Coping skills interventions, 321
Coping strategies, 192–193. *See
also* Maladaptive coping; Strategies
African American students and, 192–193
Afro, 355
emotion-focused, 96
gender and, 277
John Henryism, 193
perfectionism, 192
stress and, 95–96
women and, 277
Core self-evaluations, 86–87
Cosmopolitan, 341
Council of Graduate Schools, 215
COVID-19, 209, 215
Creative fields, 299
Creativity and shame, 120
Criterion validity, 133
Criticism, 303

Cronbach's alpha, 133, 138
Cultural misalignment, 190
Current Psychology, 345
Curricula (hidden), 325–326
Curricular integration, 326–328
Cynicism, 99, 105
medical students and, 250

D

Defensive Pessimism Questionnaire, 146
Demands, 82
Depersonalization and medical students,
250
Depression, 72, 112, 118, 318
achievement and, 118–119
African Americans and, 277
Asian American students and, 277
burnout and, 98
description of, 67
historically marginalized individuals
and, 274, 278
impostor phenomenon (IP) and, 67–68,
112, 118, 269–270, 295
mental health and, 63
perfectionism and, 71, 72
physician assistants and, 254
survivor's guilt and, 67
*Diagnostic and Statistical Manual of Mental
Disorders (DSM)*, 54, 353
Dietetics and nutrition, 255
Dimensionality, 353
Clance Impostor Phenomenon Scale
(CIPS) and, 141, 348
multidimensionality, 147
validity and, 134
Discount, 347, 353
Discriminant validity, 133
Discrimination, 273–274
African American college students and,
277
Asian American college students and,
277
impostor phenomenon (IP) and,
269–270
students of color and, 349
triggers, 273–276
Discussion, 214–216
Disengagement from work, 83, 84, 98, 105,
123
Distress. *See* Psychological distress
Divergent validity, 134

368 • *Index*

Diversity
  candidates, 271
  hires, 273
  impostor phenomenon (IP) and, 149
  in the medical fields, 246–247
  social justice training and, 287
Doctoral students, 298
  Blacks in science, technology,
    engineering, and mathematics
    (STEM), 230, 234
  fear of failure and, 206
  female, 210
  in Hispanic-serving institution (HSI), 204
  impostor phenomenon (IP) and, 203
  in science, technology, engineering, and
    mathematics (STEM), 226
Double consciousness, 271
Double impact, 271–272, 279
Du Bois, W. E. B., 271
Dunning–Kruger effect, 302

E

Early adulthood
  impostor phenomenon (IP) and, 183
  psychological vulnerability during, 183
  self-doubt and, 183
Educational interventions, 285–286, 286–
    289, 302–306
  competence distortions and, 302
  family dynamics and, 295
Education (medical), 248
EFA (exploratory factor analysis), 134
Effort–reward imbalance, 91
Emotional distress, skill-oriented programs
    for, 320
Emotional exhaustion, 93, 95, 105, 228
  burnout and, 84
  faculty and, 228
  medical students and, 250
Emotional stability, 87
Emotion-focused coping, 96
Employed populations and mental health,
    65–66
Endler Multidimensional Anxiety Scales,
    150
Energy depletion, 105
Engineering students
  impostor phenomenon (IP) and, 227
  women, 227

Environments
  factors in, 257
  high-stakes, 167
Essence Magazine, 341
Ethnic identity and affinity groups, 323
Ethnicity, 47, 170, 312
Evaluations, 115
Executive coaching, 104
Exhaustion, work related, 83
Experience, 206
Experimental findings, 115–116
Experimental studies, 259
Experts, 301
Explanatory sequential mixed-methods
    design, 207
Exploratory factor analysis (EFA), 134
Expressed self-confidence, 51
External validation, 86

F

Face validity, 133
Factors (latent constructs), 134
Faculty, 163
  academic support and, 228
  anxiety and, 228
  Black, 170
  burnout and, 228
  development programs, 328
  early-career, 172
  emotional exhaustion and, 228
  impostor phenomenon (IP) and, 165,
    228, 328
  Latina, 170
  male, 163
  in medicine, 247
  minority women, 170, 172
  positive self-talk and, 228
  publish or perish and, 228
  rank and, 228
  in science, technology, engineering, and
    mathematics (STEM), 228–230
  self-esteem and, 228
  women, 65, 162, 228
Failure
  fear of, 87, 121
  feelings, types of, 94
  terror of, 121
Fake, 347, 353
Family
  control and, 249
  dynamics, 46

educational interventions and, 295
impostor phenomenon (IP) and, 66
pressure, first-generational experiences
    of, 275
societal stereotypes and, 46
upbringing, 85
Family-to-work conflict, 93, 350
Fatigue, 105
Fear, 94, 224
    of evaluation, 224, 256
    of rejection, 94
Fear of failure, 105
    achievement and, 121
    doctoral students and, 206
    gender and, 122
    impostor phenomenon (IP) and, 121,
        206
    science, technology, engineering, and
        mathematics (STEM) and, 225
Fear of success (FOS), 94–95, 205
    femininity and, 205
    gendered occupational fields and, 205
    social rejection and, 205
Female mentorship, 205
Femininity
    fear of success (FOS) and, 205
    impostor phenomenon (IP) and, 166
FGCSs. See First-generation college
        students (FGCSs)
Field of study, 171–172
Field-specific skills, 320
First-generational experiences
    African American students and, 192
    automatic negative thoughts (ANTs)
        and, 276
    family pressure and, 275
    historically marginalized individuals
        and, 274–276
    interventions for, 275
    success stress, 89
    as triggers, 274
First-generation college students (FGCSs),
        192
    belongingness and, 192
    impostor phenomenon (IP) and, 171,
        205
    mentor networks and, 322
    in science, technology, engineering, and
        mathematics (STEM), 274–276
    women in science, technology,
        engineering, and mathematics
        (STEM), 232

Five Rs (recognition, rational thinking,
        reframing, readiness, and repetition),
        256
Fixed mindset, 317
Flexible boundaries, 100–101
Foreigner impostorism, 174
Fortunetelling, 276
FOS. See Fear of success (FOS)
Friend support, 163
Frontiers in Psychology, 345
Frustration, 105

G

Gaslighting and historically marginalized
        individuals, 273
Gay and bisexual men, 166
Gay Times, 341
Gender, 347
    academic achievement and, 113
    achievement and fear of failure and, 122
    coping strategies and, 277
    differences, conditions for, 169–172
    environment and, 169
    harassment, 233
    identity vs. role orientation, 167
    impostor phenomenon (IP) and, 46,
        162–166, 205, 311–312, 347, 355
    intersectional approaches to, 169–172
    medical students and, 249–250
    nonconformity, 166
    residents and, 252–253
    role orientation, 167
    science, technology, engineering, and
        mathematics (STEM) fields disparity
        and, 222–223
    self-efficacy and, 123
    socialization, 161
    stigma, 167
    workplace perceptions of, 168
Gendered impostor phenomenon (IP), 57
Gendered occupational fields
    fear of success (FOS) and, 205
    social stigma and, 205
Gendered traits, 173
    climate, 167–169
    feminine, 166
    impostor phenomenon (IP) and,
        166–167
    individual, 166–167
    masculine, 166
    undergraduates and, 166

370 • *Index*

Gender–racial experiences, 170
Gender stigma consciousness (GSC), 167–168, 277
Genuine self-knowledge, 61
Girl boss mentality, 174
Girl Scouts of the USA, 293
Global self-worth, 63
Grade-point average (GPA), 111, 113, 164
    medical students and, 250
    self-efficacy and, 123
    undergraduates and, 164
    undergraduates in science, technology, engineering, and mathematics (STEM) and, 225
Graduate Record Exam (GRE), 116, 117
Graduate students. *See also* Doctorial students
    anxiety and, 63
    hidden curricula and, 325–326
    in medicine, 251–252
GRE (Graduate Record Exam), 116, 117
Growth mindset, 317
GSC. *See* Gender stigma consciousness (GSC)

H

Harassment, 172
    academic, 235
    gender, 233
    workplace, 234, 279
Harvey Impostor Phenomenon Scale (HIPS), 135, 138, 206, 237, 347
    construct validity and, 138
    internal consistency of, 138
    reliability of, 138
HBCUs. *See* Historically Black colleges/institutions (HBCUs)
Health profession students, 162
Healthy confrontation, 96
HEIs (higher education institutions), 310
Helplessness, 67, 72
HEXACO-104 (Honesty–Humility, Emotionality, Extraversion, Agreeableness, Conscientiousness, Openness to Experience), 148
Hidden curricula, 325–326
Higher education
    addressing impostor phenomenon (IP) in, 312–328
    hidden curricula of, 325–326

impostor phenomenon (IP)
    manifestations in, 311–312
    interventions, 313
    management techniques vs. cures, 313
    peer mentorship and, 322
    perpetuating students' impostor cycles and, 313
Higher education institutions (HEIs), 310
High-stakes demands, 82
High-stakes environments, 167
HIPS. *See* Harvey Impostor Phenomenon Scale (HIPS)
Hispanic-serving institutions (HSIs), 204. *See also* Mixed-method study of impostor phenomenon (IP) in a Hispanic-serving institution (HSI)
    doctoral students in, 204
    impostor phenomenon (IP) and, 204, 207, 216
Hispanic students in science, technology, engineering, and mathematics (STEM), 231
Historically Black colleges/institutions (HBCUs), 183
    rigor and quality of education from, 189
Historically marginalized individuals
    anxiety and, 274
    belongingness and, 270
    burnout and, 274
    concept of success and, 270
    depression and, 274, 278
    differential career impacts and, 278
    double consciousness and, 271
    first-generational experiences, 274–276
    frequency of IP experiences, 274
    gaslighting of, 273
    impostor phenomenon (IP) and, 269–270
    institutional-level strategies to support, 327–328
    leadership and, 281
    managers and, 281
    mentorship and, 273, 280
    otherness and, 270
    psychological distress and, 278
    racial identity and, 277–278
    reducing impostor phenomenon (IP) for, 279–281
    self-esteem and, 278
    sponsorship and, 273
    supervisors and, 280
    systemic oppression and, 270

triggers for, 272–274
unsafe environments and, 272
women, 276–277
Honesty–Humility, Emotionality, Extraversion, Agreeableness, Conscientiousness, Openness to Experience (HEXACO-104), 148
Hopelessness, 67
Housemanship, 249
HSIs. *See* Hispanic-serving institutions (HSIs)
Humble realists, 302, 304
Hypervigilance, 70, 88
Hypotheses
mixed-methods question, 208
quantitative, 207–208

I

Ibrahim's Impostor Phenomenon Profile (IPP30), 134, 145–147
bifactor model of, 146
construct validity and, 146
reliability of, 145–146
Imes, Suzanne, 45, 161
Immigrant women, 174
Impostor cycle, 65, 70, 119, 274, 309
Impostor feelings. *See* Impostor phenomenon (IP)
Impostor phenomenon (IP), 45, 62, 245, 299. *See also* Depression; Gender; Interventions; Luck; Mentorship; Microaggressions; Mixed-method study of impostor phenomenon (IP) in a Hispanic-serving institution (HSI); Race; Racial discrimination; Racialized impostor phenomenon; Science, technology, engineering, and mathematics (STEM)
in academia, 204, 228
academic performance and, 164
accomplishments and, 112
achievement and mental health and, 118–120
achievement and self-efficacy and, 122–123
achievement in the academic environment and, 112, 113–114
achievement in the lab environment and, 115–116
achievement in the workplace and, 112, 114–115

achievement mediators, 118–124
African American adolescents and, 355
African Americans and, 47, 52, 269, 355
African American students and, 182–183, 183–184, 194
anxiety and, 70–71, 112, 118, 119, 295
assertiveness and, 96–97
assumptions of, 48
astronomy students and, 227–228
astrophysics students and, 227
behaviors, 49
bibliometric analysis of, 342–343
Black, Indigenous, or person of color (BIPOC) in science, technology, engineering, and mathematics (STEM) and, 223, 229–231, 233–234, 352
boundaries and, 96–97
burnout and, 83–84
Capgras syndrome vs., 55
career and, 99
career aspirations and, 165
character strengths and, 87
chronic, psychological impact of, 52
climate gendered traits and, 167–169
climate, role of on, 117
competence and, 52
conceptual and diagnostic challenges, 353
confidence and, 206
conscientiousness and, 123, 320
contextualizing, 300
contextual translation in other languages, 259
core self-evaluations and, 86
creative fields and, 299
creativity and, 120
description of, 61–62, 81
detection of, 206
discrimination and, 269–270
diversity and, 149
doctoral students and, 203
doctoral students in science, technology, engineering, and mathematics (STEM) and, 226
double impact and, 271–272, 279
early adulthood and, 183
early-career academics and, 172
effort–reward imbalance and, 91
engineering students and, 227
environmental factors and, 257

372 • *Index*

Impostor phenomenon (*continued*)
  environmental factors vs. personality
    trait, 233–234, 237
  ethnic considerations and, 47
  ethnic minorities and, 170
  etiology of, 185, 186
  experience and, 206
  experimental findings and, 115–116
  expressed self-confidence and, 51
  externally experienced, 271
  faculty and, 165, 228, 328
  family and, 46, 66, 85, 249
  fear of evaluation and, 224, 256
  fear of failure and, 121, 206
  features that accompany, 47
  female faculty members and, 65, 162
  femininity and, 166
  field of study and, 171–172
  first-generation college students
    (FGCSs) and, 171, 205, 274–276
  first-generation students in science,
    technology, engineering, and
    mathematics (STEM) and, 232,
    274–276
  fixed mindsets and, 317
  future research on, 356–357
  gay and bisexual men and, 166
  gendered, 57
  gendered traits and, 166–167
  gender identity vs. gender role
    orientation and, 167
  gender, intersectional approaches to,
    169–172
  gender–racial experiences and, 170
  gender role orientation and, 167
  gender socialization and, 161
  gender stigma consciousness and,
    167–168
  global self-worth and, 63
  grade-point average (GPA) and, 111,
    113, 164
  graduate student anxiety and, 63
  harassment and, 172, 234
  health profession students and, 162
  higher education, addressing in,
    312–328
  higher education manifestations and,
    311–312
  high-stakes environments and, 167
  Hispanic-serving institutions (HSIs) and,
    216

  Hispanic students in science, technology,
    engineering, and mathematics
    (STEM) and, 231
  historically marginalized individuals
    and, 269–270
  honors courses and, 114
  immigrant women and, 174
  impostor syndrome vs., 53–54
  indecision and, 86, 105
  individual gendered traits and, 166–167
  individual vs. socioenvironmental lens,
    324–325
  internal locus of control and, 249
  interpersonal perfectionism and, 72
  interpreting scores and, 151
  intersectional nature of for women, 174
  isolating nature of, 271
  job role-related stress and, 89–90
  job satisfaction and, 66, 350
  Latinx students in science, technology,
    engineering, and mathematics
    (STEM) and, 231, 234
  learning and development for, 104
  limitations of constructs and, 55–57
  loneliness and, 298
  maladaptive perfectionism and, 71, 122
  male faculty members and, 163
  managing, 310
  masculinity and, 166
  measurement of. *See* Clance Impostor
    Phenomenon Scale (CIPS)
  measuring in medical fields, 247
  medical culture and, 300
  medical fields and, 246–266
  medicalization of, 54
  medical professionals and, 252–255
  medical students and, 248–251
  mental health and, 62, 112, 120, 170
  mental health disorder vs., 54–55
  mental health in employed populations
    and, 65–66
  mental health of students and, 62–65,
    311–312
  mentor networks and, 321
  micromanagement and, 90
  minoritized identities and, 53, 55–56
  minority status stress and, 183
  misconceptions of, 52–55
  mixed samples and, 255–256
  Native American students in science,
    technology, engineering, and
    mathematics (STEM) and, 231

neuroticism and, 68, 249
normalization of, 297, 300, 317
occupational considerations and, 298–299
oppression and, 269–270
oppressive environments and, 278
organization culture and, 299
origins of, 185, 353
passive communication and, 95
perceived organizational support (POS) and, 66
perfectionism and, 71–73, 85, 112, 193
perfectionism vs., 301
performance anxiety and, 95
perseverance and, 98
personal relationships and, 98
postdoctoral students in science, technology, engineering, and mathematics (STEM) and, 226
prevalence of among college students, 63, 311–312
professional inefficacy and, 84
professional success and, 350
promotions at work and, 114–115
psychological disturbance and, 63
psychological safety and, 90–91
psychosocial factors and, 57
qualitatively investigating among college faculty, 66
racism and, 182, 185
reduction of, 279–281
reframing and, 314
salary and, 114
scholarly productivity and, 115
scholarship, 341–342
school-to-career pipeline and, 168
science, technology, engineering, and mathematics (STEM) faculty and, 228–230
scientific theory vs., 47–48
scores, 49
self-appraisal and, 49
self-compassion and, 318–319
self-concept and, 122
self-criticism and, 118
self-denigration and, 50
self-deprecating behaviors and, 49
self-doubt and, 52–53, 224, 225
self-efficacy and, 122–123, 225
self-esteem and, 68–69, 86
self-handicapping and, 69, 165, 206
self-presentational strategy and, 206–207

self-protection and, 69
self-regulation and, 123–124
sex disparities and, 123
sexual attention (unwanted) and, 172
sexual minority women and, 174
shame and, 118, 120
signs of, 105
social identity and, 49
socialization and, 164
social support and, 103, 165
socioeconomic status and, 174
socioracial factors and, 185
sources of, 296–297
state anxiety and, 119
strategic, 50, 58, 144
strategies to manage, 236–237, 256–258
structural inequities and, 52
students of color and, 191
suicidal ideation and, 67
systematic review of, 342
systemic factors and, 257
theoretical considerations of, 47–51
trait anxiety and, 119
trait vs. state, 150
triggers for, 272–274, 292
true, 50
undergraduates and, 162, 224–225
women and, 205, 276–277
women in science, technology, engineering, and mathematics (STEM) and, 232–234
women in the workplace and, 172–173
women of color and, 169–170, 205
workaholism and, 86
work exhaustion, 83
work–family conflict (WFC) and, 103, 350
work–life imbalance and, 91–92
work outcomes and, 66, 350
work performance and, 164
workplace behaviors and, 350
workplace culture and, 299
workplace evaluations and, 115
workplace satisfaction and, 350
younger students and, 63–64
Impostor phenomenon (IP) literature
authors, 344–345
citations, 343–344
geographic location of, 345
journal publications, 345
performance analysis of, 343
publishing patterns within, 343–345

374 • Index

Impostor phenomenon (IP) scales,
135–148. *See also* Clance Impostor
Phenomenon Scale (CIPS); Harvey
Impostor Phenomenon Scale (HIPS);
Ibrahim's Impostor Phenomenon
Profile (IPP30); Leary Impostor
Phenomenon scale; Perceived
Fraudulence Scale (PFS)
characteristics of, 136–137
Impostor Phenomenon Profiler, 348
interpreting scores and, 151
psychometrically validation of, 347
racialized, 149–150
Impostor phenomenon (IP) scores, 214
reflected appraisal and, 49
self-appraisal and, 49
Impostor Phenomenon Profiler, 348
Impostor syndrome. *See* Impostor
phenomenon (IP)
In Danger of Winning, 292
Indecision, 86, 105
Individual-level risk factors, 192–193
Inequities
access to college and, 187–188
structural, 52
Ingroup expectations, 191
Insomnia and burnout, 98
Institution-level strategies, 324–328
Intellectual fraud, 82
Intellectual incompetence
African American students, perceptions
of, 185
perfectionism and, 192
Intellectual self-doubt, 105
Internal barriers to women's occupational
achievement model, 289–292
competence and, 291, 300–301
confidence and, 300
evolution and application of, 292–304
marginalized groups and, 300
other directedness dimension of, 290–
291, 292–294
performance dimension of, 291–292,
300–304
sense of belonging and, 296
sociocultural expectations and realities
dimension of, 291, 294–300
Internal consistency, 132
Cronbach's alpha for measuring,
133–134
Harvey Impostor Phenomenon Scale
(HIPS) and, 138

Internal locus of control, 249
International Journal of Doctoral Studies,
345
*International Statistical Classification of
Diseases and Related Health Problems*,
353
Interpersonal conflict, 95
Interpersonal perfectionism, 72
Interpersonal strategies, 321–324
Interrater reliability, 132
Intersectional identities, 161
Intervention-based research, 355
Interventions, 151, 250, 302–303, 355–
356. *See also* Clinical interventions;
Educational interventions; IP/IS
intervention programs; Mindfulness-
based interventions (MBIs)
academic skills training, 320, 321
achievements lists and, 303
affinity groups, 323–324
for burnout, 84
class-based programs, 327
coaching, 356
cognitive behavioral approaches, 316
community building, 271
competence distortions and, 302
coping skills, 321
curricular integration, 326–328
elements of effective programs, 314–315
evidence-based, 314
faculty development programs, 328
for first-generational experiences, 275
fixed mindsets and, 317
higher education, 313
individual-level, 314–324
institution-level strategies, 324–328
interpersonal strategies, 321–324
for medical students, 250, 257–258
Mind–Body Wellness Course, 257
mindfulness lectures, 258
mindset-oriented, 317
online, 321
oppresive environments and, 279
peer mentorship, 322–323
physicians and, 253
pop psychology vs., 313
psychoeducational approach, 315–316
reframing and, 316
skill-oriented approach, 315–316
skill-oriented programs, 320
social capital and, 324
student-facing, 310

system-level, 279
3Cs (Clarify, Choose, Create) model, 275–276
Intrapersonal strategies, 316–321
IP/IS intervention programs, 287–289
   diverse populations and, 288
   effectiveness of, 288–289
   organizations informing, 288
   participants, 287–288
IPP30. *See* Ibrahim's Impostor Phenomenon Profile (IPP30)
Irrational rumination, 67
Irrational self-confidence, 302
Isolation, 273, 318, 326
   impostor phenomenon (IP) and, 271
   peer mentorship and, 322
   success and, 293

J

Job demands–resources model, 82
Job dissatisfaction, 99
Job performance, 103, 349
   decreased, 105
Job–person fit, 89
Job role-related stress, 89–90
Job satisfaction, 103, 349
   impostor phenomenon (IP) and, 66, 350
John Henryism, 193
Journaling, 256
Journal of Personality Assessment, 345

K

Knowledge clusters, 343, 345–354
Kolligian and Sternberg's Perceived Fraudulence Scale. *See* Perceived Fraudulence Scale (PFS)

L

Lack of motivation, 105
Latent constructs, 134
Latent state–trait theory, 150
Latinx students in science, technology, engineering, and mathematics (STEM), 231, 234
Leadership
   historically marginalized individuals and, 281
   passive, 163, 233
   transformational, 163, 233

Learned Helplessness Scale, 146
Leary Impostor Phenomenon scale, 133, 143–145
   construct validity and, 144
   participant burden and, 149
   reliability of, 144
Loneliness, 298
Longitudinal studies of medical students, 259
Luck, 224, 256, 347, 353

M

Maladaptive coping, 315
   science, technology, engineering, and mathematics (STEM) undergraduate students and, 226
Maladaptive perfectionism, 71, 112, 114, 121, 192–193, 250, 318
   impostor phenomenon (IP) and, 71, 122
   medical students and, 250
   suicidal ideation and, 72
Managers and historically marginalized individuals, 281
Marginalization, 88–89
   Black, Indigenous, or person of color (BIPOC) and, 88
   burnout and, 88
   first generation success stress, 89
   performance dimension and, 300
Marital status, 249
Masculine traits, 166
Masculinity
   impostor phenomenon (IP) and, 166
   workplace and, 168
MBIs. *See* Mindfulness-based interventions (MBIs)
MD-PhD students, 251–252
Measurement invariance, 134, 135
Measurement of impostor phenomenon (IP). *See* Clance Impostor Phenomenon Scale (CIPS)
Medical College Admission Test, 250
Medical culture, 300
Medical Education, 345
Medical education and training, 248
Medical fields
   culture of perfection in, 250
   demographics of, 246–247
   faculty in, 247
   impostor phenomenon (IP) and, 247
   racial and ethnic diversity in, 246–247
   women in, 246

376 • *Index*

Medical professionals
  physician assistants, 254
  physicians, 253–254
  residents, 252–253
  veterinarians, 254–255
Medical students, 348
  academic achievement and, 250
  burnout and, 250
  cynicism and, 250
  depersonalization and, 250
  emotional exhaustion and, 250
  gender and, 249–250
  grade point average (GPA) and, 250
  impostor phenomenon (IP) and,
    248–251
  interventions for, 250, 257–258
  longitudinal studies of, 250
  maladaptive perfectionism and, 250
  marital status and, 249–253
  mental health and, 349
  osteopathic, 250
  perfectionism and, 348
  psychological distress and, 255
  suicidal ideation and, 250, 349
  transition points and, 251
  wellness and, 250
Men's Health, 341
Mental health, 112, 327
  achievement and, 118–120
  anxiety and, 63
  burnout and, 98
  definition of, 61
  depression and, 63
  of employed populations with impostor
    phenomenon (IP), 65–66
  impostor phenomenon (IP) and, 54–55,
    62, 112, 120, 170
  medical students and, 349
  outcomes, 62
  perceived organizational support (POS)
    and, 66
  perfectionism and, 72
  racial discrimination and, 64, 191
  of students with impostor phenomenon
    (IP), 62–65, 311–312
  work related stress and, 95–96
Mental health professionals, 255
Mentor networks, 321–322
Mentorship, 103, 205, 213, 273, 325. *See
  also* Peer mentorship
  external, 104
  faculty and, 213, 236, 328

  female, 205
  historically marginalized individuals
    and, 273, 280
Microaggressions, 88, 149, 171, 191
  Black students and, 229, 234
  Latinx students and, 234
  minoritized graduate students and, 312
  as triggers, 273
Micromanagement, 90
Mind–Body Wellness Course, 257
Mindfulness, 318
Mindfulness-based interventions (MBIs),
  317–318
  evidence-based, 319
  mindfulness-based CBT, 316
  perfectionism and, 318
  racism and, 319
  self-handicapping and, 318
  shame and, 318
  superficial, 319–320
Mindfulness lectures, 258
Mindfulness training programs, 236–237
Mindreading, 276
Mindset-oriented interventions, 317
Mindset theory, 317
Minorities
  affinity groups and, 323
  faculty, 228
  graduate students, 312
  stress and, 323
Minoritized identity
  impostor phenomenon (IP) and, 53
  multiple, 55–56
Minority status stress, 312
  students of color and, 64, 183–184, 312
Mixed-methods design, 207
Mixed-methods questions, 208
Mixed-methods studies, 259
Mixed-method study of impostor
  phenomenon (IP) in a Hispanic-
  serving institution (HSI), 203–220
  COVID-19 and, 209, 215
  discussion, 214–216
  gender and, 210–211
  generational status and, 210–211
  literature review, 204–207
  method, 207–209
  mixed-methods question, 208
  program of study and, 210–211
  purpose of the study, 204
  qualitative analysis, 209
  qualitative findings, 212

qualitative questions, 208
quantitative analysis, 209
quantitative hypotheses, 207–208
quantitative results, 212
results, 209–214
sampling procedure, 208–209
setting, 204
Modeling, bifactor, 146
Morris Brown College, 286
Multiple demands, 82

N

Nap rooms, 104
National Center for Education Statistics, 181
National Center for Science and
  Engineering Statistics (NCSES), 222
National Science Foundation (NSF), 222
Native Americans in science, technology,
  engineering, and mathematics
  (STEM) careers, 231
Natural genius, 302
Natural intelligence, 168
NCSES (National Center for Science and
  Engineering Statistics), 222
Negative self-evaluation and burnout, 83
Negative self-talk, 302, 309
Neuroticism, 68, 249
Nomological validity, 135
Normalization of impostor phenomenon
  (IP), 297, 300, 317
NSF (National Science Foundation), 222
Nutrition and dietetics, 255

O

Onboarding buddy systems, 103
Online interventions, 321
Oppression
  awareness of, 287
  environments of, 270, 272, 278–279
  impostor phenomenon (IP) and,
    269–270
  systemic, 270
  as a trigger, 272
Oppressive environments, 278
  as triggers, 279
  interventions in, 279
Organization culture, 299
Other directedness, 290–291
  evolution of, 292–294
  success and, 290, 293

Otherness, 57, 246
  African American students and, 189
  historically marginalized individuals
    and, 270
  in science, technology, engineering, and
    mathematics (STEM), 235–236
  students of color and, 205
Outgroup expectations and African
  American students, 190
Overcommitment, 100
Overidentification, 85, 93, 318
Overpreparation, 69, 70, 321
Overthinking, 86
Overworking, 89

P

Participation bias, 259
Passive-aggressive communication, 95
Passive communication, 95
Passive leadership, 163, 233
Peer mentorship, 322–323
  interventions and, 322–323
  isolation and, 322
  students of color and, 322
People Magazine, 341
Pep talks, 304
Perceived Fraudulence Scale (PFS), 142–
  143, 206
  Clance Impostor Phenomenon Scale
    (CIPS) vs., 141, 347
  construct validity and, 142–143
  reliability of, 142
  subscales of, 347
Perceived organizational support (POS), 66
Perfectionism, 85, 206, 301. *See
  also* Maladaptive perfectionism
  academic achievement and, 122
  achievement and, 121, 122
  adaptive, 71
  African American students and, 193
  anxiety and, 71, 72
  burnout and, 85
  as a coping strategy, 192
  depression and, 71, 72
  description of, 71
  impostor phenomenon (IP) and, 71–73,
    85, 112, 193
  impostor phenomenon (IP) vs., 301
  intellectual incompetence and, 192
  intrapersonal and interpersonal
    characteristics of, 72

378 • *Index*

Perfectionism (*continued*)
  medical students and, 348
  mental health and, 72
  mindfulness-based interventions (MBIs) and, 318
  procrastination and, 122
  psychological distress and, 71
  science, technology, engineering, and mathematics (STEM) students and, 71, 225
  self-esteem and, 86
  socially prescribed, 256
  students and, 71–72
Perfectionistic self-presentation, 72
Performance, 291–292
  dimension, 300–301
  evolution and application of, 300–304
Performance anxiety, 70, 94–95
  workplace culture and, 104–106
Perseverance, 98
Personal control, 87
Personality and achievement, 121–122
Personality and Individual Differences, 345
Personal relationships and burnout, 98
Personal time off, 101–102
Person-centered resources
  burnout prevention and, 103–104
  flexibility and autonomy, 104
  4-day work week, 104
  mentorship, 103
  nap rooms, 104
  onboarding buddy systems, 103
  social support, 103
  team-building, 103
  work from home, 104
PFS. *See* Perceived Fraudulence Scale (PFS)
PhD Completion and Attrition, 215
Phobias. *See* State anxiety
Physical health and burnout, 97
Physician assistants, 254
Physicians, 253–254
  burnout and, 253
  identity and, 250
  interventions and, 253
  positive aspects of impostor phenomenon (IP) and, 253
  professional fulfilment and, 253
  professional identity formation and, 254
  self-esteem and, 253
  suicidal ideation and, 253
Physician–scientist identity, 252
Popper, Karl, 48

Positive self-talk, 303
  faculty and, 228
POS (perceived organizational support), 66
Postdoctoral students
  Blacks in science, technology, engineering, and mathematics (STEM), 230, 234
  in science, technology, engineering, and mathematics (STEM), 222, 226
Predictive validity vs. nomological validity, 135
Predominantly White institutions (PWIs), 183, 310
  underrepresentation of same-race peers at, 189
Presenteeism, 90
Prevention initiatives, 355
Problem-focused coping, 95
Procrastination, 86, 94, 105, 112, 123, 320, 321
  perfectionism and, 122
Professional fulfilment, 253
Professional identity formation, 251, 254
Professional inefficacy, 84
Professional success, 350
Promotions, 114–115
Proseminars, 326
Psychoeducational group experiences, 315–316
  cognitive processing therapy and, 316
  workshops, 315
Psychological distress, 255, 318
  African Americans and, 278
  African American students and, 230
  historically marginalized individuals and, 278
  medical students and, 255
  perfectionism and, 71
Psychological disturbance, 63
Psychological safety, 90–91
  burnout and, 90–91
Psychology students, 225
Psychometric scale evaluation, 132
  interitem correlations range and, 133–134
  measurement tools for, 132–135
  scale reliability and, 132–133
  scale validity and, 133–135
Psychosomatic symptoms, 63
PsycInfo, 343
Publish or perish, 228
Purposeful sampling, 208
PWIs. *See* Predominantly White institutions (PWIs)

Q

Qualitative analysis, 209
Qualitative questions, 208
Quality sleep, 102
Quantitative analysis, 209–210
Quantitative hypotheses, 207–208
Questions
  mixed-methods, 208
  qualitative, 208

R

Race and impostor phenomenon (IP), 47, 52, 53, 56, 57, 64, 230
Racial discrimination, 53, 185, 186, 190–191
  academic outcomes and, 191
  impostor phenomenon (IP) and, 57, 170, 184, 278
  institutional, 57
  mental health and, 64, 191
Racial identity, 348, 355
  academic self-concept and, 349
  affinity groups and, 323
  African Americans and, 349
  African American students and, 184
  definition of, 278
  historically marginalized individuals and, 277–278
  impostor phenomenon (IP) and, 312
  resilience and, 278
  self-concept and, 349
Racialized impostor phenomenon, 45, 47, 55–57. *See also* Impostor phenomenon (IP)
  scales, 149
Racial minorities
  hypervisbility and invisibility of, 55
  impostor phenomenon (IP) and, 47, 56, 64
  vulnerability of, 183
Racial underrepresentation, 185
Racism, 229. *See also* African American students, racism
  definition of, 181
  impostor phenomenon (IP) and, 182, 185
  mindfulness-based interventions (MBIs) and, 319
  minoritized graduate students and, 312

socioecological analysis of, 186–193
  across socioecological domains, 187
Rackham Graduate School, 309
Refinement, 356
Reflected appraisal, 49
Reframing, 316
  competence distortion and, 302
  interventions and, 316
  managing impostor phenomenon (IP) and, 314
Rejection sensitivity, 94
Relational-level risk factors, 190–191
Reliability, 132
  Clance Impostor Phenomenon Scale (CIPS) and, 139
  Harvey Impostor Phenomenon Scale (HIPS) and, 138
  Ibrahim's Impostor Phenomenon Profile (IPP30) and, 145–146
  Leary Impostor Phenomenon scale and, 144
  Perceived Fraudulence Scale (PFS) and, 142
  10-item CIPS and, 148
  types of, 132–133
Research
  expansion, 356–357
  refinement, 356
Resentment, 105
Residents, 252–253
Resilience, 256
  racial identity and, 278
Revenge bedtime procrastination, 102
Risk factors
  community-level, 189–190
  individual-level, 192–193
  relational-level, 190–191
  societal-level, 187–189
Role conflict, 92
Root-mean-square error of approximation (RMSEA), 134
Rumination, 67, 122, 197, 317, 318

S

Salary, 114
Sampling, 208–209
Scale reliability, 132–133
Scale validity, 133–135
Scholarly productivity, 115
School-to-career pipeline, 168
Science mapping, 342, 345

380 • *Index*

Science, technology, engineering, and
 mathematics (STEM), 221–244
 African American students in, 229–231,
  234, 352
 Asian students in, 236
 belonging and, 351–353
 Black, Indigenous, or person of color
  (BIPOC) individuals in, 221, 223–
  224, 229–231, 233–234, 352
 career aspirations and, 165
 Clance Impostor Phenomenon Scale
  (CIPS) and, 224
 demographics, 222–223
 disciplines included in, 222
 doctoral students in, 226
 first-generation college students
  (FGCSs) in, 232, 274–276
 gender disparity and, 222–223
 Hispanic students in, 231
 impostor phenomenon (IP) and, 171–
  172, 173–174, 221, 224–229, 299
 Latinx students in, 231, 234
 Native American students in, 231
 otherness and, 235–236
 perfectionism and, 71, 225
 postdoctoral students in, 222, 226
 self-doubt and, 224
 self-efficacy and, 225
 undergraduates, 225–226
 women in, 221, 233–234
Science, technology, engineering, and
 mathematics (STEM) faculty
 impostor phenomenon (IP) and,
  228–230
 women as, 352
Scientific theory, 47–48
Scopus, 343
Self-advocacy, 100–101
 assertive communication and, 100
 boundaries and, 100
 burnout prevention and, 100–101
 lack of, 105
Self-appraisal, 49
Self-authorship, 236
Self-awareness, 256
Self-care
 burnout prevention and, 101–103
 personal time off and, 101–102
 sleep and, 102–103
Self-compassion, 318–319
 African American students and, 318

Self-concept, 122
 racial identity and, 349
Self-confidence
 expressed, 51
 irrational, 302
 skill-oriented programs and, 320
Self-criticism, 118
 excessive, 250
 self-kindness vs., 318
Self-denigration, 50
Self-deprecating behaviors, 49
Self-discipline and academic achievement,
 124
Self-doubt, 256, 309
 burnout and, 83, 98
 early adulthood and, 183
 impostor feelings vs., 52–53
 impostor phenomenon (IP) and, 224,
  225
 intellectual, 105
 science, technology, engineering, and
  mathematics (STEM) and, 224
Self-efficacy, 87, 230
 achievement and, 122–123
 African American students and, 230
 gender and, 123
 grade-point average (GPA) and, 123
 impostor phenomenon (IP) and, 122–
  123, 225
 science, technology, engineering, and
  mathematics (STEM) and, 225
Self-esteem, 86, 230, 348
 African Americans and, 278
 African American students and, 230
 description of, 68
 faculty and, 228
 historically marginalized individuals
  and, 278
 impostor phenomenon (IP) and, 68–69,
  86
 perfectionism and, 86
 physicians and, 253
Self-evaluations
 core, 86–87
 negative and burnout, 83
Self-expectations, 72
Self-handicapping, 69, 165, 206
 mindfulness-based interventions (MBIs)
  and, 318
 science, technology, engineering, and
  mathematics (STEM) students and,
  225

Self-kindness, 318
Self-knowledge, 61
Self-perception, 61
Self-presentational strategies, 206–207
Self-presentation, perfectionistic, 72
Self-preservation
    assertiveness and, 96–97
    boundaries and, 96–97
Self-protection, 69
Self-regulation, 123–124
Self-sabotage, 105
Self-talk
    negative, 302, 309
    positive, 303
Self-worth
    global, 63
    workaholism and, 86
Sex disparities, 123
Sexual attention (unwanted), 172
Sexual harassment of women in science,
        technology, engineering, and
        mathematics (STEM), 233
Sexual minority women, 174
Shame, 117, 318
    achievement and, 120
    creativity and, 120
    impostor phenomenon (IP) and, 118,
        120
    mindfulness-based interventions (MBIs)
        and, 318
SIPS (State Impostor Phenomenon Scale),
    206
Situation-dependent boundary, 100
6-item CIPS, 148–149. *See also* Clance
        Impostor Phenomenon Scale (CIPS)
    participant burden and, 149
Skill-oriented programs, 320
Skills
    academic, 320–321
    field-specific, 320
Sleep, 102–103
Social capital, 324
Social dysfunction, 63
Social identity, 49
Socialization, 164
Social justice and diversity training, 287
Social rejection and fear of success (FOS),
    205
Social stigma and gendered occupational
        fields, 205
Social strategy and mentor networks,
    321–322

Social support
    impostor phenomenon (IP) and, 103,
        165
    workplace and, 351
Societal expectations, 301
Societal-level risk factors, 187–189
Societal stereotypes vs. family dynamics,
    46
Society, 56
Sociocultural expectations and realities,
    291
    evolution and application of, 294–300
    women and, 301
Socioecological model of health, 185–186
Socioeconomic status, 174
Soloist, 301–302
The Souls of Black Folk, 271
Sponsorship of historically marginalized
        individuals and, 273
Stability (emotional), 87
Standardized root-mean-square residual
        (SRMR), 134
State anxiety, 70, 150
    impostor phenomenon (IP) and, 119
State Impostor Phenomenon Scale (SIPS),
    206
STEM. *See* Science, technology,
        engineering, and mathematics
        (STEM)
Stereotype confirmation concern, 88
Stereotype threat, 297
Stereotyping, 234
Strategic impostorism, 50, 58, 144, 258
Strategies, 236–237. *See also* Coping
        strategies
    evidence-based, 319
    impostor phenomenon (IP) management
        and, 236–237, 256–258
    individual-level, 314–315
    institutional-level for historically
        marginalized individuals, 327–328
    institution-level, 324–328
    interpersonal, 321–324
    intrapersonal, 316–321
    mindfulness-based, 317
    self-presentational, 206–207
    social, 321
Strengths assessments, 87
Stress
    in academia, 71
    burnout and, 83, 94
    coping strategies for, 95–96

Stress (*continued*)
  first generation success, 89
  job role-related, 89–90
  management, 93–99
  work–life imbalance and, 92
  workplace-related, 95–96, 350
Stroop Color–Word Interference Test, 115
Structural inequities, 52
Students
  individual-level evidence-based
    strategies for, 314–315
  interventions for, 310
  medical and, 248–251
  mental health and, 62–65, 311–312
  nontraditional, 216
  normalizing impostor phenomenon (IP)
    and, 297
  perfectionism and, 71–72
  trait perfectionism and academic
    malfunctioning among, 71
  younger, 63–64
Students of color
  discrimination and, 349
  impostor phenomenon (IP) and, 191
  minority status stress and, 64, 183–184,
    312
  otherness and, 205
  peer mentorship and, 322
Studies, types of, 259
Success, 303
  definition of, 294
  isolating effects of, 293
  other directedness and, 293
  as a trigger, 293
Success syndrome, 94–95
Suicidal ideation, 63
  impostor phenomenon (IP) and, 67
  maladaptive perfectionism and, 72
  medical students and, 250, 349
  physicians and, 253
Superhuman, 302
Supervisors and historically marginalized
  individuals, 280
Support
  in academia, 228
  classmates and, 163
  friends and, 163
  institutional-level for historically
    marginalized individuals, 327–328

Survivor's guilt
  African Americans and, 277
  depression and, 67
Syndromes
  definition of, 286
  stigma associated with, 258
  success, 94–95
Systematic review, 342
Systemic factors and impostor
  phenomenon (IP), 257
Systemic oppression of historically
  marginalized individuals, 270

T

Team-building activities, 103
10-item CIPS (CIPS-10), 147–149
Test anxiety, 119
Test–retest reliability, 132
Text-mining, 346
Theoretical considerations of impostor
  phenomenon (IP), 47–51
Thought–Action Fusion Scale, 146
3Cs (Clarify, Choose, Create) model,
  275–276
3Ss (scroll, snack, sip), 102
Time Magazine, 341
TLI (Tucker–Lewis index), 134
Tokenism, 234
Topical trends, 345–354
  missing, 354–356
Toxic work environments, 279
Trait anxiety
  impostor phenomenon (IP) and, 119
  state anxiety vs., 70, 150
Trait perfectionism and academic
  malfunctioning, 71
Transformational leadership, 163, 233
Transient impostors, 258
Transition points, 251
Triggers, 272, 311
  discrimination, 273–276
  first-generational experiences, 274
  impostor phenomenon (IP) and, 272–
    274, 292
  microaggressions, 273
  oppression, 272
  oppressive environments, 279
  success and, 293
  toxic work environments, 279
True impostorism, 50, 144, 258
Tucker–Lewis index (TLI), 134

Index • 383

U

Undergraduates. *See also* African American students
  gendered traits and, 166
  gender identity vs. gender role orientation and, 167
  grade-point average (GPA) and, 164
  impostor phenomenon (IP) and, 162, 224–225
  medical students, 248–251
  psychology students, 225
  science, technology, engineering, and mathematics (STEM), 225–226
  science, technology, engineering, and mathematics (STEM) and Black students, 229–231
  science, technology, engineering, and mathematics (STEM) and maladaptive coping, 226
  science, technology, engineering, and mathematics (STEM) grade-point average (GPA) and, 225
United States Medical Licensing Examination Step 1, 250, 251
University of Massachusetts, Amherst, 287
University of Michigan, 309, 310

V

Validation, 86
Validity
  convergent, 133
  dimensionality and, 134
  discriminant, 133
  divergent, 134
  face, 133
  nomological, 135
  types of, 133–134
Veterinarians, 254–255
Violence in the workplace, 233
VOSviewer, 346
Vulnerability
  African American students and, 183
  early adulthood and, 183

W

Web of Science, 343
Wellness
  medical students and, 250
  residents and, 252

WFC. *See* Work–family conflict (WFC)
WHO. *See* World Health Organization (WHO)
Women
  affiliation and, 290
  astronomy students, 227
  astrophysics students, 227
  caregiving and, 290
  of color, 169–170, 205
  competence and, 300–301
  confidence and, 300
  coping strategies for, 277
  engineering students, 227
  faculty, 228
  first-generation students in science, technology, engineering, and mathematics (STEM), 232
  immigrant, 174
  impostor phenomenon (IP) and, 205, 276–277
  internal barriers to occupational achievement model and, 289–292
  in the medical fields, 246
  in science, technology, engineering, and mathematics (STEM), 221, 232–234
  science, technology, engineering, and mathematics (STEM) faculty, 352
  sexual harassment and, 233
  societal expectations and, 301
  in the workplace, 172–173
  workplace violence and, 233
Women's Health, 341
Workaholism, 86
Work disengagement. *See* Disengagement from work
Work exhaustion, 83. *See also* Burnout
Work–family conflict (WFC), 92–93, 349
  family-to-work conflict and, 93, 350
  impostor phenomenon (IP) and, 103, 350
Work–life balance, 90, 104
Work–life challenges, 82
Work–life imbalance
  boundaries and, 97
  burnout and, 91–92
  impostor phenomenon (IP) and, 91–92
  role conflict and, 92
  stress and, 92
Work outcomes, 66, 350
Work performance, 164, 350
  attributions of successful, 164

384 • *Index*

Workplace
   behaviors, 350
   burnout and, 104–106, 350
   contextual factors and, 351
   culture, 104–106, 299
   evaluations, 115
   gendered perceptions of, 168
   girl boss mentality and, 174
   harassment, 234, 279
   masculinity contest culture and, 168
   social support and, 351
   stress and, 95–96, 350
   women in, 172–173

Workplace satisfaction, 350
Workplace violence, 233
Work-related stress and mental health, 95
Work-to-family conflict, 92–93
World Health Organization (WHO), 61
   burnout, definition of, 83
   mental health, definition of, 61

Y

York University, 299
Younger students, 63–64
Young Impostor Scale, 247, 258

About the Editor

Kevin Cokley, PhD, is the University Diversity and Social Transformation Professor and professor of psychology at the University of Michigan, where he serves as associate chair of diversity initiatives for the Department of Psychology. He completed his PhD in counseling psychology from Georgia State University. His research and teaching can be broadly categorized in the area of African American psychology, with a focus on racial identity and understanding the psychological and environmental factors that impact African American students' academic achievement. He studies the psychosocial experiences of African American students and students of color and is currently exploring the impostor phenomenon and its relationship to mental health and academic outcomes. He is author of the 2014 book *The Myth of Black Anti-Intellectualism* and editor of the 2021 book *Making Black Lives Matter: Confronting Anti-Black Racism*. He has written numerous op-eds in major media outlets on topics such as critical race theory, Black people's rational mistrust of police, the aftermath of Ferguson, police and race relations, racism and White supremacy, the importance of ethnic studies, and racial disparities in school discipline. His research has been recognized in various media outlets, including the *New York Times*, *USA Today*, and *Inside Higher Education*.